The Bear

THE BEAR

HISTORY OF A FALLEN KING

Michel Pastoureau

Translated by George Holoch

The Belknap Press of Harvard University Press

CAMBRIDGE, MASSACHUSETTS, AND LONDON, ENGLAND

2011

This work, published as part of a program of aid for publication, received support from CulturesFrance and the French Ministry of Foreign Affairs.

Cet ouvrage a bénéficié du soutien des Programmes d'aide à la publication de Cultures-France/Ministère français des affaires étrangères et européennes.

This work was published with the assistance of the French Ministry of Culture—National Center for the Book.

Book Design by Dean Bornstein

Library of Congress Cataloging-in-Publication Data

Pastoureau, Michel
[L'ours : Histoire d'un roi déchu. English.]
The bear : history of a fallen king / Michel Pastoureau ; translated by George Holoch.
p.   cm.
Includes bibliographical references and index.
ISBN 978-0-674-04782-2 (alk. paper)
1. Bears—Folklore. 2. Bears—Symbolic aspects. 3. Bears—Religious aspects.
4. Christian art and symbolism. 5. Animals and civilization.
I. Holoch, George. II. Title.
GR730 . B4P3713 2011
398.24' 5259978—dc22
2011017439

Contents

No animal is more skilled at causing harm.
— Pliny the Elder, *Natural History*

The bear is the Devil.
— Saint Augustine, *Sermon on Isaiah*

But all these rough resemblances with man
make the bear all the more deformed and give
him no superiority over other animals.
— Buffon, *Histoire naturelle*

The Historian Considers the Animal

WAS Charlemagne the greatest enemy to the bear that Europe ever knew? Massacres of the beast were so numerous during his reign that the historian is entitled to pose the question. On two occasions in Germany the massacres took on a systematic character, in 773 and 785, both times after victorious campaigns against the Saxons. The future emperor, of course, never killed a bear with his own hands, even though he was, according to the chroniclers, a formidable huntsman, but soldiers acting on his orders conducted very large battues in the forests of Saxony and Thuringia.

The bears' enemies were not in fact so much Charlemagne and his troops as the prelates and clergy around them. The Church had declared war on the strongest animal on European soil and was determined to exterminate it, at least on German territory. There was a particular reason for this: In all of Saxony and the neighboring regions in the late eighth century, the bear was sometimes venerated as a god, which gave rise to forms of worship that were sometimes frenetic or demonic, particularly among warriors. Bears had to be absolutely eradicated to convert these barbarians to the religion of Christ. It was a difficult, almost impossible task, because these cults were neither recent nor superficial. They certainly pre-dated the Roman period—several Latin writers had already alluded to them—and were still present in the German heartland in the Carolingian period.

Following Tacitus, historians have written a good deal about the religious practices of the ancient Germans.[1] They have all emphasized the Germans' veneration for the forces of nature and described ceremonies associated with trees, stones, springs, and light. Some places were reserved for divination or the adoration of idols; others were used for huge assemblies at specific times (new moon, solstice, eclipse); still others were notable burial sites. Everywhere, rituals involving the use of fire and blood paid homage to various divinities. Dancing, trances, masks, and disguises were frequent. Bishops and their missionaries did not find it easy to put an end to these practices. They gradually succeeded by replacing sacred trees and springs with Christian places of worship, then by transforming a large number of pagan gods and heroes into saints, and finally by blessing or sanctifying most daily activities. But this Christianization remained uneven for a very long time, and it wasn't really until after the year 1000 that the last remnants of the old religion disappeared.[2]

While modern historians have written extensively about the worship of trees and springs, they have had much less to say about bear worship, as though it had been negligible or confined to certain tribes. But this was not the case. As chronicles and capitularies clearly attest, bear worship was widespread in both Germany and Scandinavia. It was denounced early on by several missionaries who had ventured well beyond the Rhine. In 742, for example, Saint Boniface, on a mission to Saxony, wrote a long letter to his friend Daniel, Bishop of Winchester, in which he mentioned among the "appalling rituals of the pagans" the practice of disguising oneself as a bear and drinking the animal's blood before going into battle.[3] Thirty years later, in an official list prepared by prelates of the pagan superstitions of the Saxons to be combatted, the same practices were again denounced, along with others that were even more barbaric.[4]

These customs were nothing new. From time immemorial the bear had been a particularly admired creature throughout the Germanic world. Stronger than any animal, it was the king of the forest and of all the animals. Warriors sought to imitate it and to imbue themselves with its powers through particularly savage rituals. Clan chiefs and kings adopted the bear as their primary symbol and attempted to seize hold of its powers through the use of weapons and emblems. But the Germans' veneration for the bear did not stop there. In their eyes, it was not only an invincible animal and the incarnation of brute strength; it was also a being apart, an intermediary creature between the animal and human worlds, and even an ancestor or relative of humans. As such, many beliefs collected around

2

the bear and it was subject to several taboos, particularly with respect to its name. In addition, the male bear was supposed to be attracted by young women and to feel sexual desire for them: it often sought them out, sometimes carried them off and raped them, whereupon the women gave birth to creatures that were half man and half bear, who were always indomitable warriors and even the founders of prestigious family lines. The border between human and animal was in this instance much more uncertain than the one described by monotheistic religions.

In the eyes of the Church, all of this was absolutely horrifying, all the more because worship of the great wild beast of the forest was not confined to the Germanic world. It was also found among Slavs and to a lesser extent among Celts. The Celts, of course, had been Christianized for several centuries, and their old animal cults had gradually adopted discreet forms, surviving primarily in poetry and oral tradition. But this was not true of the Slavs, and they admired the bear as much as the Germans did. Indeed, in a large part of non-Mediterranean Europe in the Carolingian period, the bear continued to be seen as a divine figure, an ancestral god whose worship took on various forms but remained solidly rooted, impeding the conversion of pagan peoples. Almost everywhere, from the Alps to the Baltic, the bear stood as a rival to Christ. The Church thought it appropriate to declare war on the bear, to fight him by all means possible, and to bring him down from his throne and his altars.

The struggle of the medieval Church against the bear forms the central section of this book. Undertaken very early, even before the reign of Charlemagne, it lasted for nearly a millennium, through the High Middle Ages and the feudal period, coming to an end only in the thirteenth century when the last traces of the ancient ursine cults disappeared and throughout Europe an exotic animal from eastern tradition, the lion, definitively seized the title of king of the animals, until then held by the bear. It was, of course, a symbolic title, but one that involved cultural phenomena of great import covering an extended period of time. Hence, my study begins long before Christianity, deep in prehistory, when bears and humans of the Paleolithic shared the same territory and the same prey, sometimes the same caves, and probably the same fears. The study continues well beyond the Middle Ages to inquire into the fate of the bear after it fell from its throne: deprived of all prestige, transformed into a circus animal, often humiliated or ridiculed, it nevertheless continued to occupy a key place in the human imagination. Along the way, the bear gradually became a subject of dream and fantasy once more and took its revenge in the twentieth century by changing into a veritable fetish: the teddy bear. The circle seems complete. The bear has become what it had been thirty, fifty, or eighty thousand years before the present day: a companion to man, a relative, an ancestor, a double, and perhaps a god or a tutelary divinity.

The subject of this history is an animal—not an individual animal but a species, the brown bear—studied over time in its relations with the societies in Europe that approached, feared, confronted, thought about, or dramatized it. A wild animal as the subject of a work of history is not common. Historians usually direct their investigations and reflections toward men, territories, and periods, as well as toward the events and challenges facing them. Until recently, historians had barely considered animals, leaving them to collections of anecdotes and curious tales, as they had the habit of doing with every subject they thought frivolous or marginal. Only a few historians of religion had been interested in one or another specific issue that might involve the study of an animal. But devoting a thesis or a scholarly book to an animal was really unthinkable. I still remember the difficulties I encountered at the École des Chartes in the late 1960s to gain approval for a thesis subject dealing with the medieval heraldic bestiary.[5] Not only was a subject of this kind hardly acceptable because it revolved around a discipline that was considered archaic—heraldry—but in addition it seemed puerile because it dealt with animals, that is, contemptible creatures that had no role to play in the foreground of historical research.

Since then the situation has fortunately changed. Thanks to the work of some pioneering historians and increasingly common collaboration with scholars from other fields (anthropology, ethnology, linguistics, zoology),[6] the animal has gradually become a recognized subject of history.

The study of animals is even at the forefront of research, at the intersection of several disciplines, a place where real discoveries are made. This study can only be interdisciplinary. Considered in relation to humankind, animals are involved in all the major issues of social, economic, material, cultural, religious, and symbolic history. They are present everywhere and constantly raise essential and complex questions for the scholar.

After writing my thesis and a number of articles on the relations between man and animal, I intend in this book to show how the animal has become in itself a subject of history. The book is based on lengthy research and preceded by several years of seminars at the École Pratique des Hautes Études and the École des Hautes Études en Sciences Sociales. I chose the bear because I have been considering the problem of the king of the animals in the Western tradition for four decades. The lion was not always king: the bear preceded him for several millennia, and the eagle, symbol of all the empires, was a later competitor. As early as 1969, while still a student working on medieval armorial bestiary, for which the lion was already king, I noticed that in the twelfth and thirteenth centuries several German and Danish families whose names suggested the idea of king or chief (Königsbach, Königstein, Kungslena, Herrsching) had a bear in their coats of arms.[7] Why a bear and not a lion? Trying to learn more, I went back in time, widened my investigation, and finally arrived at the conviction that, in a large part of Europe, the bear had been king of the beasts long before the lion. Over the years, my research on this question, covering periods before and after the Middle Ages, turned into a veritable symbolic history of the bear in European societies. Prehistorians and ethnologists had published books and articles on the bear, and it seemed to me that I ought to do the same. Although there are still many disputes among prehistorians about the relations between man and bear in the Paleolithic (was there a cult or not?), and though I don't always agree with the role ethnologists attribute to the bear (the animal is sometimes recruited in the service of regionalist causes foreign to me), their work on the subject is generally of high quality. It is now up to the historian to make a contribution. Studies of the bear and its place in various cultures have until now seldom been approached from a diachronic perspective. It is time to place these studies in historical context and to reiterate that history is never immobile.

The book you are about to read is neither a work of zoology nor a work of ethnology, even though both disciplines have been extensively drawn upon. It is primarily a work of history, constructed around a chronological sequence and emphasizing periods of change, particularly the central Middle Ages (eleventh to thirteenth centuries). There was a change in relations between man and bear, but also a change in all systems of values and perceptual phenomena associated with the animal world. Although the bear is the focus of this investigation, it is impossible to consider it in isolation. It has to be set within a wider set of issues, the focal point of which is obviously not the animal but man; not individual man, on whom the historian of ancient times has little grasp, but man living in society, the primary object of all historical investigations. In addition, the bear plays its role and takes on its full meaning only insofar as it is connected with or opposed to one or more other animals. As a result, in what follows, the bear is accompanied by many other animals: first the mammoth, the bison, and the horse; then the boar, the stag, the wolf, the crow, and the fox; later, the bull, the ass, the pig, the goat, the dog, and the ram; and finally, the lion, the eagle, the leopard, the elephant, the rhinoceros, the monkey, and a few others, the whole constituting not a fauna but a veritable bestiary, the one that Europeans forged over time and made into the primary arena for their symbolic impulses.

This history of the bear in relation to humankind is limited to Europe. It would hardly have been reasonable to extend it to other continents. To be able to describe clearly the place of an animal in any given society, one has to know the various characteristics, social structures, and forms of behavior of that society. One scholar may be able to do that for one or two societies, perhaps seen over a long period of time, but it is impossible on a planetary scale. In addition, historians are not obsessed with archetypes or invariants and have trouble believing in a universal symbolic system. They know that, on the contrary, everything in this area is cultural. While the comparative study of societies is legitimate and even necessary, and while it brings to light unquestionable points of similarity or resemblance (some examples are found in the last chapter), it cannot and should not mask the ocean of differences, in space as well as time.

Finally, in addition to being limited to Europe, this study concerns only the brown bear. This was indeed for centuries the only species known to the various societies under consideration. The notions of genus, family, species, and sub-species are themselves strongly cultural and should be handled with caution. The historian of animals is not a zoologist. He or she cannot project into the past our current definitions and classifications as such. They were not those of the societies that came before us and will probably not be those of societies that come after us. From my perspective as a historian, what we know today are not truths but only stages in the developing evolution of knowledge. This is why, in considering the bear, I have refrained from using modern scientific terms or concepts, such as "mammal" or "plantigrade," unknown before the eighteenth century. Besides, these have nothing to do with the symbolic history of animals, whose taxonomies are entirely different.

In fact, as surprising as they may seem to us, the classifications and the views that past societies adopted with regard to animals are still authentic historical documents, often of great interest. They have to be set in their context and interpreted in light of past, not current, knowledge. Although this is both obvious and necessary, it is unfortunately not accepted by all zoologists and not even by all historians of science. For example, two well-known historians wrote this not long ago about medieval bestiaries: "The Middle Ages was a sterile and decadent period, particularly from the scientific point of view. In the case of zoology, it preserved most of the absurd fables of Antiquity, invented others, and had no ability to conduct real observations . . . The inanities one encounters in the bestiaries clearly show the credulity of those who wrote, read, or propagated them . . . We will not dwell on this literature, which has more to do with folklore than with science."[8]

One would like to know what "real observations" are, and what is meant by "inanities." The men of the Middle Ages were perfectly capable of observing beings and things, but the exact and the true were not located on the same level, and it was not through observation that one achieved knowledge, much less attained the truth. Remarks like these, in any event, show that their authors have understood nothing about what history is. The past, particularly the distant past, cannot be understood—and even less judged—by the yardstick of the sensibilities, values, and knowledge of the present. In this area, what is "scientifically correct" is not only deplorable but also the source of many errors, confusions, and absurdities. Natural and biological sciences cannot and should not impose their convictions on the social sciences. Besides, what is natural history but a form of cultural history of a particular type?

I

THE BEAR VENERATED
FROM THE PALEOLITHIC
TO THE FEUDAL ERA

❖ I ❖

The First God?

T HE oldest trace of the symbolic ties between man and bear seems to date from approximately 80,000 years ago in Périgord, in the cave of Regourdou, where a Neanderthal grave is connected to the grave of a brown bear under a single slab between two blocks of stone, thereby indicating the special status of the animal.[1] We have preserved no certain trace, either archeological or anthropological, of the animal's prior relations with the Neanderthals; we can only try to imagine them on the basis of a few collections of skulls and bones in alpine caves, and venture the hypothesis that the bear may already have been seen in the Middle Paleolithic as an animal apart. However, there is no evidence to establish that these collections were deposited by men. Beginning with the Upper Paleolithic, approximately 30,000 years ago, evidence becomes more plentiful and solid, showing how in some regions and in certain periods men and bears inhabited the same territories, frequented the same caves, hunted the same prey, struggled against the same dangers, and probably had both economic and symbolic relations with one another. For that period, everything seems to confirm that the bear was no longer considered an animal like other animals, that it occupied a special place between the worlds of beasts and men, and that it may have served as a mediator with the beyond. Does this mean it is legitimate to say there was a prehistoric cult of the bear, practiced in several regions of the northern hemisphere in the Paleolithic period? The question provoked, and continues to provoke, passionate controversy among prehistorians.

Supporters and opponents of a cult of the bear conduct aggressive debates on the subject with a vehemence that surprises the outside observer. As a medieval historian, a specialist in more recent periods and used to more peaceful controversies, I am obviously in no position to say who is right. But in my view, this dispute, which has occupied an essential place in prehistoric studies for nearly a century, is itself a particularly instructive historiographical document on the role played by the bear in the imagination of ancient peoples. This is particularly the case because the scientific debate seems to have adopted particular and passionate, almost religious forms, with dogmas and prohibitions, chapels and excommunications.

Painted and Engraved Images

According to current science, the cave bear *(Ursus spelaeus)* was not the direct ancestor of the brown bear *(Ursus arctos),* the subject of this book. But they may have had a common ancestor, the *Ursus etruscus,* which became extinct during the Pliocene, and both were abundant in the environment of Neanderthal and Cro-Magnon man. What was discovered in the cave of Regourdou was certainly the grave of a brown bear, but the images that appear in wall art and in portable art (figurines and the like) during the Upper Paleolithic from 35,000 BC are primarily of cave bears. There are observable differences between the two animals, notably in size: the cave bear was significantly larger (up to eleven-and-a-half feet for an upright male), more massive, and heavier (1,100 to 1,300 pounds) than the brown bear, who grew to nearly seven to seven-and-a-half feet and weighed between 550 and 660 pounds. Its dentition was also different; the cave bear had molars with large chewing surfaces, suggesting a more vegetarian diet than that of its cousin. Finally—and this can be clearly seen in cave paintings—the form of the head is different in the two animals: the cave bear had a prominent frontal lump and a clear demarcation between forehead and snout, two traits much less marked in the brown bear. Until about 20,000 BC the brown bear was depicted less often than the cave bear, perhaps because it did not hibernate in caves. The cave bear hibernated every winter and left many traces behind. But for unknown reasons, it disappeared relatively early, between 15,000 and 12,000 BC.[2]

That said, the bear was not the star of the artistic bestiary of the Paleolithic, at least not quantitatively. The two animals most frequently drawn, painted, or engraved on cave walls were the horse and the bison.

Thereafter came the mammoth, the ibex, the stag, the reindeer, and the aurochs. Less frequent were the cat family and rhinoceroses, and even less frequent, birds and fish. Out of forty-four sites in Western Europe, the examples of bears tallied represent about two percent of the identifiable animals, a percentage much lower than that of the large herbivores and roughly equivalent to that of lions and other big cats.[3] It is, moreover, not always easy to distinguish among animals, and some bears still await identification as such.[4] To do this, it is indispensable to go to the sites and study the volumes and configurations, and not rely, as so often happens, on summaries or photographs. Several caves rich in images of bears have not yet been completely studied. This is true of the Chauvet cave in Ardèche, which contains both the oldest (between 32,000 and 30,000 BC) and the most numerous (at least twelve examples identified) of all the cave wall images of bears known to this day. Because of the strange bear skulls that were deposited there—perhaps ritually—this cave, more than any other, suggests the existence of a bear cult; or, more cautiously, adopting the expression of Jean Clottes, at least it has the strongest "bear smell."[5]

Images of bears—engraved or painted, sometimes engraved and painted—are found in only one-tenth of the approximately three hundred known decorated European Paleolithic caves. Sometimes they are the central subject of a scene,[6] sometimes they appear in a chamber or cavity reserved for them, and sometimes they seem to be a marginal motif amid other motifs. In that instance it is legitimate to wonder about the presence of a single image of a bear among other species represented by several images: does this single bear—discreet, and apparently of little significance—really play a less important role than the surrounding animals, or is it rather highlighted by its singleness? The question is worth asking. In portable art, on the other hand, the bear is usually represented alone, engraved on a block of schist, on a fragment of bone, antler, or ivory, sometimes sculpted in stone or modeled in clay.[7]

In both wall art and portable art, in any event, the bear is represented in a greater variety of postures than any other animal. It is also always the animal with the most stylized, schematized design. It is well known that in historical time, the simplification of forms in the representation of an animal is generally proportional to the place the animal occupies in the world of symbols. Was this already the case in the Paleolithic? The bear, finally, is the only animal represented full face in clay modeling (bringing together both full-face and profile views) as well as in painting and engraving. The problem is to determine whether this is the animal itself or a man disguised as a bear, as has been suggested for several finds.[8]

In some cases, the entire bear is not represented, only a specific, identifiable part of its body: sometimes it is headless, sometimes without paws, and sometimes the head and paws are engraved separately. In other cases, the bear is riddled with holes or overlaid with lines, as though there had been an intent to show it pierced by arrows, wounded, or sacrificed.[9] Some of these "wounded" bears even seem to be spitting blood through their mouths or nostrils. The problem is to determine whether the drawing of the animal and the overlaying lines were done at the same time. Nothing is less certain. Finally and above all, the bear is, except for man, the only living creature that is shown upright, standing on its hind legs. All these characteristics are remarkable and unquestionably contribute to giving this animal a special status. They also raise the question of the functions of the bestiary represented deep in the caves. For it is indeed a bestiary, and it is far from having revealed all its mysteries.

This is not the place to dwell on the meaning or meanings of the art of the caves; that art raises very complex questions for prehistorians that they have been debating since the late nineteenth century. It is nevertheless worth summarizing the principal positions because they make it easier to understand the disputes surrounding the cult of the bear.[10]

While the theory of representation for esthetic pleasure alone, art for art's sake so to speak, was wisely and swiftly abandoned, the theory of images connected to hunting rituals, favored by Abbé Breuil (1877–1961) and some of his disciples, had a longer life. In this view, animal images had the function of protecting hunters, influencing the course of events, harnessing various transcendental forces; for that very reason, the act of representation took on more importance than the resulting painted or engraved image. In fact, many images are carelessly superimposed, others located in spots where it is impossible to see them, or seem absolutely not made to be seen. But representations of hunted or dead animals are very rare, and actual hunting scenes practically nonexistent. The hypothesis of magical action through images was therefore finally abandoned in turn. The same thing occurred—and in this case probably a little too quickly— with the theory of representation of myths connected to the origins of a group or "clan"; and with the theory of totemic meaning, each animal supposedly constituting the emblem or the totem of one of the groups or clans frequenting a particular cave at a certain time. They have been supplanted by more semiological explanations, sometimes called "structuralist," based on the study of frequencies and rarity, associations and oppositions, distributions in the cave, close associations and distances, and animal categorizations and social classifications.[11] This is a methodologically exemplary hypothesis that established order in the repertory of images and signs, but it must be acknowledged that it usually ran into dead ends. More recently, the hypothesis of images linked to shamanistic rituals has had strong supporters (and vehement opponents): the cave is seen as a passageway toward the beyond and the cosmos; the succession of chambers, corridors, and vestibules is a kind of path of initiation; the images, some of which seem to come out of the rock and others to float on the surface, represent the visions of the shaman in the course of the different phases of his trance. The hypothesis is attractive, and in the case of some writers,[12] it has the virtue of restoring the bear to its rightful place—at the heart of relations between men, gods, and beasts—but it is as uncertain as the others.

Given our current knowledge, a comprehensive and unambiguous interpretation of Paleolithic cave art is an impossible task. But this does not mean that the art is devoid of functions or meanings.

Skulls and Bones

"Cavemen" never really lived in the caves whose walls they decorated. They were disturbing, inhospitable places, always difficult to get into: the ceilings were low, the floor slippery, and the dangers numerous. In addition, they were perpetually cold, humid, and dark. Painting or engraving in the depths of a cave was a voluntary act based on precise intentions, and it required that all sorts of fears be overcome. Immune to fear and danger, bears regularly frequented caves over dozens of millennia: the brown bear in summer, for coolness and rest; the cave bear in winter, for hibernation and the birth and early care of its young. Caves have preserved abundant evidence of these frequent visits: paw prints in the clay of floor and walls; traces of fur where a bear scratched itself or marked the walls with its odor; even bits of fur trapped in clay; scratches of all kinds on walls and floors; remains of dens used over many generations. Artists sometimes integrated these traces and imprints into their paintings and carvings; in certain sites, there is thus a clear link between the physical presence of bears and the images representing them. It is possible that some caves or parts of caves were so strongly impregnated with the odor of bears that in a way it cast a spell over men who ventured into them and impelled them to depict the huge animal that was simultaneously feared, admired, and perhaps worshiped.

Usually, bears preceded men in the caves. But there are some contrary cases (Bruniquel, for example, in Tarn-et-Garonne), and others, more numerous, where bears seem to have returned after the artists did their work and added more scratches to the ones already there (this is true in the Chauvet cave). Many caves, in fact, saw the successive and alternating presence of bears and men over the very long term. But what these caves contain in the greatest abundance are neither painted or carved images nor simple imprints of paws or claws, but thousands of bones. Their large number, their accumulation in certain places, their methodical arrangement in some others all raise the question of their origin. Were these natural "deposits" from corpses of bears who died during their hibernation? Were they bear "cemeteries," purely accidental or deliberately chosen by the bears themselves, or conceived by men? Or finally, were they veritable sanctuaries where ritual ceremonies were performed in which the bear played a major role? Prehistorians have been debating these questions for three or four generations and seem nowhere near to putting an end to their controversies.

Bears were, of course, not the only animals that frequented caves, but they did so more often and, significantly, in larger numbers than the others. In the oldest sites, 80 to 90 percent of the bones found belong to bears, and in some cases the figure reaches 100 percent. Two such examples are Cueva Eiros in Spain and Dijve Babe in Slovenia, where, in addition, the quantity of bones and bone fragments is considerable.[13] Even larger quantities of bone and bone fragments are located in the cave of La Balme-à-Collomb at the foot of Mount Granier in the Massif de la Chartreuse in France. In 1988, skeletal remains were found there probably belonging to several thousand Ursidae. The site has not yet been completely inventoried, but it is possible that this number will exceed three or four thousand. Carbon 14 dating has established that bears frequented this cave over a period of more than twenty thousand years, from 45,000 to 24,000 BC.[14]

Unfortunately, not all deposits of cave bears can be precisely dated. And in this case, as in others, the first problem is that of dating, which is essential to determine if one is dealing with a natural and successive accumulation over the course of several dozen or even several hundred millennia since the Middle Pleistocene,[15] or with a more recent and specific deposit more limited in time. For the majority of sites, the question is difficult to answer.

For this reason, it is the location and arrangement of bones rather than their quantity that raise the question of whether men made deposits with a magical-religious purpose. Bear bones are generally located at the deepest levels of caves. Sometimes, to reach the "sanctuary" chamber, or what is thought to be that, one has to go through a gallery in which the passageway lies between two continuous lines of bones set at the foot of the walls; sometimes, one has to clear a path amid fragments of bones forming a kind of pavement or arranged in piles at regular intervals. In certain chambers, whole bones are arranged in the shape of an arc or a semicircle; in others, they are set in a recess or on an unusual stone; in still others, bones have been found that are carved in a particular way and fitted together, sometimes painted or decorated as though they were relics or talismans.

Even more than bones and fragments of bones, skulls were subject to particular treatment: skulls deliberately covered with a mound of clay; skulls artistically piled in stone hollows; skulls set in fissures or cavities sealed by dry stones forming sorts of chests or tabernacles; skulls with the lower jaw removed and run through with a femur, a tibia, or a penis "bone"; skulls arranged in a circle or semicircle on the floor around a larger raised skull; finally, skulls set in the center of a chamber on a rocky promontory forming something like an altar. Most of these arrangements seem to be clearly ritual in nature and encourage researchers to describe them using terms borrowed from liturgical vocabulary. In every case they encourage looking at the bear as a creature apart, intermediary between the world of animals and the world of the gods. Indeed, one encounters similar evidence for no other animal. Here or there, to be sure, there have been finds of piles of reindeer bones broken into uniform fragments, skulls and tusks of mammoths arranged in unusual ways, aurochs or bison horns seemingly suspended on a wall.[16] But such instances are infrequent, difficult to date, and not at all comparable, quantitatively and qualitatively, to arrangements of bear skulls and bones. They really have no equivalents. Should one go further and speak of genuine religious practices, also suggested by the many amulets found in burial places, made out of bear fangs, claws, or tufts of fur?

A Religion of the Bear?

Several researchers have taken that step, some of them early on,[17] relying both on the evidence just mentioned—images, skulls, bones, locations, and arrangements—and on ethnological comparisons with societies that until recently practiced the cult of the bear, and sometimes even continue to do so. They include the Ainu in Japan and Sakhalin; various native peoples of Siberia such as the Ostyaks, the Evenks, and the Yakuts; the Lapps in Scandinavia; and the Inuit in Canada and Greenland. In historic time, the cult of the bear, in one form or another, has been thoroughly substantiated in several northern hemisphere societies and has been the subject of investigations and publications.[18] Does this mean it is legitimate to go back millennia and project onto societies of the Paleolithic much more recently documented beliefs and rituals? Some prehistorians believe that it is and, combining evidence and comparisons, have confirmed the existence of a paleolithic religion of the bear, perhaps connected to specific hunting techniques, the ritual deposit of the skull and bones of the animal that had been killed, and to the fabrication of tools from the bones of cave bears. Others are more cautious and follow André Leroi-Gourhan in emphasizing the oversimplification of ethnological comparisons of this kind that consist of going into raptures over a few drops of resemblance and forgetting the ocean of differences. Still others, such as F. E. Koby, have unrelentingly demonstrated the fragility or absurdity of these hypotheses: "Relations between men of the Paleolithic and bears have been exaggerated and need to be completely revised in the light of objective observations . . . Countless mistakes propagated on the subject have been accepted uncritically, giving rise to legends that become contagious as soon as they are surrounded with a mystic halo strong enough to make them attractive to the general public."[19] That is certainly true, but it would be useful to know what those "objective observations" may be.

Some important scholars have changed their opinions several times. For example, André Leroi-Gourhan (1911–1986) seems to have been troubled as a young digger by discoveries made in Burgundy, at Berzé-la-Ville,[20] and at Arcy-sur-Cure. But toward the end of his life, he proved to be hostile to the idea of a cult of the bear and used very harsh language in denouncing the "archeological novel" that this alleged cult had fostered.[21] Following him, some of his disciples have also changed their opinions on several occasions and finally saw fit to express in well-chosen words their denial of any religious practice connected to the bear. Over the decades, controversies have grown bitter, sometimes taking on a malicious and offensive character (particularly in book reviews). Today, opponents of the cult of the bear seem to be in the majority.[22] At a conference or in an article, it takes a good deal of courage to argue for the opposite point of view; for a young prehistorian, expressing the idea that prehistoric man at one time or another had a religion of the bear means opposing the dominant position, incurring the wrath of his elders, and thereby fatally damaging his career hopes. Only a few historians and ethnologists unconnected to the cruel world of prehistorians still dare to (cautiously) suggest such a hypothesis.[23]

Of course, those opposed to the idea of a cult of the bear do not deny the astonishing abundance of skulls and bones in one cave or another, but they refuse to see them as sanctuaries, identifying them only as ossuaries. They sometimes emphasize that bears came and went and moved around inside the caves incessantly and note that the animals themselves accumulated bones in piles, pushed others toward the walls, introduced still others into one or another recess or cavity. The process of sedimentation and the physical and chemical conditions for preservation did the rest: destroying bones here, preserving them there, and covering them up elsewhere. Sometimes they focus on tectonic movements after the period that men and animals occupied the caves, or else attribute the deposit of one or another collection of bones or skulls at a particular spot to rising water accidentally displacing the bones. Sometimes, finally, they point to uncertain or controversial datings and suggest that some perhaps intentional deposits should be seen not as the work of the Paleolithic but of Antiquity, the Middle Ages, or even modern times.[24]

What are the counterarguments? It is true that bears are able to grasp and move objects, make piles, and show ingenuity in shaping their habitat. It is also true that geological events, natural catastrophes, and climatic variations have changed the structure of some caves and the location of any archeological material that might be found in them. It is also true that several sites explored in the past were not treated with all the rigor that is now required: rudimentary stratigraphy, no photographs, imprecise sketches, contradictory claims. Finally, it is true that we don't know whether Neanderthals in the Middle Paleolithic really hunted cave bears and, if so, what techniques they used.[25] Bears and men were then rivals as hunters, fishers, and gatherers, and for the occupation of rock shelters. But did men hunt or fight bears, who no doubt also came to those shelters to steal food stores (grains, roots and dried meat and fish)? Even for the Upper Paleolithic and the period of Cro-Magnon man, our information about the hunting of bears is sketchy: it is based on either hypothetical hunting scenes represented in wall or portable art,[26] or on transposing known practices of the Neolithic or Protohistoric periods back several millennia. During those periods, men certainly hunted bears—brown bears—and derived many products from them: meat for food; fat for illumination (one-and-a-half to one-and-three-quarters ounces of animal fat provided light for one hour); bones not only to make various tools, weapons, or instruments, but also as fuel; and finally skin and furs (the most attractive were those in late spring and early winter) as clothing and warmth. Oetzi, the famous protohistoric hunter discovered in 1991 in the Tyrolean Alps of Italy, at more than 10,500 feet altitude, with his clothing, weapons, and all his equipment, was wearing a bearskin cap; but he lived 3,300 years before our era, not in the Paleolithic.

Are all these arguments enough to consider the hypothesis of a cult of the bear a "dead end,"[27] a "pure fantasy"?[28] Perhaps not, if one takes into account recent discoveries and reconsiders the decor and the objects in certain caves in the light of this new evidence. Probably not if, instead of confining oneself to ethnological comparisons based essentially on documentation from the nineteenth and twentieth centuries and referring to societies very distant from Europe, one finally took into consideration the European history of relations between humans and bears in Antiquity and the Middle Ages. After listening to ethnologists, perhaps the time has come to listen to historians.

Strange Designs

First I would like to consider one of the recent discoveries and some paleolithic sites that were more than simple caves frequented by bears and men, perhaps authentic sanctuaries.

The first of these sites is the Chauvet cave in Vallon-Pont-d'Arc in Ardèche, whose discovery in 1994 shocked both specialists and the general public, challenging some received ideas about the origins of cave art. Its painted and carved bestiary contains between 350 and 400 animals (they have not yet been completely catalogued). Among them, exceptionally, dangerous animals predominate (lions, panthers, bears, rhinoceroses), not the large herbivores hunted for food. The bestiary at Chauvet is the oldest one known: precise carbon 14 dating of micro-samples indicates a range between 32,410 and 30,240 BC, that is, more than fifteen thousand years before the bestiaries of Lascaux and Altamira.[29] It is also the most original, varied, and spectacular animal collection, with varying techniques and a homogeneous style, vigorous and controlled drawing in various flat tints (red, black, brown, and yellow), use of the contours of the walls to convey volumes, and use of superposition to create an effect close to modern-day perspective. Its discovery led to a reconsideration of everything written on rock art, indeed of all the textbooks on prehistory published before 1995. Needing to be revised, if not abandoned, is the idea of a "progression" in the mastery of representation over the millennia, an idea that had generally been accepted, which saw the coarsest paintings and carvings as the oldest and the most masterful or "realistic" as the most recent.[30] This is not at all the case.

The animal most abundantly represented in the Chauvet cave is not the bear but the rhinoceros, forty-seven examples of which have been counted so far; next come cats and mammoths, with thirty-six each. However, the twelve images of bears that can be seen on various walls are the most numerous ever found in a single cave. They are remarkable in their imposing size, firm outline, and red or black color. Most important, they seem to echo the many vestiges left by bears who had lived in the cave: scratches, traces of fur and rubbing, paw prints on the walls and the floor (including those of a she-bear and her cub), trails, hollows and depressions trapped in the clay, very numerous bone remnants, and a collection of at least 150 skulls. This cave does indeed "smell of bear," perhaps more than any other.[31]

But it does more than that. It puts the bear on stage and, more than anywhere else, it seems to make it an animal worthy of veneration: in the center of a circular chamber from which all bones, fragments of bones, and anything else movable was removed, a large skull is set on a block of stone with a flat surface resembling an altar; on the floor around it several dozen other skulls are arranged in a circle. This was obviously a stage setting, not the work of bears or the consequence of geological or climatic accidents, but clearly due to voluntary human action.[32] Was it the work of Cro-Magnon man or of more recent populations? Is the practically liturgical design of this "skull chamber" contemporaneous with the bestiary painted on the surrounding walls?[33] In the current state of our knowledge, it is impossible to answer; the Chauvet cave is in the process of being studied, and the study is wisely proceeding slowly. What seems certain, however, is that bears inhabited this cave before and after human intervention.

Whatever discoveries may be made in the future, the Chauvet cave has made it necessary to reconsider many opinions: for example, the a priori rejection of any form of ritual practice connected to the bear among men of the Paleolithic, or the possible existence of a cult of the bear among the Neanderthals that disappeared with them. It also leads to looking again at other sites to reconsider other evidence.

One example is the Regourdou cave mentioned at the beginning of this chapter. The presence, in an artificial pit under a large stone slab, of the graves of a Neanderthal man and a brown bear side by side, separated merely by a dry stone wall, cannot be the result of chance.[34] It was intentional and unquestionably expressed a form of religious thinking. Why did the contemporary authorities permit the site to be mutilated and a large portion of the bones to be removed? Why was Le Regourdou, which is so important for our knowledge of Neanderthal funeral practices, not purchased by the French state? Why is it necessary to go to the Field Museum in Chicago to see a mediocre reconstitution of the two vandalized graves? Is it because the site was discovered in 1957 by an unpleasant amateur, the owner of the land, Roger Constant?[35] Or is it because the discovery challenged the sacrosanct denial that there could have been ritual relations between prehistoric man and the bear at one time or another? What explains this stubborn official rejection of the idea of such a cult? Why, more broadly, is there such suspicion of all bear sites?

The situation is hardly different elsewhere. For example, the Pas de Joulié cave in Trèves, Gard, a site that has been almost completely looted, had a group of bear skulls surrounding human skulls; in the Combarelles cave in Dordogne, the walls had carvings of ten bears with very schematic designs, which have been damaged since the discovery of the site very early in the twentieth century. The cave of Trois-Frères in Ariège, which combines bear traces with several images of the animal, notably two carvings in which the bear seems to be put to death, holds as well as the celebrated and controversial image of a horned "sorcerer-god," whose hands are unquestionably ursine. It is to be hoped that the fate of the Chauvet cave and its extraordinary skull chamber will be different and will give rise to real scientific debates with no preconceived ideas or rejection of evidence.

In the meantime, if we move forward in time to the Magdalenian period and enter the cave-corridor of Montespan in Haute-Garonne, discovered in 1881 but not systematically explored until 1922 and 1923 by Norbert Casteret, we find, in a small but in every way startling chamber, the oldest statue ever made. It dates from 15,000 to 20,000 years ago, and it is the statue of a bear.[36]

It is a three-dimensional clay statue set about a meter from the wall on a kind of platform that seems to have been specially designed to hold it. One hundred ten centimeters long and sixty centimeters high, the statue represents a large animal without a head, crouching, forepaws stretched out, the left mutilated, and the right intact. The very visible digits and claws are certainly those of a bear, as the general outline of the animal suggests, with its rounded hindquarters and a posture that would be impossible for any other animal. The question of the head has caused a lot of ink to flow. Why is it missing? Was the animal ritually decapitated, or did the head never exist? The latter hypothesis now seems to have the greatest support: the severed edge of the neck is smooth and polished like the rest of the body; it is neither broken nor damaged. But toward the middle, one can see a triangular hole, as though there had been an intention to install a peg to hang something on. Sculpted fragments have been found on the floor representing lions and horses. But while the bear is a real statue that can be walked around, the other animal figures, symbolically destroyed, are attached to the wall and have the appearance of bas-reliefs. In the same chamber, the walls and the ceiling show a painted and engraved display of bison, horses, and deer, as well as various signs and spots difficult to describe, much less to interpret. But it is the bear that draws all eyes.

While it may not have lost a sculpted head, which perhaps never existed, it did lose the skull that Norbert Casteret had found on the floor between the forepaws, which was stolen a few days after the discovery. Even though it has disappeared, it helps to understand the function of a statue like this and makes it possible, if not to reconstitute, at least to imagine the rituals that were performed there, magical-religious rituals perhaps connected to the hunt. The statue was probably covered with a bearskin recently cut from an animal with the head still attached; it was used to imitate capture and killing: in the clay can still be seen the trace of blows that struck the animal in the course of these ceremonies. They were probably accompanied by dances, cries, and propitiatory gestures that were intended to make a future real hunt successful.[37]

At least sixty millennia separate the graves of Regourdou and the statue of Montespan. Between these two exceptional sites there is a good deal of evidence attesting to and displaying the privileged symbolic relations connecting bear and man—Cro-Magnon as well as Neanderthal, brown bear along with cave bear. Using the word "cult" to characterize these relations may create a debate among specialists. Seeing magical or religious motives in each representation of a bear, each remnant of bone or skull set in an unexpected place is no doubt excessive. But denying that ancient peoples in the Paleolithic considered the bear a creature apart, an animal that possessed powers that other animals did not, would be to deny the evidence and exhibit bad faith.

If men did not ritually arrange the remnants of a brown bear in Regourdou or symbolically organize the skull chamber of the Chauvet cave, the only ones who could have done so were the bears themselves. Should we conclude that prehistoric bears buried their dead? That they experienced a certain kind of religious feeling? That they practiced various rituals deep in the caves that ancient peoples, much later, ended up imitating? Should we go so far as to imagine that bears transmitted to them the idea of religion, as well as all the beliefs and rites that go along with it? Should we go that far?

I for one will not, although I know of a Russian researcher who thinks he has found vestiges of the worship of bears by bears themselves in Siberian caves of the Paleolithic that had not been penetrated by men at the time and which men had reached only in the Iron Age.[38] I prefer to remain in Europe and follow the course of time down to historic ages. In Greco-Roman, Germanic, and Celtic mythologies in the West of Antiquity and the Middle Ages, there is a good deal of evidence attesting to the existence of a cult of the bear that took on diverse forms but certainly goes far back in time. When one observes, for example, the considerable efforts expended by the medieval Church for nearly one thousand years to eradicate pagan cults connected to the bear, one senses that those cults had very deep roots, stretching back before earliest Antiquity and even to the Neolithic. Why have prehistorians shown so little interest in these cults, which have been solidly documented in historic eras? Why have they never really looked toward the European Middle Ages? Ethnological comparisons with recent practices of Asian or Amerindian societies are, of course, legitimate and sometimes fruitful, but wouldn't real historical inquiries focused on Antiquity and the Middle Ages be just as fruitful, if not more so?

Artemis, Bear Goddess

Myths always come from long ago, from archaic eras, "golden ages," or even further back, where historians rarely venture because they have only intuition to guide them, even though intuition is an indispensable research tool. Greek myths are no exception to the rule, and they are the only way to reconstitute or imagine the links that existed, from the perspective of cult or religion, between the prehistoric and the historic bear. In Greek myths, to be sure, the bear is not itself a divinity, but only an emblem of some of the gods. However, some tales involving a bear seem to have retained traces of the role it may have played in very ancient times. This is particularly the case because, in most of these myths, caves play an important and often ambivalent role: they are dark and fearsome places inhabited by monsters and evil spirits, places of ignorance, suffering, and punishment, like the cave in Plato's *Republic*. But they are also sanctuaries where humans forge alliances with the gods, harness magical powers, or draw new energies. They are also places where many heroes are born and others initiated, fortified, liberated, or metamorphosed. Entering a cave always means passing from one state to another.

The Greek bear is not the cave bear, which had become extinct between 12,000 and 15,000 BC. It is always the brown bear, the strongest of all native European animals, and along with the pig, the animal considered biologically and symbolically closest to humankind.[39] It is an emblem of several divinities, primarily the great goddess of the hunt, Artemis, twin sister of Apollo, daughter of Zeus, and goddess of the moon, the woods, and the mountains, and therefore protector of wild animals. Untamed and vindictive, Artemis has vowed to remain eternally virgin and takes pleasure only in the hunt: armed with her bow, she pursues and kills any who challenge or betray her or thwart her will. Orion and Actaeon are the most famous of her numerous victims. The first, though beloved by the goddess, challenged her at the discus or may even have tried to rape her: she had him stung by a scorpion. The second claimed to be a better hunter than she, but more significantly, surprised her when she was naked and bathing in a fountain: she changed him into a stag and had her dogs devour him. But it is the tragic story of Callisto that draws attention to the links between the goddess and bears.

Daughter of King Lycaon of Arcadia, Callisto was extraordinarily beautiful but avoided all men. She preferred to hunt in the company of Artemis, because, like the goddess herself and all her followers, she had made a vow of chastity. Zeus saw her one day and became infatuated; to approach her, he took on the form of Artemis and forced himself upon her. The young woman became pregnant and the time came when she could no longer conceal it. Violently angry, Artemis shot her with an arrow, which immediately delivered her of the child and also transformed her into a she-bear.[40] Thereafter she wandered in animal form in the mountains while her son Arcas grew up to become the king of Arcadia. One day out hunting he encountered his mother, still in the form of a she-bear. He was about to kill her when Zeus, to avoid such a crime, changed him too into a bear, or rather a bear cub; then he lifted them both into the heavens, where they became the constellations Ursa Major and Ursa

Minor.[41] In other versions, Callisto was the victim of Hera's anger, not that of Artemis. And it was the wife of Zeus who changed her into a she-bear; once Zeus had saved the animal and made her into the northern constellation, Hera asked Poseidon to prevent her from ever sinking into the ocean. That is why Ursa Major and Ursa Minor are the only constellations that always remain above the horizon.[42]

The legend of Callisto and Arcas brings out one of the three principal mythological themes associating the human being and the bear, the theme of metamorphosis. We will consider the two others later: the maternal and protective she-bear that protects and nurses a human infant; and the monstrous sexual love, sometimes fertile, between a woman and a male bear. Callisto is not the only figure in Greek mythology connected to Artemis who was changed into a bear. There is another, even more famous: Iphigenia, sacrificed by her father Agamemnon when the fleet preparing to sail for Troy was becalmed at Aulis. Artemis was holding back the winds, and the seer Calchas had explained to Agamemnon, the leader of the expedition, that to appease the anger of the goddess, he had to sacrifice his daughter to her. The fiery king of Argos at first refused. But under pressure from his brother Menelaus, he sent for Iphigenia on the pretext of betrothing her to Achilles; then he led her to the altar of the goddess, not to marry her but to immolate her. Artemis finally took pity on the girl and at the last moment changed her into a she-bear, and in that form she escaped from the priest's knife and disappeared. Artemis had taken her to Tauris (Crimea), where she made her into her principal priestess, until Iphigenia's brother Orestes one day came to free his sister. In some versions, she is not changed into a bear but a doe or a heifer before being carried off. But the bear story seems to be the oldest, the most frequent, and the most in conformity with the powers of Artemis.[43]

She is the goddess not just of wild animals but especially of bears, whose appearance she sometimes assumes. Her name itself is constructed from the Indo-European root for most of the words designating the animal (*art-, arct-, ars-, ors-, urs-*, and so on), notably the Greek word *arktos*.[44] The legend of Callisto and her son Arcas is also linked to this etymology: Arcas bears a name that directly evokes the bear, and his rich kingdom,

Arcadia, located in the center of the Peloponnesus, is etymologically "the land of the bears."[45] In his description of Greece compiled in the second century AD, the great traveler Pausanias describes how "in the past" the men of Arcadia at war against Sparta put on bearskins before going into combat.[46]

But Arcadia does not have a monopoly on bears. They are encountered practically everywhere in the toponymy of ancient Greece, primarily in mountainous country and particularly where there are sanctuaries dedicated to Artemis, whose priestesses were sometimes called "little she-bears" (arktoi).[47] The oldest of these sanctuaries was not in Arcadia but in Attica at Brauron (present-day Vravrona, not far from Athens). From the sixth century BC to the Hellenistic period, a strange spring ritual was conducted there every five years: little girls younger than ten were dressed in yellow and white, acted as priestesses, and participated in the great festivals performed in honor of the goddess. The ceremonies concluded with the sacrifice of a she-bear. It is probable that this was a toned-down form of an older ritual in which these same girls were perhaps violated and then sacrificed. The legend explained that the sanctuary at Brauron had been created to appease the anger of Artemis after the inhabitants of the village had killed a bear that had devoured a female child. The goddess had let it be known through an oracle that she demanded that the villagers ritually devote their daughters to her, first as immolated victims, later as devoted priestesses.[48]

It is probable that the tragic story of the sacrifice of Iphigenia in Aulis is connected to this tradition and that both are tied to a very old ursine myth associated with Artemis the chaste huntress and protector of wild animals. Euripides, moreover, asserts that Iphigenia herself, on her return from Tauris, established the sanctuary at Brauron and made it one of the most frequented pilgrimage sites in Antiquity.[49]

From Greek Myths to Celtic Myths

The motif of the young child sheltered and nursed by a wild animal appears in most mythologies and legends about the origins of heroes. The

Roman she-wolf remains the most famous example, but classical Antiquity produced several others just as memorable: for example, there are two stories in Greek mythology highly relevant to the subject at hand, since they feature not a she-wolf but a she-bear. The first concerns Atalanta, a heroine with extraordinary physical abilities that, in some versions, earned her a place as the only woman Jason accepted on the expedition of the Argonauts to seek the Golden Fleece. The story of Atalanta, however, began badly and ended even worse. Her father King Iasos of Arcadia (Arcadia again, the country of bears) wanted to have only sons. When Atalanta was born he abandoned her in the heart of a forest on Mount Parthenion. There she was found by a she-bear who nursed and protected her and taught her to walk. Then hunters took her in and gave her a rugged masculine upbringing. Atalanta became a formidable huntress, and like all disciples of Artemis, vowed to resist the temptations of love and to remain forever a virgin. When she grew into a beautiful and strong young woman, she was besieged by men. Several tried to violate her, and she killed all of them. Celebrated for her savage character and virile virtues, she was finally acknowledged by her father, who took it into his head to marry her off so that she would have descendants. After long refusing, Atalanta accepted, on one condition: her future husband would be the man who beat her in a footrace; men who lost would be immediately beheaded. Despite this dreadful fate, many young men competed. All of them lost and died. Then a superb suitor came forward named Hippomenes, a protégé of Aphrodite. The goddess had given him three golden apples from the garden of the Hesperides. During the race he dropped them on the ground and to everyone's surprise Atalanta stopped to pick them up; she lost time and was unable to catch up to Hippomenes. The winner of the race married the proud young woman (who probably wished for that outcome). But the newlyweds forgot to thank Aphrodite, who took revenge by turning them into lions. In some versions, Zeus, not Aphrodite, causes the metamorphosis, angered because they made love for the first time in one of his temples. In still others, it is Artemis, furious at having lost one of her protégées, who transforms the couple into animals, not lions, of course, but bears.[50]

The second tale concerns one of the most celebrated heroes of Greek mythology, Paris, the youngest son of King Priam of Troy. Before his birth, his mother Hecuba had dreamed that she would give birth not to a child but to a kind of flaming torch that would set fire to the entire city— a premonitory dream foretelling the destruction of Troy. Terrified, Priam decided to get rid of the newborn child and ordered one of his servants to kill him in the forest. But the servant took pity on the infant and exposed him alive on Mount Ida, where he came close to dying from cold and hunger. A she-bear discovered him, warmed, nursed, and cared for him.[51] Paris was later taken in by shepherds and grew into a magnificent young man. One day when Paris was tending his flock on Mount Ida, Hermes came to ask him in the name of Zeus to judge the beauty of three goddesses: Hera, Athena, and Aphrodite, each of whom claimed to be the most beautiful. Paris was to give the one he chose a golden apple. Each of the goddesses sought to seduce him and promised him a particular gift: Hera, rule over all Asia; Athena, victory in all battles; and Aphrodite, the love of the most beautiful woman in the world, Helen, wife of King Menelaus of Sparta. Paris chose Aphrodite and gave her the apple, thereby incurring the enmity of the two other goddesses. He then returned to Troy and was recognized and celebrated by his parents and brothers. He soon went off to the Peloponnesus, met the beautiful Helen, fell violently in love, seduced her, and carried her off. Thus began the Trojan War.

Countless writers since Homer have recounted and commented on the judgment of Paris, the abduction of Helen, and the ensuing dramatic events. But very few of them have pointed out that the abduction of the most beautiful woman in the world was the act not of an ordinary man but of a man who had for a time been nursed and raised by a she-bear, that is, a human being who, because of his early education, retained some traces of a certain ursine nature.[52] As I will show later, in European oral traditions, the male bear is the principal animal attracted by women; bears abduct and have intercourse with women, who then give birth to creatures that are half-human, half-bear. The tragic story of Paris thereby seems to be associated with an ursine myth from deep in the past involving the coupling of woman and wild animal, beauty and the beast. It is the oldest documented version of the many stories of thieving and raping bears appearing in tales and legends throughout Europe, from Antiquity to the present time.

Although the ursine nature of the hero is more or less masked in the story of Paris, there is another less well-known tale in Greek mythology in which sexual intercourse of a bear and a woman is expressly mentioned. This is the sad tale of Polyphonte, another girl who had taken a vow of chastity in honor of Artemis. The vow irritated Aphrodite, the goddess of love, who saw it as a kind of challenge. She tempted Polyphonte in countless ways, gave her magnificent gifts, and when she met resistance from the girl, became vindictively angry, finally causing her to conceive a monstrous passion for a bear. Polyphonte gave birth to two sons, Agrios (Savage) and Oreios (Mountain Man), prodigiously strong creatures who feared neither men nor gods. Zeus came to loathe them and ordered Hermes to kill them. Hermes did not have the time to act; the god Ares, grandfather of Polyphonte, took pity on the mother and her two sons and changed all three of them into birds; but they were fearsome birds, an owl and two vultures.[53]

Another figure in Greek mythology had sexual relations with a bear. This was not a woman, but Cephalus, a young hunter of remarkable beauty and the hero of a number of rather disparate myths. Childless, having tragically killed his beloved wife Procris by accident, and wanting to have sons, Cephalus consulted the oracle at Delphi. The oracle told him to have intercourse with the first female creature he encountered on his way home. He did as the oracle said: the creature was a she-bear, and their union produced a son, Arcisios—another name based on the word for bear—one of whose descendants was the extraordinary character Odysseus.[54]

Celtic mythology also contains tales of unions between humans and animals. But they usually involve horses: King Mark of Cornwall, for example, has a female ancestor who slept with a horse; he inherited from this union a horse's mane and ears that he vainly tries to hide. Although some heroes do have an ursine character, this is for another reason: they have been raised by a goddess or a fairy who is a protector of she-bears.

The Celtic pantheon is indeed full of feminine figures close to the Greek Artemis; several of them even have names directly associating them with the twin sister of Apollo. One example is the goddess Arduina, whose cult was located in the Ardennes region that bears her name; her alpine equivalent is Andarta, protector of both hunters and wild animals. Most important is the great goddess Artio, a veritable replica of Artemis among the Celts of southern Germany and Switzerland.[55] Her principal emblem is the bear, seen in a votive statue found, among others, in 1832 at Muri, near Bern: it represents the nourishing goddess, bearing fruit, sitting facing a bear, with the inscription DEAE ARTIONI / LICINIA SABINILLA (to the goddess Artio [from] Licinia Sabinilla). The group dates from the late second century, a period when that region of Switzerland had already been thoroughly Romanized.[56] But ancient bear cults often resisted Romanization and persisted over centuries.

The case of King Arthur, whose name is directly related to the word for bear and who will be considered later, is different. He is not a divinity but a monarch, the most famous in medieval literature. His story is partly connected to an ancient ursine myth, various traces of which are found in several Celtic legends. The figure of the king is associated with the figure of the bear, because for the Celts—as for the Germans, the Balts, and the Slavs—the bear is the king of all the animals, and hence the quintessential royal animal. He retained that status in a large part of Christian Europe throughout the High Middle Ages and even in the period immediately after the year 1000, until the Church, the sworn enemy of the bear, finally succeeded in installing on the symbolic throne another wild animal, the lion.

King of the Beasts

AT one point or another in its history, every culture chooses a "king of the beasts" and makes it the centerpiece of its symbolic bestiary. Forms of expression, oral traditions, poetic creations, and insignia and representations of all kinds grant the chosen animal superiority over all others and a central place in belief systems, forms of worship, and rituals. Despite the extreme diversity of societies, it can be said that the choice almost always derives from the same criterion: the designated animal is chosen because of its reputation, justified or not, for invincibility. Everywhere and always, the king of the beasts is the one who cannot be conquered by any other animal. The very few exceptions are circumstantial or are based on systems of reversal that merely confirm the criterion: choosing as king the weakest or most fragile animal still relies on the essential notions of strength and victory. And such instances are trivial, because the general rule, seldom infringed, is that the king is always the strongest.[1]

This means that choices are restricted. In Africa, it is sometimes the lion, sometimes the elephant, less frequently the rhinoceros; in Asia, the lion, the tiger, or the elephant. In America, the choice falls on the eagle or the bear, and, in regions where it can be found, the jaguar. In Europe, the king was for a long time the bear, and later the lion. There have been occasional scattered variants, but they are limited in time or space, whereas a "true" king of the beasts has to last and flourish in several different cultural regions. With this in mind, looking at the entire planet, there are, so to speak, only four kings of the beasts: the lion, the eagle, the bear, and the elephant. Each of them holds or held that rank not only in its place of origin but also sometimes in other cultures and on several continents. This is particularly true of the lion, which, already the king in Asia and Africa, slowly took the place of the bear in Europe.

The Herculean strength of the bear, the fact that no animal can best it (man is its only predator), and its long history of being admired and feared in all European regions were not enough to keep it on its throne. The foreign lion, preferred by the medieval Church, gradually drove it off, demonstrating that, despite the criteria set out above, cultural history always wins out over natural history. Or, more precisely, as I noted at the beginning of this book, natural history is simply one branch of cultural history.

The Strength of the Bear

No animal indigenous to Europe gave an impression of strength comparable to the bear's. All the ancient authors who wrote about the animal emphasized this impression, and it gave rise to many proverbs, images, and metaphors. The expression "as strong as a bear" exists in all European languages and matches a reality already described by Aristotle in his *History of Animals* and adopted by all his imitators and successors, notably Pliny and the medieval tradition he gave rise to.[2] The bear was the strongest of all the animals in Europe. Subsequently, modern naturalists from Gesner to Buffon explained what made up that strength, where it came from, and how it manifested itself. And although nineteenth- and twentieth-century naturalists contributed some supplementary incidental information, they hardly changed a picture that was already well established by the time of the Renaissance.

The brown bear appears first of all as a powerful and massive creature that could reach a height of eight or nine feet and a weight of 600, 800, or even 1,000 pounds. Those are, of course, record figures, at least in Europe, but it is likely that ancient and medieval bears were heavier than their present-day descendants. The bear is fattest in late autumn, when it begins hibernation. Its heavy look and clumsy appearance are accentuated by a short, thick neck of extraordinary strength and a very broad chest. Neck and chest contrast with a relatively small head and modest hindquarters. The animal's primary strength is located in the muscles of the neck, shoulders, arms, and chest. It resembles a stocky wrestler with a disproportionately large upper body. This is confirmed by anatomic analysis of its musculature, which reveals very powerful brachial, dorsal, and pectoral muscles. They are what enable the bear to carry or haul loads heavier than itself, to move gigantic blocks of stone, to break huge tree trunks, to kill a man or a large animal—cattle or wild game—with a single blow of a paw.

Despite the disproportionately small size of its head compared to its chest, the bear has very well-developed masticatory and temporal muscles. They are associated with a versatile and effective dental apparatus adapted to its omnivorous diet. First, there are incisors that are veritable pincers, enabling the animal not only to cut almost anything but also to grasp farm animals (sheep, goats, pigs) and carry them in its mouth. The canines are fearsomely sharp, and with them it lacerates and tears its prey to pieces. Finally, huge molars enable it to grind any vegetable and extract fruits from their shells. But the small size of its jaw opening means that it makes less use of its teeth than of its forepaws, particularly the left one, which it sometimes uses as a club, to attack and kill. Two writers, one medieval and the other modern,[3] have noted that the bear uses its left more often than its right paw and concluded—a bit too hastily—that it was "left-handed," a particularity which, added to many others, seemed to strengthen its troubling, not to say harmful character. Earlier cultures, notably the Christian culture of the Middle Ages, saw left-handedness as the sign of an evil nature, or indeed of a counter-nature.[4]

To its extraordinary muscular strength, the bear adds resistance to fatigue and to bad weather unmatched by any other European species. The bear seems not to be troubled by cold, rain, snow, wind, or storm; only extreme heat reduces its activity and impels it to rest. But bears generally seem to overcome all the hostile forces of nature and to look on any form of danger with contempt. No animal frightens them, not even the largest boars they encounter in the woods and that sometimes battle with them over prey, and even less the packs of wolves that attack bears in winter in groups of fifteen or twenty and try to tear them to pieces.[5] The bear fears nothing and is, indeed, practically invincible.

It is therefore hardly surprising that this animal fascinated humanity from very ancient times and became the embodiment of brute force, unconquerable courage, and superiority over all other animals. For most northern and northwestern European peoples of antiquity, who had never had any occasion to see elephants or the great beasts of Africa or Asia, the bear, present in every forest, became almost naturally the king of wild fauna and the emblem of chiefs and warriors. One after the other, Germans, Celts, Slavs, Balts, and Lapps looked on it as an animal apart, made it the central figure in their bestiary, and worshiped it in various manners. The problem remains for the historian to determine the links that may have existed between possible Paleolithic bear cults and the cults of antiquity and the High Middle Ages, well attested as early as the first millennium before our era and solidly documented in the periods preceding Christianization. Mythological narratives offer some suggestive hints, but obviously they do not make it possible to fill in the thirty or forty thousand years separating the former from the latter.

Whereas the Celts and Germans had seen pictures of lions or elephants only relatively recently, shortly before or shortly after the Roman conquests, the situation was different for the peoples of Mediterranean Europe. They had long known of the existence of the large maned cat, the huge pachyderm, and a few other exotic animals remarkable for their size, their power, or their appearance. The Romans in particular had been able to marvel at the physical presence of various species in the circus games that were larger and more savage than the European bear. Although they sometimes staged battles in the arena between bears and bulls (the bears almost always won), they especially liked to see wild animals brought from Africa or Asia fight one another or against men. Sometimes, however, curiosity made them wonder about the strength of a bear or a bull compared to that of an animal from afar, and so there were battles between bears and lions, bears and panthers, bulls and lions, bulls and an elephant, and even a bear and a rhinoceros.[6] Although bulls, fighting alone or in a group, seem never to have been victorious, a bear always won in single combat against a lion or against several panthers. But that was not enough to make the bear the king of the beasts in the eyes of the Romans. Like the Greeks—who had little fondness for animal combat—they preferred to install on the throne either the lion or, perhaps more frequently, the elephant.[7] There never seems to have been a battle between a bear and an elephant, but Martial recorded a combat in Rome late in the first century of our era between a bear and a rhinoceros: the latter won easily, piercing the bear's stomach with its horn, then lifting its wounded opponent from the ground with its snout and tossing it in the air several times.[8] A cruel humiliation for the European champion.

Aside from this battle, bears usually won glory in circus games. They never fought against one another, but against bulls, lions, or *venatores* (hunter-gladiators) helped by dogs.[9] It seems that the strongest came from Caledonia (Scotland) and Dalmatia. A mosaic fragment from the third century found in a suburb of Rodez representing Caledonian bears that had won renown in circus games preserves the names of six of them: two females (Fedra and Alecsandria) and four males (Nilus, Simplicius, Braciatus, and the champion Gloriosus).[10] Late in the following century, several letters from the consul Symmachus, prefect of Rome in 381 and 384, recount how this rich and powerful official and upholder of Roman tradition found bears for the circus games: he got them from specialized "recruiters" in Dalmatia, the *ursorum negotiatores*. He worries about a delayed shipment, fearing that during the transport someone will substitute ordinary bears for the remarkable beasts he has been promised and for which he has paid handsomely; finally, he quarrels with the dealers and, for that year, gives up receiving the huge and splendid bears from Dalmatia.[11]

The Courage of the Warrior

The warriors of Germany never heard of the defeat of the bear by the rhinoceros recounted by Martial. For several more centuries, as they had from time immemorial, they continued to hold the bear in the highest esteem. In their eyes, this almost-invincible animal, more than any other living being, embodied strength and power. Hence, they sought to compare themselves to bears, to confront and defeat them and take on their powers, and to turn the bear into both their emblem and their ancestor.

For the Germans, the bear was much more than the king of the forest or the bestiary; it was the quintessential totemic animal.[12]

For young men, for example, fighting and killing a bear was an obligatory rite of passage for admission into the world of adult warriors. More than a ceremony tied to the hunt, it was an initiation ritual that ended with hand-to-hand combat between man and beast. The young man had only his dagger to get the better of the animal, and the bear used its forepaws as a vise to try to crush the man against its chest. The young warrior had to avoid being crushed, battered, or lacerated, but it was nonetheless by allowing himself to be as closely held as possible by the beast that he would manage to stab his opponent in the belly. The bear contributed to its own death by squeezing the young warrior against itself, with his dagger coming before him. But the man often died of suffocation before he could stab the point of his weapon into the skin of the huge beast.

Tacitus does not mention this ritual in his work on the peoples of Germany, written in the late first century of our era.[13] But three centuries later, in his *Histories,* compiled around 370–380, the Roman senator and historian Ammianus Marcellinus describes how young men among the Goths similarly had to confront and defeat a bear (and a boar) before joining the community of adult men.[14] Later, various sagas and narrative texts from Iceland and Scandinavia allude to similar rituals. In his *Gesta Danorum,* which recounts the history of the Danish people from the beginning to the end of the twelfth century, the learned Saxo Grammaticus (c. 1150–c. 1220), for example, tells how a very young man named Skiold, while on a bear hunt, had to confront a huge bear unarmed and barehanded; despite this disadvantage, he managed to immobilize the animal, tie it up with his belt, and lead it toward other hunters, who killed it. This feat made him a respected adult warrior, and the memory of the glorious deed later helped him to mount the throne as the fourth king of Denmark.[15]

Real or legendary, the exploit of the young Skiold took place before the year 1000, when Scandinavia was still pagan. But even long after Christianization, defeating a bear in single combat remained for young nobles of northern Germany and Norway a mark of courage and a sign of uncommon quality as a warrior. A victory over the wild animal often foreshadowed for the victor a future as chief or king. Many chronicles and literary works tell the tale of a hero who, after defeating a bear, takes the fate of his people or his lineage in hand and finds glory. But not all these heroes were fictitious; some very real major figures of the feudal period are said to have defeated a bear in their youth, and by this deed to have come to the notice of their elders or their peers. These tales, a legacy of German and Scandinavian societies of antiquity and the High Middle Ages, were found not only in Germany, Denmark, and Iceland; they also circulated in Scotland, England, France, and even in the Holy Land, showing that medieval Christian culture, child of the Bible and the Greco-Roman world, was also long imbued with "barbarian" traditions.[16] An often-cited example is that of Baldwin Iron-Arm, first "Count" of Flanders (died c. 878): when still young, toward the middle of the ninth century, he defeated a bear that had been terrifying the Bruges region, an exploit that brought him to the attention of King Charles the Bald, of whom he became both the son-in-law and the vassal.[17] But the most famous medieval example was not Baldwin but the later one of Godfrey of Bouillon.

The episode occurred during the First Crusade, in the spring of 1099, a few weeks before the crusaders captured Jerusalem. Godfrey, Duke of Lower Lorraine and Bouillon, was merely one leader of the crusade among others. He had come to the Holy Land with his two brothers, Eustace and Baldwin of Boulogne, at the head of a large contingent of crusaders from Flanders, Hainaut, Brabant, and the Meuse valley. For the past two years he had distinguished himself in the fight between Franks and Muslims by numerous exploits, notably during the capture of Nicaea in June 1097. But more than his successes against the enemies of the Christian faith, it was his victory over a bear that definitively turned him into the sole leader of the crusade, then the defender of the Holy Sepulcher of Jerusalem, and finally after his death a legendary figure, almost a saint. The chronicler Albert of Aachen, canon at Aix-la-Chapelle, was the first to provide a detailed account of the combat between the duke and the animal. Godfrey was riding alone in a wood when he saw a bear of extraordinary size with exceedingly long and sharp teeth and claws attacking a pilgrim. He immediately came to the help of the unfortunate victim and confronted the huge beast. The bear first attacked the horse, which it soon killed and tore to pieces; then it threw itself on the rider, who had fallen to the ground armed with only a sword. They engaged in a violent hand-to-hand combat that lasted for a considerable time, with the advantage shifting back and forth between the animal and the duke. Finally, Godfrey succeeded in mortally wounding the bear in the head and neck; but he felt his strength ebbing and was about to perish, smothered by the dying monster, which was gripping him with its forepaws, when one of his companions named Husechin, alerted by the great uproar, came on the scene and freed the duke from the mortal clasp of the beast. The two men then killed the bear, "saying they had never seen anything like it in size."[18]

Albert's account, written between 1120 and 1130 and repeated by several chroniclers of the twelfth and thirteenth centuries, notably by William of Tyre,[19] is clearly nothing but a series of clichés intended to bring out Godfrey's courage and prowess. The fact that he was not able to completely vanquish the enormous animal adds a touch of truth and humanity to the story and makes the hero's exploit even more credible, but that hardly changes the lengthy accumulation of commonplaces that make up the meticulous description of the battle, intended to emphasize the victor's uncommon qualities. A few days later, in the wake of the capture of Jerusalem on July 15, 1099, Godfrey was elected king of the new Frankish state of the Holy Land by the principal leaders of the crusade. But he considered himself unworthy of so high a title and adopted that of mere "defender of the Holy Sepulcher." He died a short time later, in the spring of 1100. Thereafter, historians and chroniclers were prolific about his deeds of battle, before and during the crusade, and gave prominence to his valor, generosity, and great piety, with the aim of making him the picture of the perfect Christian knight. In the fourteenth century, this earned him a place in the exemplary company of the "Nine Worthies," in which he was, along with Charlemagne and King Arthur, one of the three

Christian worthies.[20] This was a surprising posthumous fate for a prince who was a younger son in the family, but legend set him on an equal footing with the great Emperor of the West and the prestigious sovereign of medieval literature.

The historical reality was obviously somewhat different from legendary and literary traditions. The real Godfrey of Bouillon was perhaps a man of sincere piety and remarkable physical strength. But he was also and primarily a hesitant leader, a brutal warrior, and a mediocre politician. Furthermore, the victorious combat with the bear that his earliest biographers and most historians of the crusades bring to the fore probably never happened. But the episode was necessary to distinguish the Duke of Bouillon from the other Frankish leaders in order to make him the first "king" of Jerusalem. His exploit accords not only with the Germanic tradition of singular combat between the leader and the bear; it also echoes the biblical passage that recounts how the young David, while still a shepherd, successfully defended his flock against a fearsome bear and a lion who were threatening to devour his sheep (1 Samuel 17.34–35). Victorious over the beast, Godfrey appeared to be a new David. One can also observe that in certain late chronicles, compiled in the fourteenth and fifteenth centuries, at a time when a victory over a bear was seldom any longer a remarkable deed of arms for a king or a Christian knight, accounts of the episode replaced the bear with a lion.

The Berserkers

Although it was not the first, Godfrey of Bouillon's exploit functioned as a model that recurred over several decades in chronicles, chansons de geste, and courtly romances. There is a long list of literary or legendary heroes who, over the course of the twelfth century, confronted a bear or an ursine monster, beginning with the greatest of them: Roland, Tristan, Lancelot, Yvain, and King Arthur himself.[21] But this obligatory ritual had now been Christianized and had preserved nothing of the savage trance that possessed warriors confronting the beast in pagan Germanic traditions. Several sagas and epic poems, certain narrative and mythological texts, and a few iconographic representations have preserved traces of the various practices through which those warriors, before or after the battle, sought to fill themselves with the beast's powers. These practices could not help but terrify bishops and clergy, who did everything possible to put an end to them as soon as the regions concerned were Christianized.[22]

The most savage of these practices was drinking the animal's blood and eating its flesh, a kind of ritual meal of a strongly totemic (in the anthropological sense) character, which helped to symbolically transform the warrior into a bear, to endow him with the animal's strength and thereby make him invincible.[23] An ancient version of the *Landnàmabok* (Book of the Colonization of Iceland),[24] for example, tells how a figure named Odd attacked a colossal bear that had killed his father and brother, slew and butchered it, and ate all its flesh, thereby transforming himself into a kind of unconquerable half-man half-animal. Thereafter, out of a spirit of vengeance, he tried to kill as many bears as possible until the day he died.[25] Later on, in the late twelfth century, in a compilation of excerpts from various sagas, Saxo Grammaticus explains how "some ancient Danish warriors" used to drink the blood of the bears they had defeated to become as fearsome as the beasts; he even explains that a bath in the animal's blood could be joined with or replace the bloody drink.[26] In the *Nibelungenlied*, the final form of which dates from around 1200, Siegfried proceeds in practically the same way when he bathes in the blood of the dragon he has just killed, thereby covering his body with a coating that makes him invulnerable; unfortunately, a lime leaf fell between his shoulders, and that is where the traitor Hagen succeeds in killing him with a sword blow.

By the Carolingian period, the prelates of Germany prohibited the eating of bear meat, which smacked too much of pagan customs.[27] But the repetition of these prohibitions, which extended to Scandinavia after the year 1000, demonstrates that they were seldom respected. Toward the end of the twelfth century, the Benedictine abbess Hildegard of Bingen, whose interests were at the same time mystical, moral, and medical, remarked on how dangerous it was to eat the flesh of the bear: "it is an impure meat that inflames the senses, leads to sin, and can cause death."[28]

It is likely, however, that the ritual absorption of bear's blood gradually faded in Christian lands, and that in the feudal period, in Germany as in Denmark, eating the animal's meat was nothing more than a simple custom with no totemic, savage, or bloodthirsty aspects. In the late Middle Ages, eating bear remained an aristocratic habit in several regions, not only in the north. In several Tyrol and Piedmont valleys, for example, the village communities had to supply to their lord every year a certain number of bear paws (the best cut), which he ate publicly in a kind of symbolic meal.[29] This was a last vestige of age-old practices that had more or less lost any meaning, but also important evidence of the battle against the bear still being waged in mountain country by lords and by peasants.

Earlier, among the ancient Scandinavians, the most famous and probably most frequent ursine ritual was not consumption of the flesh and blood of the animal but disguise using the animal's skin. The sagas and tales of Norse mythology present heroes going into combat wearing the skin of the animal they have killed. This garment of fur imbues them with the power of the beast, protects them from adversity, and endows them with incomparable strength. The most fearsome of these warriors were the Berserkers, who were soldiers of Odin, the chief divinity of the Norse pantheon, a cruel, treacherous, and cynical god, secretive and omniscient. The great Icelandic writer Snorri Sturluson, in *Ynglinga Saga,* the first part of his long *Heimskringla Saga,* written between 1220 and 1230, probably provided the best description of the Berserker: They "went to battle without coats of mail and acted like mad dogs or wolves. They bit their shields and were as strong as bears or bulls. They killed people, and neither fire nor iron affected them. This is called berserker rage."[30]

Snorri Sturluson was not the only one to portray the battle fury of these young warriors of Odin. They were mentioned as early as the ninth century and up to the thirteenth in several texts that emphasize their semibestial nature and the savage trance that possessed them. They are also represented in some artifacts. One can recognize three Berserkers among the famous chess pieces made of walrus tusks, which were carved in Norway toward the middle of the twelfth century and found in the sand dunes of Lewis Island off the western coast of Scotland, now preserved in the British Museum. The three pawns, wearing long tunics made of fur, are pictured in such a state of rage that they are biting their shields.[31] Like all Berserkers they are dual creatures, not werewolves like those encountered later in *courtois* literature but "were-bears," specific to the Norse and Germanic worlds.[32] Several writers explain that Berserkers went into battle imitating the gait and the groans of the bear; others that they ate human flesh; still others that they were metamorphosed into bears in the course of a magical-religious ceremony in which cries, chants, dances, potions, and drugs brought them to a state of frenetic excitement, as though they were possessed. They felt themselves transformed into wild beasts, lost any social sense, reached an extreme degree of savagery and aggressiveness, and felt no more fear or pity. Like the bear, they were or felt themselves to be invulnerable. Sometimes in this trance state, they imagined they had a bear for an ancestor, and they invoked its memory and asked it for courage and protection.[33] To describe this same state, some writers call the young warriors of Odin not "bear shirts" (Berserkers) but "wolf cloaks" *(Ulfhednir),* because they wore wolf skins when they entered a trance or went into combat.[34] This was nevertheless not as frequent, because in the pagan cultures of northern Europe the wolf was a particularly negative animal, simultaneously cowardly, hideous, and pitiless.[35]

These warrior rituals are worth comparing to well-attested shamanistic practices in more recent periods among several hunting peoples of northern Asia and America. These peoples believed in animal spirits, notably those of the bear, as both ancestor and totem. To enter into contact with these spirits and secure protection and benefits from them, shamans engaged in various rituals involving ecstasy and trance; they would, for example, put on the skin of the animal concerned and imitate its cries and behavior, start frenetically dancing, enter into a state approaching possession, leave their human state, and finally reach the spirit-world.[36] In the course of this journey into the beyond, they liberated themselves almost entirely from physical contingencies, exactly as the Berserkers did.

The Powers of the Name

There were other customs, more peaceful and better documented, among the ancient Germans and Scandinavians that brought out the bonds uniting the bear and the warrior. There was, for example, the custom of carrying on one's person a bear's teeth or claws, talismans that had already been used by men of the Paleolithic. There was above all the habit of using in combat signs, weapons, and armor decorated with the image of a bear, which clearly functioned not as decoration but as protection; it was both emblematic and prophylactic. The bear was, of course, not the only animal used for this purpose. Other animal figures expressed the identity of the group or clan, sometimes that of a single warrior; they evoked the totem-animal, called forth its protection, captured its strength, and terrified the enemy. The number of animals in this bestiary was limited: crow, eagle, stag, boar, or bear. Employed less often were wolf, horse, bull, falcon, lion, panther, dragon, and griffin.[37]

The presence of the last four animals, along with the extremely stylized depiction of motifs and scenes, demonstrates that the warrior imagery of northern Europe was influenced early on by the art of Central Asia and Siberia without passing through the reductive mold of Roman or Byzantine art.

The bear occupied the central place in this bestiary. It was found on banners, helmets, and swords, as well as on belt buckles and metal plates reinforcing breastplates or armor. It was found less frequently on clasps and absent from brooches and jewelry. It played a clearly military role. Moreover, archeological investigation has never uncovered a woman's jewel or an accessory for a female costume decorated with a bear. For periods preceding Christianization, the bulk of our information comes from abundant funerary material found in tombs. Decorations on various objects show bears entire or just their upper halves. They are sometimes depicted alone, sometimes accompanying or surrounding a warrior, as on the famous Torslunda plate, found on the island of Öland in the Baltic Sea, probably dating from the late sixth century of our era.[38] The two bears are clearly recognizable. Indeed, the same attributes always enable one to identify the animal: clearly marked hairiness; short tail; small, rounded ears; aggressive attitude, and huge paws. The bear is the image of the warrior, or better, the warrior himself, who has decorated his weapons and his armor with the image of the wild beast to take on its name, its appearance, its courage, and its strength.[39] In the sagas, where accounts of dreams are frequent, it is not unusual for a chief or a hero to see a bear in a dream warning him of impending danger; or the bear is an image of a dead guardian ancestor; or else, the hero himself in his dream takes on the appearance of a bear to confront his enemies, generally represented as wolves. Narrative traces and uses of insignia come together to bring out the complete assimilation of bear and warrior.

Anthroponymy, perhaps even more than archeology, iconography, and literature, gives us a sense of the magical aspect of this assimilation. Bearing a name based on that of the bear means turning oneself into that animal and profiting from all the powers it has. But here, too, it should be pointed out that the bear was not the only animal used; among Germanic and Scandinavian peoples, personal names taken from fauna are numerous, perhaps more numerous than in any other European society. Six animals are particularly involved: first the crow, emblem of Odin, chief god in the Norse pantheon; followed by the bear and the boar, models of courage and indomitable force; finally, for various reasons, the stag, the eagle, and the wolf. But in northern Germany and Scandinavia, the bear is probably the most common.[40] There are countless simple or compound names based on the roots *Ber, Bern, Bera, Born, Beorn, Per, Pern, Björn,* and so on, all forms derived from the word for bear. With a few exceptions, they are masculine names. Moreover, the war god Thor was early on given as surname the common name for bear in Old Norse: *björn (Thorbjörn);* in northern Europe, the god of warriors, thunder, and lightning was a thoroughly ursine god.[41]

After Christianization, some pagan names became Christian given names and adopted Latin forms: *Adalbero, Ansperus, Asbornus, Bernardus, Bernuardus, Bernhelmis, Gerbernus, Osbernus, Perngerus, Reinbernus, Torbiornus;* this occurred in the face of opposition from many bishops who, until the end of the Carolingian era in Germany and the twelfth century in Scandinavia, wanted the newly baptized to adopt the name of an apostle or a major saint rather than keeping a name "calling to mind wild animals, violence, blood, and war."[42] It was a futile effort. Most of these names persisted and sometimes even became those of great personages in the service of the Church, such as Archbishop Adalbéron of Reims (d. 988) and Bishop Bernward of Hildesheim (d. 1022); not to mention the great Saint Bernard (1091–1153), who on several occasions denounced the presence of paintings and sculptures of wild animals in monastic churches, even though he himself bore a name that meant "strong as a bear." Perhaps it was too difficult for the austere and punctilious Abbé of Clairvaux to acknowledge the connotations of his name.

In Germanic languages, the word for bear (*Bär* in German, long written *Beer*) has a sound suggesting strength and violence. It should be compared with the word for boar *(Eber),* its cousin and rival in the realm of animal symbolism,[43] and with the word designating the lord or war leader, *Baro* or *Bero*, which gave to Old French *ber*, preserved in modern French in the accusative *baron.* These various words probably have a common etymology, to be found in the neighborhood of the root **ghwer* or **bher*, which in proto-Germanic means "the strong," "the violent," "one who strikes and kills." But some philologists have suggested another track, simpler and just as interesting: the Germanic bear derives its name from its dark fur, *der Bär* meaning "the brown," "the dark," "one who glows with a dark light"; the word would then be connected to the large family of Indo-European terms constructed from the Sanskrit root **par* or **bar*, that means both "brown" and "brilliant." In the same family is the adjective *barun (braun)*, attested in several old Germanic languages, also meaning both "brown" and "brilliant." At an early date the word entered Latin *(brunnus)* and then the Romance languages *(brun, bruno)* to enrich the Latin lexical palette—that had long been poor, dull, and imprecise—with shades between red and black. The bear is dark, of course, but also glossy and gleaming. For ancient societies that made much more subtle distinctions than we do between the light and the luminous and the luminous and the brilliant, the bear's fur could be simultaneously dark and gleaming. Moreover, in ancient societies, the bear was a lunar animal and thereby often a creature of light, a cold and nocturnal light.

Taboos about the Name

Whatever one makes of these etymological hypotheses, they do have the virtue of drawing attention to an essential problem, the name of the bear. This problem shows the special status of the bear in the cultures of northern Europe, where pronouncing its name could not be done lightly, negligently, or indifferently, as for any other species. Rather, the name had to be used with the greatest caution, spoken with respect or even, where possible, avoided and replaced with metaphors or periphrastic expressions. For hunting peoples, as I have repeatedly noted, the bear was in no way an animal like the others. It was not only the king of the forest but also an intermediate creature between the worlds of beasts, men, and gods. For that very reason, its name was early on surrounded by certain taboos, which led to the creation of various nominative formulations to designate it.[44]

In Germanic as well as in Baltic and Slavic languages, the bear is designated by a word that does not belong to the large Indo-European family of words for bear. This family is based on the root *rks-, *arks-, or *orks-, which may suggest onomatopoetically the sound of the bear grunting, but also refers to the idea of light, since the bear is associated with the moon and with the constellation that bears its name. In many languages, from northern India to the Atlantic, terms designating the bear come in a variety of forms derived from that root. In ancient languages, they include: Sanskrit rksah, Persian khers, Armenian ardch, Ossetian ars, Greek arktos, Latin ursus, Old Irish art, and Middle Welsh arth; and for modern languages: Italian orso, French ours, Castilian oso, Portuguese urso, Catalan òs, Modern Greek arkouda, and Breton arzh.

Nothing of the kind appears in Germanic, Baltic, and Slavic languages. These languages may, of course, have had a term related to the same Indo-European lexical family, but it disappeared very early on, since the respect due the bear, or the fear or veneration it aroused, was a bar to saying the word. Hence, other words or expressions replaced it: nicknames or allusive or descriptive circumlocutions. The Germans, as I have noted, chose to bring out the animal's fur and to give it the name "brown": *bher* or *berun* in proto-Germanic, *bëro* in Middle High German, *bera* in Anglo-Saxon, *björn* in Old Norse and Icelandic, *Bär* in Modern German, *bear* in English, *beer* in Dutch, *björn* in Swedish, and so on. The term sometimes even became a proper name, as in the oldest branches and versions of the *Roman de Renart,* in which the bear is named *Brun.*

Slavic terms were even more picturesque: the bear became "the honey eater," "the honey thief," even "the honey master": *medvèdi* in Old Slavic, *medved'* in Slovenian, *vedmid'* in Ukrainian, and *niedzwiedz* in Polish. Likewise, in Baltic languages, the bear was designated as "the licker," "the one who licks with its tongue": *loki* in Old Lithuanian, *lokys* in Modern Lithuanian, *clokis* in Old Prussian, and *lacis* in Latvian. Was this another allusion to the honey-eating bear or to a very old and widespread belief echoing the image of the she-bear licking its stillborn cubs to give them form and life?

These were not the only languages that tabooed the name of the bear. In other languages, Indo-European or not, the original name of the bear evolved and was rejected in favor of a substitute. In various dialects used by the Lapps, for example, for whom the bear hunt was a fundamental ritual of the social system, the animal answered to several names, all of which were highly metaphoric: "the grandfather," "the ancestor," "the old one of the forest," "the old furred one," "the one that sleeps in the winter," "the one that walks with a light step," or "the one that hears everything."[45] Avoidances and replacements of this kind are found in the languages of all bear-hunting peoples from Siberia to North America: "the old uncle," "honey paw," "broad foot," "light foot," "the glory of the forest." For the Lapps as well, the real name of the bear was not to be spoken but replaced by circumlocutions or nicknames, for otherwise the animal would enter into a violent rage and refuse to allow itself to be killed, and the hunters would come back empty-handed, which would be catastrophic for the group or clan.[46]

Linguists and philologists have long been interested in animals and plants whose names, in one society or another, were generally not to be spoken by particular individuals, or at a particular time of year, or in a specific situation. The unnamed are always animals or plants (especially trees) imbued with great symbolic power that play an important role in beliefs, traditions, and cultural practices. In societies of the northern hemisphere, the animals whose names are most frequently taboo are the bear and the snake—the bear because it represents much more than an animal, either an ancient god or an ancestor of man; the snake because it embodies all the forces of Evil. Speaking its name helps to make it appear or brings misfortune, so that it is better to say "the crawler," "the repugnant one," "the slimy one," or "the greenish one." These lexical prohibitions sometimes extend to certain objects—among the Lapps and the Samoyed, for example, hunting weapons and tools used to kill and butcher the bear—or even to some proper names of places, persons, or divinities that similarly must be replaced by nicknames or circumlocutions.[47]

Arthur the Bear-King

The bear occupied a symbolic position of the first rank among the ancient Celts, comparable to the one it held for the Germans and the Slavs. For the Celts, however, it seemed to have been less frequently associated with the idea of strength, war, or violence, and more with the idea of power and sovereignty. Celtic warriors, to be sure, sometimes carried bear teeth and claws into battle as amulets, as well as weapons and shields decorated with the image of the animal. But while they sometimes adopted the name of the bear—less often than the Germans or Scandinavians—they lacked the capacity to transform themselves into a furious and indomitable beast, as the Berserkers did in dreams, accesses of fury, or trance states. As fiery as they might be, Celtic warriors never attained the intermediate state between human and ursine nature, a state that several German researchers have designated by two highly unusual and practically untranslatable words: *Bärenhaftigkeit,* "bearhood," and *Bärenfähigkeit,* "capacity to become a bear."[48]

Some prohibitions and circumlocutions in ancient Celtic languages nonetheless give a sense of how special an animal the bear was for the Celts, simultaneously feared, admired, and respected. Instead of speaking or writing its name, they chose to use its nickname: *math* or *matu,* which in Irish and Welsh means "male," "virile," and "kindly." In this instance, as in other cultures, the bear is the quintessentially virile animal, the *masle beste* as it was later known in Middle French. It was better to win its favor by calling it "kindly" than to incur its anger by calling it by a name it did not want to hear. The same was true for Matugenos, the god of the Gauls whose name was based on the same root (literally "born of a bear") and who was a warrior god as strong as a bear; it was better to have him with you than against you. In addition to the terms *math* and *matu,* Old Irish and Old Welsh also use metaphoric expressions to designate the animal indirectly: for example, the compound word *mêlfochyn* (literally, "honey pig"), that brings out both the bear's inordinate love of honey and, as in Germanic traditions, its close relationship to the pig.[49]

But unlike the bear of the Germans and the Vikings, the Celtic bear is more of a lord than a warrior. It is often a king and sometimes even a god. In the last chapter, I referred to several Celtic goddesses related to the Greek Artemis who had names directly linked to the bear: Artio, Arduina, and Andarta.[50] They were very ancient Celtic divinities whose worship had followed the migrations of the Celts from Central Europe to the far West; in various forms, traces of them can be found in Bohemia and Switzerland, as well as in Ireland and Wales.[51]

But the legendary King Arthur, along with Charlemagne, was the major royal figure in medieval literature. His origins were unquestionably Celtic and his name was identical to that of the bear, *art* in Irish, *artos* in Gaulish, *arth* in Welsh, and *arzh* in Breton.[52] In Welsh and Irish mythology, the original Arthur seems to have been a bear-king, perhaps even, like the goddess Artio, an ursine divinity who was later transformed into a legendary monarch and then gradually lost most of his original nature.[53] In Latin narrative texts of the Christian High Middle Ages, this animal nature has almost ceased to surface. It was still more discreet in the courtly romances written in vernacular languages in the twelfth and thirteenth centuries. Most writers no longer understood the mythological patterns and themes around which the story of Arthur and his knights had once been constructed. In their novelistic writing and rewriting, they reduced the mythological components and changed them into mere literary motifs.

Indeed, the major classic Arthurian romances never present Arthur as a bear-king, not to mention a bear-god. Moreover, the few episodes in the romances involving a bear do not concern Arthur directly, but his female associates or his principal knights. Hence it is essentially his name that associates him with the animal. This was in fact clearly noted by an anonymous English scholar of the thirteenth century in a marginal gloss on a manuscript page of the *Historia Britonum* by Geoffrey of Monmouth. Opposite the word "Artur," the gloss reads: "[The name] Artur, expressed in Latin, sounds like the name of a fearsome bear."[54] This shows that in this period the etymological or simply phonic relationship between the name of the king and the name of the animal was still clearly understood in English scholarly circles.[55]

While Arthur is never transformed into a bear in the chivalric romances and never confronts the beast in single combat,[56] the literary texts nonetheless give occasional, perhaps involuntary, glimpses of some discreet evidence of his former animal nature. While fading, this mythological origin has left traces in oral traditions and in folklore. As the work of R. S. Loomis and his disciples showed long ago,[57] folklore often influenced the formal presentation of a particular passage or literary motif, at first sight difficult to understand, but easier to interpret if one keeps in mind the first identity of King Arthur and his principal companions in the ancient Celtic myths.

The most obvious example is found in an episode connected to the death of the king, recounted in several romances, notably in the most famous, *La Mort le roi Artu,* a remarkable work by an anonymous author written around 1220—it is the finest romance of the Middle Ages written in French. The episode in question is close to the end: the king is lying down, severely wounded; one of his faithful companions, Lucan the Butler, approaches, in tears, to say a final farewell. Arthur stands up to embrace him, "holding him so tightly against his chest that he smothers him, crushes his heart and kills him."[58] This is a strange and dramatic event, unexpected, serving no plot purpose, but an event that recalls that Arthur was in origin a bear-king endowed with superhuman strength: like the animal, he could kill his enemy in hand to hand combat simply by pressing him against his chest. The king is not aware of his animal strength, but even as he is dying, he retains the power to cause death by a mere embrace, a power that no human being possesses.[59]

A historian is entitled to raise the question of how the thirteenth-century public that heard or read this passage might understand or interpret it. The death of the king's butler is particularly enigmatic, as is his epitaph a few lines later: "Here lies Lucan the Butler whom King Arthur crushed in his arms."[60] Was the public aware of or did it guess Arthur's ursine antecedents? Did some erudite scholar supply the necessary explanations? That is hardly likely. It must be acknowledged that literature is literature, not a learned commentary on one myth or another, and that this passage, along with many others, was all the more enchanting for the aristocratic public of the thirteenth century because it preserved a strong element of strangeness.

In the vast corpus of Arthurian texts scholarship has uncovered other indications—often discreet—of the ancient animal origin of King Arthur, especially those related to the calendar. An example is the date of the king's "death." It occurs a few days after the great battle of Salisbury, which signals the twilight of Arthurian knighthood and the end of the adventure of the Round Table. According to the author of *La Mort le roi Artu* and of several other works,[61] this battle took place on All Saints' Day. Arthur thus died in early November, a point in the pagan calendar when, almost everywhere in Europe, various age-old festivals were celebrated in honor of the bear's annual hibernation. The Church, horrified by the barbaric rituals that accompanied these festivals, tried to eradicate them from a very early date. To this end it placed feast days for saints that had names or stories associated with bears at those dates (Ursula, Ursinus, Mathurin, and so on). And it chose the date of the most important of these pagan festivals, November 11, as the feast day for one of the Church's most prestigious saints, Saint Martin, whose name gradually became one of the proper names given to the bear in folklore.[62]

In literary traditions then, the death of the king occurs around November 11, at the time of the great fall festival of the bear. But according to those same traditions, Arthur did not really die; he was only gravely wounded and his half-sister Morgane came to heal him and take him to the island of Avalon, a place of waiting and rest located in the Other World. Like the hibernating bear, the bear-king has gone to sleep in the autumn mists; and like any messianic hero, he awaits his return to the living to reign again and lead his people on the path to salvation.[63]

Another essential event in the story of Arthur takes place on the day of a great festival of the bear: the test of the magic sword, the symbol of sovereignty. The one who is able to remove the sword from the stone in which it is implanted will become the legitimate king. By succeeding in removing the weapon from the block of stone, something no lord or knight had been able to do, the young Arthur accomplishes a rite of passage, is recognized as the son of King Uther Pendragon, and becomes the ruler of the kingdom of Logres (that is, Great Britain). Several medieval writers set this episode on Christmas Day; others, forty days later, at Candlemas. Still others say that Arthur accomplished his feat twice, at Christmas and at Candlemas, February 2.[64] In the traditional rural calendar, February 2 was the day on which the supposed end of the bear's hibernation was celebrated; it was a festival marked by particularly savage and transgressive rites. To put an end to them, the Church of the High Middle Ages had had to strike a decisive blow and set that as the date for a great feast day for Christ (the Presentation of Jesus at the Temple), a great feast day for the Virgin Mary (the Purification of the Virgin), and to Christianize a folk celebration, the feast of the candles (Candlemas). These calendar issues and the difficulties the Church encountered in eradicating various ursine cults that had survived in Christendom will be considered later. It suffices to note now, following Philippe Walter, the exemplary symbolic link between the moment the bear ends its hibernation and the moment when the young Arthur, the bear-king, comes out of the shadows, is recognized, and can begin his reign in the full light of day.[65]

A Royal Animal

Ancient divinity, venerated creature, invincible beast, master of the forest, embodiment of strength and courage, the bear was not only the king of the beasts, but also the animal symbol of all kings. Although the case of Arthur, in whom bear and king were one, was unique among northern European societies—Celtic, Germanic, Scandinavian, Baltic, or Slavic— the northern bear was everywhere an emblem of the chief, a symbol of authority, an image of sovereignty. Long after the Christianization of all these populations, vestiges of this phenomenon could be found in most of the kingdoms of the West. For instance, at Aix-la-Chapelle, among various antique objects related to authority was a large bronze she-bear, probably brought from Gaul during the reign of Charles the Bald.[66] The bear remained a royal animal in the ninth century, despite the war that Charlemagne and the Church had waged against it. And it remained royal for more than three centuries.

I have already noted that, among the Germans, victory over a bear made a young man into an adult warrior, often a chief, and sometimes a king. Still in the late eleventh century, in the Holy Land itself, combat with a bear helped Godfrey of Bouillon to mount the throne of Jerusalem.[67] Elsewhere during the same period, hunting practices continued these rituals in less pagan but just as perilous forms: the bear remained, along with the boar, the quintessentially noble game animal.

This was already clearly true in antiquity, for the Celts and the Germans as well as the Romans. In the late Roman Empire in particular, emperors and their entourage liked to hunt bear. It was considered a fearsome and admired animal, a dangerous opponent that fought to the end and died instead of fleeing or giving up. For that reason, it was respected and sought after. This was especially true because the bear hunt was usually conducted on foot and ended in hand-to-hand combat, face to face, breath to breath. The beating of the animal was done with dogs, but only a man was to face the final attack of the furious beast: disdaining its blows, its cries, and its odor, the hunter would seek to finish it off with a spear or a knife, striking at the neck, the throat, or between the eyes.

During the last centuries of the Roman Empire and throughout the High Middle Ages, defeating a bear was always considered an exploit worthy of a king. Hunting stags (not to mention deer) was abandoned because the animal was considered cowardly. It fled before dogs, and then surrendered and allowed itself to be killed. In its image, soldiers lacking courage who fled in the face of the enemy were called *cervi*.[68] Moreover, venison was long considered soft and unhealthy; unlike bear meat, it was not served at the tables of emperors and kings.[69] Finally, deer inhabited land on which aristocratic hunting parties were infrequent; they preferred darker and rougher terrain. Pursuing or hunting down a stag was therefore an activity that won neither glory nor pleasure. And that remained true until the twelfth or thirteenth century, that is, until the moment when the medieval Church, having failed in its efforts to ban all hunting, managed to impose the stag hunt as the royal hunt and to devalue that of the bear and the boar.[70]

For the time being, before and after the year 1000, hunting a bear, confronting it, and killing it in single combat remained an act of bravery characteristic of a chief or a hero. Kings, as I have noted, were obliged to accomplish the deed. But that was not enough: they also had to surround themselves with a menagerie containing one or more bears, necessary symbols of power. By doing so, they perpetuated the practices of the barbarian chiefs and Roman emperors of the fourth and fifth centuries, who liked to exhibit bears and watch them fight against other animals. Several Roman writers remarked on the peculiar, morbid interest of Emperor Valentinian I (364–375) for the bears that had been given to him by a German princeling, Macrian, a chief of the Alemanni. He spent "considerable sums" to lodge and feed them; he had them sleep in his room as sentinels; sometimes he amused himself by watching them tear to pieces prisoners under sentence of death.[71]

Like those of antiquity, medieval menageries were political tools.[72] For a long time, only kings, princes, and great lords, secular or ecclesiastical, were rich enough to own menageries.[73] Beginning in the thirteenth century, some cities and even some great abbeys imitated them. There was no attempt to satisfy the curiosity of a public eager to see ferocious or unusual animals; the purpose was to host the living symbols of authority that only the most powerful could buy, give, or exchange. In this sense, every menagerie was a "treasure," that is, a tool of government.

It is unfortunately difficult to establish the typology of these medieval menageries:[74] the few documents that mention them provide scanty information and the vocabulary designating them is unstable and ambiguous.[75] We lack in particular real inventories or lists that would indicate the composition of the menagerie of a particular prince at a particular place and at a particular time. One would also like to know more about the relative proportions of animals that were indigenous and exotic, wild and "domestic" (a notion to be used cautiously in speaking of the Middle Ages),[76] dangerous and inoffensive, and those held as single specimens compared to those held in large numbers. It would also be useful to know how the menageries (and the numerous aviaries) were organized, and how animals were acquired, exchanged, and named (some animals were given proper names).[77] Some menageries were fixed, more were itinerant; some could be seen only by the prince and his entourage, whereas others were accessible to the public under various conditions. In the menageries of the High Middle Ages, bears predominated, followed by boars and lions. In the feudal period, boars were seldom seen, but bears remained numerous, and there were increasing numbers of lions, leopards, and panthers. In the late Middle Ages, exotic animals from the north (moose, reindeer, elk), from Asia (elephants, camels), or from Africa (elephants, dromedaries, monkeys, antelopes, wild asses, and even giraffes) were more and more in demand.[78]

But up to the twelfth century, every royal or princely menagerie had to contain one or more bears. That animal was the finest gift one king could make to another in Western Europe. The bear that was given, of course, had to be remarkable in one way or another, either for its size, its fur, or its origin. The king of Norway, for example, once gave the gift of a polar bear, a wonder that Aristotle himself had never mentioned.[79] The first one seen in the temperate zone of Europe was probably the one sent to the king of England by Haakon IV in 1251. Contemporaries were impressed by this polar bear, and it left documentary traces: one chronicler tells how it had to be bathed daily in the Thames, another tells us that it was given the nickname *Piscator* (Fisher), and yet another indicates the daily wages of its guardian and even the cost of the muzzle and the long chain that were made to keep it from swimming away.[80]

Throughout the Middle Ages, it was not uncommon for a peace treaty or an alliance between two lords to involve gifts for their menageries.[81] Until the twelfth century, if monarchs were concerned, the gift generally had to be a bear. In the *Chanson de Roland,* for example, the Saracen King Marsile sends to Charlemagne, with whom he wants to make peace, a collection of sumptuous gifts that the author enumerates three times: bears always come at the head of the list.[82] But this is a work of literature, probably written toward the end of the eleventh century or the beginning of the twelfth. In reality, Oriental princes also offered lions, leopards, panthers, and even elephants, such as the famous Abul-Abbas that Harun al-Rashid, the Caliph of Baghdad, sent to Charlemagne in 801.[83]

Two centuries later, in 1051, when Anna Yaroslavna, daughter of the grand prince of Kiev, arrived in Reims to marry King Henri I of France, she was accompanied not by an elephant but by two male bears of a gigantic size unknown in the West. According to the chroniclers, they came from "Great Tartary,"[84] a fabulous origin which made them veritable *mirabilia* and bestowed on them an incomparable pedigree. It is also possible that an attempt was immediately made to mate them with she-bears in the royal menagerie—about which we know nothing for the period—in order to obtain one or more unusual bear lineages, as seems to have happened a few years earlier when Anna's elder sister married King Harald of Norway.[85] In the Middle Ages, and later under the Ancien Régime, the marriage of a prince and a princess was sometimes accompanied by the mating of several pairs of animals offered by each of the parties (horses, dogs, and even remarkable cattle or pigs). They might be seen as metaphoric marriages of a kind, ones that strengthened the union of two lineages or two dynasties and brought out the symbolic relationship between humans and certain animals.

In the feudal period, among the animals seen as ancestors, parents, or supposed "cousins" of humans, the bear occupied the first rank.

3

The Relative of Man

W HAT animal is the one that most resembles man? The answers
to this question have varied widely according to time and place,
since every society had its own bestiary, taxonomies, and conceptions of
the relationship between men and beasts. In Europe, however, in historic
times, only three animals have been really considered to be bound by ties
of resemblance, proximity, or kinship to human beings: the bear, the pig,
and the monkey.

For Aristotle and Pliny, the monkey was the closest to humans.[1] This
idea found support in some zoological learning in the High Middle Ages,
but it considerably troubled Christian values, not only because man had
been created in the image of God and any animal of any species was an
imperfect creature that could not resemble him, but also because, for medieval sensibilities, the monkey no doubt represented everything that was
most ugly, vile, and diabolical;[2] it was an obscene and repugnant creature
that it was impossible to associate with the human species. In that case,
how was it possible to reconcile Aristotelian knowledge, which was gradually being rediscovered and increasingly admired, with the values and
convictions of Christianity? Scholasticism finally found a solution in the
mid-thirteenth century: the monkey did not resemble man *per naturam*
(by nature) but *per imitationem* (by imitation); it seemed to resemble man
when it really did not resemble him at all.[3] It "simulated," as the word
for monkey in Latin indicated: *simius*. It therefore seemed even more demonic, because it tricked and deceived. It was the very image of the Devil
(*figura diaboli*) that sought to "ape" God, and it remained so until well into
the modern period. It was not until the eighteenth century that it again became possible to conceive of the hypothesis of an anatomical kinship between man and monkey, thereby laying the groundwork for Darwin, who

published the first edition of *On the Origin of Species* in 1859, overturning all theories dealing with transformism and relations among living things.

The Relationship of Appearances

In the Middle Ages imitation was considered a sin, a great sin, because it struck a blow against the order established by the Creator. Jongleurs, actors, and the like, who used imitation or disguise, were morally reprehensible and socially marginalized. In iconography, the monkey gradually became their emblem, as it did from the mid-sixteenth century on for other imitators—now a bit more tolerated—such as painters and sculptors.

The case of the pig was more ambiguous than that of the monkey. Greek medicine considered the pig the animal closest to man because of its internal organization, notably with regard to the anatomy of the major organs and the functioning of the digestive system. This was fully confirmed by contemporary medicine, which took much more from pigs than from monkeys (organ and skin grafts, tissue, dressings for wounds, and essential products such as insulin and anticoagulants).[4] It is possible that the ancient and long-lasting taboos related to the pig in several cultures had their roots in this close biological relationship with humans. On this subject, Arabic medicine differed little from Greek medicine: pig and man had similar anatomy. And medieval Christian medicine, the heir of both, also taught that the pig was "internally" the animal that most resembled man. Moreover, since the Church prohibited the dissection of the human body, at least up to the fourteenth century, human anatomy was often learned through the dissection of a sow or a boar.[5] But that was not done without some reluctance: the pig was in no way an admirable animal. It was an impure creature, an emblem of dirtiness *(sorditas)* and gluttony *(gula)*, sometimes of laziness *(pigritia)* and debauchery *(luxuria);* like the monkey, it found a place in the Devil's bestiary. This is why, although doctors knew that the pig was anatomically a cousin to man, they did not declare that fact too openly and allowed clerics to assert that the animal that most resembled humans was neither the pig nor the monkey, but the bear.[6]

Indeed, at first glance, no other animal has such a distinctly anthropomorphic appearance. Although more massive, the bear is built like a man: it has the same stature and the same silhouette, since, unlike most quadrupeds, it can remain vertical; moreover, when it walks, it places the entire foot on the ground, including the heel. Medieval writers, of course, did not characterize it as "plantigrade," a term unknown to them, but they knew this was a particular trait that it alone shared with humans. The same writers also remarked that once stripped of its fur, a bear's body was identical to a man's body.[7] This made rituals of disguise all the easier. "Playing the bear"—*ursum facere*, as the prelates who denounced the practice throughout the Middle Ages called it—was an easy exercise, easier than "playing" the stag, the ass, or the bull, three other animals targeted by these prohibitions. To transform oneself into a bear, one merely had to put on a furry garment, draw in one's shoulders, and walk with legs far apart.

But the bear did not appear only as a man in disguise; it also behaved physically like a man. It could stand, sit, lie on its side or stomach, run, swim, dive, roll, climb, jump, and even dance. An anonymous twelfth-century writer notes the contrast between the apparent heaviness of the animal and its agility, its speed, and its ability to bob and weave and avoid obstacles. Another observes with admiration that the bear is the only animal that frequently lifts its head to contemplate the sky and the stars. Still another draws the reader's attention to the diversity of the colors of its fur and makes a comparison with the diversity of shades of men's beards and hair: black, brown, tawny, red, blond, gray.[8] Most important, everyone remarked on how the bear used its front paws to grasp, hold, or throw an object, delicately pick berries, skillfully catch fish in flowing water, or, in contrast, savagely massacre hives to gather honey.[9] Bears' gluttony was proverbial and it made them careless, though they were generally considered to be sensible. On many occasions in the *Roman de Renart* Brun the bear is the victim of his inordinate love of honey and finds himself trapped by the fox, shaved or beaten by peasants, mocked by the lioness, and ridiculed in front of all the other animals.

Modern zoologists have contributed some qualifications and details to the overly anthropomorphic picture presented by ancient and medieval writers. Although the bear can hold itself upright (especially to see and to smell), it almost never moves as a biped. But it is true that it can climb trees, swim well, and catch fish. It often adopts a sitting position (notably to wait), and it can walk backward and go down a ladder like a man with its back in the open (which no other animal can do). Above all, it has remarkable manual skill: it can open a door, untie a knot, and use a stone as a hammer. Despite its huge paws, it picks raspberries and carefully dissects the fish it catches, a little like a monkey peeling a banana. But not all naturalists are enraptured by these comparisons between bears and men. Some prefer to bring out the differences rather than the resemblances; others emphasize the crude, exaggerated, or troubling character of those resemblances. In the eighteenth century, for example, Buffon, who did not like the bear (probably because he never succeeded in fitting it into his zoological system) refused to allow himself to be carried away by comparisons that he found excessive: after describing in detail the anatomical similarities that seemed to make the bear a cousin to man, he concluded by declaring that "these crude resemblances make it only more deformed and give it no superiority over other animals."[10] But this was a superiority that many ancient and medieval writers had recognized, at least up to the thirteenth century.

Diet was another area that established a kinship between bears and humans. Medieval writers said little about it,[11] although there was one who claimed that bear meat had the same taste as human flesh,[12] but modern scholarship has given it detailed attention. There are indeed very few truly omnivorous animals, and they include bears and men. With respect to the animal, however, certain qualifications are necessary. Not only does its diet vary according to season and location, but also and above all, it has evolved over the centuries: the prehistoric brown bear was clearly carnivorous; the present-day brown bear is largely vegetarian. The long war that men conducted against bears drove it out of many regions, made it a creature of the mountains, and gradually changed its diet, forcing it to replace the flesh of wild or domestic animals with increasingly varied plants.[13]

Animal Experimentation in the Twelfth Century

Today the bear is no longer considered to be the animal closest to man; the monkey and the pig have clearly overtaken it in that role, and they have become of constantly growing interest for medical experimentation and research. Incidentally, this is truer of the pig than of the monkey, not only because it is an abundant species, not costly to use, and not at all threatened with extinction, but also because contemporary science recognizes that it is more biologically and pharmaceutically useful, even though the percentage of DNA shared by man and monkey (specifically the chimpanzee) is slightly higher than that shared by man and pig.[14]

Things were different in the twelfth century. The pharmacopoeia derived none of its products from monkeys—that was unthinkable—but it did take a certain number from pigs and bears. Bear grease was particularly sought after to relieve eye disease, treat burns, cure ulcers and various skin diseases, and even to make hair grow.[15] Of the two animals, the bear was probably considered closer to humans; for even though doctors in Byzantium, Salerno, and elsewhere dissected sow cadavers to study internal female anatomy, they conducted bold experiments more frequently on the wild beast than on the domestic animal.[16]

The story of the bear of King Baldwin of Jerusalem provides a striking example.[17] We know the story from several chroniclers and it echoes the story of Godfrey of Bouillon's bear recounted earlier.[18] Baldwin was, in fact, Godfrey's younger brother. When Godfrey died in July 1100, Baldwin became the first Frankish king of the kingdom of Jerusalem and devoted the eighteen years of his reign (1100–1118) to pursuing the war against the Muslims and expanding his possessions. He was a conquering king, a valiant knight, and an exemplary Christian.[19] The chroniclers admired him and sought to endow him with the same prestige as his brother, the chief hero of the First Crusade. Since Godfrey had triumphed over a monstrous bear, so Baldwin, to be fully his equal and successor, also had to have an ursine legend. However, probably based on a real event, the legend did not take the form of a victorious battle against a ferocious bear but that of an edifying medical experiment.

In his war against the Sultan of Egypt during the summer of 1103, Baldwin was severely wounded when, like his brother a few years earlier, he braved danger to come to the aid of one of his soldiers. He suffered what appeared to be a mortal wound: a sword fragment that could not be removed remained lodged deep within it. The king sensed that he was going to die. He questioned his doctors. None of them foresaw a favorable outcome; they all prognosticated imminent death because the king had lost too much blood and the infection was continuing to spread. One of them, however, asked the king for permission to try a last-ditch experiment. For this he had to use unusual and dangerous remedies and to study the development of the wound for a few days. But the risks of death were significant, so he suggested to the king that a trial be first conducted on a Muslim prisoner wounded in the same place and in the same way, with a piece of steel embedded in his body that they would allow to fester. The king refused, not wishing to risk the life of an innocent man, even that of a captive infidel. The doctor then proposed replacing the prisoner by the bear in the royal menagerie, arguing that it was an animal very close to man and a "useless creature except for dancing and display." Baldwin agreed. The beast was given a wound identical to that of the king and it was allowed to grow infected. The doctor, whose name is not known, applied to the bear various balms and powders he had made, consulted other doctors, and prepared more balms and potions. Finally, the bear died after having howled and suffered at length. But the king's doctor had learned enough to prepare an effective remedy and apply it to his lord with not too many risks. The king was saved. To be sure, the wound never healed, but Baldwin lived for another fifteen years before it reopened in 1118, in the course of a battle in Egypt, this time causing a swift death.[20]

This story is instructive on several accounts. First it brings out Baldwin's exemplary charity—he considered the life of a Muslim prisoner more precious than his own. It also presents an example of experimental medicine, thereby demonstrating that, contrary to conventional wisdom, medieval medicine sought to increase its knowledge and relied on experiment and observation to do so. Of course, this took place in the East, where the Church had less power to block medical experiment and the study of the human body. In addition, it is probable that the king's doctor did not come from northern France, like Baldwin, the son of the Count of Boulogne, but that he was Greek, Jewish, Syrian, or Armenian. In any event, everywhere in the early twelfth century doctors were no longer satisfied with the knowledge inherited from Galen and Avicenna or the various ancient and eastern pharmacopoeias; they looked for new remedies, tested them, took risks, doubted, and made progress. They were not yet the pompous doctors of the late Middle Ages, even less the ignorant pedants of Molière. Finally, the edifying story of this cure strongly brings to the fore the supposed kinship between bears and men. The experiment was tried not on a horrible monkey or a vulgar pig, but on a bear, the king of the beasts, the admirable animal that was a necessity for every menagerie. Although the doctor considered it a useless creature, he knew that no other animal could fulfill the biological and symbolic conditions necessary for his final attempt to cure the king. Only a bear could replace a human being in this role. Only the king of the beasts could save the king of Jerusalem.

The same author told the story of Godfrey of Bouillon's victorious battle against a gigantic bear and the story of King Baldwin and the bear. His name was Guibert de Nogent, and the stories appeared in the *Gesta Dei per Francos,* compiled from 1104 to 1108 to celebrate the Crusade and the creation of the first Frankish states in the Holy Land.[21] His two bear stories were repeated, glossed, amplified, and then translated by several chroniclers of the twelfth and thirteenth centuries. But Guibert's source is unknown. He himself was a startling figure. He was the youngest child (born around 1053) of a high-ranking family in Picardy. His father died when he was still young, and as an adolescent he entered the Abbey of Saint-Germer near Beauvais, where he remained as a monk for forty years, studying, visiting many libraries, and maintaining regular contacts with intellectuals in monastic circles in northern France and southern England. Later, in 1104, he became the abbot of the small monastery at Nogent-sous-Coucy, where he remained until his death in 1124. His extensive work, written in pompous Latin, includes, in addition to his history of the First Crusade, sermons, works of exegesis, and theological treatises, all relatively ordinary. But it also includes two works unusual for a monk of the time: a pamphlet against the excessive cult of relics *(De pignoribus sanctorum)* and a sort of autobiography *(De vita sua)*, inspired by Saint Augustine's *Confessions*.[22] In the latter, Guibert tells us how his mother strongly marked his youth and his life as a monk (she set up house at the gates of the monastery, and Guibert did not really part from her until he became the abbot of Nogent when he was over fifty). He describes the dreams of this intrusive and overly beloved woman; he also reports his own, reveals his doubts, his fears (of the Devil), and his phobias (of blood). He mentions contemporary events on various occasions: the preaching of the First Crusade, which made a lasting impression on him; the horrible revolt of the commune of Laon against its bishop; the scandalous spread of new fashions in clothing, with men's clothing as extravagant as that of women.[23] Finally, he alludes to an event that he also mentions in a sermon: the cruel story of the bear that William the Conqueror, King of England and Duke of Normandy, gave to his protégé Lord Arnoul of Ardres.

This story is set around 1080. Having returned to England with the huge beast, Arnoul did not have the time to place it in his menagerie. The residents of Ardres, eager to see the animal, came to meet it, some of them with their dogs. Taking advantage of the fact that the bear was chained, the dogs pounced on it: "more than forty" attacked it, savagely bit it all over its body, and finally killed it. The residents of Ardres were so pleased by the spectacle of this killing that Lord Arnoul did nothing to prevent it. Later, he even acquired another bear that, several times a year, danced, did tricks, and confronted dogs—now victoriously—on the fairgrounds. In exchange, the residents of Ardres agreed to pay a tax intended for the care and feeding of the animal.[24]

The story of the cowardly murder of the lordly bear by plebeian dogs seems to have impressed Guibert, whose delicate sensibility was also troubled by the stories circulating in the monasteries in his region. These tales told of monks and novices who had seen the Devil appear in the form of a bear and had been terrified by the vision. This was no doubt the source of Guibert's interest in bears and lay behind his inclusion in the *Gesta*

Dei per Francos the two exemplary stories glorifying the two prestigious sons of the Count of Boulogne, Godfrey of Bouillon and Baldwin of Jerusalem.

The Sexuality of the Bear

Chronicles were not the only texts in the feudal period that brought out the kinship between man and bear. Bestiaries and encyclopedias did the same and delighted in highlighting some or all of the anthropomorphic characteristics of the animal discussed above, most of them already known to the Ancients and sometimes confirmed by contemporary science. But medieval bestiaries added a remarkable particularity that modern zoology has not preserved: bears did not mate like other quadrupeds but like men and women, lying down and embracing, face to face, stomach to stomach; they were the only animals to do so. The oldest mention of the practice, *more hominum,* is found in Book VIII, on quadrupeds, of Pliny's *Natural History.* His description of this unusual conduct forms the opening of the long chapter on bears: "Bears couple in the beginning of winter, and not after the fashion of other quadrupeds; for both animals lie down and embrace each other. The female then retires by herself to a separate den, and there brings forth on the thirtieth day, mostly five young ones."[25]

This passage, for once, does not seem to have been taken from Aristotle, who merely asserted that "bears perform the operation lying prone on one another, in the same way as other quadrupeds do while standing up; that is to say, with the belly of the male pressed to the back of the female."[26] Pliny had a different source, perhaps a Greek writer whose works have not survived; unless he was following oral traditions which, as we have seen, have from time immemorial attributed human behavior to the bear; or, even more likely, he simply misread Aristotle.[27] In any event, for medieval scholarship, Pliny was an unquestionable authority, as was Aelian, who abridged and revised him in the third century. Hence, all writers who discussed bears adopted his sentence, sometimes word for word, sometimes adding a remark or a detail reinforcing the idea of sexual behavior comparable to that of humans. For example, the anonymous author of a Latin bestiary written in southern England in the early thirteenth century asserts: "Bears do not couple like other animals but face to face, grasping and embracing one another as men and women do. Pleasure lasts longer for them than for any other species and is accompanied by caresses and playfulness similar to those of two lovers."[28]

To the usual way of thinking, this coupling of bears in the human manner was a wonder of nature, a "marvel." It distanced the beast from the animal world and moved it closer to the world of men, thereby fostering a large number of beliefs, legends, and images. In the late Middle Ages, for example, some illuminators liked to show bears engaging in lovemaking unlike that of other wild beasts or indeed of any other animal.[29] For clergy and theologians, however, such behavior had something troubling about it, even monstrous; far from heightening its status, the behavior helped to harm the bear's image and consign it to the infernal bestiary. These sexual practices seemed contrary to the natural order desired and created by God; they could only be the consequence of a vicious nature and the cause of very great sins, notably of lust, constantly associated with the bear when the scholastic system of the seven deadly sins was established. Of course, the bear was not the only animal serving as an emblem of lust (the ram, the ass, the monkey, the dog, and a few others kept it company in that role). Four more of the seven sins were also attributed to it (anger, gluttony, envy, and sloth). But perhaps more than anything else, it was the bear's lewdness, its love of debauchery, and its supposedly abnormal sexuality that helped to demonize it.[30]

Medieval Christian culture did not invent all of this. In the third century of our era, in his treatise on hunting, written in Greek and dedicated to the emperor Caracalla, Oppian had already pointed out the sexual appetite of bears, particularly of she-bears: "Bears are obsessed by carnal love and indulge in it without restraint; the females, unable to curb their desire, pursue the males day and night and refuse to interrupt their lovemaking once it has begun."[31] This was echoed in the late fifteenth century by a remark in an anonymous bestiary: "Bears have a hot temperament and constantly seek the pleasure of love. Once they set to it, nothing stops them, not even the baying of dogs or the threats of hunters."[32] Between these two dates, many writers strove to bring out the lewd nature of the bear; the female was particularly targeted. Several encyclopedists explained that the mother was to blame for the fact that her cubs were born small and unformed, with no eyes or hair and practically lifeless, because she did not have the patience to go through the normal gestation period. And the reason she was so impatient to give birth was because the male refused to mate with her while she was pregnant. Since the pleasures of the flesh were dearer to her than the joys of maternity, she hastened to give birth, producing nearly stillborn cubs, and then hurried to rejoin the male to fornicate with him again.[33]

This image of the bad mother was, however, corrected by other writers, who were more numerous and more faithful to ancient traditions. Quoting various passages from Aristotle, Pliny, Ovid, and Aelian,[34] and relying on a well-known verse from the Bible ("like a she-bear robbed of her cubs"),[35] they explained that, on the contrary, by patiently licking her lifeless cubs, the she-bear brought them back to life, warmed them, and gave them form and strength; thereafter, she kept them with her for many months and courageously defended them against predators. For some Fathers of the Church, this act of resurrection earned the exemplary mother a place in the divine bestiary.[36] For others, such as Saint Ambrose,[37] the behavior of the she-bear was akin to repentance or even conversion: having become aware of her misdeeds, she abandoned her vicious nature and became an example worthy of imitation. For still others, the return to life of the stillborn cubs was equivalent to a baptism: their flesh took shape, their breath came to life, and their eyes were opened, like the children of God when they received baptismal anointment.[38] Some writers even drew attention to the fertilizing role of the tongue, an organ that ancient sensibilities often considered a source of life and an instrument of knowledge. For primitive Christianity, the tongue had to do with the Word and with Creation, sometimes with the fire of the Holy Spirit. It was primarily later scholastic morality that invented the notion of "sins of the tongue" and saw the organ as a perfidious tool at the service of falsehood and arrogance.[39] In the early seventh century, Isidore of Seville had not yet gone down that path. Like Saint Ambrose, he considered the mother's licking of the cubs a second birth; playing with the words *orsus* ("born") and *ursus* ("bear"), he even detected the origin of the term designating the animal in this phonic resemblance: *"ursus fertur dictus quod ore suo formet fetus, quasi orsus"* ("The bear is said to be so called because it shapes its offspring in its 'own mouth'").[40] This phonic etymology was later adopted by all the bestiaries and treatises of zoology down to the Renaissance.

I will come back to the ambivalent symbolism of the bear. It should be noted here, however, that the belief in the coupling of male and female in the human manner, face to face, belly to belly, had an extremely long life. It did not begin to be really called into question until the seventeenth century, and it was still reported in the eighteenth century by Buffon, although he himself scarcely believed it: "Bears seek each other in autumn, the female is said to be more ardent than the male: it is claimed that she lies on her back to receive him, that she embraces him tightly and holds him for a long time. But it is more certain that they couple in the manner of quadrupeds."[41] Zoologists later definitively rejected the idea of coitus *ad modum hominem* and ended the reputation for debauchery and lewdness that surrounded the sexuality of she-bears. They established on the contrary that the female went into heat only once a year, in late spring or early summer, that she was often monogamous, seeking out the same male every year (which was not always possible), and that the two coupled just like other terrestrial mammals. What did differentiate them was the length of copulation, longer than that of other wild animals. As for the cubs, they were not born after thirty days as Pliny had asserted and Aristotle had already surmised,[42] but at the end of eight or nine months. They were certainly very small in proportion to an adult bear, but thanks to the care lavished by their mother, they quickly reached a size that enabled them to perform all the activities of young wild animals.[43]

Bears and Women

The vices associated with bears that have just been described concerned primarily females. But males were far from above reproach. For many medieval writers, the bear was the very image of uncontrolled anger, blind violence, and brutal desire, and therefore a grave danger for human beings—for women more than for men. An ancient belief, which came down to the Middle Ages from various sources and was passed on to modern times, held that bears were fond of girls and young women. A bear would sometimes be a lover or seducer, more often an abductor and rapist; he would seize them and carry them off to his den where he would have monstrous sexual relations with them, which sometimes resulted in half-human, half-bear offspring. There were such tales of abduction in Greek mythology, but they were not very explicit. The Greeks preferred to skirt around them, as in descriptions of the rituals of Brauron, where young girls sacrificed to Artemis, goddess of bears. Or else they chose to mask them, as in Paris's abduction of Helen. Of course the proud and handsome young man, son of Priam and Hecuba, bore no resemblance to a bear; but it will be recalled that he had been abandoned at birth in the forest on Mount Ida and nourished with bear's milk. This animal milk bestowed on him a more-or-less ursine nature, and as an adult, like most male bears in mythological tales, he abducted a young woman, the most beautiful in the world, and made her his companion. The abduction of Helen took place without violence, but it was an abduction, and it brought about the ruin of Troy.

Celtic and Germanic mythologies were less discreet. They did not hesitate to give prominence to stories of bears raping women and to the exploits of heroes or misdeeds of monsters born from those unnatural unions. Despite the vigilant filter of Christianity, these stories left fairly numerous traces down to the feudal period, primarily in sagas, epics, and chivalric romances, but also in the genealogies of the most prestigious royal dynasties.

One example is a little-known Arthurian romance in verse by an anonymous English or Norman author of the late twelfth or early thirteenth century, *Yder*.[44] The name is that of a young nobleman who, like Perceval in the *Conte du Graal* by Chrétien de Troyes, written a few years earlier, does not know who his father is and goes to King Arthur's court to be made a knight. The overly warm interest Guinevere takes in him provokes the jealousy of Arthur and several knights of the Round Table, particularly the king's nephew Gawain and the villainous steward Kei. Arthur refuses to dub Yder until he has proved himself. Yder is disappointed, but a dramatic event soon gives him the opportunity to demonstrate his strength and courage. One day when he is in a tower room with Guinevere, Gawain, and several noble young ladies of the queen's entourage, a big bear comes into the room—"no-one ever saw a bigger one." It is the bear from the royal menagerie that has broken its chains and escaped from its pen. The ladies are terrified. Gawain looks for a weapon to strike the bear, but finds none in the room. Then Yder attacks the angry bear and they engage in a furious hand-to-hand battle. The two wrestlers occupy the center of the room; the ladies are pressed against the walls; Guinevere screams; Gawain remains paralyzed. The battle is long and its outcome uncertain. Finally, Yder manages to escape from the arms and claws of the animal, grasps it by the head and the skin of its back, and drags it up to a window, where, in a show of superhuman strength, he lifts it and hurls it into space. The bear lands on a rock in the trench, where the dogs hurl themselves at it; the romance is silent about the animal's fate.[45] But it gives prominence to Yder's exploit, pointing out that he was "molt prisiez" (greatly admired) at court, particularly by the ladies and by Guinevere. But Yder's heart beat for another queen, Guenloie, whom he finally marries after accomplishing other deeds, winning Gawain's friendship, and being dubbed a knight. But Arthur—the bear-king—remains hostile to him to the end.

The bear episode is the heart of the romance, a receptacle for various themes and motifs inherited from very old traditions. The battle of the young Yder against the fearsome beast obviously represents a rite of passage, the exploit required to become a knight. It echoes at a distance of several centuries the battles that young men in pagan Germany had to wage against a bear or a boar to become adult warriors.[46] For a Christian audience, it would also recall the Bible verses telling how David, when still a shepherd, defended his flock against a bear (1 Samuel 17.34–35). Further, the bear in the menagerie is the emblematic animal that every king has to own to assert his power and display his majesty. In the late twelfth century, Arthur does not escape from the custom and, like all monarchs in the West, he has a bear. This would probably no longer be necessary a few decades later when the lion had definitively replaced the bear in the symbolic role of king of the beasts. In this dramatic episode, however, the most remarkable element is neither the presence of a bear in the royal menagerie nor young Yder's victory over the beast, but the fact that after breaking its chains and escaping confinement, the bear does not run off into the forest to recover its freedom and return to the wild, but climbs directly into the tower and rushes toward the ladies' chamber. The bear in *Yder* is, like many others, a dangerous lover of women. Feminine flesh is more important to it than its freedom. The text of the romance even specifies that the bear is old and blind and that he found the ladies' chamber with his sense of smell.[47] This is a troubling, almost diabolical detail that is at the same time very modern. The *odor di femina* obsesses and guides it.

Even though they contain no similar episodes and do not mention the word *bear*, several other Arthurian romances of the twelfth century, like *Yder*, seem marked by an obscure and persistent "ursine" atmosphere.[48] This probably derives from the original mythology of King Arthur, not yet fully Christianized but already thoroughly masked, as well as from his name, directly constructed from the name of the bear, as the preceding chapter showed. Arthur, king and man, remains more or less a bear. This is why he does not like Yder, conqueror of the beast and champion of the ladies. But Arthur does not confront Yder directly: Yder's battle against a real animal is a necessary displacement, almost a transference in the psychoanalytic sense. Yder believed he had found a substitute father in Arthur to replace the one he had never known; but like all the heroes of the Round Table romances—an admirable aspect of these tales—Yder is mistaken, about himself and about others. Arthur does not have and does not want a child; he is a bear, a rival, a jealous man, an enemy.[49]

The figure of Tristan is just as ambiguous as Arthur, at least in the older versions of his legend. They are discreet about his parentage: he is known to have an uncle, King Mark of Cornwall, his mother's brother, but his father is as yet unknown.[50] A text difficult to date, however, gives him a father: Urgan le Velu, a sort of hairy giant whom Tristan kills, unaware of their kinship.[51] The favorite hero of the medieval audience, the prince so mad with love he dies from it, the wild man who goes off to the woods, sometimes alone, sometimes with Queen Iseult, to escape from King Mark, would thus be the son of a man covered with hair, perhaps a man-bear, born from the union of a wild animal and a woman. And as the grandson of a bear, Tristan would have retained something of that animal nature, particularly when he takes refuge in the depths of the forest among other wild animals. Of course, most literary texts gloss over any allusion to this old ursine character of mythic origin, but in the earliest romances and verse fragments of the twelfth century some traces remain.[52]

Literary texts were not the only documents in the years between 1170 and 1200 to evoke the attraction male bears felt for queens or young women—an attraction that may also have been considered reciprocal. Chronicles also provide several accounts of various unions between woman and beast. In the chronicle by the celebrated English monk and illuminator Matthew Paris, compiled a few decades later, there is mention of a tournament near London in the early summer of 1215, in the midst of a civil war. The great English barons had rebelled against King John, who had been defeated at the Battle of Bouvines the year before. The barons had deposed him and called to the throne Prince Louis, son of the king of France. While awaiting his arrival and the resumption of hostilities against the supporters of King John, the barons organized a huge tournament that was to last for a week at Hounslow, a London suburb. The heralds of arms were instructed to proclaim it throughout the region and to explain that whoever fought best would receive an exceptional reward of great price: a bear that a generous lady would send to the victor.[53]

We don't know the identity of this lady (the chronicle says *"quaedam domina,"* "a certain lady"). We also don't know whether the tournament actually took place. Finally, we don't know whether the prize to be given to the victor was to be a real live flesh-and-blood bear or rather a semblance of a bear, a straw or wax model, or even a wooden object representing the animal and constituting a symbolic gift. It was not uncommon at the time for the knight who had fought best in a tournament to receive as a reward a falcon or a pike, two warrior animals; but they were semblances—carved, modeled, or sculpted—not real animals.[54] It is impossible to determine whether that was the case for this bear. Matthew Paris wrote thirty or forty years after the events he reports. He does not dwell on the tournament itself but comments ironically and foreshadows a reversal of the situation: "Such were the trivial and frivolous amusements of the barons, who were unaware that at the same time, John and his allies were setting subtle snares for them." His notation of the prize to be given to the victor has a twofold interest. On one hand, it shows that a bear was still at this time a gift of great value, an emblem of strength and courage, an image of victory; on the other, it suggests that ladies hold symbolic power over bears, that they are the bears' mistresses or queens and that they may dispose of them "freely."[55] We would like to know the identity of this lady, this mysterious *"quaedam domina"* the text mentions, but we never will.

Debates about Sperm

Can a woman procreate with a bear? Mythologies, tales and legends, literary texts, and oral traditions assert the fact with no hesitation: yes, such a union is fertile and produces half-human, half-animal creatures whose fate is always out of the ordinary; there are fairly numerous ancient and medieval examples. But medicine in the Middle Ages has little to say on the subject, at least learned medicine. When it discusses sexuality and procreation it suggests that, except in rare cases (monsters), the union of a human and an animal is infertile. Curiously, some theologians adopted a more nuanced position.

Consider the point of view of one of the most remarkable intellectuals of the first half of the thirteenth century, William of Auvergne, bishop of Paris (1228–1249).[56] His work was extensive and is of great interest for the study of the encounter between theological thought, still strongly Augustinian, and Aristotelian natural philosophy, recently translated or retranslated, in the years from 1230 to 1250.[57] One of William of Auvergne's works directly raises the question of the union between a human and an animal, *De universo creaturarum*, given its final form around 1240. This is a treatise on the created world, divided into two major sections: the corporeal world and the spiritual world. Animals occupy a significant place, and the author examines not only the differences in nature between human and animal bodies, but also the souls of animals and their possible capacity to distinguish between Good and Evil. This provides him with the opportunity to record several beliefs and practices that today would come under the category of "folklore." In the course of doing so, he has provided historians with documentary material not found anywhere else. On several occasions, he reiterates the fact that animals were created perfect to serve mankind; hence, sin is unknown to them. Man, on the other hand, is sinful, and by committing sin, he has lost some of his power over animals.[58]

The last part of the book is entirely devoted to demons. William returns to a theological question that had long been debated: can demons mate with humans? If so, is the resulting offspring human in nature? Is it subject to sin and to the resurrection of the flesh? The bishop of Paris answers all three questions in the negative. But he goes further, and wonders what happens when a demon steals animal semen to mate with a woman, or—and this is the most interesting remark for my purposes—when an animal itself, not in any way a demon, mates with a human being.[59] On this question, he reports an *exemplum notissimum,* that is, a well-known exemplary story:

> One day in Saxony, a bear of enormous strength abducted the wife of a knight and imprisoned her in the cave where he usually hibernated. She was a woman of very great beauty, so that after a time her body awakened the bear's concupiscence. He raped her, and in his infernal den, had sexual relations with her for several years. Three sons were born of this union. Happily, one day woodsmen freed the woman and her sons; she returned to her husband and lodged her sons near the château in the sight of everyone; later, they were even knighted in the presence of the great Saxon barons. They did not differ from other knights except for their abundant hairiness and their habit of inclining their heads slightly to the left, in the manner of bears. They were, besides, given the name of their father and were called *Ursini,* sons of the bear.[60]

This *exemplum,* relatively ordinary compared to similar tales found in earlier and contemporaneous literary and narrative texts, nonetheless provides William of Auvergne with the opportunity to discuss animal nature and, in a striking and unexpected conclusion, to point out that the bear is in no way an ordinary animal. After pointing out all the physical resemblances with humans (silhouette, standing position, prehensile grip, mating practices, and so on), he asserts that the flesh of the bear has the same taste as human flesh, and for that reason many people refuse to eat it because it would be cannibalism; conversely, a man devoured by a bear is a victim of cannibalism.

Pursuing his breathtaking speculations and returning to the story of the Saxon woman abducted and raped by a wild animal, William of Auvergne acknowledges that bear sperm is almost identical to human sperm, that bear and woman are interfertile, and that the offspring of their union are not at all monsters *("monstri")* but fully human *("veri homines"),* and that they must be acknowledged and accepted as such, and baptized and raised as other children. Unlike animals, these beings know Good and Evil, are affected by original sin and the resurrection of the body; they have feelings, fears, joys. Unlike mules, the offspring of cross-species mating, children born from a bear and a woman can procreate and have descendants. Finally, engaging in subtle casuistry, the bishop of Paris makes a sharp distinction between the case of a woman raped by a bear and that of a man mating with a she-bear. The first case is not entirely a crime against nature, because the male bear is sexually very close to man; the second case, however, involves the commission of an act of true bestiality, because the she-bear is little different from other female animals and in no way resembles a woman.[61]

Sons of Bears

Despite this thoroughly extraordinary view, found in the work of no other theologians, William of Auvergne was not alone in thinking that creatures born from the union of a woman and a bear could be fertile and have descendants. Several texts of the feudal period share that view. The most surprising document is probably the chronicle by Saxo Grammaticus, already mentioned in the preceding chapter. In his *Gesta Danorum,* the great Scandinavian scholar recounts that the great-grandfather of the prestigious King Sven II Estridsen of Denmark (1047–1076) was the son of a bear. The wild animal had abducted a young woman and "married" her in his cave. After some time, a hunter succeeded in rescuing her and killing the beast. But the woman was pregnant and soon gave birth to a son, who was given the name Torgils Sprakeleg *("Thurgillis dictus Sprakeleg")*. He did not differ from other children except for his fierce and aggressive character. When he became an adult, he avenged his father by killing the hunter; thereafter, he led a life like that of other young nobles. He took a wife, had a son, and then a grandson, Count Ulfo, *jarl* of Roskilde, who married the sister of the king of Denmark and was the father of King Sven.[62]

Saxo Grammaticus did not invent this dynastic legend. He adopted it from several earlier sources and in turn passed it on to his successors: annalists, chroniclers, and historians. In the official genealogies compiled at the Danish court throughout the thirteenth century—the great century of genealogies in Scandinavia—the bear as ancestor of a king held an acknowledged place. No one doubted that a bear was one of the founders of the Danish dynasty; some writers even omitted a generation and made the son of the animal the father of Count Ulfo, hence Sven's grandfather.[63] Far from damaging it, this animal ancestry seems to have given a mythical prestige to the Danish dynasty that roused the envy of the kings of Sweden and Norway, to the point that from 1260 on the kings of Norway also claimed descent from that founding bear, recalling that one of the nieces of Count Ulfo married King Harald III of Norway (1047–1066). In Sweden, where genealogies going back more than four generations could not be produced, the preferred path was to point out that several kings of Denmark had also ruled Sweden, that the two dynasties were closely related, and that they had common ancestors, which was true.[64]

Oddly, no monk or priest before the end of the Middle Ages seems to have denounced the alleged ursine origins of the kings of Denmark, Norway, and perhaps Sweden. In the sixteenth century, Olaus Magnus, the last archbishop of Uppsala, having taken refuge in Rome after being driven out by the Reformation, was still alluding to it in his long and fascinating history of the northern peoples, *Historia de gentibus septentrionali-bus*. He even provides details not reported by Saxo Grammaticus, notably on the bear's sexual appetite, the way he inseminated the young woman, and the role of dogs in his capture.[65] Moreover, Saxo and his sources had invented nothing; as early as the eleventh century, literary and narrative texts were in circulation that included a bear among the ancestors of various celebrated figures. For example, in the Latin gest of the deeds of Duke Siward, the Danish companion of King Canute the Great, who had defeated the Anglo-Saxons in northern England in the years 1020–1030, the anonymous author explains that the duke's father had bear's ears, the last bodily inheritance of a bear ancestor that had procreated with a woman.[66] This father with bear's ears was named Beorn Bereson, and it is probable that the legend of an animal ancestor was built around his name (Beorn) or that of his father (Bero)—two names that directly evoke the bear. Incidentally, in chronicles as in sagas, characters supposed to have a bear for an ancestor are almost always figures with ursine names. Symbolically, the name is supposed to be the consequence or the sign of this kinship link, but historically it is almost always the cause. Genealogy does not create the name, but the reverse.[67]

This was not a specifically Scandinavian phenomenon. In late thirteenth-century Italy, a similar legend arose around the name of the prestigious Roman Orsini family, which gave the Church three popes and many cardinals. The name clearly recalled that of the bear, and around 1280 people began saying that an Orsini ancestor had had close relations with a she-bear. Two versions of the nature of those relations were in circulation: the appalling one spoke of procreation by the man with the beast; the other, more acceptable and patterned after Roman mythology, told of an infant abandoned in the forest given shelter by a bear and nursed with her milk. In the late Middle Ages, the Colonna family, hereditary enemies of the Orsini, put in circulation pamphlets featuring the first version and declaring that the Orsini, *"figli dell'orsa,"* were monstrous beings, the offspring of a union between a man and an animal. The Orsini obviously preferred the second version, which made them resemble the kings of Rome, descendants of Romulus. This was the legend they had copied, and they displayed their emblematic animal, the she-bear, everywhere to carry, accompany, or replace their armorial bearings.[68] In reality, it seems that the true eponymous ancestor of the Orsini was a certain Orso, the restless and ambitious nephew of Pope Celestine III (1191–1198). Before the end of the twelfth century, the family to which he belonged was merely a branch with no specific name of the huge clan of the Boboni-Boveschi.[69] In addition, in the feudal period in Rome and central Italy, the baptismal name Orso was not unusual. But, in this instance, it enabled the creation of a myth, a legend, and images and emblems.

Further back in time and in a more northern part of Europe before the year 1000, similar tales can be found in several literary texts arising from oral traditions. One example is the oldest European epic in a vernacular language, *Beowulf*. The epic was written in Old English, but England is completely absent from the narrative, which recounts the deeds of a preternaturally strong prince who kills, in succession, two monsters and a dragon. His name, Beowulf, that is, "the wolf of the bees," or "the enemy of the bees," was one of the epithets sometimes given to bears by the Germans, for whom pronouncing the real name of the animal was taboo. Beowulf is a bear, or rather the son of a bear and a woman, which explains his extraordinary strength, his savage nature, and at the same time his sense of Good and Evil and his already Christian sentiments. The story takes place in Denmark and southern Sweden; the tale was probably transmitted orally to northern England at the time of the Germanic invasions of Great Britain.[70] The poet who set it down in Old English seems to have been a native of Yorkshire or Northumberland. He was educated, probably a member of the clergy, with a majestic and colorful style. He was equally acquainted with Germanic legends and ancient epics. He may have written in the late seventh century, or more likely in the eighth or early ninth.[71]

Later sagas also relate deeds (or misdeeds) of creatures who are half-man, half-bear. Sometimes, they are not sons of an animal and a woman but heroes transformed into bears by an evil spell: for example, Bjarski ("little bear"), transformed into a bear by his stepmother whose advances he has rejected; or Bodvar, a young hunter given bear's feet because he has violated a prohibition and eaten the hindquarters of a bear that was unjustly killed. Sometimes, they are dead men reincarnated in the body of a bear who return to Earth to torment their enemies.[72]

Animal Boundaries

How could clerics in the feudal period allow the circulation in Christian lands of stories that presented bears and men as similar beings, kin, interfertile? They ran counter to the teachings of the Fathers of the Church and all the theology flowing from those teachings. That theology had consistently contrasted man, created in the image of God, to the animal, an inferior and subject creature; there could be no kinship between them. Moreover, the Church harshly condemned any behavior that might create confusion. This meant, for example, repeated—and ineffective—prohibitions of animal disguises,[73] the imitation of animal behavior, the celebration of animals, and especially carrying on illicit relations with them, ranging from excessive affection for certain individual animals (horses, falcons, dogs) to the most infamous crimes, such as witchcraft and bestiality.

This was the prevailing position. But some theologians followed another path, more discreet but perhaps more suggestive of modernity. It was both Aristotelian and Pauline. From Aristotle came the idea of a community of living things, an idea scattered through several of his works and reaffirmed in *De anima*. The Middle Ages inherited this idea in several stages, the last and most important of which occurred in the thirteenth century.[74] The assimilation of the Aristotelian heritage in this area was, it should be said, facilitated by the existence within the Christian tradition of an attitude toward the animal world that was roughly comparable, although for very different reasons. This attitude, the most well-known example of which is the legend of Francis of Assisi,[75] had its source in several verses of Saint Paul, particularly in a passage from the Epistle to the Romans: "The creature itself also shall be delivered from the bondage of corruption into the glorious liberty of the children of God" (Romans 8.21).[76] This sentence strongly affected the theologians who commented on it.[77] Some of them inquired about the meaning of those words: they wondered whether Christ had really come to save *all* creatures and whether *all* animals were truly "children of God." That Jesus was born in a stable seemed to several authors to be proof that the Savior had come to Earth *also* to save animals.[78] Other theologians, enamored of casuistry, posed questions that were debated at the University of Paris in the middle of the thirteenth century. For example, regarding the future life of animals: Were they resurrected after death? Did they go to heaven? Was there a special place reserved for them? Was this true for all animals or only for one individual from each species? And with regard to their life on Earth, the questions were: Can they work on Sunday? Should they be required to observe fast days? And most important, should they be treated in this life as morally responsible beings?[79]

That said, all prelates and theologians did not ask themselves these questions. For most of them, animals were servile creatures with no kinship, biological or spiritual, with human beings. Anything that might encourage that belief had to be combated, particularly when the animal in question, like the bear, bore a dangerous resemblance to man. From the Carolingian period to the beginning of modern times, all the playful or festive rituals that involved physical contact with a bear or the disguise of a man as a bear were targeted. Archbishop Hincmar of Reims (845–882), for example, in a famous capitulary of 852–853, vigorously denounced, among other practices, "vile games with a bear" (*"turpia joca cum urso"*) and demanded that the bishops of his province not tolerate such turpitudes under any circumstances.[80] He provides no details about these "vile games," but it can be imagined that they were dances or mimes performed at carnival time and still containing, in the late ninth century, powerful remnants of paganism, perhaps even simulations of copulation. A few decades later, Bishop Adalbéron of Laon, despite his strongly ursine name, also denounced games and masquerades in which men disguised themselves as bears or danced with bears.[81] It was a wasted effort. The bear was the quintessential animal for disguises—resembling as it did a man in disguise—and until the end of the Middle Ages, and even later, many prelates repeated, although they were not really obeyed, that a good Christian should not "play the bear."[82]

The bear, of course, was not the only animal concerned by these prohibitions, but it was the one that always came at the head of the list when the same prelates cited examples of animal disguises it was particularly vile and dangerous to adopt. As I have noted, the animals most often mentioned were the stag, the bull, the ass, and the boar. Why those? It was not a contrast between the domestic and the wild worlds, since the list contained three wild animals and two domestic animals. On the other hand, it is noteworthy that these five male animals had the reputation of having a heightened sexuality, or indeed, in the case of the bear and the ass, an abnormal sexuality; they were potential sexual partners for women, as recounted in several stories handed down from antiquity, in the tradition of Ovid's *Metamorphoses* and *The Golden Ass* of Apuleius. In addition, these five animals all had bodies that were neither smooth nor homogeneous, but rather bristly, aggressive, endowed with appendices and protuberances: fur and claws for the bear, antlers and penis for the stag, horns and tail for the bull, bristles and tusks for the boar. These were no doubt the primary attributes of animality for medieval sensibilities: an animal that was fully animal, that is, dangerous for humans, particularly for women, a being that has not only a frenzied sexuality but also well-marked protuberances: fur, horns, claws, teeth, tail. All these attributes, easy to imitate with mere pieces of wood, metal, or cloth, enabled men to disguise themselves quickly and easily and then, for the time of a ritual, to become a bear, a stag, a bull, an ass, or a boar.

These games and rituals, which took place at specific moments in the calendar (carnival, winter and summer solstices), were neither neutral nor innocent, but on the contrary always strongly transgressive. "Playing the bear" or "playing the stag" meant not only disguising oneself as a bear or a stag; it also involved manifesting uncontrolled sexual desire and, as in the Lupercalia of ancient Rome,[83] pouncing on women or girls, carrying them away from prying eyes, and raping them, or indulging in shared but prohibited pleasure with them. Women were always the victims, real or symbolic, of these masquerades that featured strongly sexed animals. Hence, attempts had to be made to keep women away, exactly as they were to be kept away from hunts, where large game was not only a mortal danger to them but also a sexual danger. Many priests and monks of the High Middle Ages believed that one had to go further and simply prohibit all these pagan rituals inherited from barbaric societies and contrary to all Christian values.

The Church tried to do this beginning in the Carolingian period, and it attacked first the animal that was considered most dangerous because it was closest to the human species: the bear.

II

THE BEAR COMBATTED
FROM CHARLEMAGNE
TO SAINT LOUIS

4

The Saint Stronger than the Beast

KING of the beasts, present in every land, dreadful and dreaded, emblem of chiefs and warriors, symbol of extreme savagery and heightened sexuality, presumed cousin or ancestor of man, an object of veneration and pagan ceremonies throughout northern Europe, lover of girls and young women with whom it was thought he mated, the bear necessarily terrified the Church of the High Middle Ages. The Church saw the bear as the most dangerous of all indigenous animals and even as a creature of the Devil. This was not because it was endowed with such prodigious strength that no other animal could defeat it but primarily because it strangely resembled man, so much so that human conduct was attributed to it. It was also the animal around which clustered oral traditions, uncontrollable beliefs, and the superstitions that were the most difficult to eradicate.

The Church therefore went to war early against this creature, striving to remove it from its throne and replace it with another wild animal, more distant and hence more subject to control: the lion, king of the bestiary of the East and the central figure of all written traditions—biblical, Greek, and Roman. This war against the bear, which ended with a new king of the beasts in all European societies, lasted not for a few decades but for several centuries, almost a millennium. To bring it to a successful conclusion, priests and theologians had recourse to various methods. Some were employed sequentially, some simultaneously.

The first was to eliminate the physical presence of the bear by organizing battues and huge massacres, chiefly in the Germanic countries. A second strategy was used at the same time: the bear was portrayed as a submissive, tamed, almost "domesticated" (in the medieval sense of the word) animal.[1] Beginning in the seventh and eighth centuries, hagiography was used for that purpose. Many saints' lives told how a man of God, by his example, his virtues, or his power, had succeeded in defeating the savage beast and forcing it to obey him. Subsequently, relying on the Bible (in which the bear is always seen in a bad light) and on a sentence from Saint Augustine commenting on the combat of the young David against a bear threatening his flock, theologians and preachers made the animal the embodiment of numerous vices and gave it a privileged place in the satanic bestiary. Moreover, they claimed, the Devil often took the form of a threatening bear to torment sinful men or those who doubted God, particularly monks whom Satan sought to induce to renounce their vows. Finally, after taming and demonizing the bear, priests and monks sought to humiliate and ridicule it. This generally occurred after the year 1000. Ecclesiastical authorities, usually hostile to all animal spectacles, made an exception for the disgraced beast and no longer opposed exhibitions of bears. Captured, muzzled, and chained, the animal accompanied jongleurs and tumblers from château to château, fair to fair, market to market, and gradually lost its rank as a royal animal, admired and feared, and became a mere circus animal, dancing, doing tricks, and amusing the public.

At the turn of the twelfth and thirteenth centuries, the battle seemed finally to have been won: the bear had preserved practically nothing of its former role as king of the beasts. Everything was ready for the consecration of another wild animal and the replacement of the "lion of the North" by the lion of the South.

The Lion of the North

Going back a few centuries, Charlemagne organized great campaigns of bear massacres in Germany in the years 772–773, 782–785, and 794–799. These slaughters were one element in a general policy of the eradication of pagan cults, particularly those having to do with the forces of nature. The Christian religion everywhere replaced or at least overlaid the old cults. Just as thousands of trees were cut down in Saxony and Westphalia, stones displaced or made into buildings, springs diverted or turned into fountains, sacred places turned into chapels, so thousands of bears were massacred. The beast that was too much venerated by the Germans seemed to be an enemy of Christ. So, victims of a major program of evangelization, the bears of northern Germany saw their numbers decrease significantly in the course of thirty years. The decline was speeded by the simultaneous battle against trees and forests, which forced bears to move, change territory, take refuge in still-wooded hills, and then to emigrate toward the mountains to the south.

Charlemagne and his missionaries were imitated a few decades later by other evangelizers who killed bears or cleared forests. To the east, Slavic and Baltic bears were similarly victims of the inroads of Christianity. To the north, the conversion of the Scandinavian countries was less brutal, but bears suffered from the retreat of forests, laid waste by heavy consumption of wood. Indeed, the great clearings everywhere in the West, consequences of demographic growth, changed the forest landscape, plant covering, and the habits of animal populations after the year 1000. The bear gradually disappeared from plains areas and became exclusively a mountain animal, coming down only when food was too scarce.[2] At the same time, although the bear remained omnivorous, its diet changed: 80 percent carnivorous in antiquity, the European brown bear was probably only 40 percent carnivorous in the late Middle Ages. This evolution, moreover, continued into modern times, so that today something between 85 and 90 percent of the diet of the few brown bears still living in the wild in Europe is vegetarian.[3]

France is a prime example of the decline and eventual disappearance of bears in certain regions in the course of the Middle Ages. Bears were present everywhere in independent Gaul, including in the great wooded plains near the seacoasts. This was no longer true in Roman Gaul: bears were scarcely to be found in northwestern France and on the Atlantic coast. By the end of the Carolingian period, they seem to have disappeared west of a line running from Flanders to Bordeaux, a tendency that accelerated after the year 1000: in the kingdom of France, bears frequented primarily the marches of the east and the northeast, as well as mountainous regions. The clearings of the feudal period and subsequent deforestation made them retreat a little further toward the lands of the

Holy Roman Empire and the Iberian peninsula, so that in the late Middle Ages there were practically no bears west of a line running from the Ardennes to the Pyrenees. Even where there was reforestation, as in various regions of Normandy, Berry, and the Île-de-France, bears did not return. In modern times, bears moved a bit higher into mountain forests; then they disappeared from the Massif Central, probably in the seventeenth century, and can now be found only in the Vosges, the Jura, the Alps, and the Pyrenees.[4] A memory of the bear's presence nonetheless remained everywhere. Even though the bear may have disappeared from one area or another, that did not mean that it stopped playing a role in imagination, ritual, or social symbolism. Quite the contrary, folk practices featuring the bear remained very much alive in several regions in eighteenth-century France that had not seen bears for a long time (Brittany, Berry, Artois). Such practices were sometimes even more vigorous than in mountain regions where bears were still physically present.[5]

In the Middle Ages, systematic slaughter and large-scale clearings were not the only causes of the decline in numbers of bears in Western Europe since the end of antiquity. Hunting also played a role, at least up to the twelfth and thirteenth centuries, when the stag definitively became the royal game animal in place of the bear and the boar. Before then, hunting a bear was an obligatory aristocratic ritual that, as in pagan Germany, sometimes ended in savage hand-to-hand combat between man and beast. But hunting was also a way of eliminating the great beast, which was harmful, dangerous, and too abundant in some areas, and to take from it various products that were of use in material culture. This meant not so much the meat, which was of course edible but very fatty and hard to preserve, as the skin, hide, fat, bile, fur, teeth, and claws. Medical practitioners were especially eager to get ingredients from bears, to which they attributed various prophylactic and therapeutic virtues, particularly the bile, which was supposed to be effective against sterility, baldness, epilepsy, rabies, and gout.[6] Similarly, but in a more symbolic register, bear teeth and claws were worn around the neck or next to certain parts of the body as amulets to ward off evil or danger, a practice that endured throughout the High Middle Ages. Amulets played a role not only in the

Germanic world; warriors and hunters of the north made abundant use of them. They also wore caps, gloves, and shoes made in whole or in part from bear fur, which was not as stiff and abrasive as boar bristles and was more protective against cold and damp.

The skin provided the greatest benefit and was sometimes preserved whole in Church or princely treasures.[7] Of course, it was not until the Romantic period that a bearskin became a trophy hung on a wall or set on the floor as a rug, which explains the anachronism of all the movie or cartoon images featuring the great hall of a medieval castle decorated with a bearskin spread before the hearth. It was, however, a really useful product, especially if the fur was separated from the hide. With the hide, which was thick and firm, one could make shoes and boots of high quality that were solid and waterproof. But it was a hide hard to work with that required long softening before it could be shaped.

Bear meat, on the other hand, kept badly, even when it was salted. It was soft, rather bland, and very oily, and fat and lean were barely distinguishable. In the nineteenth century, Alexandre Dumas described it as a strange dish—hence succulent for him—in his culinary dictionary, but it is possible he never tasted it, even during his travels in Switzerland and Russia, and that he was more taken with the idea of eating a bear than with the meat itself.[8] In any event, in the Middle Ages, lords and poachers much preferred boar meat. Eating bear was more a symbolic than a culinary act, more virile than tasty: it was a way of ingesting the animal's strength, not of enjoying its meat. The best bit seems to have been the thigh, sometimes made into a ham. The rest was given to the huntsmen's dogs, who often didn't want it (whereas they were wild about anything that came from a stag) and left it in turn to wild or domestic pigs, which would eat any kind of flesh.[9] I have already noted that in the late Middle Ages and the early modern period, a bear paw was still feudal dues in some Alpine valleys. Village communities had to provide several of them to their lords.[10] It was obviously in no way a dietary necessity but a symbolic gesture inherited from former times: the lord merely pretended to eat the paw in a sort of ritual meal, or else he displayed it for several days as a trophy at the entry to his dwelling. This practice was unknown elsewhere,[11] and products derived from bears seem to have disappeared relatively early from the list of feudal dues. This was especially so because in a large part of Eastern Europe, among the Slavs and even in Byzantium, the bear remained an animal that was both admired and taboo, whose flesh it was unthinkable to eat.[12]

One of the strategies used by the Church to bring the bear down from his throne consisted, as I have noted, of making him lose symbolically his strength and arrogance by presenting him as an animal for which man should feel no fear, an animal that he could easily overcome. Not any man, of course, not even a king, a warrior, or a simple hunter, but the exemplary man, "the man of God" *(vir Dei),* the perfect model for every Christian life: the saint. Hence, at the very moment Charlemagne's armies were exterminating thousands of bears in Saxon forests, hagiographers were given the task of presenting stories in which the king of the beasts was defeated, tamed, or humiliated by a saint who was stronger and more admirable than the animal. The oldest of these stories can be read in several saints' lives well prior to the German campaigns, as early as the sixth or seventh century, and they appear again after the year 1000, sometimes as late as the twelfth century. But the basic typological core around which most of the stories were built was developed in the Carolingian period.

Bears were not the only animals involved. The hagiography of the High Middle Ages is full of episodes in which animals intervene in various ways, and they often later become iconographic emblems of saints: Saint Benedict's crow, the dragon of Saint Martha and Saint Margaret, the deer of Saint Eustace, the horse of Saint Eligius, Saint Genevieve's lamb, and many others—the list is practically endless.[13] But whatever the fate reserved for them, these animals featured in saints' lives and collections of miracles are always a source of instruction, and seem to express two strains of thought and sensibility that are apparently contradictory. On the one hand, a hagiography had to establish as sharp a contrast as possible between man, who was created in God's image, and animal, subordinate and imperfect, if not impure. But on the other hand, in some texts there is a more or less diffuse sense of a true unity of the living world and a kinship—not merely biological—between man and animal.

The first strain was dominant and explains why animals were so often invoked as elements in a tale. Establishing a systematic contrast between man and animal, and making the animal an inferior creature or a foil, necessarily involved talking about animals constantly and referring to them on any pretext; they became a favored site for every metaphor and every comparison. In short, they were the focus of "thinking symbolically," to adopt the well-known formulation of Claude Lévi-Strauss.[14] This strain of thinking also encouraged the harsh repression of any behavior that could create confusion between human beings and an animal species. The second strain of thought was more discreet, but it fostered many questions about the relationships between humans and animals—debates, for example, about the souls of animals or the crimes of bestiality.

The questions and many speculations that medieval theologians expressed about animals clearly show that Christianity was the source of a remarkable improvement in their status. Biblical and Greco-Roman antiquity had ignored or despised them; the Christian Middle Ages moved them into the foreground. Hagiographies were particularly loquacious about animals, particularly in the Carolingian period and around the year 1000. They delighted in rewriting old tales and multiplying episodes involving animals in order to bring out the various powers of the saints: Saints could protect against savage beasts, remedy any harm they might have caused, give them orders, take care of them, exchange charitable deeds with them, and perform miracles and conversions of all kinds. The model of the holy hermit exacting obedience from one or another fearsome beast was a favorite recurrent feature.

The Bear as Companion to the Saint

More than the bishop or the abbot, the hermit was the one who had the closest relationships with animals, especially with the bear, which could in some ways also be considered a kind of hermit: it lived in solitude, in the heart of the forest, removed from the world and its dangers and temptations. The two saints who best embody this figure of the hermit who withdrew to the wilderness and lived in community with wild beasts were Saint Anthony (c. 251–352), the founder of Christian monasticism, and his follower Saint Blaise, who died in 316. Before becoming bishop of Sebastea in Armenia, Blaise had chosen to live in the forest "among bears, lions, tigers, and panthers."[15] At least, that is what his biographers say, and images often represent his early life in that way, before he was found by hunters and brought into town. Among his various animal companions, words and pictures often give bears the most prominent place.[16]

But the example of Blaise is not an isolated one. There were many saints, real or legendary, who had something to do with bears in the course of their lives. Drawing up a list of them is an almost impossible task, because alongside the "great" saints who were honored in several different regions, there was a crowd of local saints, whose names, lives, and miracles are little known, uncertain, or the result of mistakes, doublings, vagueness, or confusion. However, great or small, these "saints with bears" were not all hermits living in solitude in the forest, the western equivalent of the "wilderness" of the early days of Christianity. Some of them traveled extensively. Among the oldest *vitae* containing one or more episodes with bears are those of Saint Columban and his disciple Saint Gall, two Irish monks who went on a mission to the continent to evangelize regions not yet won over to Christianity and to found monasteries there.

Born around 540, long a monk in Bangor in the north of the island, around the age of forty Columban felt a calling to go on a "peregrination of God" *(peregrinatio Dei)*, that is, to go into exile to preach the Gospel. He set off for Gaul with twelve disciples. Welcomed by the king of the Burgundians, he established three monasteries in the Vosges, including the monastery of Luxeuil, which became a major center of monastic reform. But he soon quarreled with Brunhild, the dreadful Queen of Austrasia, and had to resume his journeying. Columban went first to Lake Constance, where he converted the last remaining pagan Alamanni, and then to Lombardy where, with the permission of King Agilulf, he established the monastery of Bobbio, near Pavia. He died there in the following year, 615, after compiling monastic rules marked by such great severity that they were later replaced everywhere by the rules of Saint Benedict.[17]

On the road to Switzerland, as he was crossing the Jura, Saint Columban was caught in a violent storm and sought refuge in a cave. The cave was inhabited by a bear who had no intention of sharing his abode. The animal took on a menacing air and tried to drive off the holy monk. But Columban, not at all frightened by the angry beast, responded just as belligerently; then with God's help, and using more gentle words, he succeeded in dominating the bear and forced it to grant him a place in the cave. Later on, relations between man and beast became more peaceable, and Columban, who stayed in the spot for some time, lived with it and even succeeded in causing a spring to appear in the depths of the cave.[18]

This episode, recounted in the oldest version of the *vita* of Saint Columban, compiled by Jonas of Bobbio shortly after the saint's death,[19] became early on a *topos* in hagiographies of the High Middle Ages: a monk taming a bear became the archetypal image of the saint stronger than the strongest beast, exacting obedience and sometimes aid from the animal, not by force of arms or through physical strength but by the force of words. Several other "men of God," beginning with Saint Gall, Columban's chief disciple, obtained comparable results and transformed terrifying bears into good-natured and helpful companions. Yet, going far back into the past, this episode of the cave seems to be an unconscious echo of an ancient time, when bears and men of the Paleolithic frequented the same caves, struggled to find refuge in them, or even, less often and more briefly, stayed in them together, in a sense joining forces against the rigors of the climate and the dangers of the moment.

This was also the one episode out of the long and tumultuous life of Columban that iconography adopted as the inevitable image of the hermit saint—although he was a particularly nomadic monk—thereby making the bear his special emblem.[20] Columban thus appears to have been one of the first "saints with bears." It is true that another episode in his *vita*, also reported by Jonas of Bobbio but omitted by most later writers, featured a second bear, less famous than the first. One extremely cold day in the Vosges forest, at the time he was abbot of Luxeuil, Columban saw a pack of wolves attacking a deer. They killed it but could not feast on it because a bear put them to flight (an important point: a bear is stronger than a pack of wolves), seized the dead animal, and got ready to devour it. The holy abbot approached the beast and asked it to spare the deer's hide, which could, he said, be used by his monks to cover books and make shoes. He was so persuasive that the bear obeyed and ate only the flesh, taking care not to damage the hide.[21] An edifying story, once again showing the superiority of the man of God over the savage beast.

In this role, Saint Gall (c. 560–c. 645) went beyond his master. Saint Gall was founder and head of one of the richest and most glorious abbeys in Roman Christendom, the one that bears his name in eastern Switzerland. Having traveled from Ireland with Columban and his companions, Gall spent a short time at Luxeuil and then, followed by a single disciple, he left the abbey in the Vosges and set out for the Alps. Not far from Lake Constance, where the two men had halted to share a frugal meal, a lame and starving bear that had come down from the mountains tried to seize their food. Not at all afraid, unlike his companion, Saint Gall spoke to the beast and ordered it to fetch wood and revive the fire. Against all expectations, the bear complied. The man of God rewarded it by giving it bread and removing a large thorn that had wounded its paw. From then on, the bear shared the saint's life, obeyed him with docility, and then helped him build a hermitage that later became the huge and flourishing Abbey of Saint Gall.[22] A late legend even claims that the bear became the first monk in the abbey.

Several of these marvelous episodes are clichés borrowed from other saints' lives; they were to have a long life and were found in various hagiographies up to modern times. For example, the companionship between bear and saint was obviously copied from the story of Columban, Gall's model and master. As for the thorn removed from the paw,[23] it echoes the story of Saint Jerome removing a thorn from a lion's paw, after which the lion became his chief companion at table. The theme of the animal builder is more widespread: it is found in various saints' lives and collections of miracles (Gerold, Ghislain, Severin). And the bear as a monk or cleric is encountered in some branches of the *Roman de Renart* at the turn of the twelfth and thirteenth centuries, when Brun, victim of the fox's nasty tricks, enters a monastery or becomes the chaplain of King Noble.[24]

In contrast, the bear coming down from the mountains is perhaps a realistic touch, attesting as early as the High Middle Ages to the disappearance of the animal from the plains regions.

But these are narrative details. The principal idea is that of the encounter between the man of God and the king of the beasts, between the divine order and the natural and wild order. This is an idea that is found in all the stories that bring into contact a bear and a saint, from the Merovingian era to the heart of the Middle Ages: the saint dominates the beast; he tames its violence, gives it orders, exacts obedience, makes it work, transforms it into a domestic animal, and even into a real companion; sometimes he converts it to Christianity. All these themes, diffused by hagiography, iconography, and preaching, had the primary function of battling against pagan bear cults, particularly in the Germanic world and in mountainous regions.[25]

For this reason, they appeared early on in the iconography of Saint Gall, the founder of an abbey that was influential not only in all Switzerland but also throughout Western Christendom. There again, the saint was stronger than the beast. In the anonymous early life, compiled at the monastery of Saint Gall around 770, in the huge *vita* written by the monk Walafrid Strabo in 833–834,[26] and for several centuries thereafter, the illustrations present only the episode of the bear and show it obeying the saint and working under his orders. This is the scene one sees, for example, on a famous ivory plate binding made at Saint Gall in the early tenth century, covering a book of the Gospels.[27] And this was the scene that became the emblematic image of the powerful abbey, appearing on its great seal. The mold for this seal, engraved around 1320, represents the saint seated, dressed as an abbot, holding out a loaf of bread to a bear at work, standing erect and carrying the trunk of a tree, the symbolic "cornerstone" of the future monastery.[28]

Carrying the Baggage, Pulling the Plow

Hagiography and iconography feature other working bears, but they are doing so against their will: not at all familiars or companions to a saint, they have been forced to obey and serve him. The most frequent theme is that of the bear carrying the traveling man of God's baggage. The archetype is found in the story of Corbinian, apostle to Bavaria and a prestigious saint, honored throughout the Alpine region. Born near Melun, France around 675, Corbinian was given the mission by Pope Gregory II to evangelize Bavaria, a mission he executed perfectly. He became the first bishop of Freising and founded several monasteries in his enormous diocese before his death in 725. One day on his way to Rome, accompanied by a mule carrying his baggage, not far from the Brenner Pass Corbinian encountered a colossal bear that, scorning the priest, attacked the mule and devoured it. Furious, the saint forced the beast to take the place of its victim and carry his baggage all the way to Rome.[29] The indomitable king of the beasts thus found itself degraded to the status of a miserable beast of burden: admiring it or fostering its cult, as was still being done in most Alpine valleys not yet fully Christianized, no longer made any sense.

The theme of the bear transformed into a beast of burden can also be found in some other saints' lives that were more or less widely diffused. The outline of the story is almost always the same: the saint goes on a journey with a domestic animal (donkey, mule, ox) carrying his gear; a hungry bear appears on the scene and devours the animal, and the saint forces the bear to take the animal's place and carry his baggage. For example, in the life of Saint Amand, bishop of Maastricht (647–675) and apostle to Flanders, Hainaut, and Limburg, the bear devours a donkey while the traveler is asleep. The same thing occurs in the life of Saint Humbert (died c. 680), abbot of Maroilles in Hainaut; in that of Saint Remaclus (died c. 670), founder of the abbey of Stavelot in the Ardennes; in that of Saint Sylvester, a fourth-century pope; and that of Saint Valerius, his contemporary, bishop of Saint-Lizier in the Pyrenees. The *vita* of Valerius adds an interesting detail: the donkey had been a gift from his friend Martin, the great and prestigious archbishop of Tours, and as a token of his gratitude, the humble Valerius had given the animal the name Martin and used it as a mount to visit his mountain parishes. It was during one of these pastoral visits that the donkey was devoured one night by a bear; the next morning the holy bishop forced the wild beast to stand in for the mount he had killed.[30]

A related story is found in the life of another priest who was also a legendary friend of Saint Martin: Saint Maximinus, archbishop of Trier in the fourth century. The two saints went on a pilgrimage to Rome with two donkeys carrying their baggage; along came a bear that devoured Maximinus's donkey. Maximinus did not know what to do, but Martin intervened, and with his great authority forced the bear to carry his companion's baggage. It is not out of the question that this episode, found in the earliest version of the *vita* of Saint Maximinus, compiled in the fifth century,[31] though not in the life of Saint Martin written by Sulpicius Severus, was the source of the *topos* that turns up later in many saints' lives. This legend also makes it easier to understand why many bears in medieval traditions were given the name Martin.[32] But there were additional reasons for choosing that name: for one thing, the proper name Martinus includes the root *art-*, which, as I have noted, was the word for bear in most Indo-European languages, notably in Greek and the Celtic languages;[33] further, the great fall festival of the bear preparing to hibernate fell on Saint Martin's Day, November 11.[34]

Carrying the saint's baggage was thus a relatively frequent activity for bears in the High Middle Ages, at least in hagiographic accounts. But pulling a plow was almost as frequent. The model here was an episode from the life and miracles of Saint Eligius. Eligius (c. 558–660), bishop of Noyon, was adviser to King Dagobert and a skillful blacksmith and noted goldsmith. He also worked in the fields. One day as he was plowing, a bear came on the scene and seized one of the two oxen yoked to the plow and carried it off to devour it in his cave. Following its tracks, the saint found the beast in its den and ordered it to replace the dead ox; the bear obeyed and set to work: it pulled the plow alongside the surviving ox and led an exemplary life until the day of its death.[35] Later, Ourscamp abbey was established in the field where the miracle took place, the name itself retaining a memory of the event (*ursus / campus*, bear / field).

A related story is told in the lives of Saint Claude, archbishop of Besançon (c. 680–690) and patron saint of Franche-Comté;[36] of Saint James, first bishop of Tarentaise; and of some other saints—monks, abbots, or bishops. The case of Saint Arigius is probably the most original, because his legend brings together several ursine themes featuring a wagon, a plow, or a cart. Arigius, the rather legendary first bishop of Gap, was returning from Rome and had placed his heavy baggage in a wagon pulled by two oxen. Along came a bear who ate one of the two animals; the saint immediately forced the bear to replace its victim. The beast obeyed, and, with the help of the surviving ox, willingly pulled the wagon to Gap. It subsequently became attached to the priest, helped him in his work in the fields, pulled the plow, and guarded the sheep. When Arigius died, the bear, it was said, went to the church, attended the funeral mass, and, going before the funeral wagon, led the cortege to the cemetery. It returned every year until its death on the bishop's name day, May 1.[37]

Guarding the Sheep, Founding an Abbey

Another saint was similarly escorted to his final resting place by a bear: Saint Vincentian (c. 623–c. 700), but in that case the animal was forced to act against its will. A hermit in a Limousin forest, Vincentian died at an advanced age and was mourned throughout the region. Saint Rusticus, bishop of Limoges, had the body placed on a funeral wagon pulled by two huge oxen. On the way to the cemetery, one of the oxen was carried off and eaten by a bear. Saint Rusticus and his curate Saint Savinien found the beast in its lair and ordered it to harness itself to the wagon in place of the ox. Conquered by the words of the men of God, the animal obeyed, with some grumbling. Two murals have partially preserved the memory of this tale in two parish churches in the dioceses of Tulle and Limoges. The treasury of the church of Saint Vincentian in Corrèze also holds a beautiful enameled reliquary of the early thirteenth century with a medallion representing the wagon pulled by an ox and a bear.[38]

Bears transformed into shepherds were also not infrequent. In the life of Saint Florentius of Saumur, for example, recounted in the remarkable *Dialogues* of Pope Gregory the Great, not only does the beast guard the sheep, but it even provokes jealousy among the saint's companions. Florentius had come from Austria to Anjou with a disciple named Eutychius. They both became hermits on the banks of the Loire, not far from Saumur. But Eutychius was called to be abbot of a nearby monastery and Florentius found himself alone. He became friendly with a bear that rendered him various services, guarding the hermitage, watching over and protecting the sheep, and never thinking of making a meal of them. Jealous of such a marvel, Eutychius and his monks killed the bear. Florentius mourned the animal and gave it a Christian burial; then he cursed the monks and called down leprosy upon them.[39]

The image of a bear guarding the sheep at the request of a man of God is particularly instructive. It brings to the fore the miraculous powers of the saint: he alone can bring together and unite contraries. The same idea occurs in other tales in which an animal gives up following its natural inclinations and stops behaving like a savage beast: one saint or another, for example, keeps a bear from killing, devouring, threatening, or simply stealing and pilfering. In the life and miracles of Magnus, a seventh-century saint particularly venerated in Bavaria and the Tyrol, he forbids a bear to eat his apples; instead he has the animal work with him in the orchard and transforms him into a gardener. I should note in passing that this Magnus (there are several others) was a companion of Columban and Gall and that his legend and iconography, like theirs, include a bear. The twelve monks that had traveled from Bangor, Ireland to Gaul and the Alps around 580 seem to have had as duties—at least if the hagiographic accounts are to be believed—not only the evangelization of the countryside, the foundation of monasteries, and the reform of the clergy, but also the eradication of the last bear cults.

For collections of miracles, a particular case was that of a bear sparing its victim in a circus game or in a pit of the condemned. Several young Christian women condemned to the torture of being devoured were treated gently or saved by a bear who was supposed to be their executioner: examples are Euphemia, Landrada, and Thecla.[40] To them may be added Columba, who was not spared by a bear but protected by a she-bear, first from the prostitution to which Emperor Aurelian had condemned her, and then from a fire that destroyed her prison; she finally had her head cut off. I might note here that two saints that have a bear as their emblem are nearly homonyms: Columba and Columban. One might add another Columba (masculine) (c. 521–597), also an Irish missionary, who founded the monastery of Iona in Scotland. He had a bear among his emblems, although the reason for this is not very clear. It may have arisen from word play—in what language?—between the saint's name and the name of the animal. Or else it might be a meeting of opposites: a Latin name, evoking the pure and peaceful dove, and a wild and cruel beast.

It will be recalled that Saint Gall's bear helped him build his hermitage at the location of the future abbey in eastern Switzerland.[41] There were other bears that, while not becoming masons or carpenters, contributed to the foundation of a church or a monastery. For example, Saint Severin's bear (fifth century) allowed a hermitage to take the place of his modest den beneath a rocky shelter; and there was the bear of Saint Ghislain (eighth century), patron saint of Mons and Hainaut. This bear indicated to the saint the spot where he should establish a monastery, the future abbey of Ursidongue; an eagle sent by God confirmed the choice. Even more famous was the she-bear of Saint Richardis. The daughter of a powerful Alsatian count, Richardis married Emperor Charles the Fat (881–887); later, accused of adultery, she submitted herself to the judgment of God and victoriously underwent the ordeal by fire. Withdrawn from the world, she saw in a dream Saint Odile, her relative, who asked her to establish a monastery at the spot where she would see a marvel. Soon thereafter, Richardis came upon a she-bear with her cubs. The she-bear seemed to trace the boundaries of an enclosure on the ground with her claws. This was where the empress established the abbey of Andlau, to which she retired, and where she died in 896.

In another version of the legend, not as old but more widespread, the she-bear did not trace an enclosure but scratched the ground, groaning all the while; Richardis discovered that the bear was preparing to bury the dead cub lying beside her. Overcome with pity, the saint began to pray and obtained the cub's resurrection. As a token of thanks, she had a church built on the spot, and then a monastery. In the crypt of the church of Saint Pierre et Saint Paul in Andlau, completed in the late ninth century, one can still see a large stone she-bear preserving the memory of the event; it seems to have been carved in the Romanesque period and is the abbey's emblematic animal. In addition, several documents in the archives indicate that in the late Middle Ages, the abbey was home to a living she-bear and that every week the bakers of the town of Andlau had to deliver a certain number of loaves to feed it.[42] Archeologists, who hardly believe either the saint's vision or the legend of the bear, have uncovered beneath the foundations of the church the remnants of a Celtic sanctuary: it is possible that this sanctuary was consecrated to the goddess Artio.[43]

Saints as Successors to Bears

Telling tales about men of God who were stronger than wild animals (not only bears, but also wolves, boars, eagles, and even crows) and who succeeded in exacting obedience from them or making use of their strength and natural cunning certainly helped weaken the veneration bestowed on those animals by populations that had only recently and superficially been converted to Christianity. But that was hardly enough for the bear, and the Church of the High Middle Ages had to go further in its hagiographic strategies to eliminate the last remnants of the ancient bear cults. To do this, as I have noted, some priests early on came up with the idea of using the calendar: at various times of year when games and rituals connected to admiration of the invincible beast took place, they set either feast days of very great saints or those of more local or regional saints, all of whom in one way or another had some connection to bears.

An exemplary case in this regard is Saint Martin, whose principal feast day, at first somewhat fluctuating, was definitively set at November 11, the supposed date of the death of the holy archbishop of Tours in 397. There was no element of chance in this date. In a large part of the temperate zone of Europe peasants celebrated on that day the moment when the bear was supposed to sense the first cold spell of winter, go into his den, and begin the long period of sleep: twice forty days of hibernation. The date was also the one when, in rural areas, outside activities gradually began to come to an end and each peasant brought in his cattle, his grain, and his tools before himself taking shelter with his family. The conduct of the bear going into hibernation was in a sense a symbolic image of this significant moment in the calendar: the movement from outside to inside, or even the passage from life to death.[44] This is why many rites and ceremonies associated the bear with various autumn festivals. These were pagan rites, of course, noisy, violent, transgressive, sometimes dangerous or sexual, consisting of dances, disguises, or masquerades, that could not help but frighten monks and priests.

The bishops of several dioceses in Gaul, rather than celebrating the festival of the bear, proposed as early as the fifth century to celebrate the festival of Martin, the great saint, sometimes called the thirteenth apostle, the evangelizer of the countryside, the founder of numerous parishes, and the future patron saint of the French monarchy (in the late Middle Ages, four thousand churches in the kingdom of France were consecrated to him). Indeed, it took all the prestige of Martin, his miracles, and his legend, to put an end to a particularly persistent festival of the bear. The choice was especially appropriate because the saint had several links to the bear: I have noted that Martin, on his voyage to Rome, forced a bear to carry the baggage of Saint Maximinus in place of the donkey the beast had devoured; I have also pointed out that the name *Martin* echoes words designating the bear in several Indo-European languages (root *art-*), particularly Celtic languages. Gradually, the example of Gaul was imitated in a large part of Western Europe: November 11, once a festival celebrating the hibernation of the bear, became almost everywhere Saint Martin's Day, a key date in hagiographic, economic, and popular calendars. On that day, which marked the symbolic onset of the cold season, great fairs and all kinds of festivities took place: debts were paid, provisions stored, there were feasts, people ate goose, they drank a lot—in Middle French, the verb *martiner* meant "indulge in excessive drink"[45]—and, as on Saint John's Day, celebratory bonfires were lit.[46]

The success of this peaceful and relatively rapid substitution—the change seems to have been completed by the Carolingian period—encouraged similar action for other local festivals or ceremonies involving a bear cult. These ceremonies took place at various moments in the calendar, but they were especially numerous in the month of September, as well as throughout the period when the bear was supposed to be hibernating, from November to February. It was therefore those dates that the Church chose for feast days of saints who had tamed a bear or had a special relationship with the animal, whether hostile or benevolent. This concerned not only all the saints already mentioned, but also many local saints the cult or memory of whom did not extend beyond the confines of a diocese or even a few parishes. Examples in the order of the calendar from September to February of major or minor "ursine" Saints' Days include Remaclus (September 3), Magnus (September 6), Corbinian (September 8), Euphemia (September 16), Lambert (September 17), Richardis (September 18), Florentius (September 22), Thecla (September 23), Ghislain (October 9), Gall (October 16), Martin (November 11), Columban (November 23), Eligius (December 1), Columba (December 31), Vincentian (January 2), Romedius (January 15), Valerius (January 29), Blaise (February 3), Aventinus (February 4), Amand and Vaast (February 6), and Valentine (February 14).

To this list should be added the saints whose names are directly constructed from the Latin word for bear, *ursus*. Most of them are purely legendary, created out of whole cloth by the Church to replace, in one diocese or another, the memory of a particularly admired bear: Saint Ursus the Theban, a soldier in the Theban legion, companion of Maurice, venerated throughout northern Switzerland (September 30); Saint Ursicinus II, protector of cattle in the Tyrol (October 2); Saint Ursinus, first bishop of Bourges, and patron saint of Berry (November 9); Saint Ursicinus, apostle to Friuli (December 1); Saint Ursicinus, the legendary bishop of Ravenna (December 13); Saint Ursicinus, a disciple of Columban who may have been a monk at Luxeuil (December 28); Saint Ursus of Aosta, whose cult extended to both sides of the Alps (February 1); as well as other Saints Ursus, Ursinus, and Ursicinus, not forgetting the great Saint Ursula (October 21), virgin martyr and patron saint of Cologne, venerated throughout the Rhine Valley, the Netherlands, northern France, and as far as Venice.

A New Calendar

Indeed, from the earliest days of Christianity, the Church had adopted the practice of manipulating or changing the calendar. It intended to get rid of Roman festivals and replace them with Christian counterparts.[47] In towns, that was done gradually and without too much difficulty between the third and fifth centuries. In the countryside, however, things were different. Along with official festivals, whether religious or civic, many pagan festivals survived, linked to the passing of the seasons, the cycle of nature, the position of the stars (solstices, equinoxes), or to customs or beliefs derived from mythological traditions. Eliminating them was not so easy, particularly since they corresponded to various mythologies (Celtic, Germanic, Slavic) and they were distributed throughout the year. In addition, they did not always fall on precise dates, but rather at points in the calendar varying with latitude and the cycles of the moon. Hence, for the new Christian festivals, choices differed from one diocese to the next before dates common to all Roman Christendom were settled on, sometimes belatedly.

Beginning in the fifth century, however, the rise of the cult of saints and the gradual establishment of a large number of feast days intended to honor them provided effective solutions to these calendar problems. Some particularly venerated saints, indeed, were honored with several feast days: celebrations were held for their conversion, their passion, their Deposition, their principal miracles, and the translation of their relics; as for the minor saints, in the parishes for which they were patron saints, they had a summer and a winter feast day. In addition, the same saint was not always celebrated on the same dates from one diocese to the next and, to give more solemnity to the rituals and more freedom to the festivities, it was not unusual, if a feast day fell during the week, for it to be changed to the following Sunday. There was gradually established a vast network of Christian feast days that completely overlay the old Roman and barbarian calendars. That enabled the Church to suppress—if not to truly eradicate—most cults devoted to pagan divinities, mythological creatures, stars, forces of nature, and, most important, animals. Gradually, in every diocese, in every parish, a feast day decided upon and consecrated by the Church was superimposed over an old barbarian festival and finally replaced it.

This new Christian calendar, reinforced by hagiographic accounts pointing out how much stronger were men of God than savage beasts, made it possible to fight successfully against the last remaining bear cults. The old ursine ceremonies were succeeded by festivals glorifying saints who had been able to make themselves obeyed, respected, helped, or loved by a bear. The hero of the day was thus no longer the bear but the saint. A careful study of the new calendar, incidentally, shows that all periods of the year did not have the same concentration of ancient cults. Three times seem to have been particularly important: the month of September as a whole, mid-November, and the end of January and the beginning of February. It was at those points that the Church had to establish the largest number of feast days for "ursine" saints.

I mentioned earlier the pagan bear festivals tied to the month of November and the choice of the eleventh of that month as Saint Martin's Day. I will consider later the even more important period of the beginning of February. There remains the month of September. Why were there so many bear festivals at that time of year? Why was it necessary to call on such a large number of saints—almost one every day—to eliminate or replace the beast? Was September, like November and February, a "month of bears"? Was it the entire month, or only around the equinox? What of the end of the month, so full of pagan festivals that the Church had to set at that time one of the most important Christian festivals of the year, the feast of the archangel Michael, chief of the heavenly host, on the twenty-ninth? In the current state of our knowledge, it is difficult to answer these questions, since specialists in ancient mythological calendars and their "folk" continuations have shown little interest in them.[48]

Geography, in contrast, poses fewer problems than chronology. If one considers only local and regional saints whose lives or miracles involve one or more bears, one observes that they are particularly numerous in a few regions of Europe: on the one hand, mountain ranges, especially the central part of the Alpine crescent; on the other, a rather vast territory corresponding to the present-day Ardennes and its borderlands. These were two zones where, before Christianization, Celtic goddesses, cousins of Greek Artemis, had been worshiped: Artio (Switzerland, Vorarlberg, Tyrol) and Arduina (Ardennes). Had the Celtic divinities associated with bears resisted Christianization more successfully than those of the Germans and the Slavs?

From the Feast of the Bears to the Feast of the Candles

The traditional rural calendar that the medieval Church sought to replace with a Christian calendar fixed somewhere near the middle of November as the time when the bear went into hibernation. This event, as I have noted, was gradually replaced by Saint Martin's Day. Even more enduring, however, were the festivals celebrating the moment when the bear awoke and came out of its den to see whether winter had ended. Depending on regions and latitudes, that occurred about forty days after the winter solstice, toward the very end of January or at the beginning of February, and sometimes lasted a week. It was during this period of the calendar that, throughout Europe, the principal ursine ceremonies inherited from the ancient cults were celebrated; they prefigured the later excesses of Carnival.[49] On those dates, the Church of the High Middle Ages therefore had to intervene even more forcefully and establish a large number of "bear" saints' days: some whose cult was widespread, such as Blaise (February 3) or Valentine (February 14), but also and most numerous, regional saints such as, for the region of Moselle and Artois, Amand (February 6) and Vaast (also February 6). Even more numerous were feast days of local saints, such as Valerius (January 29), Ursicinus (January 31), Agrepe (February 1), Ursus of Aosta (February 1), Aventinus of Troyes (February 4), and many others, particularly in Alpine valleys and mountain regions.

Such efforts were not sufficient. In that part of the calendar, there remained a date unlike any other, the date when the bear, having completed its winter sleep, came out of its den, observed the sky, the clouds, and the winds. On this day it was supposed to make a decision about the continuation of its hibernation. If the sky was clear and the sun shining, it judged

that winter was not over; after licking its left paw, spinning around, breaking a few branches, and groaning several times, it returned to its lair and
fell into another sleep of forty days. But if the sky was gray or cloudy, if it
was raining or snowing, the bear judged that the end of winter was near;
it did not return to sleep but stayed outside, went to take a purifying bath,
began its search for food, and calmly awaited good weather.

In many temperate regions of Europe, this major event in animal life
was supposed to occur on February 2, sometimes February 3. On that
day in rural societies, feasts and celebrations commemorated the bear's
coming out. Songs, dances, games and ursine masquerades played a large
role in these ceremonies. But what terrified monks and priests most of all
were simulations of abductions and rapes. Men covered themselves with
fur and pretended to abduct girls or young women and then mate with
them. Attested in the archdiocese of Reims in the Carolingian period,[50]
documented in Alpine valleys beginning in the fourteenth and fifteenth
centuries,[51] these games and simulations were still taking place—as a kind
of folk custom—in several areas of the Pyrenees in the late twentieth
century, much to the delight of ethnologists.[52] The question obviously
remains as to what may have survived of medieval practices in these modern games, more or less artificial and given excess media attention. Probably nothing.[53]

Early on—as early as the fifth century—the Church sought to Christianize the date of February 2, when pagan rituals seemed even more
vigorous and transgressive than at any other time of year. It was especially important because not only the end of the bear's hibernation was
involved. The memory of Roman Lupercalia and their accompanying
fertility rites in mid-February had not completely disappeared, at least in
scholarly tradition; nor perhaps had the great festival of Proserpina, the
Roman goddess of the underworld, at the beginning of the same month.[54]
But most important, in all northern and northwestern Europe, various
purification rituals celebrated the end of winter and the return of light.
Among the Celts, for example, the great festival of Imbolc took place on
February 1, glorifying a mother goddess whose name varied;[55] the Church
settled on that date for the feast of Saint Brigid, patron saint of Ireland and

a Christianized figure of several divinities in the Celtic pantheon. On the following day, February 2, to suppress all pagan cults and rites, whether or not they were linked to the bear, the Church set two Christian festivals associated with the life of Christ and the life of the Virgin: the Presentation of Jesus at the Temple and the Purification of Mary. Two great festivals for a single day: liturgists and theologians had struck forcefully.[56]

But once again this was not enough. Not only did the practices and beliefs linked to the end of the bear's hibernation not disappear completely—far from it—but festivals celebrating the return of light and the sun were still very much alive in the northern countryside. They generally featured bonfires and torchlight processions. In the fifth century, to put an end to these festivities, Pope Gelasius instituted the Christian Feast of the Candles *(festa candelarum)*. Several of his successors in the sixth and seventh centuries made the meaning of this new feast more explicit and sought to bring out its Christian aspect, which was not always obvious, by associating it with the Presentation of the Infant Jesus at the Temple. Processions with candles or torches—now solemnly blessed—were not suppressed but redirected: leaving from the parish church, they were supposed to pass by every house in the village, with the mission of dissipating the darkness, driving off evil spirits, and protecting against bad weather. A third Christian feast thus found its place on February 2: Chandeleur (Candlemas).

In most rural areas of Gaul and then France, however, where the memory of the bear was still very much alive, this feast was often called, from the twelfth to the eighteenth centuries, not Chandeleur but Chandelours, a popular term bringing together in a single word the memory of ancient cults around that date devoted to fire and light, the return of fertility, and especially the bear *(ours)* coming out of hibernation. Although it had been Christianized, the Feast of the Candles remained in many regions a more or less ursine festival.[57]

✤ 5 ✤

The Bear in the House of the Devil

HE long war against the bear that had preoccupied the Latin church
for nearly a millennium had begun with the physical elimination of
the animal and continued with its symbolic defeat by the saint. Beginning with the Carolingian period the warfare was pursued through constant and tenacious demonization. Several writers in the early centuries
of Christianity had already classified the bear among the harmful animals
and, adopting an enigmatic sentence from Pliny, had seen it as a particularly wicked creature. Later on, some Church Fathers, commenting on
one or another scriptural passage mentioning bears, did not hesitate to
include them in the infernal bestiary where they now kept company with
wolves, snakes, dragons, and other fearsome creatures. But the decisive
step was taken at the turn of the fourth and fifth centuries. As was often
the case, it was Saint Augustine who delivered the decisive verdict around
which the entire Christian symbolism of the animal would be constructed
for several centuries: *"ursus est diabolus,"* "the bear is the Devil."

The Devil was not really the creation of Christianity, but he was practically unknown in the Jewish religion and barely appears in the Old Testament, at least in the form given to him by Christian traditions. In the
Bible, the Gospels, chiefly, reveal his existence, and Revelation gives him
a prominent place. Thereafter, the Church Fathers made him into a demonic force that dares to defy God. A dualistic conception of the universe,
presenting a confrontation between a principle of good and a principle of
evil, was totally foreign to the Old Testament. Medieval theology is more
ambiguous on this point. God, of course, remained omnipotent, but for
Christianity there was indeed a maleficent being who was inferior to God
while enjoying a certain freedom: Satan.

Satan did not lead an isolated existence: he was accompanied by a retinue of demons, monsters, and animals that had issued from the infernal depths to seduce, pervert, or torment humanity. Weak and sinful men and women saw these creatures rise up before them everywhere, particularly in the late Carolingian period and around the year 1000, when Satan and his acolytes became ubiquitous, both in the world of priests and monks and in the secular world. They represented the threat of eternal damnation and drove Christians to conversion. And beginning around this time, among the creatures accompanying the Devil, or even more often, serving him as an emblem or mask, the bear occupied the first rank. It embodied almost all the vices and all the forces of evil.

The Biblical Record

The Church Fathers and their successors in the feudal period, however, had only a meager biblical record on the basis of which to make the bear into a diabolical animal. It did not play a major role in scripture, and the passages on which exegesis and symbolic interpretation could be based were few. It is true that difficult problems of vocabulary and translation arose in this area, especially with respect to the Old Testament. The Hebrew versions of various books, and even the Greek Septuagint, gave precise names to only a small number of species of wild animal. The texts frequently used vague or metaphorical expressions, such as "an animal living in the woods," "a very cruel crawling beast," "a wild beast enemy to man." The lion itself was not always designated by a single term—as domestic animals usually were—but with a variety of words, some generic, others precise and carefully distinguishing the lion from the lioness and the lion cub.[1] In many cases, the first Latin translations, and then the Vulgate, were the first to introduce genuine species names, and instead of saying "a frightful beast," "a gigantic creature," or "a monster of the deep," preferred "a crocodile," "an elephant," or "a hippopotamus." A historian is thus obliged to attempt to identify the different versions and translations used by one medieval theologian or another who comments on a biblical passage and draws from it material involving animal symbolism: in relation to older versions, his language may be strongly affected by the choice of too explicit a term or by an erroneous interpretation of an uncertain formulation.[2] These problems, it seems, did not arise with respect to the bear. The biblical passages in which bears are present are few in number and not open to confusion or questioning. The Hebrew word for bear, *do'b,* is restricted to that animal and always corresponds to the Greek *arktos* and the Latin *ursus.* There is no ambiguity of vocabulary, unlike what occurs for the wolf, the jackal, the hyena, the snake, the whale, the falcon, and other dangerous and feared animals.

Of the passages mentioning bears, the most famous and the one most often glossed by the Church Fathers is the one that tells how young David, still a shepherd, fought valiantly against a bear and a lion that were stealing his sheep and decimating his flock (1 Samuel 17.34–37). The bear is paired with the lion, as though the two kings of the beasts in the eastern and western traditions had joined their destructive forces to attack the young shepherd and his flock, typological prefigurations of Christ and his believers. On several occasions elsewhere in the Old Testament the bear and the lion are an inseparable couple or else are named one after the other to signify great danger or the intervention of the forces of evil. It would be worth undertaking a scrupulous heuristic and philological analysis of the texts, their various states, versions, and translations, in order to inventory the passages in which one finds the sequence *bear / lion* and those where one finds the reverse, *lion / bear.* Word order and list structures are never neutral, especially when, as in this instance, it is a question of determining which is the strongest and hence, here, the most diabolical of all animals.

The other biblical passage featuring a bear also received comment in the Middle Ages, but less often: it involves a she-bear, just as fearsome as the male. The passage occurs in the story of the prophet Elisha, disciple of Elijah. One day when Elisha was traveling to Bethel, near Mount Carmel he came upon some young boys who mocked his baldness and insulted him by calling him "bald head." The prophet cursed them in the name of the Lord, since it was not right to mock a man of God with impunity; two she-bears immediately came out of a wood and devoured the children in front of Elisha, who did nothing to stop them (2 Kings 2.23–24).[3] The Church Fathers explained that this episode foreshadowed the insults and abuse Christ suffered in his Passion, and they did not hesitate to bring out the phonic and etymological—hence strongly symbolic—link in Latin between the words *calvus* (bald) and *Calvaria* (Calvary). Some very learned exegetes even pointed out that among the Hebrews baldness was considered shameful, and that calling a man "bald head" was a serious insult.[4] It will be seen later, with regard to the bear's hairiness, that this passage should also be interpreted as a meeting of extremes: the man of God with a bare, smooth scalp, and the savage beast whose body is covered in thick, bristling fur. Here it should be noted that the she-bear is as dangerous as the male, that she can be a source of danger, punishment, or vengeance, and that she is an instrument of death.

On several occasions, biblical verses bring to the fore, with images or comparisons, this dangerous aspect of the bear, a savage, fierce, cruel animal (Daniel 7.5; Proverbs 28.15; Hosea 13.8), unpredictable like the snake, pitiless like the lion (Amos 5.19), particularly fearsome when it is hungry (Lamentations 3.10), or, for the female, when her cubs have been taken from her (Proverbs 17.12). The fearsome animal was indeed physically present in Palestine and Syria in biblical times; it was still there in the late eleventh century at the time of the First Crusade. Smaller than today's brown bear, it sometimes attacked people and constantly attacked sheep, goats, and beehives. Hence it was a necessary element in every evil bestiary. In one of his dreams, the prophet Daniel sees four terrifying beasts coming out of the sea representing the four kingdoms that were enemies of Israel: the lion symbolized Babylon; the leopard, Persia; the monstrous "beast" with ten horns, Greece; and the bear, the kingdom of the Medes (Daniel 7.1–8 and 15–22). This is echoed in Revelation by the vision of John, who also sees a horrifying beast come out of the sea that has not only seven heads and ten horns, but also the lion's huge jaw, the leopard's troubling spots, and the powerful paws of the bear (Revelation 13.1–2).

For medieval theologians, these biblical passages, though few in number, constituted effective grounds on which to construct, organize, and comment on the diabolical image of the bear.

Two Enemies of the Bear: Pliny and Augustine

To accomplish this demonization of the bear, these theologians also had at their disposal a corpus of texts from pagan writers that were no more favorable to bears than their biblical counterparts. Aristotle makes no moral judgment about the animal, but on several occasions describes its strange hibernation practices as well as its dietary habits, which he considers surprising for a quadruped;[5] the Christian Middle Ages interpreted all these traits as troubling or diabolical.

But more than Aristotle, whose complete zoological works were rediscovered late, in several stages,[6] it was especially Pliny the Elder (who died in the eruption of Vesuvius in 79 AD) who helped shape for more than a millennium the negative symbolism of the bear. His *Natural History,* compiled beginning in the late forties of the first century AD, thirty-seven volumes of which have survived, is one of the founding texts of medieval knowledge. It was an "authority" that was not really challenged before the seventeenth century. And Pliny was particularly loquacious about animals, both in the zoological portion[7] of the work and in its medical portion,[8] which was longer but more confused, as well as in countless examples, anecdotes, remarks, stories, and comparisons distributed throughout the work. The writers of the High Middle Ages borrowed frequently from him, particularly the authors of bestiaries and encyclopedias. They sometimes did so directly, but more often they relied on one of his "abridgers," Solinius, a writer of whom nothing is known except that in the third century he compiled a curious *Polyhistor* that abridged Pliny's text and classified the materials he borrowed from Pliny geographically.[9]

Book VII of the *Natural History,* on "terrestrial animals," begins not with the bear but with the elephant, "the largest of them all, and in intelligence . . . the nearest to man." Then, following a rather loose organization, come dragons and snakes, lions and panthers, various quadrupeds of Africa and Asia, and then, in the second part, wild and domestic animals found in Europe. Among these wild animals, the first chapter is devoted to stags,[10] the second to bears. Pliny provides abundant information about them, largely derived from Aristotle, but also from Theophrastus, Virgil, Varro, Ovid, and various hunting treatises.

Unlike other chapters, the one dealing with bears is relatively well constructed. Pliny follows the animal through the seasons: autumn allows him to discuss mating and gestation; winter, hibernation and all the marvels related to it; spring, the animal's dietary habits and its inordinate fondness for honey; summer, its capture and its place in circus games and its resemblance to man. The bear appears as a creature of the calendar, closely linked to the cycle of the seasons, and above all as a highly anthropomorphic animal. Its "portrait" was thus traced for fifteen centuries. But as a conclusion, and in a rather unexpected manner given what has gone before, Pliny brusquely expresses a very negative opinion: "In no other animal is stupidity found more adroit in devising mischief."[11] This terrible sentence, which seems to have been borrowed from no predecessor but is attributable to Pliny himself, determined by itself, or almost, the fate of the bear in the medieval Christian bestiary.

The *Natural History* was in fact a text that the Church Fathers and their successors read attentively and copied frequently up to the fourteenth century. The number of surviving medieval manuscripts—more than three hundred—demonstrates its success and its influence;[12] and although the oldest manuscripts do not contain all thirty-seven books, all of them copy the famous eighth book, on terrestrial animals, and hence its chapter on bears, which is my concern here. Among the Church Fathers, Jerome and Augustine seem to have been very assiduous readers of Pliny. The former, who called the *Natural History* an "admirable" work *("opus mirandum et pulcherrimum")*[13] looked in it for information or glosses to interpret the passages in the Bible concerning animals, plants, and precious stones.[14] He read it primarily as a philologist, but he thereby established a solid and lasting link between pagan encyclopedic knowledge and sacred texts. Besides, for Jerome as for other Christian writers, the Bible was an immense encyclopedia; it was therefore legitimate to establish comparisons between the two texts. Augustine thought differently. He was not a philologist, and he knew no Hebrew and little Greek. Unlike Jerome, he spent little time on the literal meaning of the biblical text,[15] but was rather constantly seeking its allegorical and mystical meaning. His exegesis was always aimed at showing how the text was "inspired," how one needed to seek there—there and not elsewhere—the truth of beings and of things. More than Jerome, he sought to define the limits of profane knowledge and, in this instance, to show how skeptical and pessimistic a writer Pliny was,[16] denying as he did the existence of any divinity.[17]

But Augustine differed from Jerome—and from Ambrose—in another way, his personal view of animals, which he seemed to consider with suspicion, and some even with horror. As a theologian, he was far removed from the Christian current of thought derived from Saint Paul which, beyond the requisite acknowledgment of the hierarchical nature of the Creator's work, was sometimes timidly inclined to consider that there was also a community among all living beings.[18] In Augustine's view, one ought not to confuse man, created in God's image, with the animal, a subject and imperfect, if not impure, creature; fostering confusion between human and animal nature was an abomination.[19] In fact, it seemed that animals personally disgusted or frightened him. What episode in his childhood or youth could explain this rejection and fear of animals? The *Confessions,* though full of autobiographical details, says nothing about it. But it is legitimate to wonder about this Augustinian zoophobia that recurs almost everywhere in his work and had a powerful influence on medieval thought and symbolism. It seems out of place in a writer who constantly repeats that "the created world is infinitely good because it is the work of God."

Two animals were the particular targets of Augustine's hostility: the lion and the bear. Moreover, he barely distinguished one from another. For example, in a sermon on Isaiah, written in 414 or 415, commenting on David's victorious battle against the bear and the lion just discussed (1 Samuel 17.34–37), the two beasts are equally evil: they are enemies of God and of the just, instruments of the Devil; the strength of the bear lies in its paws, that of the lion in his jaw. For Augustine, David's exploit in rescuing his flock is to be compared to Christ's descent into Hell, because "the Devil himself is incarnated in these two animals."[20] This assertion recurs on several occasions in Augustine's exegetical works and for a long time permeated medieval discourse. The bear was the principal victim, but the lion also suffered: once identified with the Devil by Augustine, the lion was forced to wait for nearly eight centuries before being definitively acknowledged as the king of the beasts throughout Christian Europe. The lion's fate will be considered in the following chapter. I will focus here on the bear and the bishop of Hippo's hatred for the animal. It is certainly possible that Augustine had seen bears in North Africa and that he or someone in his circle had been attacked by one. In the fourth and fifth centuries, bears were indeed numerous in the territory corresponding to present-day Tunisia and its borderlands. Solinius, for example, devotes a long chapter to "Numidian bears," a now-extinct species that seems to have been smaller but more dangerous for people than the brown bear familiar to us.[21] But Augustine's aversion to the animal is not to be sought in the woods and forests surrounding the city of Hippo. It is to be found in books, beginning with the Bible, with its negative image of the beast, and continuing with Pliny's *Natural History*, which the scholarly Augustine read assiduously. The last sentence in Pliny's chapter on bears quoted above, "In no other animal is stupidity found more adroit in devising mischief,"[22] certainly had an effect, convincing him that bears were really very harmful. But other passages must have struck him just as forcefully, notably those in which Pliny points out the physical resemblances between bears and men and describes the way the male and female couple: lying down face to face, stomach to stomach, embracing *more hominum*.[23] Of course, bears do not mate in that way: Pliny was mistaken, as I have noted,[24] probably because he misunderstood an obscure passage in Aristotle. But Augustine did not know that; he trusted Pliny, as did all writers who spoke of bears mating down to the seventeenth century. For a theologian who was continually asserting that man and beast could in no way be confused with one another, that human and animal nature were completely different, this was a scandal, a crime, a transgression of the order intended by the Creator, something truly diabolical: *"ursus est diabolus,"* "the bear is the Devil."[25]

Beginning in the Carolingian period, many writers adopted this expression from Augustine, thereby contributing to the demonization of the

Bear skull set on a rocky outcropping, surrounded by other skulls. Chauvet Cave, Ardèche, "skull chamber" (−34,000 / −32,000). Photograph courtesy of Jean Clottes.

The she-bear who nursed the infant Atalanta. Greek ceramic fragment, third century AD. Amsterdam, Allard Pierson Museum.

Rock art: brown bear and cave bear in the Chauvet Cave (−34,000 / −32,000).
Photographs courtesy of Jean Clottes.

The she-bear of the Celtic goddess Artio. Bronze votive figurine, late second century AD, found at Muri, near Bern. Photograph by S. Rebsamen. Bern, Historisches Museum, Inv. 524 Z.

A Scandinavian warrior battling two bears. Bronze (helmet?) plate from the late sixth century, found at Torslunda, Öland Island, Sweden. Stockholm, Historika Museet.

Chess piece made of walrus tusk, Trondheim c. 1160–1170: Berserker wearing a "bear shirt" and biting the top of his shield. London, British Museum. Iv. Cat. 123. © The Trustees of the British Museum. All rights reserved.

Bear hunt. Painting from the *Codex Manesse,* Zurich or Constance, c. 1300–1310.
Heidelberg, Universitätsbibliothek, Codex Palatinus Germanicus, 848, fol. 90
(Hawart). Courtesy of AKG Images.

Bear among lions and griffins. Carved trumeau from the interior portal (stone), French school, twelfth century. Souillac, France, Abbey Church. © Paul Maeyaert / The Bridgeman Art Library International.

Sale of bear meat at a butcher's stall. Miniature from an illuminated manuscript of the *Chronique du concile de Constance* by Ulrich Richental, Constance, c. 1450–1460. Constance, Rosgartenmuseum, Konstanzer Codex I, fol. 24.

She-bear licking her cub. Miniature from an English illuminated bestiary, c. 1190–1200. State Public Library, Saint Petersburg, ms. Saltykov-Shechedrin, Q. v. V. 1, fol. 16 v°. Courtesy of the Russian National Museum.

Pair of bears playing and mating *more hominum*. Grisaille miniature from a manuscript of the *Livre de la chasse* by Gaston Phébus, Avignon, late fourteenth century. Paris, Bibliothèque nationale de France (BNF), ms. Fr. 619, fol. 15 v°.

The murder of Thomas Becket. Among the assassins is Reginald FitzUrse, identifiable from his shield with a bear. Miniature from an illuminated manuscript of the life of Saint Thomas Becket, c. 1200. London, British Library, ms. Harley 5102, fol. 32.

"Diabolical" crest with a bear muzzle. Coat of arms of the Teufel family in the manuscript of *Wappenrolle von Zurich,* c. 1325–1335. Zurich, Swiss National Museum.

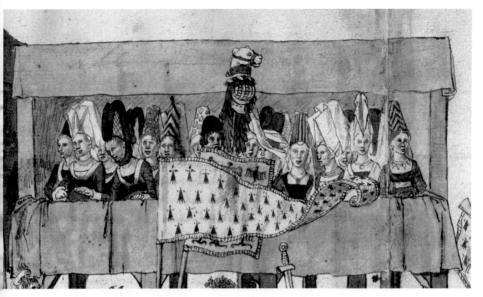

A bear crest given by the ladies to the victor in a tournament. Detail of a large painting in a manuscript of the *Livre des tournois* of King René of Anjou, Provence, c. 1460. Paris, BNF, ms. Fr. 2695, fol. 97 v°–98.

The bears of Bern carrying the city's banner going off to battle (the battle of Laupen, 1339). Allegorical painting in a manuscript of the *Spiezer Chronik* by Diebold Schilling, dated 1485. Bern, Stadtbibiliothek, ms. H. h. I, 16, fol. 227.

Combat of David against a bear and a lion. Miniature from an illuminated manuscript of a *Speculum humanae salvationis,* Constance, c. 1320.
Kremsmünster, Austria, Stiftsbibliothek, Codex 242, fol. 19.

The prophet Elisha and two she-bears devouring children who had mocked him. Painting from a manuscript of the historiated *Chronique* of Rudolf von Ems, dated 1459. Colmar, Bibliothèque municipale, ms. 305, fol. 384 v°.

Bear banner of the canton of Appenzell, eastern Switzerland, c. 1470–
1480. Zurich, Swiss National Museum.

The Devil in bear form. Psalter from Polling, southwestern Germany, after 1235. Bayer, Bayerische Staatsbibliothek München, Clm 11308, fol. 10v.

bear. The most influential of them was perhaps Rabanus Maurus, abbot of Fulda and later archbishop of Mainz. Around 840, he compiled a long encyclopedic and symbolic treatise, De universo or De rerum naturis, that had a long and abundant posterity. The work is lacking in originality, but it has the distinctive characteristic of fusing into a single text the encyclopedic discourse of Pliny, the etymological discourse of Isidore of Seville,[26] and the exegetical, allegorical, or moral discourse of the principal Latin Church Fathers.[27] By doing so, he provided posterity with rich material that was reused on many occasions, notably by the authors of Latin prose bestiaries in the eleventh and twelfth centuries. The space given to animals in De universo is indeed considerable. For Rabanus Maurus, and for all his imitators in the course of four centuries, animals were favored sources of meaning: it was therefore necessary to study their "properties" (physical aspects, mores, behavior, supposed qualities and defects) in order to derive from them moral and theological interpretations and thereby accede to the hidden truths of nature and the world.

Like Augustine, Rabanus Maurus saw in the bear an image of the Devil seeking to deceive men and turn them away from God. But, like Pliny, he also saw it as a cruel and merciless animal, particularly inclined to do evil, and whose wickedness recalled that of "fierce and bloodthirsty princes."[28] Commenting on the scriptural passage quoted above (2 Kings 2.23–24), in which two she-bears devour children who had ridiculed the baldness of the prophet Elisha, Rabanus Maurus identifies the two beasts with the Roman emperors Vespasian and Titus, respectively enemies of the Christian and Jewish peoples.[29] This is the man of the Church speaking who, at the dawn of the feudal period, is already defending the fragile flock of the faithful against the rapacity and brutality of the powerful. For the clergy, the bear was the image of Satan, the prince of devils; but a few decades later, when the Carolingian Empire fell apart and gave way to a multitude of particularly greedy and ferocious local powers, it would also become an image of the plundering baron, the lord who feared neither God nor man.

The Devil and His Bestiary

In the feudal period, the Devil became ubiquitous, spreading his misdeeds everywhere and extending his empire. Medieval Christianity was, of course, far removed from Manichaeanism. Theologians considered that it was perhaps the greatest of all heresies to believe in the existence of two divinities and to set Satan and God on the same plane. Satan was in no way God's equal: he was a fallen creature, the leader of the rebel angels, who occupied in the infernal hierarchy a place comparable to that held by Saint Michael in the celestial hierarchy. Revelation foresaw his ephemeral reign, which would precede the end of time. But in the daily life of clergy and monks, as in that of ordinary men and women, the situation was different: the Devil, endowed with considerable powers, almost as great as those of God himself, was constantly on the prowl, using every trick to draw weak and sinful men to his side. Hence, the entire realm of moral life was made up of a black-and-white confrontation between good and evil; on Judgment Day, the elect on one side would go to Paradise and the damned on the other would be cast into Hell.

The name *Satan* is of biblical origin. It is derived from a Hebrew word meaning "adversary" and is used in the Book of Job to characterize the angel sent to put Job to the test. It was the Church Fathers who made Satan the proper name of the leader of the rebel angels, opposing God and embodying the forces of evil. But it was a learned and rare term; in Latin and vernacular texts of the feudal period, the word "Devil" *(diabolus)* is much more frequent. It is of Greek origin *(diabolos)* and was an adjective before it became a noun. In Ancient Greek, it characterized any individual who inspired hatred, disorder, or envy, and, by extension, a deceiver or slanderer. Moreover, Greek iconography of the satyr (a sort of rustic spirit, a companion of Dionysus, with hairy ears, faun's horns, and goat's feet and tail) provided several aspects of the way Christian art represented the Devil.

This imagery emerged gradually between the sixth and eleventh centuries but long remained unstable and polymorphous. In Romanesque art, however, the image of the Devil definitively assumes a hideous and bestial aspect. His body is usually thin and withered to emphasize that he comes from the kingdom of the dead; he is naked, covered with hair like a bear or pustules like a dragon, sometimes spotted or striped like a leopard, and always revolting; attached to his back are a goat's or a monkey's tail and two bat wings recalling his condition as a fallen angel; his feet sometimes resemble those of a goat, sometimes those of a bear. His head is dark and massive, with pointed horns and hair standing on end evoking the flames of Hell; his face, sometimes featuring the snout of a bear or a pig, grimaces, with the mouth stretched to the ears, offering a distorted and cruel appearance.

Like the Devil, the demons, "who are legion," smaller in size and under his command, were naked, hairy, and hideous figures. Like him, they had bestial features and might have on some other part of their bodies, usually the most obscene, a second or third face in the form of a mask as revolting as the face on their head. They tormented men, took possession of their bodies, spread vices and abuse, set fires, unleashed storms, and propagated epidemics. Above all, they watched for the failings of the weak or ill and attempted to seize the sinful soul of the dying as it was about to leave the body. One overcame them through prayer and faith in Christ. One defended against their attacks with the light of candles, the sound of bells, and the sprinkling of holy water. Exorcisms—gestures made and apotropaic formulas pronounced by the bishop or his representative—were also a way of driving them off or expelling them from the bodies of the possessed, as Christ had done on several occasions.

To reach his goals, that is to turn monks and believers away from the paths leading to the good and to salvation in Christ, the Devil used every variety of deception, disguise, and temptation. Those that several great saints, such as Anthony and Margaret, had to face were famous. Christ himself had resisted the Devil three times in the desert and then, on his descent into Limbo, trampled him underfoot and shattered the gates of Hell. But not everyone was Saint Anthony or Saint Margaret, and every man, woman, priest, and monk lived in perpetual fear of seeing the Evil One appear and of not having the strength to resist him.

What was worse was that often the Devil assumed a disguise to deceive men and women. He might take on the appearance of a seductive young woman or a handsome young man (or even of Christ himself), or, more often, the form of an animal, generally frightening or repulsive. The list of animal forms he could assume was a long one, and were those one might expect, animals that for one reason or another were condemned or despised by medieval culture and sensibility. They were actual animals, such as the snake, the goat, the monkey, the whale, the cat, or the toad; but also fantastic animals such as the manticore, the basilisk, or the dragon; or else semihuman monsters, such as the satyr, the centaur, and the siren; or creatures that were so composite it was impossible to give them a name. Satan's bestiary was concerned not so much with animals as with animality. An arm, a foot, a mouth, hair, or horns were enough to create that animality, as was any shift away from the "ordinary" anatomy of any particular creature.

But whatever the diversity of this bestiary, its leading figure in the feudal period was unquestionably the bear. Satan often assumed ursine traits, particularly the snout, hair, and feet, not only in material images, painted or sculpted; but also and especially in fantasy images—those produced by dreams and visions—Satan almost always appeared in the form of a bear to threaten or torment men. Besides, the boundary between immaterial and material images was porous, and the Devil-bear experienced no difficulty in moving from one to the other.[30]

Dreams of Bears

People dreamed a lot in the feudal West, and monasteries seem to have been particularly fertile soil for this activity. Monks dreamed more than the secular clergy or ordinary mortals. Only kings, especially in chronicles and literary works, offered some competition in this area. Dreaming was not yet considered to be an individual expression, connected to the body and a matter of concern for medicine or psychology. It was primarily a collective phenomenon, almost a cultural system, that was located in a given milieu where it fulfilled precise functions. Saints' dreams were of divine origin and differed little from prophetic visions; kings' dreams were premonitory and had to be interpreted with care; the dreams of monks—the most numerous—were, on the other hand, only dark illusions, inspired by the Devil.[31]

The Devil was indeed always present, either intervening directly or, more often, assuming a disguise, the better to deceive or terrify. The bear was his favorite disguise. Several accounts have survived of monastic dreams that feature the Devil in that disguise. The most remarkable is perhaps the one told by the great abbot of Cluny, Peter the Venerable, around 1130, in his *Liber de miraculis,* a vast collection of miracles assembled for purposes of edification and intended to show how the Devil, a great enemy of monks, attacked those in the prestigious abbey in Burgundy. In the collection, Peter relates various apparitions or manifestations that afflicted the monks of Cluny, either in dreams when they were asleep, or when awake. On the eve of the winter solstice (Saint-Jean d'hiver), a novice named Hermann dreamed of a colossal bear with sharp claws and thick fur that was sitting on his chest and smothering him. He awoke with the feeling that this frightful image was only a dream, but when he opened his eyes, he was terrified to see before him the bear that seemed to be suspended in the air, threatening him and growling. His screams awoke the other novices, then the monks, and finally the abbot himself. A great crowd ran to the scene and surrounded the young Hermann, thereby helping to drive off the diabolical beast.[32]

In this instance, dream and vision were joined together, and the novice seems not to have been the only one to see the Devil disguised as a bear; many others also saw him and helped to drive him off. At Cluny in the twelfth century, they knew how to put the Devil to flight, even when he assumed the monstrous appearance of a wild animal. This is at least what Peter the Venerable intended to show; he succeeded perfectly, and his example was gradually imitated in other abbeys.

A few decades later, in a Cistercian abbey this time, another Hermann was confronted with the Devil disguised as a bear. But he was not the victim of the Evil One; that fell to another monk named Henri, nicknamed "the Cheat" by the other monks. The account of this strange story comes to us from Caesar of Heisterbach (c. 1180–1240), a Cistercian monk, master of a monastery of novices located near Bonn, and the author, between 1220 and 1223, of a voluminous *Dialogus miraculorum,* inspired by Peter the Venerable's collection. This, too, was a treatise for edification, presented in the form of a dialogue between a monk and a novice, intended to teach how to fight effectively against the Devil. But what makes it of interest is that it relies on about eight-hundred little stories, taking the place of *exempla* and embracing all aspects of the life of monks and of believers; some were derived from Caesar's own experience and provide original documentation for historians.[33]

Caesar tells how a pious and disciplined monk named Hermann, "recently deceased," had the gift of vision. In his abbey at Hemmenroda in Thuringia, his neighbor in the choir of the church and the refectory was a monk named Henri, who had a sinister reputation. On several occasions, Hermann saw amphoras full of wine floating in the air and surrounding Henri, thereby pointing to his fondness for drink. But one night Hermann had a much more fateful vision: while Henri was sleeping, a gigantic bear stood near his bed, put its forepaws on his chest, and approached his ear with its snout. Hermann could not hear what the bear was saying to Henri. A short time later, Henri renounced his vows, threw off his cowl, and became a jongleur. Hermann understood that it was the Devil disguised as a bear who had come to speak to Henri several nights in succession to turn him away from the holy monastic life. This Henri, of course, was not a model of virtue: not only did he drink to excess, but he was unstable, lying, fraudulent, vicious, and lascivious. He was a former Benedictine monk, who had come to the Cistercians after a brief stay with the Premonstratensians: such a career could only be the sign of weak faith and great instability. It was even said that, disguised as a nun, he had entered a convent, had dishonored several nuns, and impregnated some of them. A man of that kind, used to disguises, deceit, and perversion, could only be in turn a victim of the greatest deceiver and corruptor: Satan himself, transformed into a bear for the purpose.[34]

These two tales are not at all isolated. The twelfth century and early decades of the thirteenth have left several accounts of "dreams of bears" constructed around the same pattern: the Devil assumes that animal form the better to deceive and threaten young vulnerable monks or men and women of unsteady faith and turn them from the paths of Christ. Sometimes he acts not through dreams but in a vision; then he takes on different animal forms one after another, moving from the repulsive to the fearsome, and from the fearsome to the deadly.[35] From the tale of Saint Anthony assailed in the desert and onward, the list of animals in this infernal bestiary of visions and apparitions had grown lengthy. But in the feudal period, when the Evil One adopted a series of several animal appearances to torment a person, the most dangerous and the most frightful was always that of a bear. The bear had become the quintessentially diabolical animal.

Kings' dreams fully confirm this demonization of an animal once venerated, lord of the forest and of all savage beasts. The most striking example is found in the dreams of Charlemagne; not those of the historical Charlemagne, which are unknown, but those of the legendary and literary Charlemagne. Characters in the chansons de geste of the twelfth century dream often, more often than in courtly romances, and these dreams almost always have a premonitory meaning: they predict or foreshadow what is going to happen; but at the same time they in no way make it possible to prevent these future events from coming to pass. They are dark and troubling dreams, like those in ancient epics, and dreams in which satanic animals play an important role.[36] Charlemagne is, of course, not the only one who dreams, but his dreams have a greater symbolic force than those of his companions or enemies. In the *Chanson de Roland,* for example, the emperor dreams on four occasions,[37] and each of his dreams features one or more animals, representing either the traitor Ganelon or his Saracen allies: bears, lions, leopards, boars, dragons, griffins, and snakes.[38] The bear is the animal that occurs most frequently, and in a list it is always the one that comes first. In Charlemagne's last dream, after the dramatic battle of Ronceveaux, it expressly symbolizes the sinister Ganelon, represented in the form of a chained bear on a platform waiting to be judged in Aix-la-Chapelle. Thirty other bears come running from the Ardennes to bring him help: they are thirty of Ganelon's relatives, who will finally be found guilty with him and hanged.[39] The bear here represents not only the treacherous enemy but also an entire lineage,[40] in revolt against the suzerain. In the twelfth century, the bear had become an animal that was hateful in every way.

Brown and Hairy

The fact that Satan and his creatures could so easily be incarnated in the figure of the bear was owed primarily to Augustine and the Church Fathers, who were the first to demonize the animal and set him at the center of the infernal bestiary for several centuries. But the bear's ubiquity as a creature of evil was also due to the beast itself, which was found wherever there were woods and forests, and was everywhere dangerous and always harmful. This was no longer the biblical or patristic bear but the real one, the brown bear, the only one known in the countryside of the Christian West during the High Middle Ages and the feudal period: a bear of flesh and fur, larger and wilder than the bear that still inhabits in small numbers a few wooded mountains on the old continent. The medieval bear had a more carnivorous diet than today's brown bear; it was taller and heavier, its coat was darker, its fur stiffer, and its claws sharper.[41] That bear shared with the Devil, or at least with the image retained of the Devil, several physical attributes that facilitated Satan's disguise as a bear as well as the transformation of the beast into a demonic creature, notably its dark color and its thick fur.[42] The bear, huge, brown, and hairy as it was, could only be diabolical.

In medieval bestiaries, all animals with dark fur or feathers were, for one reason or another, troubling and harmful. They were thought to have privileged relations with the world of night and death, and brown animals were often considered worse than black ones because they seemed to unite the color of darkness and the color of the flames of Hell. On the medieval color chart, brown was located halfway between red and black. It was not a "real" color, what is known today as a primary color,[43] but a color made by mixing others. For that reason it could not but be devalued. Symbolically it seemed to bring together the negative aspects of red (anger, violence, lust) and the negative aspects of black (sin, darkness, death).[44] In addition, it was not pleasing to the eye, because it seemed dirty, dull, impure, and painters and dyers experienced great difficulty in creating monochromatic, solid, and saturated brown tones. In the medieval sensibility, brown had completely lost the shiny and luminous nature it had sometimes possessed for the ancients, which was the origin of the word designating it in Germanic languages: *braun*.

Etymologically, the term *braun*—or at least the term that preceded it in Proto-Germanic—means "burned," "brilliant," and "dark."[45] There was nothing resembling that in the medieval vocabulary of browns, either in Latin or in vernacular languages: brown did not glow; rather, it always denoted or connoted something extinguished, dull, obscure, and soiled. Besides, even in Latin, naming the color brown was not an easy exercise, which is confirmed by the abundance and imprecision of terms used. All of them referred to the dark and melancholy nuances of brown, never to its lighter or more attractive aspects;[46] what would have corresponded to our light brown, ochre, or beige was never named, either in classical or medieval Latin, or in vernacular languages before the fifteenth century. Was this a problem of vocabulary, perception, or sensibility? In aristocratic society, no one dressed in brown; it was a color that was considered very ugly, reserved for villeins, and adopted out of humility beginning in the twelfth century by several monastic and religious orders wishing to distinguish themselves from Benedictine black and Cistercian white, and thereby attempt to rediscover the poverty of early Christian life.[47]

The bear, the quintessential brown animal, was therefore a victim of its color. The Latin adjective most often used to characterize the shade of his pelt—*fuscus*—was also the one most frequently applied to the Devil, to demons, and to the pagans of Africa and Asia to denote the dark color of their skin. It was a pejorative term—more pejorative than *niger* ("black")—facilitating a pun on *suffocare* ("strangle," "smother") and making it possible to emphasize the harmful character of anyone naturally associated with the color. And this was true of the bear more than of any other creature. Not only, as noted above, did the bear owe to its brown color its common name in Germanic languages (*Bär, bear, bern, brern, björn*), but brown also informed its proper names starting in the twelfth and thirteenth centuries. In animal stories, fables, and the *Roman de Renart*, bears were *Braun* or *Bruno* in German, *Bruin* in Dutch, *Brun* in French and Anglo-Norman, and *Bruno* in Italian. Thereafter, everywhere in Western Europe, *Brun* became the usual proper name of the bear in oral traditions and literary texts. The name was so widespread that it sometimes tended to turn back into a common noun in Romance languages: in French, for example, some writers of the fifteenth century said not *un ours* but *un brun*.[48] It was not a particularly positive name. In no way did it evoke the old king of the beasts and his coat of light, but rather a heavy, clumsy animal, often ridiculous and ill-treated, victim of his gluttony and of the tricks played on him by the fox, the wolf, dogs, and peasants. Being named *Brun* thus had nothing royal or admirable about it for either beast or man. In the Arthurian romances of the twelfth and thirteenth centuries, for example, all the knights—and there are a fair number of them—who, like the bear in the *Roman de Renart*, are named *Brun* are negative characters, sometimes further emphasized by the adjective accompanying their name: Brun the Black, Brun the Savage, Brun the Haughty, Brun the Merciless, Brun without Joy.[49]

For some writers, the bear's dark coat was also related to his winter sleep. What did he really do between the months of November and February? "No one knows," said the Dominican Vincent of Beauvais in the middle of the thirteenth century; several cataloguing chapters of his *Speculum naturale* summarize everything that was known or thought to be known about bears at the time.[50] On the other hand, a contemporaneous writer, unfortunately anonymous, doubted that the bear really slept during this supposed hibernation. He thought the bear did not stay in his den, but went to Hell. That's where he had commerce with the Devil and acquired the deadly color that clothed him, a color compound of red and black, in the image of the infernal flames that burned in the darkness and produced no light.[51]

The Skin of the Beast

But the bear was not just dark, like the Devil and like Hell; he was also hairy, like all wild creatures, enemies of man and of the Church. He was the very archetype of these creatures; the expression "hairy as a bear" was found in several languages, and a well-known biblical passage lay at the source of various developments that medieval symbolism devoted to hairiness. Genesis relates that Rebecca, the wife of Isaac, gave birth to twins, and the one considered the eldest because he came out of his mother's womb first was "red and hairy like a [bear's] skin." He was named Esau and was noted neither for his intelligence nor his wisdom. One night, returning hungry from the hunt, he traded his birthright for a mere dish of lentils that his brother Jacob was about to eat (Genesis 25.29–34). This was a truly sacrilegious deed.[52] This same Jacob, a clever and ambitious young man, Rebecca's favorite son, also replaced his brother in his father's affections by passing himself off as his brother. Isaac was blind, and it was by touching the hairy skin (like that of a bear) of his elder son Esau that he used to identify him and distinguish him from Jacob. But one day, advised by Rebecca, Jason put on a goatskin tunic, tricked his father into taking him for Esau and, in his brother's place, received his father's blessing and the inheritance that went with it (Genesis 27.1–45). From then on, Esau held Jacob as a mortal enemy, so that Jacob had to flee and take refuge with his uncle Laban in the land of the Arameans.

For the Church Fathers and the commentators on Genesis, Esau is a negative figure. He is foolish, gluttonous, brutal, and vindictive, as though his hairiness and ursine appearance had endowed him with all the vices of the beast. Despite his crafty spirit, Jacob is viewed in a more favorable light. In the story of the two brothers, it seems that Esau owes his bad reputation not to his hateful conduct, nor even to his status as a hunter (like all hunters he carries within himself something of the savage and unruly), but precisely to his physical appearance: for medieval sensibilities, being red and hairy from birth could only be the sign of an evil nature and a tragic fate.[53] Red hair was an expression of a false and violent character, and hairiness of a coarse, impure, and almost bestial temperament. To be sure, there was hair and hair: the stiff bristles of the boar could not be compared to the soft and supple wool of the lamb. But in the Middle Ages, on the human body, hair was always connected to animality, and that could only be diabolical.

This was evidenced by the prohibition, repeated frequently from the Carolingian period to the beginning of modern times, against animal disguises or the imitation of animal behavior. As already noted, bishops, councils, and theologians constantly condemned any practice involving the adoption of an animal appearance for a performance, a masquerade, or a seasonal festival. They saw these practices, not without reason, as survivals of idolatrous rituals that it was absolutely necessary to eradicate. But they also saw them as a dangerous confusion between human and animal nature, that is, an intolerable violation of the order intended by the Creator. For medieval Christianity, man was not an animal: he was created in the image of God and had only a distant connection to animals, imperfect creatures subject to his will. Everything in a man's appearance that seemed to bring him too close to animals was abominable, notably, hair, a tail, and horns.[54]

Until the thirteenth century, the animal most often condemned for this reason by the bishops, the central figure in the bestiary of prohibited disguises, remained the bear. Disguising oneself as a bear, "acting the bear" *(ursum facere)* as the Latin texts say, was in the eyes of the clergy even more reprehensible than disguising oneself as a donkey, a stag, or a bull because, again, "the bear is the Devil." It was also a more frequent practice. Perhaps it was the easiest disguise to assume because of the bear's anthropomorphic appearance. Finally, it was more dangerous behavior. In the feudal period many beliefs persisted that considered the bear a relative or a "cousin" of man, or else that saw a bear as a human being transformed into a wild beast: under the coat of fur perhaps was hidden the naked body of a damned soul or an unfortunate victim of an evil spell who could no longer resume his human appearance. It was better not to play thoughtlessly at "acting the bear," better not to tempt the Devil and his evil spells.[55]

In iconography, the Devil was never hairless. He might, of course, be smooth or slippery, but his body or his head always had, here and there, some tufts of hair that expressed his bestiality. This aspect found its primary expression not in teeth or claws, nor even in aggressive horns or the grimacing mask of a face, but in hair. Hair "made" the beast in the culture of the Christian Middle Ages. For that very reason, the bear was the most bestial animal that images—material or dreamed—could present, much more than the lion, the wolf, or the leopard. Drawing a bear, dreaming of a bear, disguising oneself as a bear all meant revealing a dark and hairy form, all the more troubling in the case of a disguise because it was located at the juncture of animal and human and was reduced to a mere skin, apparently—but only apparently—devoid of any life.

In ancient traditions, the bear was the animal that had the closest connection to the motif of skin and hair. I have already mentioned the Berserkers, the fierce warriors of Odin who went into battle naked under "bear shirts," that is, clothed in a bearskin that communicated the animal's strength to them. In Scandinavia and Lapland until modern times some hunters continued to do the same and put on a bearskin before tracking the beast in the forest.[56] The Middle Ages preserved the memory of the figure of the invincible bear that had come from the north and was linked to the metamorphoses of the warrior or the hunter; but under the influence of the Church, it gradually made it into a figure of ridicule. For example, in the Alsatian version of the *Roman de Renart,* composed in the late twelfth century by the poet-knight Henri de Glichezâre, Brun the bear, King Noble's chaplain, is sent on a diplomatic mission to Renart to negotiate a peace treaty. More cunning than ever, the fox offers the bear a "good meal of honey" and draws him to a forked tree where Brun, a victim of his gluttony and his corpulence, finds himself wedged between the two sides of the trunk. Renart mocks him and leaves him trapped in the tree. Brun's howls finally attract a group of peasants. Delighted with the windfall, they knock the bear out, strip him of his fur, and scalp him. The hairy animal, the king of the forest, is left bare, hairless, and bald. Women and children mock him and cut off his ears.[57]

I have mentioned the cruel Bible story in Kings that similarly associated the bear with the theme of baldness: the story of the prophet Elisha on the road to Bethel meeting children who mock his baldness.[58] But as always in ancient traditions, the bear there is not the victim but the attacker: two she-bears devour the children. From the twelfth century on, iconography was fond of depicting this episode and emphasizing the contrast between the abundant fur of the two animals and the prophet's bald head, whereas theologians, for rather obscure reasons, saw it as a prefiguration of the scourging of Christ.[59]

Though troubling on the living animal, the bear's coat, once removed from the dead animal, became a source of wealth. Throughout the Middle Ages, bearskin was sought after and was the object of an active trade between Slavic and Scandinavian countries and the West. Lübeck, Bergen, Trondheim, and Novgorod were the major centers for the shipment of bearskins to Germany, Flanders, and England. Even though it was difficult to work, because it was thick and sturdy, bear hide made excellent boots and shoes, while the fur, dense, warm, and waterproof, was used to make clothing and hats.[60] It is softer than literary works or hunting treatises say, because they lump together with identical disgust the stiff and sharp bristles of the boar and the softer and finer fur of the king of the forest. Sometimes the skin of a bear that was remarkable because of its size or color became the subject of a story or a legend and was preserved for that reason among various *curiosa* in the treasure of a church or a palace, along with an ostrich egg, a giant's bone, a dragon's claw, and the horn of a unicorn.[61] But that became rare after the fourteenth century: other "marvels" that were more exotic or more spectacular now attracted prelates and princes, such as the prestigious crocodiles "boiled in oil" (that is, stuffed), star attractions of the early cabinets of curiosities in the sixteenth and seventeenth centuries. Yet in some mountain regions the skin of one or more bears remained well into modern times a feudal tribute due from villagers to their lord: it was still a way of fighting against an animal considered harmful and of securing without expense a certain number of products that could be used for clothing and food.[62]

Moreover, it may have been during the peasant battues of feudal origin that the expression "sell the bear's skin before having killed the beast" arose. It was unknown in Ancient and Medieval Latin and is solidly attested in the vernacular only beginning in the fifteenth century, in the form *marchander la peau de l'ours jusques ad ce que la bête fust morte* ("sell the bearskin before the animal is dead").[63] Here too, men whose hopes had been disappointed seemed to be victims of the ruses of the bear and those of the Devil.

6

The Coronation of the Lion

THE long war that the Church had been fighting against the bear since the Merovingian period really began to bear fruit after the year 1000. Physically eliminated by systematic hunts, symbolically vanquished by a large number of saints, demonized by texts, images, and sermons, in the High Middle Ages the bear finally descended from his throne and joined the parade of ordinary animals, taking its place among large game animals alongside the stag and the boar. This dethronement took place slowly, of course, and was never complete. In the feudal period, the bear still preserved certain features of his former rank as royal animal, both admired and feared. But he was no longer the great and venerated wild beast of European forests, the god of warriors, the founding ancestor of several prestigious primitive dynasties, such as those of the kings of Denmark and Norway, the margraves of Brandenburg, the counts of Toulouse, and even King Arthur. His throne was increasingly unstable, so much so that at the turn of the twelfth and thirteenth centuries, he was forced to abdicate. The Church had achieved its goal.

But however symbolic the throne, it could not remain unoccupied. Popular beliefs and habitual ways of thinking would unfailingly have installed another animal in his place, perhaps just as dangerous as the bear or even more pernicious, like the fox, another incarnation of the Evil One, or more venomous, like the vile, perfidious snake. Priests and monks took the matter seriously and decided to install another wild animal on the imaginary throne, invincible like the bear and therefore legitimately an object of fear, admiration, and respect, but completely absent from European forests: the lion.

The ground had in reality been prepared over the course of several centuries. The Church did not decide suddenly in the years between 1150 and 1200 to replace the bear with the lion. It was rather a long-range maneuver that began in the Carolingian period and was conducted simultaneously with three other strategies described earlier: fighting, taming, and demonizing the bear. But it was not an easy task. The lion did belong to written tradition and therefore seemed easier to master or manipulate than the bear. But like the bear, it played an ambivalent role in animal symbolism, notably the symbolism the Christian West had inherited from the Bible: there was a good lion and a bad lion. In a Europe thoroughly Christianized, how was it possible to crown as king of the beasts a wild animal that to a large degree still belonged to the devil's bestiary? How could he be stripped of his negative characteristics? Codes had to be violated, experiments undertaken, and resistances overcome. The lion had to be discussed at every opportunity, and the good lions carefully distinguished from the bad. Finally, the true nature of the bad lions had to be changed.

Any researcher familiar with medieval documents knows that from the age of Charlemagne to that of Saint Louis, in France and in neighboring countries, lions were encountered everywhere, in all places and circumstances: real lions of flesh and fur, but also lions that were painted, carved, modeled, embroidered, woven, described, recounted, thought about, and dreamed. Before and after the year 1000, the West mirrored the life of the lion as much as the bear, and the steady rise of the former was both a cause and a reflection of the inexorable decline of the latter.

A Threefold Legacy

Before studying the promotion of the lion in detail and setting out the broad lines of lion symbolism in medieval traditions, it is worth mentioning the lion's place in the three cultures to which the Christian West was heir: biblical, Greco-Roman, and barbarian.

In biblical times, wild lions were still living in Palestine and throughout the Middle East. This lion was smaller than the African lion, and it attacked livestock much more frequently than people.[1] It had been abundant for several centuries, but was less so at the time of the Roman conquest. It had practically disappeared by the time of the Crusades. The

Bible mentions it frequently and emphasizes its strength. Defeating a lion is an exploit, and all the heroes endowed with great strength are compared to lions. Symbolically, however, the lion is an ambiguous animal, who can be beneficial or harmful, more often the latter. Cruel, brutal, cunning, impious, the lion embodies the forces of evil, the enemies of Israel, tyrants and bad kings, and men living in sin. The Psalms and the prophets devote a good deal of space to what they present as a dangerous creature from whom one should flee while begging for divine protection: "Save me from the lion's mouth," begs the psalmist (Psalms 22.21); the prayer was echoed by many writers of the High Middle Ages. The New Testament followed suit, making the lion an image of the Devil: "Be vigilant, because your adversary the devil, as a roaring lion, walketh about, seeking whom he may devour" (1 Peter 5.8). But the Bible also has a good lion, more discreet, who puts his strength at the service of the common good and whose roaring expresses the word of God. He is the bravest of the animals (Proverbs 30.30) and the emblem of the tribe of Judah, the most powerful in Israel (Genesis 49.9). For that reason, he is associated with David and his descendants, and even with Christ: "Weep not: behold, the Lion of the tribe of Juda, the Root of David, hath prevailed to open the book, and to loose the seven seals thereof" (Revelation 5.5).

In their wild state, lions had long disappeared from Europe, probably for several millennia before our era. Romans imported them in large quantities from North Africa or Asia Minor, sometimes from even farther, for the circus games. This is probably why, like the biblical voices, classical writers were loquacious about the lion. They knew it well; many of them gave it a kind of primacy over the other animals. None of them, however, not even Aristotle, expressly declared that the lion was the "king of the beasts." Pliny seemed to prefer the elephant in that role, and he begins Book VIII of his *Natural History,* on the quadrupeds, with that animal.[2] But when Isidore of Seville writes of wild animals in the *Etymologies,* compiled five centuries later, he begins with the lion. He calls him the "ruler of all the beasts" and expressly bestows on him the title of "king" *(rex).*[3] This was an Eastern tradition, perhaps more Persian than Indian.[4] And it was practically unknown to the Greek and Roman writers of classical antiquity, hardly present in biblical texts, but it penetrated into the West beginning in the late Roman Empire. Isidore seems to have been the first Christian writer to express it so clearly.

There was nothing comparable among the Celts, whose mythology long remained impermeable to Mediterranean and Eastern traditions. The Celts were ignorant of the lion before Christianization. It played no role in their animal symbolism. The first rank was occupied by the bear (King Arthur's name, as I have noted, evokes the bear, a royal animal), but several other animals in the mythological bestiary offered strong competition: the boar, the stag, the crow, and even the salmon.[5]

German traditions were more complex and nuanced. The lion appears nowhere in the oldest strata of German and Scandinavian mythology. But very early on, well before Christianization, the Germans of the Black Sea region, who had commercial and cultural contacts with the societies of the Middle East and Central Asia, imported into the West the figures of the lion and the griffin, etched in metal, carved in ivory, or embroidered on cloth. These images quickly took on a symbolic dimension compatible with Germanic traditions. The mane, in particular, gave value to the lion, because long and full hair was among the Germans always a sign of strength and power. So when the first Christian missionaries came to Germany bearing with them the Bible and its long parade of lions, the animal was already well known to the pagan natives, although it occupied a modest place in animal emblematics and heraldry compared to those of the bear and the boar, and even the wolf, the crow, or the stag.

An Ambivalent Symbolism

The ambivalent character of the biblical lion also appears in Christian symbolism of the High Middle Ages. Following Augustine, a declared enemy of the lion and of all savage beasts, most Church Fathers saw it as a diabolical animal: violent, ferocious, and bloodthirsty. Its strength is rarely used to serve the good, its mouth resembles the pit of hell; any battle against a lion is a battle against Satan, and vanquishing a lion, as David and Samson had, is a rite of passage that consecrates heroes and saints.

But a few writers—Ambrose, Origen, Rabanus Maurus[6]—adopted a different view. Relying primarily on the New Testament, they saw the lion as the "lord of the wild beasts" *("dominus bestiarum")*, even as a more or less Christological figure. They thereby laid the groundwork for the growth in the lion's prestige in Christian symbolism by the end of the Carolingian period, and especially from the eleventh century on.[7]

This increased prestige was heavily influenced by Latin bestiaries derived from the Greek *Physiologus* compiled in Alexandria in the second century AD.[8] Following Eastern traditions, the lion is almost always presented there as the "king of all the wild beasts" *("rex omnium bestiarum")*, but not yet as "king of all the animals."[9] This phrase was not used until the great encyclopedias of the thirteenth century by Thomas de Cantimpré, Bartholomaeus Anglicus, and Vincent of Beauvais, compiled between 1240 and 1260.[10] All three call the lion "king of the animals" *("rex animalium")* and write at length about him, more than about any other animal. They emphasize his strength, courage, generosity, and magnanimity, all qualities inherent in kings, and with which, in the oldest branches of the *Roman de Renart* (c. 1175–1180), King Noble, that is, the lion, is abundantly endowed.

Meanwhile, also under the influence of bestiaries, the lion was definitively given genuine Christological symbolism. Each of his wonderful "properties" inherited from Eastern traditions was connected to Christ. The lion wiping away his tracks with his tail to fool hunters was Jesus concealing his divinity by being born of Mary: he became man in secret the better to deceive the devil. The lion who spares a defeated enemy was the Lord who, in his mercy, forgives the repentant sinner. The lion who sleeps with his eyes open is Christ in his tomb: his human form sleeps, but his divine nature keeps watch. The lion who breathes life into his stillborn cubs on the third day is the very image of the Resurrection.[11]

But once the lion had found his definitive place in the bestiary of Christ—sometimes even being identified with the Savior—a delicate question arose for theologians and artists: what should be done about the negative aspects of the animal? What of the bad lion mentioned by the Psalms, Saint Augustine, most Church Fathers, and, following them, a large part of the monastic culture of the High Middle Ages? Authors of bestiaries, creators of emblems and symbols, painters, and illustrators seem to have hesitated a long time, unable to resolve this essential question. Then, as the eleventh century gave way to the twelfth, they finally found a solution. They made the bad lion an entirely separate animal, with his own name and attributes, so as not to be confused with the Christological lion, who was then on the way to becoming the king of the animals. They found an animal to serve as a kind of escape hatch for the former "bad lion" that had become an autonomous species in the course of a few decades—the leopard. Not the real leopard, the one we know as a cousin of the panther, but an imaginary leopard, the supposed offspring of the guilty mating of a lioness and a *pardus,* an enigmatic animal sometimes presented as a male panther. The leopard preserved some of the properties and formal aspects of the lion (but not the mane) but was endowed with a very bad nature; the lion, by means of this subtle lexical shift alone, was freed of it. From then on, there was no longer a good and a bad lion; there was the just and generous lion and the cruel and harmful leopard. The sculpted bestiary provides ample evidence of these changes. In the Romanesque period, all or almost all lions are negative; in the Gothic period, they are so no longer, having been replaced in that role by the leopard.

Before this occurred in sculpture, by the middle of the twelfth century, literary texts and early heraldry delighted in featuring the new leopard, making him a fallen lion, a demi-lion, or even an enemy of the lion. In that role, he was sometimes a cousin or ally of the dragon, or even a kind of dragon of a special type.[12] The leopard became the quintessentially negative animal, the one who appeared on the hero's path to lead him to death, or in the coat of arms of treacherous knights, pagan enemies of the crusaders, and all those who embodied the forces of evil.[13]

The Birth of Armorial Bearings

The earliest armorial bearings, or coats of arms, real or imaginary, provide a particularly fruitful source of documentation for studying the various changes that affected animal symbolism in the course of the twelfth century, particularly those I am concerned with here: the promotion of the lion, the "creation" of the leopard, and the devaluation of the bear.

Coats of arms can be defined as emblems in color, specific to an individual, a family, or a community; their composition obeys the particular rules of heraldry. Much ink has flowed on the question of their origin. By the late Middle Ages, treatises of heraldry had proposed several hypotheses, and their number continued to grow in the following centuries. Some purely fanciful ones, such as attributing the invention of coats of arms to Adam, Alexander, Julius Caesar, or King Arthur, were rejected early on. Others, based on more serious arguments, had longer lives but were gradually undermined by the work of heraldry experts in the late nineteenth and early twentieth centuries.

Three theories that were long in favor have now been abandoned. First, the idea that there was a direct and continuous relation between the military or family emblems used in Greco-Roman antiquity and the earliest coats of arms in the twelfth century. Also abandoned was the theory of a special influence of runes, barbarian insignia, and German and Scandinavian emblems of the first millennium on the formation of feudal heraldic imagery. Finally, and most important, because it lasted the longest, was the theory of an Eastern origin, based on the adoption of a Muslim or Byzantine custom by Westerners during the First Crusade. This theory prevailed for a long time, but it has now been rejected by all specialists. They have agreed that the appearance of coats of arms in Western Europe was connected to transformations in feudal society after the year one thousand and to the evolution of military equipment between the late eleventh century and the first decades of the twelfth. There were no coats of arms at the time of the First Crusade (1096–1099), but they were already in place by the time of the Second (1147–1149).[14]

Between those two dates, Western combatants, made unrecognizable by the cowls on their chain mail and the nosepieces of their helmets, gradually developed the habit of placing on the large surface of their almond-shaped shields figures that could serve as signs of recognition in the heart of the melee of battles or tournaments. These figures were geometric, animal, or floral. They were painted in color and became actual coats of arms once the same person began to use them constantly. Their imagery obeyed a few simple, fixed, and recurrent principles. This occurred shortly before the middle of the twelfth century.

But this material cause, related to the evolution of military equipment, does not explain everything. The appearance of coats of arms was more deeply connected to the new order governing Western society in the feudal period. Like the patronymic family names that arose at the same time, or the iconographic attributes that were beginning to proliferate in pictures, heraldry provided new signs of identity for a society in the process of reorganization. It helped situate individuals within groups, and groups within the social system as a whole. For this reason, coats of arms, which at first were individual emblems, were soon grafted onto kinship. By the second half of the twelfth century, their use in a family became hereditary, and this characteristic gave them their final form.[15]

First used by princes and great nobles, coats of arms were gradually adopted by the Western aristocracy as a whole. By the early thirteenth century, all lower and mid-level nobles had them. Over the decades, their use extended to noncombatants, to nonnobles, and to various corporate entities. Seals were the primary means of extending the use of coats of arms to noncombatants. Lords and knights were soon not content with merely painting on their shields the coat of arms they had adopted; they also showed it on their banners, on their horse's saddle cloth, and then on various possessions, primarily their seal, symbol of their legal status. Gradually, anyone who had a seal adopted the habit of filling its surface with armorial bearings in imitation of princes and great lords. There is a significant figure related to this: we know about a million coats of arms for medieval Europe. Three-fourths of them are known through seals, and nearly half are coats of arms of nonnobles.

There is no certain geographical origin for coats of arms. They appeared simultaneously in various regions of Western Europe: areas between the Loire and the Rhine, southern England, Switzerland, northern Italy. By the late thirteenth century, the entire West had taken up this new fashion, and it even began to reach into Eastern Christendom. Geographic and social distribution was accompanied by material distribution. More and more objects, fabrics, clothing, and monuments were covered with coats of arms, which played three roles: signs of identity, marks of command or ownership, and ornamental motifs. Their use was so widespread in social life and material culture that by the twelfth century they were attributed to imaginary characters, heroes of romances, legendary figures, mythological creatures, and personified vices and virtues.[16]

The Heraldic Bestiary

Coats of arms appeared, then, at a time when the symbolism and imaginative use of the lion were rapidly growing as those of the bear were clearly declining. In the second half of the twelfth century, in all French and Anglo-Norman literary works, the shield of the lion became the stereotypical shield of the Christian knight, now opposed to the shield of the dragon (or leopard) of the pagan warrior.[17] Only Germanic regions resisted this proliferation of lions and maintained a connection with the mythological bestiary of ancient pagan Germany for a few decades. In the early thirteenth century, the bear and the boar were still the conventional emblems of literary heroes, but that did not last long. By the middle of the century, a hero as prestigious as Tristan, for example, abandoned in Germany and Scandinavia his traditional boar shield and adopted a lion shield, as he had done the century before in France and England, and would a little later in Austria and northern Italy.[18]

The lion was the most frequent figure in medieval coats of arms, in all periods and for all social categories: nearly 15 percent featured one. This was a considerable proportion, since the figure in second position, the *fasce* (a geometric figure represented by a horizontal band), reached only 6 percent, and the eagle, the lion's only real rival in the heraldic bestiary, did not go beyond 3 percent. This primacy of the lion appeared everywhere, in northern and southern Europe, in noble and nonnoble coats of arms, in coats of arms of individuals and of corporate entities, and in real and imaginary heraldry.[19] The famous proverb: "Whoever has no arms bears a lion" appeared in literature in the thirteenth century and was still being justifiably quoted by heraldic manuals in the sixteenth and seventeenth centuries. It should also be noted that, apart from the emperor and the king of France, all the dynasties of Western Christendom at one time or another in their history had a lion in their coats of arms.[20]

Statistically first, the lion was also first in the writings of heralds of arms and writers describing the fauna of heraldry. Beginning in the thirteenth century, they all agreed in making him king of the beasts and the quintessential heraldic figure.[21] Like bestiaries and encyclopedias, they attributed to the lion all the virtues of the chief or the king: strength, courage, pride, generosity, and justice.

This was not true for the leopard, a new animal in the emblematic and symbolic bestiary of the twelfth century.[22] From the formal point of view, of course, the heraldic leopard was only a lion represented in a particular position: the head always facing forward and the body in profile, most often horizontally, whereas the lion always had head and body in profile.[23] It was this frontward facing position of the head that created meaning: in the zoomorphic iconography of the Middle Ages, it was almost always pejorative.[24] Because he faced forward, while the lion was in profile, the leopard on coats of arms was indeed a bad lion. During the same period the leopard in literature and in zoology books was always presented as the bastard offspring of a lioness and a *pardus*.[25] One might also wonder whether the countless wild animals in Roman sculpture that are presented face forward and jaws wide, ready to devour, are not sometimes "leopards" rather than lions.

While granting first place to the lion, far ahead of all other animals, heraldry granted the bear only a very discreet role. Heraldry arrived too late in the world of lords and knights to make the bear a rival to the lion. The first coats of arms would have had to appear around the time of Charlemagne, or at the latest around the year 1000, for the heraldic bear to have played a role comparable to that of the lion. Its average frequency of appearance in medieval coats of arms barely exceeded five out of one thousand (except perhaps in northern Spain and certain regions of Germany), while the comparable figure for the lion was 15 percent. The difference was considerable. The heraldic bear was in fact primarily a speaking figure: his name was a pun on that of the owner of the coat of arms.[26] The earliest-known coats of arms charged with a bear are of this type. They occur in an English miniature painted in the region of Canterbury between 1190 and 1200 that depicts the murder of Archbishop Thomas Becket (1170). The chief of the assassins, the celebrated and fearsome Reginald FitzUrse, was distinguished by an escutcheon adorned with a muzzled bear.[27] This was an expressive coat of arms, perhaps created after the death of Reginald to serve as an iconographic emblem in the scene frequently depicted of the murder of the archbishop in his cathedral. Whether or not he bore this coat of arms is a difficult but not essential question. It is the oldest coat of arms with a bear that has come down to us, and it inaugurated a series in which the animal "spoke" the name of the owner: an individual name, family name, name of a fief, or name of a community. Physical persons were not in fact the only ones who used a bear in their coats of arms. Cities (Bern, Berlin, Madrid), abbeys (Ourscamp, Sainte-Ursanne), and brotherhoods (that of Saint Ursin in Bourges, for example) did the same thing.

Heraldry did not, however, completely obscure the old warlike aspect of the bear. The animal was sometimes used as a crest atop the helmet, perhaps a remnant of the old "bear helmets" of the High Middle Ages in Germany and Scandinavia.[28] But it is worth emphasizing that some German and Swedish coats of arms display the former royal dignity of the animal. They are the ones in which the bear on the escutcheon "speaks" with an anthroponym evoking the idea of king: *Königsberg, Könnecke, Kungslena, Herringa*. Heraldry here gives evidence of the last remnants of an oral tradition in the process of disappearing.[29] Everywhere else, it was the lion who played the role of king of the beasts, even in northern Germany, where the long-running conflict (c. 1164–1168) between the powerful Henry the Lion, Duke of Saxony (1129–1195), and the no less powerful margrave of Brandenburg, Albert the Bear, ended with Henry's victory.[30] From the perspective I am concerned with, the victory had a symbolic value: thereafter, no German dynasty would be nicknamed "Bear." But there were many, in imitation of the prestigious Henry, Duke of Saxony and Bavaria, that were given the nickname "Lion." This was not restricted to Germany. A few years later, King Richard of England and King William of Scotland, while still alive, were given by chroniclers a nickname taken from the lion, not the bear: "Lionheart" for Richard and "the Generous Lion" for William.[31]

From then on, the lion extended his empire everywhere.

Noah's Ark

The lion established his presence particularly in images and in works of art. Indeed, if seeing a living lion was still an unusual spectacle in the twelfth century, despite traveling menageries and animal showmen, seeing a painted, carved, embroidered, or modeled lion had become relatively common, even among peasant populations. Whether still Romanesque or already Gothic, many churches displayed a large number of lions both inside and outside, in the nave as well as the choir, on floors, walls, ceilings, doors, and windows, on tombstones and funerary monuments, on objects and vestments used in worship services, and even in holy books: entire lions or hybrid lions, crossed with other animals or showing only the head, represented alone or as part of a scene.

In this lavish setting, where considerable space was given over to the bestiary, so much so as to provoke the hostility of some prelates,[32] carved lions are now more numerous than painted lions. Some of the latter have disappeared, however, and it is not certain that the carved animals that we take for lions were really thought of and accepted as such. They are sometimes relatively indeterminate felines, or even simply quadrupeds to which it is hardly possible to attach the name of a species. Sometimes as well, we have a tendency to confuse the lion and the bear, since the two animals are a pair in the Bible, in patristic texts, and in the associated iconography—only the mane and long tail make it possible to identify the lion with certainty.[33] Even more often, we are tempted to give the name *lion* to any beast or monster with a gaping jaw appearing to swallow or vomit out a human being; in some cases, the identification is improper because it is too precise.[34]

All the same, from the eleventh and twelfth centuries lions abounded, not only in sculpture but in all forms of artistic creation. In illuminations, for example, the lion was now the animal most often represented. In some manuscripts it was even found on every page: in the principal miniature, in the secondary decoration, and especially in the historiated letter, which was often in animal or specifically leonine form. Indeed, whatever the medium or technique used, the lion gradually became the most prominent animal in the images of the bestiary, very far ahead of all the other animals. The times and places when one's eyes did not encounter one or more lions were very rare. The image became a part of daily life, and it raises a question for the historian about the aptness of the now familiar opposition between "native" and "exotic" animals. For feudal societies, the lion was not really an exotic animal, even though it had not been native to Europe for several millennia. The lion could be seen every day and everywhere, represented on a great many monuments, objects, precious fabrics, and works of art.

Perhaps better than any other, one iconographic theme makes it possible to assess the increasingly important place granted to the lion in images between the Carolingian period and the thirteenth century: Noah's Ark.[35] It was represented frequently in various media, often featuring a carefully selected bestiary, forming a kind of ideal menagerie. The text of Genesis in fact mentions no names of species for the animals in the ark, simply presenting God's command to Noah: "And of every living thing of all flesh, two of every sort shalt thou bring into the ark, to keep them alive with thee; they shall be male and female. Of fowls after their kind, and of cattle after their kind, of every creeping thing of the earth after his kind, two of every sort shall come unto thee, to keep them alive. And take thou unto thee of all food that is eaten, and thou shalt gather it to thee; and it shall be for food for thee, and for them" (Genesis 6.19–21).[36]

Artists and illuminators were therefore relatively free to choose the animals they would put in the ark, and their choices obviously reflected the value systems, ways of thinking and feeling, knowledge, and zoological classifications that differed according to era, region, and social milieu. The usually limited space at their disposal to represent the ark and its inhabitants limited their number, but the lack of precision in the biblical text left them wide freedom of choice.

Indeed, from the ninth to the thirteenth centuries, images of the ark floating on the waters of the flood do not always show identifiable animals.[37] But when they are identifiable—four times out of five—the bear and the lion are always among them. They are generally accompanied by a few other quadrupeds (to use a medieval concept), the list of which is variable—the most frequent are the boar and the stag. For the purposes of iconography, an animal is first of all a quadruped, and wild quadrupeds seem more "animal" than the others. Domestic species, sometimes difficult to identify with precision,[38] occupy only second place. Birds are rare (present in only one-fourth of the images), apart from the crow and the dove, essential figures in the story of the flood. Small rodents and snakes occur even less frequently. And insects (in the modern sense) and fish are never depicted, except for fish shown under the ark in the middle of the water. In nearly one-third of the examples, a pair of each animal species is not shown, but a single, sexually undifferentiated representative. Even in large-scale images, the ark rarely holds more than a dozen different species; the number is often limited to four or five, sometimes fewer. On the other hand, less numerous and more recent images presenting the entrance or exit of the animals depict a richer and more diversified fauna. They also make it possible to study certain hierarchies in the animal world: at the top come the bear and the lion, followed by large game (stag, boar), and then domestic animals; closing the parade are small animals, rats, "worms," and snakes.[39]

These hierarchies are instructive in various ways, particularly because they evolved over time. In the rare images of the ark before the year 1000 there seems to have been only one king or chief of the animals: the bear, as in the ancient traditions of all northern Europe. But in the feudal period, the bear gradually gave way before the lion in the distribution of places in the ark and it was lowered by one rank, sometimes several, in the entry or exit procession. The first role now always devolved on the lion. After the thirteenth century, new species made their appearance (elephant, camel, monkey, unicorn, and a few others), but that did not challenge now well-established classifications: the lion remained the central figure in the bestiary of the ark, and the bear became more and more discreet. And even though the bestiary grew more exotic, the border between real and fantastic animals remained blurred until the seventeenth century. Finally, in the late Middle Ages, an animal that had long been absent from the ark made a conspicuous entrance: the horse. For feudal sensibilities, the horse was more than an animal, it was a companion to man. This is why texts and images were sometimes reluctant to include it in bestiaries. Its place was not among the animals but alongside humans. From the fourteenth century on, this particular view of the horse declined; it seemed to again become an animal like the others, and thus to find its place among the animals of the ark, along with the lion, the stag, the bull, and the boar, and there it remained.

Princely Menageries

Heraldry and iconography are not the only documentary sources that bring out the promotion of the lion and the devaluation of the bear beginning in the twelfth century. Other evidence confirms this unavoidable development and even points to its acceleration between 1180 and 1200: for example, the royal and princely menageries discussed earlier.[40] In the Carolingian period, and again in the early feudal period, as I have noted, every menagerie had to include one or more bears, and the finest gift a king could give to another king was a bear, if possible notable because of its size, its fur, or its origin. It is clear that in the second half of the twelfth century, and even more in the thirteenth, this was no longer the case. The bear was no longer a royal gift, except in a few literary works behind the times with regard to actual practice. Among Christian monarchs, only the king of Norway continued to offer his polar bears, exceptional animals captured on the ice fields of the far north. We know from a chronicler that the menagerie of Emperor Frederick II in Palermo contained a "gigantic bear as white as snow" (*"ursus albus sicut nivea magnitudinis insolite"*) that King Haakon IV of Norway had sent to him in 1235 on the occasion of his marriage to Isabella of England, a remarkable gift that excited the curiosity of the residents of Palermo for several years—no chronicler tells us how the bear withstood the Sicilian climate, but it appears that the animal had a rather long life.[41] A few years later, the same Haakon IV gave King Henry III of England, Frederick II's brother-in-law, another, smaller, polar bear, probably from Spitzbergen, that I have already mentioned: it was given the name *Piscator,* Fisher.[42]

Toward the middle of the thirteenth century, these two polar bears were *curiosa exotica* of the kind that every menagerie of any importance had to possess in order to effectively function as an emblem of power. Owning a brown bear had become totally banal and held very little interest. Kings and princes gave up that animal, abandoning it to the menageries of towns and petty lords, or even to jongleurs, tumblers, and animal showmen who traveled from one village fair to the next. Lions, not bears, were now what every princely menagerie had to contain. It would be useful to know in detail the composition of thirteenth-century menageries, but, in the absence of plentiful documentation, we have only an approximate idea. Thanks to narrative texts and a few accounting archives, we know that they contained many lions that had to be fed, cared for, guarded, and replaced. Lions, but also panthers, leopards, and even some "tigers," about which we can guess that they were not the animals we know by that name. When medieval images intend to depict tigers, they never show felines resembling our Asian tigers, but quadrupeds with dark, sometimes spotted fur, resembling large wolves with enormous teeth and claws.[43] In the closing years of the fourteenth century, King Charles VI of France adopted the "tiger" as an emblem that he used, among others, as a personal "device." Narrative texts and accounting documents frequently mention this "tiger," but images never represent it as a large, striped wild animal, but rather as a kind of fox or wolf (the latter was, incidentally, the device of the king's brother, Louis d'Orléans).[44]

We know that there were many lions in princely menageries and that on some days the town public could come to see them. We also know that lions were often given as gifts between monarchs and that African lions, larger and rarer, were sought after more than those from the Middle East. Once again, in the first half of the thirteenth century, it was Emperor Frederick II's Palermo menagerie that held the largest number of them. It even functioned as a distribution center for other royal menageries. The major supplier of lions and other wild animals to the West was at the time the sultan of Egypt, with whom Frederick II had a privileged relationship.[45] In Europe, Venice and Byzantium were also markets well supplied with wild animals imported from Asia and Africa. Among them, archive documents frequently mention lions, panthers, and leopards, but never bears, which could have been brought from the Caucasus or Anatolia— two regions that had huge ones—or from even farther off. In the middle of the thirteenth century, a brown bear, even a remarkable one, no longer had market value since it was no longer an animal that conferred prestige.

The decline is confirmed by many texts—literary, narrative, and even hagiographic. A young warrior aspiring to knighthood would not now confront a bear to demonstrate his strength and courage, as was still sometimes the case in the twelfth century, but a lion, or possibly a dragon. Moreover, in Arthurian romances, kings, sons of kings, and confirmed knights, such as Lancelot, Tristan, Gawain, and all the knights of the Round Table, did the same thing: vanquishing a lion had become the quintessential exploit. The romance *Yder*, written between 1190 and 1210, which I have discussed at length earlier,[46] was one of the last to give an account of the admirable prowess involved in victory over a bear.

A lion, never a bear, now sometimes became the hero's companion, accompanied him on the road of adventure, protected him, and served as his emblem. The model—a very early one—can be found in the romance by Chrétien de Troyes, *Le Chevalier au Lion*, written between 1177 and 1181. The hero, Yvain, makes a lion his companion. Similarly, in saints' lives and hagiographic accounts, stories of bears that were frequent in the High Middle Ages became increasingly rare, replaced in the thirteenth century by stories featuring lions, notably in episodes in which the saint, doomed to being devoured, is spared by wild beasts. Between 1230 and 1250, being threatened and then spared by a bear was no longer very wondrous or miraculous. But being spared by a lion, the new king of the beasts, gave sainthood a new dimension that was particularly glorious.

Even the Bible reflected these new hierarchies. In the various passages of the Old Testament where the text, in one way or another, talks of wild beasts and cites primarily the bear and the lion, maleficent and fearsome animals, medieval Greek and Latin versions prior to the thirteenth century used, at random it appears, sometimes the sequence bear / lion, sometimes the sequence lion / bear. Thereafter, it seems that the new versions and translations of the Bible, notably those done in Paris, were careful to favor the sequence lion / bear, as though the lion now had always to come before the bear.[47] The same hierarchy can be found in other categories of texts that contain lists of animals. In some manuscripts of encyclopedias and works of zoology, where chapters are organized alphabetically according to the first letter of the animal concerned, it even happens that the chapter on the lion—and that one alone—is not placed under the letter L *(leo),* but taken out of alphabetical order and set at the front of the book, before the chapters devoted to animals whose names begin with A. The primacy of the king of the beasts is expressed in taxonomies as in all other fields of knowledge.

The Resurrection of the Flesh

The replacement of the bear with the lion on the animal throne was a long-term phenomenon, the apex of which was undoubtedly the twelfth century, at least in Western Europe. The evidence that has just been mentioned even seems to show that the last decades of that century and the first decades of the next were the decisive years, the years of definitive change. There are, however, some documents that lead a historian to think that, in several domains, the change took place earlier, probably at the turn of the eleventh and twelfth centuries. This was, for example, the case for theology, always loquacious on the animal world—a privileged locus for all sorts of examples and comparisons—and reflective of various value systems that it did not always create but that it often helped to promote.

With regard to the new superiority of the lion over the bear, one "manual" of theology is particularly instructive, the *Elucidarium* of Honorius Augustodunensis.[48] It preceded the evidence provided by ursine anthroponymy, heraldry, and iconography since it was compiled between 1100 and 1105, before being partially adopted and developed in a work by the same writer, *Clavis Physicae,*[49] written between 1120 and 1130. We know little about this eclectic writer who was a talented theologian. It used to be thought that he was a schoolmaster from Autun; it is now agreed that he had no connection to Autun, nor even to Augsburg, despite the adjective "Augustodunensis" often attached to his name by medieval scribes, and that he was rather a monk of British origin who had come to the Continent and was living as a recluse in a monastery near Regensburg. In any event, he was an important writer, particularly because he had gifts as a pedagogue and a popularizer. He was quoted, and indeed pillaged, by a good number of theologians until well into the fourteenth century.[50]

Writing on the problem of the resurrection of the flesh—a theme of great topicality for theologians in the early twelfth century—Honorius came to speak of the act of devouring. He wondered particularly about the mystery of the human body that, torn to pieces by a wild animal, could miraculously recover its integrity at the moment of resurrection. This was in fact a question that had long been debated in Christian theology.[51] The Church Fathers of the High Middle Ages (Tertullian, Origen, Methodius, Gregory of Nyssa, Jerome) were already asking it with reference to martyrdom. How did the bodies of torture victims, after being fragmented by the executioner's axe, torn apart by the teeth of wild animals, or reduced to ashes by the flames of the stake, recover their integrity at the threshold of eternal life? To this complex, almost insoluble question, the Church Fathers had provided diverse and sometimes contradictory answers, giving rise to several long-lasting polemics, primarily between supporters of Origen's arguments and supporters of Jerome's. In the fifth century, Augustine had proposed a middle way, but had pointed out, in agreement with Jerome, that integrity of body and soul was indispensable to fully constitute a "person" (in the eschatological sense that medieval theology gave to that term).[52] Then the debate had subsided to an extent and had produced little in the way of polemics during the Carolingian period, although in the ninth century, Johannes Scotus Erigena had proposed some new hypotheses in *De divisione naturae.*[53]

The controversy returned to the front of the stage in the early twelfth century, in connection with the theology of martyrdom, the cult of relics, and the mystery of the Eucharist.[54] Honorius echoed it in his *Elucidarium*. Referring to bodies that had been devoured by a wild beast—there was a lot of devouring in the Romanesque era, as sculpted bestiary shows—[55] he even offers some examples, which he does not elaborate on, that might be called "case studies."[56] On this occasion, unlike his predecessors, he names three animal species: wolf, bear, lion. Honorius first presents the case of a man who has been devoured by a wolf: the flesh of man and wolf, he asserts, necessarily end up being mixed together, at least partially. What will happen at the moment of the resurrection of the flesh? How will human and animal flesh be separated? How will the body of the man recover its integrity? Honorius does not provide unambiguous answers to these questions, but in his attempt to indicate the importance of the problem he has brought up, he goes further and wonders what would happen if the wolf who had eaten a man were in turn devoured by a bear: once again, the flesh of the bear would be mixed with that of the wolf, which has already been mixed with the flesh of the man. How would the flesh of the three be distinguished on the day of resurrection? How could the body of the man be separated from those of the wolf and the bear to recover its total integrity? One senses that the questions are becoming more and more specious. But Honorius doesn't stop there. Carried away by an irresistible impulse toward increasingly extravagant casuistry, he extends his questioning still further, deliberately complicates the problem, and very seriously wonders what would happen if the bear were in turn devoured by a lion.[57]

Honorius stops there; he even seems overwhelmed by the complexity of the questions he has raised. Indeed, from a strictly theological point of view, they are arduous and passionately interesting. In succeeding decades they led scholasticism toward extraordinarily subtle analyses to avoid having Christian dogma trap itself by becoming locked within inextricable arguments. This is not the place to dwell on that matter; other researchers have considered the question, some of them in remarkable fashion.[58] For my purposes, the examples presented by Honorius represent a cultural and historical document of great importance. They bring out a hierarchy in the animal world that was entirely new in the early twelfth century and was to last until modern times, even up to the present: the bear is stronger than the wolf, which was known for a long time,[59] but not as strong as the lion, a novelty when compared to prior value systems. Honorius was the first writer to clearly assert the superiority of the lion over the bear: "What if the bear in turn were devoured by a lion?"[60] A lion was now able to defeat and devour a bear.

Never would a writer of antiquity, the High Middle Ages, or even around the year 1000 have written such a sentence. From time immemorial the bear had been invincible, as indeed had the lion. But the two animals, not frequenting the same geographic areas or the same realms of knowledge or the imagination, could hardly encounter much less confront one another. Christian theology had now decided otherwise. It had early on declared war on the bear, fought it on every field, devalued it in every domain, and then proclaimed the superiority of another beast that it had similarly hated in the past. For the Church in the early twelfth century, the bear was no longer the king of the beasts. The lion, even though not fully freed of its negative aspects (that would not come until the "invention" of the leopard a few decades later) had already seized the bear's throne.

III

THE BEAR DETHRONED
FROM THE LATE MIDDLE AGES
TO THE PRESENT

7

A Humiliated Animal

ALLEN from his throne, left out of Noah's Ark and princely menageries, forgotten by kings, replaced or overtaken by the lion, the bear
of the 1200s was no longer the invincible beast venerated by warriors and
hunters a few centuries earlier. He had almost become a wild animal like
the others, a "rather common beast," as books of venery later called him,
notably the one that Gaston Phébus compiled between 1385 and 1388.[1] In
many regions, bears still haunted forests, came into villages, stole honey
and chickens, and sometimes killed a few lambs, but they hardly frightened anyone any more. One could even see a bear wearing a muzzle,
dancing or doing tricks in a village square, forced to obey not saints or
heroes but a mere jongleur or a vulgar animal showman with a monkey
on his shoulder or hares popping out of his clothing.

Many documents attest to this swift and profound devaluation of the
bear at the turn of the thirteenth century. But one in particular brings out
better than any other the inoffensive and resigned, if not frankly coarse
and stupid, character that now belonged to the bear, while at the same
time discreetly recalling his old role as king of the beasts. This is a literary
text, or rather a set of literary texts, simultaneously homogeneous and
disparate, in which the characters are animals and the bear one of the
chief protagonists: the *Roman de Renart*.

A New Bestiary

For a historian of animals and of the systems of values that the central
Middle Ages conferred on them, the *Roman de Renart* is a particularly fertile field of inquiry, a veritable laboratory in whose byways it is worth
lingering. The set of animals presented in the various French branches of
the *Roman,* compiled between approximately 1175 and 1250, is not based

on an abundant and diversified fauna mixing wild and domestic animals, but makes up a carefully organized, selected, and hierarchical bestiary. Compared to other categories of texts or documents concerning or mentioning animals, this bestiary provides original information largely derived from secular culture. Written in the heart of the Middle Ages, it expressed a new way of looking, new sensibilities, and new meanings. Or rather, it expressed a way of looking and sensibilities that had previously remained in the shadows, obscured by the religious bestiary and religious symbolism, and later by the bestiary of emblems and coats of arms. Neither is at work in the *Roman de Renart*.

Unfortunately, specialists have paid little attention to this bestiary and this aspect of the work, because they have legitimately given priority to the difficult task of preparing editions of the texts making up the set of branches, as well as to questions of literary history, sources, revisions, imitations, and the study of language. Scholars have long debated whether these animal tales in the vernacular, to which thirteenth-century scribes sometimes gave the title *Roman de Renart*, were a product of learned or "popular" culture. In the Romantic period, the great Jakob Grimm looked for the sources of these texts in the oral traditions of primitive Germany and pointed out that the proper names given to most of the protagonists were of Germanic origin.[2] First of all was the name given the fox, the protagonist of the tales: *Reinhard* (or *Reginhard*)[3] passed into French in the form *Renart*, a proper name that became so proverbial that early on it was transformed into a common noun—*renard*—which replaced in common speech the old term for fox, *goupil,* derived from the Latin *vulpes*.[4] Gaston Paris later restored France as the place of origin of the *Roman* and emphasized its folk sources.[5] His student Léopold Sudre extended the study to animal tales from more distant cultures—Slavic, Scandinavian, Asian— and again emphasized the role of oral traditions that he wrongly identified as "popular collective creations."[6] But on the eve of the First World War, the thesis of Lucien Foulet produced a radical reversal and convincingly drew attention to the written sources and Latin precursors of the *Roman* (fables, fable collections, and animal stories composed in monasteries).[7] He pointed in particular to the role played by a long burlesque poem, *Ysengrimus,* written in Latin around 1150 by a monk in Ghent, that recounted the misadventures of the wolf and the fox.[8]

Today, although the theses of Lucien Foulet have been qualified, no specialist sees the *Roman de Renart* as a "popular" work. This is learned, sometimes very learned, literature, whose most direct sources are to be found in texts, not in oral transmission. Moreover, the authors of the various branches were all clerics and the fact that their language is sometimes foul and their satiric verve increasingly grating from branch to branch and decade after decade does not mean that this was literature that came from the people or was written for the people. Quite the opposite. The language of the *Roman de Renart* is a difficult language distinct from the language of the jongleurs and even more from that of the villeins.[9] It remains to determine who was the intended audience for this literature, why it was so widely diffused throughout Europe in the late Middle Ages and early modern period, and how it ended up constituting a common fund of themes and motifs (literary, as well as iconographic, emblematic, and proverbial) despite the relatively small number of surviving manuscripts—very few in comparison to those of the *Roman de la Rose* or of Arthurian literature.

Returning to the animals, if all the branches of the *Roman de Renart* are taken into consideration, their number is high but not unlimited, and only fifteen or twenty animals play major roles. In this list, there is a mixture both wild and domestic, indigenous and exotic, companions of men and feared by men. But these are modern categories that should not be projected as such onto medieval documents, at least not without taking precautions. I have pointed out that the lion, although not indigenous to Europe, was nonetheless part of daily life in feudal society. The notion of "exotic" species in the current sense was not always pertinent in the Christian West of the twelfth and thirteenth centuries. The same holds true even more strongly for the notion of "domestic" animal. In the usage and taxonomies of this period, "domestic" *(domestica)* refers to all the animals living in and around the house *(domus):* not only dogs, horses, oxen, pigs, and all those we now consider domestic, but also foxes, weasels, crows, blackbirds, magpies, mice, moles, hedgehogs, and others that were all familiar in the house, on the farm, in the garden, or in the henhouse. The word "familiar" is no doubt the one that best translates the Latin word *domesticus*.[10] It should also be recalled that some animals we cherish today may have been disliked, rejected, or despised in the feudal period. For example, cats did not enter houses and become human companions before the late Middle Ages when, after the great epidemics of plague in the fourteenth century, it was discovered that they were more effective than weasels to drive out rats and mice.[11] Earlier, cats were disliked, and the cat in the *Roman de Renart,* Tibert, a sly and slippery feline who is still very wild, is sometimes as cunning as Renart, or even clearly diabolical.[12]

Almost all the animals of farm, fields, and woods are found in this selective bestiary. But birds are less numerous than quadrupeds, and fish and reptiles are excluded (at least as characters). The great absent figure is the eagle, a prime figure in religious and emblematic bestiaries of the time. Its absence is hard to interpret. Was it too great a rival for the lion, since it could also claim the title of king of the beasts? What role might have been attributed to it in this animal society in which each one occupies a precise place and function? Where should it be situated hierarchically in relation to the lion (the king), the bear (sometimes the vice-king), the wolf (the constable), the stag (the steward), the donkey (the archpriest), the boar, the rooster, and even the dog and cat (all great barons), or the modest snail (the standard-bearer)?

Indeed, the animals of the *Roman de Renart* are not only animals. They are also characters and "types": allegorical and moral types, but social types above all.[13] They represent feudal society, with a king at its head, its court, clergy, and barons, with the minor characters representing the people. Renart himself is the embodiment of a minor rebel lord, who is very individualistic and does not respect the rules of customary law. Indeed, he sets himself outside any hierarchical relationship of loyalty as a vassal. His den is both a real den that he shares in part with his cousin Grimbert, the badger, and an authentic fortified castle, the impregnable castle of Maupertuis, where he takes refuge with his family when he is threatened. Among the animals that can also be understood as masks, that is, as disguised humans,[14] the principal ones are strongly individualized with a proper name, a title or a function, family relationships, and character traits that reappear from one branch to another of the *Roman*. In this society, where improbabilities are not unusual—the rooster kills a buffalo, the wolf and the sheep are friends, the fox wants to devour the crow—real men (peasants, hunters, priests, monks) are also present and deal with these more or less humanized animals. Yet, and this is the magic of the work, both the medieval and the modern reader feel perfectly at home in that world.

The Wolf, the Lion, and the Fox

Although they were all compiled by clerics, the various branches of the *Roman de Renart* expressed not so much a clerical or monastic imagination as a secular and rural imagination. The bestiary they offered was not that of church or monastery, even less that of court and city, but rather that of village and countryside, revised and supplemented by book learning. In this way, the *Roman* contributed to the cultural history of animals a good deal of new information more in touch with real practices and beliefs than those transmitted by works of theology, hagiographical narratives, or epic literature. In this regard the example of the wolf is remarkable. For exegesis and religious symbolism, Latin bestiaries, and encyclopedias, the wolf was a fearsome animal that threatened and devoured men. In the *Roman de Renart,* in contrast, Isengrin is a stupid and laughable animal, blinded by anger and resentment, always ready to fall into the traps the fox sets for him. He is a victim, constantly humiliated, mystified, wounded, and beaten, but a victim who hardly inspires pity because he is always in a ridiculous position. This presentation of a wolf mocked by everyone was not, as is often thought, a protective reaction, but the image of a certain reality. There was little fear of the wolf in the countryside in the twelfth and thirteenth centuries, at least in the West. That did not come until the late Middle Ages and even more in modern times. Fear of the wolf, a major factor in peasant sensibility, is linked to crisis periods (climatic, agricultural, social), not to times of economic prosperity or demographic expansion.[15] It was not accidental that the story of the beast of the Gévaudan took place in the France of the eighteenth not the thirteenth century. In the French countryside in the feudal period, people feared the Devil, dragons, the Wild Hunt, and night hunting, but not really the wolf.[16] This is fully confirmed by the *Roman de Renart*.

On another level, the work features an animal that had previously been a rather discreet presence in theological treatises, works of zoology, and literary texts: the fox. Only ancient fables had given it a prominent role in the animal repertory. It is probable that this new, or renewed, attention to the fox was in response to a fact of rural life, perhaps connected to recent clearances, the conquest of new territories, the creation of villages, and the dispersal of habitat. Foxes were part of daily life, stayed close to the farm, made visits to the garden and the henhouse, and were harmful to everyone. At the scale of the village, the fox was the image of the Evil One. Peasants tried to fight against its misdeeds, and petty lords liked to hunt it if they were unable to go after bigger game.

But more remarkable than the portrayal of the fox and the wolf is that of the lion. Representations of lions were not more or less realistic accounts of country life but rather cultural documents. In the *Roman*, animals that do not belong to the local fauna are rare: the lion, the leopard, the camel, and the monkey.[17] Although any peasant could see them painted or sculpted in his parish church, they represent the slender contribution from books, or from dreams, to a bestiary that came primarily from fields, woods, and farm. Among these nonindigenous animals, the *Roman de Renart* chose its king: the lion. In doing so it once again showed itself to be in touch with recent history, learned history this time, because it was in the twelfth century that the Church had definitively installed the lion in place of the bear on the animal throne. In the *Roman*, the bear appears diminished compared to the lion, although in a late branch of the Dutch version, the bear still timidly plays the role of vice-king.[18]

The lion, however, is every inch a king. He was already that in the Latin *Ysengrimus*, composed a generation before the first branches of *Renart*. There he was named *Rufinus*, in reference to the reddish *(rufus)* or tawny color of his coat.[19] But he was not yet a king in Aesop's fables or in their oldest adaptations in vernacular languages. It was thus toward the middle of the twelfth century that medieval literature for the first time made the lion the king of the beasts.

In the *Roman de Renart*, the lion is not named *Rufinus* or *Rufin*, the vernacular equivalent, but *Noble*, a much more flattering term. Aware of his royal prerogatives, concerned with his duties, the lion exercises his office with majesty and authority. His primary activity is to dispense justice and to ensure respect for the law in order to maintain peace among his subjects (a difficult task) and guarantee them a degree of well-being. Of course, the lion-king does not have only positive qualities—he is sometimes vain, irascible, vindictive—but he is a just and good-natured sovereign, often conciliatory, always skillful, and even subtle. He seems to have a weakness for Renart, although the fox is a fractious and perverse vassal who both amuses and annoys him. Further, while in many respects Noble is still a feudal king, surrounded by barons from whom he must take counsel, he is also an image of the contemporary king of France, a monarch whose powers were growing in scope and who was seeking to reduce those of the overly powerful lords. He draws them to his court, makes them his principal officers, puts himself forward as the arbiter of all conflicts, appoints ambassadors, summons the army, and makes war. With the lioness, Madame Fière, he forms a respected couple, although she, younger than her husband, is proud, fickle, and unfaithful (she has Renart as a lover in several episodes), like the Queen Guinevere of the Arthurian romances.

Some scholars have seen in King Noble not a lion but "an idealized form of dog."[20] This interpretation seems hardly plausible and is even anachronistic. For one thing, there are several dogs among the other characters of the *Roman*—notably Roonel, one of the barons of the court—and their role is not particularly emphasized. Moreover, King Noble has all the attributes of a lion in his physical appearance, his character, and his conduct. Any literary work is always the child of its time, and when the various branches of the *Roman* were compiled, everything conspired to make the lion the king of the beasts. This was not at all true of the dog, an animal in no way remarkable at the time, either in daily life or in imagination.

The Fall of a King

The portrayal of the bear in the *Roman de Renart* also belongs to the new systems of value of animal symbolism emerging in the late twelfth and early thirteenth century. He had irremediably descended from his throne, on which the lion was seated for a long time to come. But while the *Roman* provides solid evidence of this devaluation of the bear, desired and carried out by the Church, it also to a great extent helped to accentuate and even accelerate it, and then to transform it into a genuine fall that quickly spread to other areas of secular literature and learning. With regard to the cultural history of the bear in Western Europe, there is a "before" the *Roman de Renart*, and there is an "after."

The bear of the *Renart*, present in all the principal branches, the protagonist of several of them, has the name *Brun*, probably in reference to the color of his fur. Similarly, the squirrel is named *Rousseau*, the boar *Beaucent*, and the vixen *Hermeline*, all names that in one way or another evoke the coats of those animals. But it is possible that the name *Brun*, which was already given to the bear in some predecessors of *Renart* written in German-language countries, was chosen for other, more learned reasons, and that it is merely the French version of the given name *Bruno*, well attested in the countries of the Holy Roman Empire and often given to the great bishops who belonged to the Ottonian imperial family. The bear of the *Roman* and the animal tales that preceded it sometimes plays the role of a chaplain or a prelate. This may be a distorted memory or a satirical image of one of the bishops named Bruno.[21] The sources of the *Roman de Renart* were not only literature and folklore, but history as well.[22]

That said, in the various branches, Brun the bear is not always a chaplain or a prelate. He is also one of the principal barons of King Noble, sometimes replacing him when he is absent. He is usually the one the king sends on embassies, whom he consults in his council, or to whom he imprudently entrusts a battle group of the royal army. But while the bear's titles and functions are diverse, his character traits are stable from branch to branch, perhaps more stable than those of any other character.

Unfortunately for him, they are anything but flattering traits. The bear of the *Roman de Renart* is a stupid animal, ridiculous, humiliated, a constant victim of the fox, and an object of contempt and derision from the other animals. No branch brings to the fore his proverbial strength, his legendary courage, or his invincible nature.[23] All that has gone. His character is made up of purely negative aspects, and these are what were retained by posterity, sometimes completely obscuring the old qualities of the implacable and royal bear. Thereafter, in fables as in proverbs and images, the bear was usually a coarse, solitary, irascible, and stupid creature.

The only quality of Brun in the *Roman* is his unconditional fidelity to King Noble. Otherwise, he is portrayed as a collection of defects and vices. To start with, there is his love of eating, not to say gluttony. Brun is willing to do anything for a little honey, and that is what leads him into many of his scrapes. Then he is naïve, or even foolish. The bear is presented as one of the most witless of the lion's vassals and subjects. With his heavy body and slow-moving mind, he can do nothing against the keenness of the fox, the cleverness of the cat, or the wisdom of the stag. Even worse, he is obstinate and fixed in his thinking. That makes him litigious and resentful, obsessed like the wolf—of whom he sometimes seems to be a double—by the fact that Renart escapes punishment. Finally, and this is one of the most original traits the *Roman* attributes to the bear, Brun is fearful and sensitive. He faints on learning overly painful news and is afraid of everything, particularly villeins and hunters, whom he flees or hides from. In previous literary texts and oral traditions, bears never fled and were never afraid, but fought face to face until death. The *Roman de Renart* inaugurated the theme of the fearful bear, who flees from hunters, peasants, dogs, and many other animals.

Several branches add to this negative moral portrait an unflattering physical image. Brun is obese, clumsy, awkward; he has trouble moving, cannot run, and, in several episodes, gets stuck in a split tree trunk or at the bottom of a ditch. For medieval sensibilities, being unable to get loose, being blocked or stuck was a ridiculous situation, perhaps quintessentially ridiculous, even more degrading when it was put on show, as in a pillory. This happens to the bear on several occasions, and not only when he is in flight or a victim of the fox's tricks. In a late branch preserved in only one manuscript, *Renart magicien*, ridicule turns into shame and becomes scatological: during a banquet presided over by the king and queen featuring a contest in which each animal has to show what he can do, Brun offers to dance and do acrobatics; but his first somersault turns into a brutal fall followed by a particularly noisy fart that humiliates him in front of the entire court. "A fine tumble the tumble by the one who plays the trumpet with his bottom as he executes it," ironically comments Queen Fière, whom he was trying to seduce.[24] The dishonor is absolute.

The Death of the Bear

In some episodes humiliation is joined by mutilation, a frequent theme throughout the *Roman*. The bear is not its only victim: Isengrin, Renart, and Tibert lose their tails, Roonel an ear, and Brichemer his antlers. Sometimes they suffer more or less serious wounds inflicted by dogs or villeins, sometimes the fox himself mutilates his enemies, as when Isengrin has to leave his tail in a frozen pond, or Tibert his in a chest that Renart suddenly slams shut. On another occasion, pretending to be a doctor, Renart cuts up the wolf and the stag supposedly to treat the lion with their skin.[25] But the mutilations suffered by the bear are more severe: Brun is the only one to be truly scalped.

This takes place in the first branch, the most well known, devoted to Renart's trial. The rooster Chantecler has told Noble and the court how Renart had slaughtered his sister, the hen Coupée, and her entire family. Brun is sent to Maupertuis to bring back the fox, who has been summoned to appear. But on the way Renart explains to Brun that he knows a place where you can get honey. The always gluttonous bear is eager to get there. The fox leads him to a split oak on which woodsmen have set two wedges to keep the parts separated. Renart tells Brun the honey is behind the tree. As soon as Brun has stuck his snout and his front paws through the gap, Renart removes the wedges. The branches close up and the bear is caught. After crying out in vain and then falling asleep, he is surprised in that uncomfortable and ridiculous position by peasants, who try to kill him. After desperate efforts, Brun manages to get loose, but leaves behind in the tree the skin from his head and his front paws. Later, in his flight, he suffers the brutality of a priest and the sarcasms of Renart, who, seeing his bloody head, asks him what monastic order he belongs to with his "red hood"—an irony again pointing to the link between the bear and the clergy. Brun finally reaches the court where, exhausted, humiliated, mutilated, he faints. The other animals make fun of him: never had they seen such a horrible animal.[26]

Isengrin is the only one who suffers an even more frightful mutilation, castration. The scene is not directly described but narrated by Renart to his wife Hermeline. He has made the wolf lose his genitals—the text does not say how—and the wolf can no longer have sexual relations with the she-wolf; Hermeline laughs at the tale.[27] The *Roman* never visits a similar fate on Brun, but a little-known bawdy tale from the 1240s inspired by one of the late branches of the *Renart* describes how a bear has himself voluntarily castrated by a peasant, "in order to be as strong as an ox," and offers in exchange to perform the same service for the man the next day. The peasant agrees, to get rid of the animal. His wife shows up the next day and explains—showing the bear the evidence—that he / she is already castrated, and the bear believes her.[28] In this tale he no longer has anything of the fearsome beast, but resembles the Brun of the *Roman de Renart*. He is a naïve and stupid animal who never frightens anyone and has even lost his legendary strength, because he wants to become "as strong as an ox." Toward the middle of the thirteenth century, the bear in *Renart,* slow and heavy in body and mind, victim of his gluttony and stupidity, a whipping-boy for men and other animals, had become a kind of archetype or model frequently imitated by other texts featuring other bears.

But humiliation and castration are nothing, or not much, in comparison to what happens to Brun in the branch of the *Roman* traditionally given the title *Renart et le vilain Liétard.*[29] Written around 1200 by an author who says he is a "priest from La Croix-en-Brie," it is from the literary point of view one of the best written and most original branches, involving only four characters: the bear, the fox, a rich peasant, and his wife.

One day working in the fields, a villein named Liétard gets angry at

Rougel, one of his eight oxen, whom he considers lazy. He curses him and goes so far as to hope a bear devours him. Brun, who is lurking in the area, hears Liétard's words. He takes them literally and immediately offers to devour the ox his master wished dead. Terrified, Liétard tries to gain time, argues, quibbles, and suggests the bear come for the ox the next day. Brun agrees and leaves. While he is bemoaning the fate of his poor Rougel, the peasant sees Renart approaching; hidden in a thicket, he has seen and heard everything. He offers to help Liétard deceive the bear if he gives Renart his rooster Blanchard in exchange. The agreement is made, and Renart explains his plan: when Brun comes to get the ox, Renart, hidden in the nearby wood, will imitate the noise of a hunt and thereby frighten the bear, who will try to hide. Liétard, well armed, will take advantage of this to kill him. This is exactly what happens the next day. When Brun comes to get what he is owed, Renart, "expert in the art of sounding the horn and hallooing," makes an unholy uproar in the neighboring wood. Liétard explains it is a bear hunt organized by "the formidable Count Thibaud," a great hunter and enemy of bears. He advises Brun to hide in a newly plowed wide furrow. The bear, not very reassured, does so. Immediately Liétard stuns him with an ax and cuts his throat with a huge knife. When night falls, with the help of his wife and son, he carries the bear carcass home, cuts it into pieces, and salts it. The peasant profits doubly, because his ox is safe and the threatening bear has been turned into an abundant supply of meat for the winter. Liétard even saves his rooster. When Renart comes to claim his reward, the villein pretends to have forgotten their agreement and, encouraged by his wife, who is even more treacherous than he, lets loose his dogs and forces the fox to run away. Wounded, deceived by someone slyer than he, Renart takes refuge in Maupertuis and decides to exact revenge.[30]

At first sight, the episode, which continues with Renart's vengeance and victory, seems relatively anodyne, facetious and mocking, faithful to the spirit and the framework of the first branches of the *Roman*. But it differs in the death of one of the protagonists, and not the least of them: Brun, the most loyal of King Noble's courtiers, his first baron and advisor, sometimes his chaplain, often his ambassador. In the entire work, the bear is the only major character who dies. This happens in a manner that is far from royal or princely. It is a miserable end for an animal who was once admired, venerated, and confronted in single combat by the boldest kings and warriors, who were all "as strong as bears."

At the turn of the twelfth and thirteenth centuries, this death of the bear in *Renart* was not merely anecdotal, and not devoid of significance. On the contrary, it was a symbolic disappearance showing that the old bear, king of the beasts, had definitively ceased to exist and had given way to a clumsy, naïve, and ridiculous animal. The death of Brun, recounted by a minor priest from Brie, is one of the first pieces of literary evidence for this, and it was deliberately grotesque. The wild beast that was once known as the ancestor or the cousin of man, who abducted and raped young women to found dynasties, who was an object of worship and of ancient beliefs, is not killed in heroic battle but in a cowardly way, with his throat slit in the furrow of a field, and then turned into game and salted away to be used as winter food for the greedy family of a coarse and wily peasant. It is difficult to imagine a more ignoble end for the former king of the beasts.

A Circus Animal

From the beginning of the thirteenth century, the time of the bear's majesty was finished. The wild beast was humiliated not just in fables and animal tales, but in other literary texts, proverbs, images, and even in daily life. Bears could be seen in fairs and marketplaces, chained, muzzled, dancing or performing pitiful acrobatic tricks, accompanying jongleurs and tumblers, following their orders like sad, resigned clowns. A collar and chain prevented the bear from escaping, the muzzle kept it from biting, dogs no longer feared it, and even children could come close to defy, touch, and tease it, or, less often, feed it and feel pity for it. Only young women had to keep some distance. Not because there was any danger of the animal breaking his chain to capture them, violate them, or run off with them, but rather because the sexual desire that traditionally drew the bear to the woman was seen as a reciprocal desire. Seeing a male bear too close up, even if he were chained, might awaken in girls and young women a kind of bestial and repressed lust. It was better to keep them at a distance from the beast, even though he had become an inoffensive instrument for a miserable animal showman.

Here again, the Church was partly responsible for this decline. Although it had always been hostile to animal shows, although theologians since the days of primitive Christianity had condemned all the games and practices that associated men and animals in a single ritual, and although some bishops and abbots even denounced the use of names, insignia, clothing, or disguises taken from the animal world, a degree of tolerance gradually grew up toward bear handlers. Anything was appropriate to desacralize the indigenous great beast and put an end to the bear cults that still existed. Allowing the faithful to contemplate a solidly chained bear obeying grotesque characters, sometimes performing crude acrobatics, spinning in circles, trying to walk on his hands, collapsing, groaning, provoking laughter and mockery from the audience, all taken together could not fail to devalue and hold up to ridicule an animal that had once been venerated. So the Church tolerated these spectacles. Taking advantage of this unexpected indulgence, bear handlers proliferated starting in the twelfth century, first in mountain regions, where bear cubs were numerous and easy to capture, then in the late Middle Ages and the early modern period in all areas, especially where bears were no longer physically present.

But these animal showmen belonged to a particularly despised social category, connected to the motley world of *joculatores* and *histriones*, that is, the jongleurs, tumblers, and conjurors, wanderers who put on shows and expected a recompense. They profited both from the credulity of the public and the possible generosity of the petty lords they amused or to whom they brought news. Their activities were so varied that it is almost impossible to establish a typology or even a simple list of them. Some were mere mimes and entertainers, playing the clown, telling jokes, imitating famous people, making fun of everything and everyone, including themselves: these were the jongleurs. Others danced and performed acrobatics or contortions, often with the help of a stick *(bâton)*, hence the name *bateleur* (tumbler). Still others played an instrument, sang, and recited fables and tales, sometimes taking their stories from hagiography or epic. Many also performed tricks and feats of prestidigitation, stole objects, pulled animals from their hats or clothing, abused and amused their audience, and sometimes used the opportunity to rob them.[31] Others, finally, exhibited odd, funny, or learned animals. Among them, bear handlers enjoyed some prestige, at least more than leaders of monkeys and dogs or conjurors with hares and squirrels.

One might note in passing that all these animals were great reprobates to which bestiaries and encyclopedias attributed negative symbolism. The dog was less a faithful human companion than a vile and impure creature. The hare, which was thought to be a hermaphrodite in the Middle Ages, was the perfect image of exacerbated or even deviant sexuality. The monkey, even more abominable, represented the quintessentially diabolical animal. He was hypocritical, deceptive, obscene, and frighteningly ugly. As for the squirrel, he was not the charming, happy, and playful animal we know. Medieval culture thought of him as "the monkey of the forest,"[32] and he had the reputation of being lazy, lubricious, stupid, and greedy. The bulk of his time was spent sleeping, teasing his companions, playing, and cavorting in the trees. Besides, he stored much more food than he needed—a very grave sin—and he didn't even remember his hiding places—a sign of great foolishness. In addition, his red coat was the external sign of this evil nature.[33]

Performers who traveled from fair to fair with animals like this could only be seen themselves as maleficent creatures. Monks and prelates accused them not only of being liars, cheaters, thieves, lazy, and drunken—relatively common misbehavior for marginal figures and commoners—but also of being unattached, free, vagabonds, of earning money easily without really working, by gesticulating, mocking, or joking, and above all by exhibiting vile animals. Associating the bear with them therefore effectively helped to devalue the animal and, through a kind of osmosis, to project onto him all the vices imputed to his masters and companions in misfortune. Only his great size and anthropomorphic aspect conferred on him a certain superiority, or at least stimulated greater curiosity in the public. In the thirteenth and fourteenth centuries, there was not much of an audience for monkeys, hares, or squirrels, even if they were more or less "wise"; curiosity had faded. But audiences did gather to see a bear who could stand, climb on a beam, do somersaults, and try to learn the alphabet.

More than archive documents and better than literary texts or chronicles, images help the historian to grasp the different stages of this transformation of the king of the forest into an animal of fairs and marketplaces. In illuminated books in particular, the illuminated letters and miniatures show that this devaluation, rarely attested before the year 1000, became more frequent toward the end of the eleventh century,[34] then became general a century later. Thereafter it was rare to come across a bear not provided with a collar, a chain, and a muzzle. Of course, the animal did not always perform tricks or acrobatics, but he was no longer free and wild. He obeyed a master, a jongleur or a tumbler, and ended up as one of their iconographic attributes. Sculpture confirms the evidence of illuminated books. It was in the course of the twelfth century that the bear ceased to be a fearsome beast and gradually became a circus animal. He started to appear standing, contorting himself, holding himself upside down, head down, forepaws on the ground and rear paws in the air. Sometimes he is wearing a blindfold or seems to have been blinded. But unlike the donkey or the pig, the bear never appears as an animal musician, even though, because of his remarkably sharp hearing, he was thought to have a close connection to music. When he danced to the sound of an instrument, it was always played by a man, never by another bear, nor in fact by any other animal.

Starting in the thirteenth century, a relatively frequent theme in iconography was the *ours bêté* (baited bear). This strange expression turns up in literary texts, where it is difficult to interpret. It is easier to understand in images. It is a captive bear chained to a solid post, his head enclosed in a muzzle, who is attacked by several dogs who wound him, sometimes mortally, with their repeated biting. This violent image seems to represent a real practice, a spectacle the public was fond of. I related earlier the fate of the bear King William of England gave to the lord of Ardres in the late eleventh century: it was lacerated and killed by the dogs belonging to the residents of the town.[35] This is the oldest evidence of that cruel custom, which was not confined to fairgrounds and village squares, but was also practiced within the walls of châteaus. The author of the chanson de geste *Renaut de Montauban*, who wrote in the second half of the thirteenth century, tells, for example, how Count Aymon de Dordonne has "ses urs combattre et ses grans ors beter" (his bears fight and his great bears baited).[36] The practice of baiting bears had a long life, since bearbaiting is mentioned by Froissart in the late fourteenth century.[37] It is also pictured in the marginal ornaments of several French and English illuminated manuscripts of the fourteenth and fifteenth centuries.[38]

From Oafishness to Melancholy

The Middle Ages did not invent games and spectacles featuring bears. They were frequent in ancient Rome, especially from the last century of the Republic on. In the circus arena, bears were practically invincible, especially the giant bears imported from Caledonia (Scotland), Dalmatia, and the Carpathians. They did not fight against each other but against bulls, lions, or specialized gladiators assisted by dogs. Outside the arena, mere exhibitions replaced combat. But bears did not perform dances or acrobatics, as they did starting in the twelfth and thirteenth centuries. Nor did they get up on platforms or stools, but remained locked behind bars or isolated at the bottom of a ditch. The Roman audience came to see wild and dangerous animals, remarkable for their size, their strength, or their coats. The performing carnival bear was a creation of medieval Christendom.

The Christian emperors were in fact the first to limit and then ban circus games where, according to Tertullian, who exaggerates a bit, one could see "entrails of the . . . bears loaded with human viscera."[39] In 326, Constantine issued an edict forbidding the penalty of *damnatio ad bestias,* and in 404 Emperor Honorius abolished all gladiatorial combat. But we owe to the medieval Church the abolition of battles between animals, which were considered spectacles.[40] Starting in the ninth century, the Church prohibited all forms of "games with bears"[41] and tolerated them only in menageries, and even there with some reluctance. Although these prohibitions had to be repeated many times before they were respected, the bear's prestige suffered from them. As time passed, he had fewer and fewer occasions to demonstrate his strength and superiority over all other animals. In the ancient arenas, he triumphed over other wild animals, including the lion, at least in single combat. But in medieval churches and abbeys, the rivalry between bear and lion was no longer a physical rivalry, but a learned, bookish, iconographic, and symbolic opposition. The bear could not win at this game because the clergy wanted the lion's victory and used all the means at their disposal to help it along. If the public in the feudal era had really had the opportunity to witness a physical confrontation between a bear and a lion, it is probable that the bear would have been the victor. In that event, Brun would have occupied Noble's throne in the *Roman de Renart,* and the chief animal in the heraldic bestiary would have been the bear, not the lion. Moreover, no writer would have dared, like Honorius in his *Elucidarium,* to suggest that lions could devour bears. But that was not the case, even though some chansons de geste and chivalric romances of the late twelfth century still mention an enigmatic game "of bears and lions."[42] What was involved was probably not, as some scholars have thought, battles between real bears and lions, organized as spectacles to divert an aristocratic public eager to see flesh and blood animals in combat, but rather tournaments in which, in a confused and violent melee, two groups of knights in two camps confronted one another, each distinguished by a zoomorphic name or insignia: bears and lions. Once again, wild animal reality had given way to a staging of emblems and symbols.

A few decades later, the bear was no longer associated with anything kingly or even lordly. Alive, the great beast was reduced to exhibiting itself in fairgrounds and market squares, where it demonstrated that it was not strong and courageous but slow-witted and clumsy. It was asked to violate its nature, to spin in circles, dance, waddle, walk on its hands, and balance on a ball or a board. It was not made for this kind of exercise and could only show itself to be inept and clumsy, often falling, always groaning, and hence provoking laughter and sarcasm. This image of the graceless, clumsy bear did the species considerable harm, and, in the thirteenth and fourteenth centuries, almost became an archetypal image. Bears could only be awkward, ill-at-ease, clumsy. The larger and stronger they were, the more they aped humans, the more intense was the pleasure of the audience and the ridiculousness of the animals.

There is only one step from awkwardness to foolishness. And that step was swiftly taken in the late twelfth century, as shown by the oldest branches of the *Roman de Renart* and, a few decades later, in fables, proverbs, and images. One theme recurred often: the bear trying to learn the letters of the alphabet and practicing reading, an impossible task that became proverbial and was staged to express the idea of vain and absurd conduct. In the satirical images of the late Middle Ages, trying to teach a bear to read was as aberrant as shoeing geese, or as absurd as a one-legged man chasing a hare. These three scenes were sometimes painted together in marginal decorations of illuminated manuscripts or carved on the misericords of church choir stalls, along with other proverbs mocking unreasonable activities: feeding crows or putting pants on donkeys. The bear was heavy and clumsy in body, therefore heavy and slow in spirit. It could never learn to read.

It is striking that this devaluation of the bear, linked to its weight and corpulence, took place at a time—the turn of the twelfth and thirteenth centuries—when in systems of value concerning the human body, obesity was becoming a sin, particularly for kings and princes, if not for priests.[43] A century earlier, a monarch or a great lord was still held in high regard if he was big and fat. Several Western kings were obese: in France, Henri I, Philippe I, Louis VI le Gros; in England, William the Conqueror, William the Red, Henry I; in Germany, Emperors Henry IV and Henry V. Their obesity did no damage to their prestige. But beginning in the 1200s the glorious image of the corpulent king was finished. From then on, a monarch worthy of the name was expected to be svelte, slender, and temperate in the pleasures of food and drink—Saint Louis in the thirteenth century was a perfect example. Obesity had become incompatible with nobility of body and spirit, and even with a noble heart and ethics, and this lasted for several centuries. A kind of "antifat" sectarianism is rooted in this period, at least in the West. Being obese from then on meant being ugly, vulgar, lazy, uneducated, and stupid. The few counterexamples only confirmed this grim rule, or were highly exceptional cases. The best known was Saint Thomas Aquinas, "the fattest man who ever was," according to one of his biographers,[44] but also one of the greatest theologians of all time.

It is thus possible that somewhere between 1180 and 1200 the bear's corpulence damaged him and helped deprive him of his title as king of the beasts. The supple and agile body of the lion was more fitting for that role. For the same reasons, it could never be assumed by the elephant, despite all the virtues attributed to him by bestiaries and animal symbolism: chastity, fidelity, generosity, intelligence, memory. As for the bear's clumsiness, particularly visible when he was forced to ape men, at best it could make him a priest fond of eating—which is what he often is in the *Roman de Renart*—at worst, and more often, a buffoon, etymologically a creature who was bloated *(bouffi)*, full of hot air and futility.[45] This is what the bear became from the thirteenth century on, at least from the point of view of the men who had captured and chained him. But this transformation of the former king of the beasts into a circus animal, or even a ridiculous entertainer, perhaps did not occur without a certain feeling of guilt. In the late Middle Ages, and in modern times, many writers and artists, as they represent the comical character of the bear, cannot help but point to his resignation, suffering, and sadness.

By dethroning and desacralizing the bear, medieval Christendom made him a melancholy animal, perhaps the quintessentially melancholic animal, and hence—disregarding the anachronism—a sort of romantic hero. After removing the bear from his throne, the Church in the thirteenth century hounded him, and ended up attributing to him all vices, if not all sins.

A Vicious Creature

In the Middle Ages, moral theology carefully distinguished vice from sin. The former was rooted in the very nature of the individual concerned. It was hard for him to repress and control it, and even more to free himself from it. Sin, in contrast, arose from free and voluntary conduct (even though sometimes inspired by the Devil). It was an offense against God; given the will, one should be able to refrain from sin, correct oneself, or, in case of failure, confess. Hence, sinning was more serious than being endowed by nature with any particular vice, although the boundary between the two realms was not always well defined and sin was often presented as the consequence of vice.

Sin was long an act limited to men and women; animals, exempt from original sin, did not sin, did not commit offenses against God. They were merely imperfect creatures, who were more or less vicious, more or less "filled with vices," as Augustine says *("animalia vitiis contenta")*,[46] depending on species. It was not until the thirteenth century that theology, followed by law, began to look at some "superior" animals as moral and perfectible beings, able to understand good and evil, and that could therefore, individually and under certain conditions, be brought before a court, imprisoned, tried, and punished because they had committed crimes or sins. In 1254, for example, a sow in a village north of Paris, a dependency of Saint-Martin-des-Champs, was tried, hanged, and burned for having knocked down, killed, and half-eaten a young child. To the crime was added a sin against the law of God and the Church: not only had it committed infanticide, but it had consumed its terrible meal on Friday, a fast day.[47]

For the Church Fathers and the theologians of the High Middle Ages, the bear was a creature inhabited by many vices, perhaps more than any other animal. Since he was the king of the forest, the king of the pagan bestiary of Germanic, Celtic, Slavic, and Scandinavian Europe, it was necessary to attribute almost all the vices to him to bring him down from his throne. There was indeed a long list of vices attributed to him by the Patristic writings, the penitentials, and works of zoology. All of them focus on the notions of violence *(violentia)*, anger *(ira)*, wild fury *(furor)*, cruelty *(saevitia)*, voracity *(voracitas)*, and rapaciousness *(rapacitas)*. The bear was the strongest of all animals, but his strength was evil and it made him fearsome, dangerous, violent, and unpredictable. Everyone ought to be afraid of him, run from him, or put him to death.

Later, around the year 1000, the bear was more directly associated with the Devil, of whom he gradually became an emblem, a tool, or a disguise. Thereafter, the vices monks and priests attributed to him were not just physical, but also moral: deceit *(fraus)*, lust *(libido)*, gluttony *(gula)*, sloth *(acedia)*, and loss of self-control *(intemperantia)*. The bear was not yet committing sin, in the Christian sense of the word, but his vices were presented as tendencies to do evil, repeatedly and almost consciously. A remarkable example taken from the dual series of vices, ancient and modern, was provided by Peter Damian, one of the precursors of the great reform of the Church in the mid-eleventh century. In his treatise *De bono religiosi status*, compiled around 1060, he denounces forty-one vices that stain human existence, and associates each of these vices with one or more animals. The bear is separated into male and female, the former embodying *furor,* that is, violence, anger, and wild, uncontrolled strength, while the latter embodies *libido,* that is, sexual appetite. Following many other writers, Peter Damian explains why the female bear gives birth much too soon to unshaped and almost stillborn cubs. It is because while she is pregnant, the male does not want to cover her; the she-bear, who likes nothing better than fornication, hurries to get rid of her offspring and goes in search of the male. She is a bad mother. However, seeing the state in which her cubs are born, she repents, forgets her sexual appetites, licks and warms her cubs to give them shape and restore them to life.[48]

The same idea appeared a century later in the work of Hildegard of Bingen (1098–1179). In various writings, notably the *Physica,*[49] the great Benedictine abbess speaks copiously about animals, their properties, their mores, and their meaning. The bear is one of the major figures in her bestiary. He is in her view an ambivalent animal, as shown by the female who revives her cubs after having expelled them from her womb before the proper date. The male is a solitary being, sometimes peaceable and taciturn, sometimes violent and angry, depending on how well his mother licked him when he was a cub. But it is better to keep away from him, especially if you are a girl or a young woman, because he is unpredictable and a lover of female flesh. Indeed, Hildegard sees the bear primarily as a harmful and fearsome animal, whose principal vices are anger (ira), lust (libido), and, a novelty compared to her predecessors, treachery (perfidia).[50]

A curious allegorical poem composed between 1235 and 1240 presents the vice of treachery alone to discredit the bear: the *Tournoiement Anté-christ* by Huon de Méry.[51] We know nothing of the author, except what he tells us in his poem. He describes himself as a poor knight from the Beau-vaisis who, to fulfill his feudal obligations, has had to join the royal army at war with Pierre Mauclerc, Duke of Brittany. In the course of this expe-dition, Huon, who had read a good deal of Chrétien de Troyes, claims to have traveled through the famous and mysterious forest of Brocéliande and to have drunk from the equally famous fountain of Barenton. After having drunk, he went through a terrible storm, then had a vision: two armies about to clash, the army of God and the army of the Antichrist. In the former were the angels, archangels, virtues, and several knights of the Round Table (who fought very badly and almost caused the defeat of the divine army). In the latter were the pagan gods (primarily those of Greco-Roman mythology), numerous vices, half-wild peasants, and "Bourguignons." The battle is akin to a Psychomachia, an epic battle of good against evil, virtues against vices, themes cherished by the literature and iconography of the first half of the thirteenth century.

More than the battles themselves, the author dwells on descriptions of the fighters' equipment, mainly the shields, banners, gonfalons, and horses' coverings. His heraldic knowledge enables him to attribute to each vice and each virtue several symbolic figures and colors.[52] The shields of the vices are particularly interesting. Gluttony sports an entirely red shield, "devoured by gules"; pride bears the same shield but decorated with a lion rampant "with an insolent tail"; adultery holds a shield show-ing the door of a brothel; sloth, a shield with six sleeping dormice; cow-ardice, a shield of aspen with the image of a hare. Huon de Méry inaugu-rated a new form of heraldic symbolism by playing on the music and the multiple meanings of terms of coats of arms. The bear is called on only once, but to play a very poor role. Designated by the name *Brun* from the *Roman de Renart,* he is associated with a ferocious dog to make up the armorial bearings of treachery: "Treachery, which hates Piety, was escorted by a mob of Bourguignons and carried an indented shield bearing a threatening red mastiff and Brun without Pity, emblem of treachery."[53] A negative color, a troubling dividing line (the indented heraldic line is a saw-toothed line), two fearsome beasts: Treachery's shield is one of the worst in the infernal troop. Fortunately, the divine army triumphs and the poet awakens. Troubled in heart and soul by this eschatological vision, he gives up the state of knighthood and takes monastic vows.

Huon de Méry's poem is not an isolated case in the literature of the early thirteenth century. Other allegorical or narrative works present animals incarnating the Devil in his various aspects. In the *Vengeance Radiguel*, for example, a chivalric romance sometimes attributed to Raoul de Houdenc, composed in the early years of the century, a treacherous knight, the owner of magic weapons and of a bear trained to do evil, uses the animal to take his opponents off guard and submit them to his will.[54] The bear of this terrible Guengasouain is the flesh and blood ancestor or cousin of the one proudly flaunted on the shield of treachery in the *Tournoiement Antéchrist* a few years later.

Five Sins out of Seven

As the decades passed, this prolific and unstable bestiary of vices from the High Middle Ages, essentially derived from patristic writings, tended toward a tighter organization, more mechanical and modern, the system of the seven deadly sins. The spread of the practice of the new private confession, imposed by the Fourth Lateran Council in 1215, brought about the formulation of new models of questioning and, for that purpose, the preparation of new manuals for the use of confessors. In order to avoid excessively long and detailed questioning, confessors began to use outlines in which the offenses to be detected among the faithful were grouped into seven major categories, at first variable and then tending to stabilize after the middle of the thirteenth century.[55] According to scholastic principles of classification, each of the seven major sins was subdivided into seven sub-sins, and each of those in turn further subdivided into seven sub-sub-sins. The whole formed a veritable "tree of sins" *(arbor peccatorum)*, with branches and sub-branches. Around 1260–1270, the basic list of the seven sins was definitively set as a counterpart to the long-established seven cardinal virtues. They were for the most part sins of the laity, sins of the world rather than truly spiritual sins: pride *(superbia)*, greed *(avaritia)*, lust *(luxuria)*, anger *(ira)*, gluttony *(gula)*, envy *(invidia)*, and sloth *(acedia)*.[56] A mnemonic for this list consisted of the first letters of the Latin names for the sins, which produced *saligia*, easy to remember because it meant nothing in medieval Latin. But it did express a certain hierarchy of seriousness, with pride as the supreme sin. In any event, this was the order in which confessors were expected to question the faithful.[57]

The old bestiary of vices was gradually grafted onto this new system, and each of the seven major sins—not yet called "capital" or "deadly"— was associated with a certain number of animals that were both its emblem and its embodiment. Various late medieval documents make it possible to establish a list of animals corresponding to each particular sin. There are texts: bestiaries and encyclopedias, allegorical and moral literature, penitentials and confessors' manuals, collections of *exempla*, surveys and treatises on vices, books of medicine and physiognomy. There are also proverbs and expressions, turns of phrase, puns, names and surnames, imaginary armorial bearings, not to mention all the evidence provided by iconography—painted, carved, woven, sculpted, or engraved.[58] In Germanic countries, for example, original and often little-known material is provided by treatises of psychomachia and etymachia, allegorical and didactic works that describe symbolic jousts between the seven virtues (three theological and four cardinal) and the seven major sins.[59] These works produced a relatively abundant iconography, particularly in illuminated manuscripts and on tapestries, as well as real jousts reenacted during carnival.[60] Every virtue and sin is represented mounted, in full heraldic costume, carrying shield, banner, and crest; four different animals are associated with him: his mount, the one that decorates his shield, the one that forms his crest, and the one shown on his banner.[61] The whole makes up a kind of moral bestiary within which certain animals can be found on the side of the virtues as well as the vices (lion, eagle, horse), whereas others are always negative (fox, monkey, bear, pig, dog).

This psychomachia bestiary, although confined to German-speaking countries, differs little from what is found elsewhere in most texts and images in the late Middle Ages. Concentrating on sins alone and sketching a summary of all the sources leads to the following: the animals most often associated with pride are the lion, eagle, peacock, horse, and camel; with greed, the squirrel, mole, monkey, and ant; with lust—with which the bestiary overflows—the goat, bear, pig, hare, and dog; with anger, the boar, bear, lion, and bull; with gluttony, the bear, pig, fox, wolf, vulture, and crow; with envy, the dog, fox, monkey, bear, and magpie; with sloth, the donkey, bear, pig, cat, and squirrel. In these lists, which could be extended,[62] several animals appear twice: lion, monkey, squirrel, dog, fox; only one, the pig, is mentioned three times. But that is nothing compared to the bear, associated with five of the seven greatest sins: lust, anger, gluttony, envy, and sloth. From the thirteenth century on, he was the star of this hateful bestiary, a sad fate for a wild animal who was once king of the beasts. He had become not only a stupid and humiliated animal but also one who was angry, lustful, gluttonous, envious, and slothful. The Church had struck very forcefully and succeeded in transforming an admired and feared animal into a grotesque and hateful creature.

It is noteworthy that, in this bestiary of the seven major sins, the two animals ordinarily considered closest to humans—bear and pig—are the most devalued. It is as though this kinship were unbearable and had to be compensated for by extreme disparagement, accompanied in the case of the bear by the rituals of extermination I discussed at the beginning of this book and, in the case of the pig, by various forms of taboo, less radical than in Jewish or Muslim societies, but common in medieval Christian societies.[63] The major monotheist religions do not like animals that nature and culture have declared to be "cousins" or "relatives" of man. The pig was a victim of this in biblical Antiquity. The bear suffered in turn in the heart of the Christian Middle Ages. And the great apes suffered the same fate a few centuries later. It has never been a good idea to resemble human beings too closely.

8

Princes' Whims, Ladies' Fantasies

B Y the late Middle Ages, the Church had achieved its goal. It had, of
course, not yet conquered the Devil, but it had definitively overcome the bear, which it saw as the Devil's most dangerous accomplice.
Dethroned, pursued, condemned, the great beast of the forest had fled to
the mountains. Not only did he no longer frighten anyone, but he himself
was fearful and avoided contact with men. He no longer came to villages
and farms, and seldom approached sheep or cattle. It had become unusual
to come across a bear on the road, and perhaps even more unusual to
organize a battue to flush one out. Even in words and images, his presence had become more discreet. He had everywhere given way to other
animals, notably the stag, the most sought-after game, and especially the
wolf. Little feared by men and women of the feudal period, the wolf had
now become a ubiquitous enemy in country life and would remain so
until the nineteenth century. Even in the infernal bestiary, the bear was no
longer in the front rank. Satan preferred to assume other animal disguises
(goat, wolf, dog, owl), and in the new witches' sabbath rituals he played a
very modest role.

But this retreat did not mean that the bear had disappeared from
the world of the imagination. Quite the contrary. The more discreet his
place became in royal menageries, noble hunts, and rural life, the more
it seemed to grow in the world of dreams and signs. Gone from many
regions, neglected by kings and princes, hard to observe or study, the bear
gradually turned into an animal of fiction, an exotic creature, a subject
of dreams and fantasies, some dynastic or emblematic, others fanciful or
playful, and still others strongly erotic.

Hunting and Psychoanalysis in the Fourteenth Century

The most troubling bear dream was one of a hunter, Pierre de Béarn, the half-brother of Gaston Phébus, Count of Foix and Viscount of Béarn. His distressing story is told by Jean Froissart, whose long chronicles are one of the best narrative sources for knowledge about fourteenth-century aristocratic society. The chronicler spent three months (November 1388–February 1389) at Gaston's court at Orthez of which he gave a detailed account, perhaps making up the most brilliant and least conventional segment of his work, at least for a modern reader. Born in Valenciennes in the north, Froissart is both surprised and charmed by the conduct of the *gentil* Count of Foix and his court. The prince above all fascinates him: he is a man full of contradictions, courteous and brutal, seductive and vindictive, a lover of poetry and music who indulges in the most violent activities. He has a fine library but also several kennels, raises boars, rides aimlessly through his forests, works at night, sleeps through part of the day, is surrounded by favorites, but changes them often.[1] At the court, the chronicler notes the importance of meals, spectacles, dancing, and especially the hunt. Hunting, much more than tournaments, occupied the attention of southern lords, including Gaston, one of the greatest huntsmen of his time and the author of the *Livre de la chasse,* which has survived in several sumptuously illuminated manuscripts. As he takes his leave, Froissart offers the prince who has been such an excellent host four large greyhounds, which he has named himself: Tristan, Roland, Hector, and Brun—two literary heroes, an ancient knight, and a creature taken from the *Roman de Renart.* At first sight, Brun the bear, the fox's perpetual victim, does not appear to be at the same level of renown as the three others nor to merit giving his name to a princely greyhound. But it is possible that in the late fourteenth century, in the mountain country of the south, his prestige had not been so undermined as it had in the northern plains. This is in any event suggested by the chapters devoted to the bear—a combative and fearsome game animal—in Gaston Phébus's hunting treatise.[2]

As the guest of a society foreign to him, Froissart takes an interest in everything, especially in questions of genealogy and rank; kin connections and networks occupy his full attention. To satisfy his curiosity, he questions an "old squire" at length about the identity and personality of Pierre de Béarn, the bastard half-brother of the Count of Foix, whose behavior seems to him peculiar and who, he is surprised to see, has no wife or children. The squire then tells him of the sad fate of this man whose wife has left him and who is suffering from a strange disease.[3]

Pierre is the bastard son of Gaston II, Count of Foix (1308–1343) and a woman "whose name must be unspoken." As a young captain in the château of Lourdes, Pierre was married to Dame Florence, daughter of Count Jean de Biscay, a neighbor and ally of the Count of Foix. A fanatical hunter, a few years earlier he had accomplished an exploit that was the source of his fame and of all his misfortunes: he confronted a gigantic bear alone in the mountains. After interminable hand-to-hand combat of unparalleled violence, he succeeded in vanquishing the beast with no help but that of his good "espée de Bourdiaux" (Bordeaux sword). But ever since that memorable day, every night, while deep in sleep, he gets up, takes his sword, fights in the empty air, and raises "un tel terribouris et un tel tempestement" (such a racket and an uproar) that it seems as though all the devils of hell are in the room with him. Pierre is indeed a somnambulist and every night thinks he is reliving his battle with the bear. But his suffering does not end there. The day he killed the great beast and brought the body to the château of Biscay to show it to his people and his wife, she fainted when she saw it. She was carried to her room, where she remained practically insensible for two days. When she recovered, she asked her husband to allow her to go on a pilgrimage to Santiago de Compostela as soon as possible, accompanied by their two young children. A strange request in the circumstances, but it was nonetheless granted. She left immediately, not only with her children but also with "all her treasure, gold, silver, jewels, because she knew she would never return." Indeed, she was never seen again, not in Biscay, nor in Béarn, nor in the Comté of Foix. Abandoned, the victim of his sleepwalking, Pierre sank into melancholy and soon came to live with his half-brother Gaston Phébus.

The tale told by the "old squire" is rather confused, perhaps deliberately, and Froissart does not grasp all its subtleties. Is Pierre de Béarn possessed? Does he take himself for a bear? Or else, every night, when he is seized by his "fantasy"—the term Froissart uses—does he think he is fighting the bear? And how can the conduct of his wife Florence be explained? Why this fainting fit, real or feigned? Why does she run away? Why does she refuse to come back to her husband? On the last point, the squire provides some details, both troubling and obscure. One day when the Count of Biscay, Florence's father, was hunting in the mountains, he too came face to face with a bear. He was about to do battle with it when the animal began to speak and said to him: "You hunt me although I mean you no harm. You will come to an evil end."[4] And indeed, a short time later the Count of Biscay was imprisoned through treachery and beheaded by his worst enemy Peter the Cruel, King of Castile.

The squire's explanations do not make it clear whether Florence was afraid of her sleepwalking and violent husband, or whether she had been terrorized by the bear Pierre had killed, which reminded her of the other bear, who had predicted her father's unjust death. Perhaps husband and bear were one, as Michel Zink judiciously suggests.[5] Doesn't Pierre de Béarn, whom Froissart constantly calls "Pierre de Berne," as everyone apparently did at the court of Orthez, have an ursine name? Of course the wordplay on *Berne* and *Bär* (German name for bear) is intelligible only in Germanic languages, but for the chronicler from the north, who knew Dutch and German, it was perfectly clear. Pierre is himself a kind of bear, or at least he takes himself for a bear, perhaps for the one he killed, or even the one who predicted the death of his wife's father. Moreover, the animal interests Froissart much more than the fate of Florence of Biscay or of her father. At the end of his conversation with the squire, he wonders whether the bears of the Pyrenees were not originally knights who, in the ancient times of paganism, wounded some god or goddess while hunting in these forests, and for that offense were turned into bears. He takes the opportunity to tell the squire, who does not know it, the story of the hunter Actaeon, changed into a stag by the goddess Diana (Artemis) whom he had come upon bathing naked in a pool. Froissart thereby shows his erudition, his knowledge of ancient myths—to which he alludes frequently in his poetic works—but he does not specify that Actaeon was later torn to pieces and killed by his own hounds.[6]

This episode, which describes somnambulism and metempsychosis, or at least what took their place in the late Middle Ages, is probably the most unusual episode in the *Chroniques*. Aside from its dream and psychoanalytic aspect (disregarding the anachronism), it echoes the rites of passage of young warriors and hunters of pagan Germany discussed earlier. Confronting and defeating a bear in single combat was a rite required for entry into adulthood.[7] Pierre de Béarn is, of course, an adult when he combats the terrible beast, but from the dynastic point of view he is still a minor because he is merely the bastard son of the preceding Count of Foix: he has no hope of succeeding his brother Gaston Phébus, even though, at the time Froissart arrives at the court of Orthez, Gaston has just lost his only son in tragic circumstances.[8] Hence, Pierre has a better claim to some rights in Biscay on account of his wife.[9] But to do that he would have to be acknowledged as a true lord, accomplish an exploit, demonstrate manly strength, in short, kill a bear. He does so, but it drives him mad, because this act of valor probably goes beyond his capacities as a hunter and his psychic, dynastic, and political possibilities.

Moreover, the bear Pierre fights every night in his dreams, like his counterpart that predicted the sordid death of the Count of Biscay a few years earlier, echoes the bears of the feudal period, whose form the Devil assumed to torment monks, knights, and kings in their sleep. For many writers, whether at night in a room or during the day in the heart of the forest, any bear encountered was always more or less a phantom, and behind the animal was often hidden a spirit or a ghost. The kinship of man and bear was too close for the "semblance" of the animal not to conceal some wandering soul awaiting judgment. Froissart's speculations about ancient gods punishing excessively bold or insolent knights are therefore not incongruous, just a little archaic and bound by Ovidian tradition. Unless, and this may be the case, they are tinged with slight irony. The chronicler-poet sometimes liked to mock his interlocutors, his audience, and himself.

The Glory of the Stag

Turning momentarily from the bear to the stag, in the late Middle Ages the decline of the former greatly contributed to the increased prestige of the latter, as though the two animals held in common a certain symbolic potential that they had to share. The more the bear was devalued or faded into the background, the more the stag moved to the front of the stage, starting with the stage of venery.

Neglected as a game animal throughout the High Middle Ages because it was a fearful animal quick to flee, the stag became an animal for the royal hunt starting in the thirteenth century. In that role, it replaced not only the bear but also the boar, as all the hunting treatises demonstrate. Writers now began with the stag hunt and spent more time on it than on any other. Some, like the anonymous author of the *Chace dou cerf*,[10] compiled in the second half of the thirteenth century, even devote an entire poem or a specific book to the stag alone, something the bear and the boar no longer could expect. Most important, the stag is never discussed in negative terms and hunting it is valued from every point of view. This is what Gaston Phébus wrote in his *Livre de la chasse* between 1387 and 1389: "The stag hunt is a good hunt, because it is a fine thing to seek a stag, a fine thing to trick him, a fine thing to let him run, a fine thing to hunt him and hunt him again . . . and a fine thing to skin him well and to cut him up . . . He is a fine and pleasing animal, and I claim that this is the noblest hunt."[11]

The same or similar language is found in other hunting writers of the fourteenth century, notably Henri de Ferrières, a Norman gentleman about whom almost nothing is known, but who was the author of a famous book, *Les Livres du roy Modus et de la royne Ratio*, written some time between 1360 and 1379. This volume enjoyed considerable success until the early modern period. Although a precise chronology cannot be established, it is likely that in France and England stag hunting became more prestigious than bear and boar hunting between the late twelfth century and the middle of the thirteenth, while in Italy and Germany this reversal of the hierarchy took place later, perhaps toward the end of the fourteenth century or early in the fifteenth, and in Spain and Portugal still later, at the dawn of modern times.[12]

The role of the clergy in the promotion of the stag as a noble game animal was essential. For the Church, an enemy of all hunting,[13] the stag hunt was a lesser evil. It was less savage than the bear hunt or the boar hunt and did not end with bloody hand-to-hand combat between man and beast. In addition it caused fewer deaths of men and dogs, gave rise to fewer cries of rage and animal stench, and relied primarily on the fatigue of men, dogs, and the game to bring matters to an end. It was, of course, not as peaceable as hunting birds, and it even had a furious aspect in the fall, with the bellowing of stags in rut, when the full-grown males were at their most sexually excited. But at any time of year, the pursuit of the stag did not plunge hunters into a state approaching trance or fury, as could happen in close combat with a bear or a boar. In short, it seemed to be more civilized, under better control.

Above all, the symbolism of the stag made it possible to give this hunt a Christian dimension. The Church Fathers and the Latin bestiaries that followed them relied on various ancient traditions that saw the stag as a solar animal, a creature of light, a mediator between heaven and earth. This produced all the hagiographic and later literary legends built around the golden, white, winged, wondrous stag encountered by a hunter and bearing a luminous cross between his antlers. In medieval stories, the saint is always the antithesis of the hunter; with the stag, the hunter can become a saint. For example, in the legend of Eustace, a Roman general and a fanatical hunter, one day he sees a crucifix between the antlers of a stag he was pursuing. After this vision, he is converted along with his entire family.[14] And later, in the related legend of Hubert, son of the Duke of Aquitaine, Hubert has the same vision while hunting on a Good Friday. He reforms his life, goes to evangelize the Ardennes, and becomes the first Bishop of Liège.[15]

Deliberately disregarding the negative and sexual aspects of the symbolism of the stag,[16] medieval theologians turned it into a pure and virtuous animal, an image of the resurrection (every year its antlers grew again), an emblem or a substitute for Christ, like the lamb and the unicorn. In carrying this out, they did not hesitate to play on words to establish a connection between *servus* (one of the attributes of Christ) and *cervus* (stag). In this connection they recalled Pliny's statement that the stag is the enemy of the snake, that is, the devil,[17] and glossed a verse of Psalm 42, in which the soul of the just man seeks the Lord like a thirsty stag seeking water from a spring.[18] For these theologians, the stag was the Savior. Books on hunting easily adopted the comparison: the stag was a sacrificial animal, a game animal ritually sacrificed, following precise codes and customs, and its death was made parallel to the Passion of Christ. Literary works relied on the same play on words between *servus* and *cervus* to turn the stag hunt into a metaphor for redemptive love, or the animal into the image of the lover who is the servant *(servus)* of his lady.[19]

This positive symbolism was not confined to the realms of hagiography, letters, and art, but spread to the world of emblems. Two monarchs in the late fourteenth century, for example, made the stag their favorite emblematic animal and frequently represented it on ceremonial and court insignia and clothing: a stag lying down, collared and chained, for Richard II of England (1377–1399); a winged stag for Charles VI of France (1380–1422). According to legend, Charles VI encountered a winged stag following his coronation when he was hunting in the forest of Senlis.[20] A soon as he became king, Charles VII, the son of Charles VI, whose legitimacy had been questioned, swiftly made his father's emblematic animal his own: the winged stag became his favorite badge and a rallying sign for his supporters for nearly a decade. Once he was crowned in Reims in 1429, thanks to Joan of Arc, Charles VII even made winged stags the supporters for the arms of France: a winged stag was shown on either side of the crown with three fleurs-de-lis, which they seemed to hold and protect. The place given the animal was all the more prestigious because in the two preceding reigns two angels had played the same role. Subsequently, Louis XI and Charles VIII continued, more discreetly, to make stags the supporters for the arms of France.[21]

Popes themselves seem not to have been indifferent to the powerful Christian symbolism of the stag. The most remarkable example in the fourteenth century was provided by Clement VI (1342–1352), an authoritarian pontiff, a clever politician, and a lavish prince of the Church. He had the palace in Avignon partially rebuilt and included in his private apartments a kind of *studiolo* whose secular décor, showing scenes of fishing and hunting, earned it the name "chamber of the stag." A now heavily damaged fresco on one of the walls of a stag hunt painted by Matteo Giovanetti seemed to echo the "deer park" that covered a portion of the gardens of the pontifical palace. The animals were under the surveillance of a "keeper of stags" *(custos cervorum),* well paid according to accounting records.[22] But the relationship between Clement VI and the stag took on a still more intimate and more symbolic cast at the time of his funeral.[23] In his will, the pope had asked to be buried naked, his "body sewn in the skin of a stag." This was done nine days after his death on December 6, 1352, and he was buried in that final garment the following April in the abbey church of La Chaise-Dieu. Although it was mutilated during the Wars of Religion, his splendid tomb can still be seen. This surprising choice, unique in its time, can be explained not so much by the astringent and anti-plague qualities of stag skin (Clement VI was the pope of the Black Plague), nor even by a genuine desire for humility, but rather by the Christological aspect of the animal, both an image of the Savior and a symbol of resurrection.[24]

A New System of Emblems

Despite the stag's growing prestige, there were still some personages of rank in the fourteenth century who remained loyal to the bear and still built their symbolic world around that animal's former glory. One of them was well known to Froissart and all the contemporary chroniclers. Unlike Pierre de Béarn, he was not a petty lord from the south, fragile, ill born, and with meager resources, but an illustrious "prince of the fleurs-de-lis," son, brother, and uncle of kings: Jean de France, Duke of Berry, son of King Jean le Bon (1350–1364), brother of King Charles V (1364–1380), and uncle of King Charles VI (1380–1422). He is a familiar figure because on various occasions he stood on "the second step of the throne,"[25] and left many traces in archives and documents. He has for a long time rightly been a focus of interest for historians. His powerful personality marked the history of the kingdom for more than six decades, at a time when it was experiencing profound crises—political, dynastic, military, social, economic, and even climatic. Not that Jean was a great politician, much less a brilliant war leader, but he was a clever diplomat and a sensitive patron of the arts. It was in this realm that he played an essential role, the greatest of his time, and through it he came down to posterity. Born in 1340, dying in 1416, Jean lived longer than most of his contemporaries, and throughout his adult life conducted himself as a man of power and money, impassioned and greedy, a lover of the beautiful and the new, a protector of artists and men of letters, a patron, builder, collector, and bibliophile.[26]

He was also—and this is less well known—a prince who was a friend to bears at a time when the great beast of the forest, the former king of the beasts, no longer charmed anyone, especially not kings and great lords, all absorbed by their horses, dogs, and falcons, owning lions and panthers, with leopards and genets as companions, and setting out in search of richly colored and chattering birds from the wondrous Indies or mysterious Africa. Aviaries and parrots were in fashion, and in princely menageries bears were no longer an attraction, except for Jean de Berry.

This attraction to a neglected or even despised animal probably originated in England, at the court of King Edward III, where Jean stayed for more than four years as a young man, from 1360 to 1364. He lived in London with several other French princes serving as "hostages" until the huge ransom for King Jean le Bon of France, captured at the battle of Poitiers in 1356 and then released, was paid. Jean de Berry's English prison was more or less a gilded cage. He lived in a residence specially reserved for him, was free in his movements and activities, could visit the countryside around London, but had to return "dedans le soleil couchant" (before sunset). It was a form of house arrest. According to legend, during his London stay, Jean de Berry had a love affair with an enigmatic English lady named "Urcine" or "des Ursines." Out of love for her, he was said to have adopted during these years of forced exile the two animal emblems that he maintained until he died: the bear and the swan, phonically producing the name *Urcine* (*ours* + *cygne*). Two emblems, a play on words, a young imprisoned prince, the name and the memory of a beautiful lady: the story is seductive. But the documents contradict it.

In the 1360s, the adoption by princes of individual emblems that they chose freely and which they used unrestrainedly, whether or not in association with their family coats of arms, was a new fashion that appears to have sprung up at the English court a short time earlier. It was intended to compensate for a certain rigidity of the traditional heraldic system that had come into being around the middle of the twelfth century, had been codified since the early thirteenth, and functioned so well that kings, princes, and lords were no longer free to choose or to modify their armorial bearings as they wished: they were hereditary and tied to kin relations. Nobles received them as a legacy at the same time as they received their names, their fiefs, and their titles, and they had to conform to custom, respect the rules of heraldry, and, if they were the youngest son, introduce on their shield a *brisure* (cadency), a modification (generally the addition of a small figure) indicating their place and rank within the lineage to which they belonged. Jean de Berry, who was a youngest son, therefore bore the arms of France, *d'azur semé de fleurs de lis d'or* (azure strewn with fleurs-de-lis of gold), *brisées* (modified) with a *bordure engrelée de gueules* (a red border defined by a line indented by semicircles). He was not free to change it.

Princely heraldry was so rigorously regulated and controlled that it needed safety valves. It did not allow those who used armorial bearings—as had been true in early heraldry—to reveal anything but their identity. Their aspirations, their plans, their exploits, their love affairs, the ideas they held dear or that were their emblematic "impulses" had to be expressed in other ways. First came *devises* (devices), which probably appeared in England between 1340 and 1360. This term in Anglo-Norman and Middle French designated not words, maxims, sentence fragments serving as an emblematic proclamation, but only images. In origin, the device was a stylized image (animal, vegetable, object) functioning as an emblem for anyone who used it repeatedly. Unlike armorial bearings, it was not subject to rules of composition or transmission. But since it soon became customary in the second half of the fourteenth century to associate with this image a word or group of words, or even a complete sentence, the whole (image and word) was in the end designated by the term. Device did not take on its modern meaning until the seventeenth century, when the use of the binary device became less frequent and the use of a word or a maxim alone became the norm in accompanying armorial bearings.

At the English court, like all young princes, Jean de Berry quickly succumbed to the new fashion of the device and adopted one for the first time. It may even have been suggested to him by another prince, a friend or protector. In any event, when he arrived in London on All Saints' Day in 1360, Jean's only emblem was his coat of arms. When he left for good in December 1364, he still had his armorial bearings, of course, but he also had a device: a bear, usually represented standing and sometimes holding a banner. This bear accompanied him to the end of his life and was found on countless documents, monuments, art objects, and objects of daily life.

The choice of this animal as an emblematic image can easily be understood. It was not really a reflection of symbolic considerations but rather of a simple play on words. Since mid-October 1360, Jean had been possessed of Berry, a fief he was attached to because those granted to him previously, the countships of Mâcon and subsequently of Poitiers, had soon been taken from him. This time, shortly before leaving for England, he had received the Duchy of Berry from the crown. He was attached to it, never wanted to lose it, and his new device was a way of proclaiming his attachment for all to see. In English, the first syllable of *Berry,* the name by which he was known at the court of Edward III, bore a resemblance to the word *bear.* From the phonic echo to the choice of the image was a short step that Jean must have taken very early on, probably to imitate the young English princes at court who already had devices in 1360 and 1361. Among them were the younger sons of the King of England, Lionel, Duke of Clarence; John, Count (later Duke) of Lancaster; and Edmund, Count of Cambridge (later Duke of York). Thirty or forty years earlier, in the same situation as a hostage in London, Jean de Berry would probably not have chosen a bear as a device, because the court and the aristocracy of the time spoke French; English was the language of commoners and of daily life. The wordplay on *Berry* and *bear* would have had little resonance or would have been derogatory. This was no longer true in 1360. By order of Edward III, for political reasons, the royal court of England had recently adopted English, and the aristocracy enjoyed using the formerly despised language. The wordplay on the young prince's name and the name of the great beast was now possible, and even quite up to date.[27]

The notion of a "play on words" is entirely cultural and varies according to language, era, and social milieu. Today, it is not particularly enhancing and is often associated with a pun. Individuals and groups are hesitant to adopt as an emblem an image the name of which creates a play on words with their own, especially if it seems far-fetched. In the late Middle Ages, matters were different: expressing with a single phrase the name and the emblem was a deliberate act, a highly meaningful choice, not at all derogatory. On the contrary, the emblematic or symbolic dimension was strengthened. Moreover, for several decades, heraldry had accustomed society as a whole—nobles and commoners, individuals and communities—to using "speaking" images, that is, images whose names, directly, phonically, or by allusion, were linked to the person who used them. Nearly one fourth of medieval armorial bearings were "speaking" in this way and were no less prestigious than the others. They only became so in the seventeenth century, because of the abuse that had been made of them and because of a profound change in sensibility with respect to turns of phrase.[28]

The Bear and the Swan

The oldest evidence of Jean de Berry's device is a seal on a document dated February 1365, a few months after his return from England: the bear is shown standing, holding a banner, and wearing a shield around his neck with the Berry arms.[29] It is found on several more of the duke's seals used in the 1370s and subsequently, paired with a wounded swan, on his great full-length seal, the matrix of which was probably engraved in late 1374 or early 1375. The duke is pictured standing, seen from the front, holding a scepter; in a recess to his right is a seated bear, wearing a helmet with fleurs-de-lis, and on his left a swan wearing the ducal shield of Berry around its neck.[30] Thereafter, the bear and the swan were often paired to form the two favorite devices of Duke Jean. But there were also many instances in which the bear was used alone; the bear was the earliest to appear and the animal that the duke preferred.

The swan did not appear before 1375. That is sufficient to puncture the legend of the English lady des Ursines with whom the duke is supposed to have been smitten during his captivity in London. Indeed, the legend is not attested before the middle of the fifteenth century, nearly forty years after the death of Jean de Berry in 1416. The first writer to allude to it was his great-nephew René d'Anjou, a prince and a poet of unbridled emotion, in his celebrated *Livre du coeur d'amour épris* of 1457.[31] It seems that René d'Anjou created the Lady des Ursines from a play on words involving his great-uncle's two favorite emblems, and not that Jean de Berry had chosen his emblems out of love for or in memory of an imagined mistress. The bear and the swan preceded the mistress by several decades, and the mistress in fact never existed.

Then, why the association of a bear and a swan? I have already suggested that the bear, a "speaking" image in English, echoed *Berry*. But what explains the addition of the swan? Was it an allusion to the powerful house of the Counts of Boulogne, for whom the swan had been the mythological and totemic emblem since at least the twelfth century? Indeed, widowed, in 1389, Jean de Berry married the very young Jeanne de Boulogne, heiress of the prestigious Counts of Boulogne and Auvergne.[32] But by then Jean had been using his swan device for nearly fifteen years. The solution is to be found elsewhere, perhaps again by considering the words. The patron saint of Berry was Ursin, first bishop of Bourges, to whom the duke was especially devoted. The Latin name of Saint Ursin, *Ursinus,* is a name in which could be seen, according to the lexical speculations of the time, the fusion of the words *ursus* and *cygnus,* bear and swan. It is therefore possible that it was in homage to the patron saint of Berry that the duke, already possessing a device with a bear, later chose a swan as a complementary device. Unless the solution is to be found still elsewhere, for example in the legend of the mysterious "Knight of the Swan" that preoccupied a portion of the European aristocracy throughout the fourteenth century and gave rise to many emblems.[33] Or perhaps it lies in the pair formed by the bear and the goose (a bird that is a "cousin" of the swan, formally and symbolically): the two animals had from very ancient times been associated with the festivals of Saint Martin, and scribes often confused their French names *(ours, oie).*[34]

In any event, Jean de Berry liked to display both of his devices. They functioned as signs of identity, marks of possession, emblems proclaiming his power and majesty. The bear especially was ubiquitous. It could be seen frequently sculpted in the duke's various palaces and châteaus, in Bourges, Poitiers, Riom, Mehun-sur-Yèvre, and elsewhere—some examples still survive. But it was found even more frequently painted, drawn, woven, enameled, engraved, or molded in the numerous books, documents, and art objects that belonged to him: seals and charters, illuminated manuscripts, reliquaries and gold plate, painted panels, tapestries, jewelry, necklaces, cameos, intaglio, and stones of every kind. The duke's account books and inventories reveal that the animal was also found on furniture, sheets, precious cloth, clothing, belts, hats, all "embroidered with bears," "carved with bears," "decorated with bears," "in the shape of a bear."[35] The animal might be depicted in full or only down to the waist, in one copy or many, holding an object or included in a setting. The drawing was sometimes naturalistic, sometimes stylized, notably when the animal supported or was a part of the duke's armorial bearings. The role of supporter was particularly frequent, as though here too there was a play on English words of *bear* the animal and *bear* meaning to carry: the bear bore a shield, a banner, a helmet, a collar, a weapon, an object.

Sometimes, it was not merely a supporter or a mark of possession, but a sign with an almost totemic value. Starting in the early 1400s, the bear surrounded the duke on all sides and seemed to have become his tutelary animal, almost a patron "saint." This was particularly clear toward the end of his life: Jean de Berry never took off a luxurious upturned bearskin cap—several of which he had had made in 1410 and 1411[36]—and his aging physical appearance, coarsened, heavy, with his round head and ears sticking out, made him resemble a bear. The resemblance is striking in several miniatures painted by the Limbourg brothers: a leaf added to the *Petites Heures,*[37] and especially three leaves in the *Très Riches Heures,*[38] two lavish manuscripts in which the duke had himself portrayed by his favorite painters. During these sad times for the kingdom of France, Jean, retired from political life, seemed resigned and imbued with deep melancholy, in the image of the bear, his protective animal. Further, various account books reveal that on his clothing and jewelry he sometimes paired the image of the bear with that of the columbine, the pretty blue flower that, long before Gérard de Nerval, consoled in the early fifteenth century the "blighted heart" of princes and poets.[39]

But in the collections of Jean de Berry, the bear was present not only in the form of images or emblems. He also appeared as a relic and could be found in a cabinet where curiosities taken from the animal world were numerous and varied. There were ostrich eggs, unicorn horns, coral branches, snakes' tongues, and griffins' talons, all of which were relatively common in a princely treasure of the time. But, more originally, Jean had a giant's jaw, two teeth from a "horse of the Nile" (hippopotamus), several "sea hedgehogs" (sea urchins), a large "lizard boiled in oil" (stuffed crocodile), and various bones and skins of "strange beasts," including the skin of a "wolf-stag" of great size and the skin of a polar bear "with his head."[40] In the 1400s, although the brown bear was no longer an object of curiosity, his cousin from the north, with his astonishing white fur, still fascinated.

The Bear Prince

But it was probably in his menageries, more than in his collections of books, objects, jewels, or *curiosa,* that the personality of the duke and his ursine passions were expressed in the most original way. At a time when the bear was no longer a royal gift and when princely menageries no longer held any, Jean de Berry had several and was very attached to them. There seems to have been a sharp contrast between his artistic tastes, which drew him constantly toward contemporary art, and his backward-looking fancy for a devalued animal, only good for dancing or being ridiculed at fairs. Of course, like any great lord, the duke was proud to have exotic birds in his aviary and large numbers of swans and aquatic birds swimming in his ponds. He also liked to show his visitors at Mehun-sur-Yèvre an animal that no other French prince had, a dromedary, given to him by the king of Aragon along with a large, temperamental ostrich, given by the bishop of Tournai. The ostrich had an official keeper whose name has been preserved, Guillemin Merlin.[41] But he always preferred his bears, present in both menageries: in Mehun below the château and in Bourges south of the ducal palace. Archive documents often mention bears, and three of them are even known to us by their proper names: Chapelain, Martin, and Valentin, listed here in the order in which they seem to have lived.

The three names were not chosen at random. Aside from the common sound in their last syllable, they recall three figures who had privileged re-lations with bears. The case of Martin has already been mentioned on sev-eral occasions; he was the great ursine saint whose feast day of November 11 replaced a mid-autumn pagan bear festival. Valentin was a more modest saint, but his feast day of February 14 also masked older seasonal ceremo-nies tied to the bear. There remains Chapelain, a common name before it was a proper name. This is one of the functions fulfilled by the bear at the lion's court in the *Roman de Renart*. Depending on the branch, Brun is sometimes vice-king, sometimes a baron, sometimes a messenger, and sometimes King Noble's chaplain. This role is more frequent in the later branches. Its source lay in the heavy and indolent appearance of the bear, similar to a fat and overfed cleric, but also in an episode from an earlier branch in which Brun, victimized by the fox, is scalped by peasants. His tonsure then designates him for an ecclesiastical role. Jean de Berry prob-ably paid little attention to the *Roman de Renart,* but the tradition of the "chaplain" bear was certainly still very much alive in the late fourteenth century.

Accounting records also show that the animals obeyed a "master of bears," Colin de Bleron, who served the duke for nearly two decades,[42] and that the sums spent each year to guard, lodge, and feed them, and to make collars, chains, and muzzles were relatively large.[43] This was all the more true because on top of ordinary expenses came exceptional ones, like transporting the favorite bear of the moment (first Martin, then Valentin) in a cart from Mehun to Bourges, from Bourges to Poitiers, even to Paris, and then back to Mehun; or compensating a servant or visitor who had gotten too close to a bear and been injured. In July 1398 forty-five *sous tournois* were paid to a certain Lorin Larchier "whom my lordship's bear injured . . . for him to be treated."[44] The injury must have been serious, because the sum is large. Even familiar, tamed, subject to the authority of a guardian, and accustomed to frequent princely residences, the bear remained an unpredictable and dangerous animal. It was perhaps for that reason that Jean de Berry was so attached to it. He liked to have his favorite nearby and wanted it to travel with him, a unique example among the princes of the late Middle Ages.

For his final journey into the beyond, the duke also wanted to be accompanied by his favorite bear, Valentin, who had cheered the last years of his life, which had been particularly dark. Not Valentin alive, of course, nor even Valentin in the form of a relic, enclosed with him in his tomb—that would have been true heresy—but Valentin carved in stone and set beneath his feet to keep him company on his recumbent statue of white marble. A bear beneath the feet is a unique example in all funerary sculpture. Only three animals had previously been portrayed in that location: the dragon under the feet of prelates to symbolize their victory over the forces of evil; the lion beneath the feet of kings and lords to glorify their power and signify their resurrection; and the dog beneath the feet of ladies to proclaim their faithfulness. It is true that this ternary distribution had sometimes been disturbed since the feudal period—prelates with a lion and several princes with a dog or a dragon. But no cleric or layman, no man or woman had chosen for his funerary image to keep company with a bear.

Jean de Berry's bear can still be seen in the crypt of the cathedral of Bourges, sleeping for eternity under the feet of his master. He is wearing a muzzle, but his pleasant-looking snout seems to echo the calm face of the prince, who again resembles his totem animal: the same prominent cheekbones, the same small, close-set eyes, the same round ears sticking out. At the end of his life Jean de Berry, by conscious or unconscious imitation, had assumed the appearance of a bear, and this ursine face is preserved in the marble of his tomb sculpture.

The duke's splendid tomb was sculpted by a great artist, Jean de Cambrai, who died in 1438.[45] At that date, although the recumbent statue had been completed, the monument as a whole had not. At the request of Charles VII, the duke's heir, a team of sculptors finished the tomb in the 1450s, completing the number of mourners and setting the heavy white marble statue on a large slab of black marble. It is not known whether the tomb had been begun during the lifetime of the duke. By 1405, he had decided to be buried in his Sainte-Chapelle of Bourges, adjacent to the ducal palace. In May 1416, one month before his death, he had confirmed this wish and specified that his body should under no circumstances be divided (heart, viscera)—as was sometimes the custom—to be buried in several places, for example Riom, Poitiers, and Saint-Denis. He wanted his entire body to be buried in Bourges, the capital of his beloved Duchy of Berry.[46] But nothing had been said then about the sculpted image of the bear. Was it in response to the duke's demand, to a simple wish, to the idea of a friend, or of Jean de Cambrai or one of his assistants? The choice is in fact so unusual that it must have been made by Jean de Berry himself. Everything in his life, beginning with his forced residence in England at the age of twenty, tied him to this animal. It was normal that, having become not only his favorite emblem but an authentic totem, it accompany him in death.

The Sainte-Chapelle of Bourges, heavily damaged by a violent storm, was demolished in 1757. The body and the tomb of the duke were transferred to Saint-Étienne cathedral. They are still there, in the crypt, but the tomb has been reduced to the recumbent statue alone. The magnificent mourners who supported it were victims of revolutionary vandalism, and those that survived have been scattered around Europe and the United States.[47]

Fire and Fur

The example of Jean de Berry is an isolated case in the princely world of the late Middle Ages. No other dynast or great lord shared his fascination with bears, although a few princes, such as Amédée VIII, Count of Savoy, still had one in their menagerie.[48] But, according to several literary and narrative works, all written by men, the male bear, with his virile appearance, his savage strength, and his luxuriant fur, still held a mysterious attraction for women. The bear's fur, above all, seemed to charm them, even to provoke sexual excitement. As a result, at court and in villages, young vigorous men took advantage of major seasonal festivals or even simple celebrations to disguise themselves as hairy creatures halfway between a bear and a devil or a wild man. In this animal disguise, they approached young women, performed suggestive dances in front of them, played at frightening them, and then pretended to abduct or sexually assault them—sometimes really doing so. Rituals of this kind, already attested in Greco-Roman Antiquity, continued throughout the Middle Ages and the Ancien Régime, and could still be found in European folklore in the nineteenth and twentieth centuries, especially in mountain regions during carnival.

In the late fourteenth century, a princely celebration of this kind preceding the beginning of Lent has remained famous because of its tragic end: the Bal des Ardents. It took place in January 1393 in a prince's residence in the faubourg Saint-Marcel, at the time almost in the countryside. It was a politically unsettled period. Since the preceding summer, King Charles VI had been suffering from mental illness and had been experiencing "absences" lasting several weeks, falling into fits of melancholy.[49] His uncles and his brother had ruled intermittently. In order to cheer up the king, there were many balls, diversions, and court festivals, all to the great delight of the ladies. The remarriage of a young widow, one of the queen's ladies-in-waiting, provided an opportunity to include in one of these parties a kind of masked ball. Five young lords decided to disguise themselves as wild men to frighten (or seduce) the ladies by rushing into the ballroom. Thinking they would cheer up the king, they suggested he disguise himself and join their joyous procession, and Charles VI agreed. Thus it was that six wild men invaded the ballroom, dressed in simple tunics steeped in pitch and covered in clumps of cotton and hemp imitating animal fur. Few at court had been informed of the masquerade: a few servants, a major-domo, and perhaps the young Duke Louis of Orléans, the king's brother. The surprise was great in the large, ill-lit ballroom. The ladies were seized with fear, but it was ambiguous fear, both terrifying and exciting. What did these hairy wild men want, looking like bears in heat, yelling and gesturing in front of them? Would they abduct them, fondle them, assault them? Tragedy struck suddenly: the Duke of Orléans, wanting to see these frightful creatures more clearly, grabbed a torch and brought it close to one of them, too close. The hair caught fire, and the flames quickly spread to the costumes of the five others in the midst of the frightened and helpless spectators. Panic was complete. Four of the wild men died in terrible agony, two escaped: the son of the Lord of Nantouillet, who had had the presence of mind to jump into a tub filled with water; and King Charles VI, whom the young Duchess of Berry had quickly wrapped in the train of her gown, stifling the flames.[50]

This tragic event, known to posterity as the Bal des Ardents (in Old and Middle French, the verb *ardre* means "to burn"), has provoked many commentaries and questions. What role exactly was played by the Duke of Orléans in starting the fire? Did he intentionally set one of the costumes on fire, or was it really an accident? Did he know about the masquerade? Did he know that his brother was participating? Did he want to kill him? Louis d'Orléans was not the young, amiable, and peaceable prince of romantic historiography and conventional anecdote.[51] His assassination by the Duke of Burgundy in 1407 almost turned him into a martyr. But he was in fact a dissembling, calculating, cynical figure consumed with ambition.[52] At the time of the tragedy, Charles VI had several daughters but only one son, Charles, Duke of Guyenne and Dauphin de Viennois, one year old and in fragile health (he died in 1409). If this child were to die and the mad king were to die accidentally, the king's brother Louis would inherit the throne. It is impossible to prove, but some contemporary chroniclers believed him capable of treachery and several modern historians are also persuaded that the king's brother was guilty.

In any event, I am concerned here not with Louis d'Orléans' crime but with the appearance of men disguised as savages in the midst of a princely celebration. In the late fourteenth century, wild men were in vogue. Painted, sculpted, woven, or embroidered, they could be seen everywhere: on walls, furniture, stained glass, hangings, and tapestries; in the margins of illuminated manuscripts; even in the decorations of church stalls. Festivals and spectacles featured them, and heraldry and emblems used them frequently. Wild men were on armorial bearings, held a large number of shields, and were used as crests and devices, with or without a club. Naked wild women also appeared, covered only in their hair. The vogue of this theme in images and works of art began toward the middle of the fourteenth century, shortly after the Black Plague (1346–1350). It reached its culmination in the early 1400s and lasted until the early sixteenth century.[53] At first it was connected to new or revived curiosity for strange creatures situated at the frontier of the animal world. But it was also related to tales of western travelers who were discovering unknown peoples in Asia and Africa and expanding the limits of the known world. It was sometimes accompanied by a certain moral discourse: these more or less imaginary wild men were not all negative or diabolical; like the early Christian hermits in the desert, they lived in a state of nature and had not been corrupted by dissolute mores and the pursuit of wealth. To be sure, Jean-Jacques Rousseau and the myth of the noble savage were far in the future, but the idea was already expressed by some moralists in the late Middle Ages that some wild populations might represent models for a Christian society that had fallen into licentiousness, misery, and despair. This explains the vogue for the theme.

What made the wild man fully wild for iconography were his nakedness and his hairiness: there were no clothed wild men, nor were there any who were smooth-skinned and hairless. By nature, any wild man was half man, half animal. And the most powerful manifestations of animality, as I have shown already in discussing disguises, were the parts of the body that formed protuberances: horns, teeth, claws, tail, ears, sex organs, and hair. Especially hair. Hence, the most "animal" of all the animals, and also the one closest to the wild man, was the bear, the quintessentially hairy animal. Hair seemed to establish a kind of kinship between the bear and the wild man. Besides, both were not only hairy but also woodland creatures, *enforestés,* as Old French nicely put it. They lived withdrawn in the forest *(silva)* and were therefore fully "wild" *(silvatica)* in the etymological sense.

Medieval sensibility made distinctions when hair was present on the male body. Hair that was only partial (chin, arms, legs, chest) was positive and beneficial, a sign of power, virility, even at some times an aid to seduction. But if it covered the entire body it was usually maleficent, or at least against nature, the sign of a disorderly instinctive and sensual life. It brought man close to beast. For the imagination and the world of symbols, it was obviously that excessive hairiness that intrigued and attracted the ladies, because it was unusual and it seemed to express uncommon sexual vigor. From this arose various literary and artistic themes associating the two opposites: woman and bear, or woman and wild man. On one side, smooth, gentle, and white beauty; on the other, thick, bushy, and dark hairiness. In short, Beauty and the Beast.

It is possible that this supposed attraction felt by ladies for animal hair is what saved the king of France at the Bal des Ardents. The young Duchess of Berry covered King Charles VI's disguise with the train of her gown at the very moment it caught fire. But how did she have the capacity and presence of mind to act so quickly when no other lady present was able to do the same for another "wild man"? Perhaps because the young woman, far from being revolted by the six wild men bursting into the ballroom, had rather been attracted, more or less consciously, to these hairy creatures full of life and strength. She had approached one of them before fire broke out, not knowing it was the king. Finding herself next to him, she was able to intervene at the first flame, and did not hesitate to take the immodest step of lifting her dress to cover the unfortunate man. Chance, curiosity, courage, and immodesty probably saved Charles VI.

He may also have been saved by sexuality. In January 1393, Jeanne de Boulogne, duchesse de Berry, was not yet fifteen. She had been married

three years earlier, barely aged twelve, to Jean de Berry—the bear prince—
who was then over fifty and several times a grandfather. The court and the
king himself had mocked the old prince marrying a tender child: "Good
uncle," Charles VI had said with irony, "what will you do with such a
little girl? She is only twelve. By God, it's great folly to think of it."[54] The
marriage had nonetheless taken place in June 1390. When it was consum-
mated is obviously not known. Had it been by January 1393? If so, there is
no doubt that Jeanne would have felt more troubled by a young and vigorous wild man than by her greybeard husband. And if not, perhaps it was
the awakening of her desire and her fascination for the hair that, joined
with her childish naïveté, impelled her to approach a sexually attractive
and dangerous creature.

Orson the Wild Man

Although this hypothesis may seem a little scabrous, there is nothing
anachronistic about it. There are a fairly large number of writings and
images from the fourteenth and fifteenth centuries that feature Beauty
and the Beast, some of which emphasize the attraction ladies feel for hair
and the wild creature, man or bear. The most striking example is found in
a literary work that was very widely diffused, *Valentin et Orson*. This was
a late chanson de geste, existing in several versions. The oldest, in verse,
was probably composed in the middle of the fourteenth century by an
unidentified author. It is now lost, but it survives in a German adaptation,
Valentin und Namelos, set down a few decades later. There is also a French
prose version, printed in Paris in 1486 and translated in the following century into English, Spanish, Italian, Dutch, and even Swedish. The story,
constructed around the themes of the wild man, twins, and the unjustly
accused wife, is full of adventures and was read throughout Europe.[55] The
following summary is based on the prose versions.

Everything begins in Constantinople—an imaginary Constantinople—where the Empress Bélissant is courted by the archbishop but rejects
his advances; he then accuses her of adultery before the emperor. The
emperor believes the archbishop rather than his wife, and the empress

is forced to flee, accompanied by a single squire, to seek refuge in Gaul with her brother King Pépin. The journey is particularly difficult because Bélissant is pregnant. Having nearly reached the end of her journey, she gives birth beneath an oak in the forest of Orléans, alone, to twins. Unfortunately, almost immediately, a huge she-bear springs forth and carries off one of the boys in her mouth. Leaving the other one, Bélissant goes in pursuit of the beast, in vain. When she returns to the oak, the second boy has also disappeared. Bélissant is in despair, and she also learns from her squire, who had gone to seek help, that her brother Pépin sides with the emperor and does not want to take her in. Overwhelmed, Bélissant leaves the forest and then Gaul and takes refuge in Portugal.

In the meanwhile, the first twin has not been devoured by the she-bear but is nursed, licked, and kept warm by her. The animal becomes his adoptive mother and the cubs his foster brothers. He is raised in the forest among wild animals. He lives naked, does not know how to speak, and has no contact with humans. But "maternal" milk has given him a totally hairy body and prodigious strength. He is half man, half bear. When he reaches adolescence, he becomes aggressive and creates a reign of terror in the whole forest of Orléans, attacking hunters and travelers, destroying beehives, devouring livestock, and killing woodsmen. He has become a scourge for the entire region and, because of his appearance and conduct, has been given the name Wild Man. No one can defeat him.

His twin brother, who had disappeared in the forest, was rescued by King Pépin and his men who were hunting that day near Orléans. He has been given the name Valentin, because he was found on that saint's feast day. Raised at court, beloved and protected by the king—who does not know Valentin is his nephew—he grows up to be one of the best knights in Gaul. Wishing to show his gratitude to his adoptive father, he decides one day to put an end to the misfortunes affecting the forest of Orléans and to confront the Wild Man. He does so alone, not wishing to send any companion to a probable death. The encounter and the combat between the brothers are dramatic. Valentin fights with a long sword, the Wild Man at first with his bare hands, and then with an uprooted tree trunk. Valentin, speaks, curses, prays, begs. The Wild Man can only groan, but the voice of Valentin troubles him. Finally the Wild Man is wounded by Valentin's sword, bleeds copiously, and has to stop fighting. Valentin, victorious, chains him securely and brings him back to the king's court, where he himself is welcomed as a hero.

But although he has been defeated, the Wild Man is also greeted as a hero. His brutal appearance, his unknown identity, and his uncertain nature provoke not only curiosity but also fascination and even desire. For he is indeed a man, a naked and bestial man, covered with hair and resembling a bear. The ladies are very troubled by him. A few weeks later it is discovered that the Wild Man is having sexual relations with one of them, causing jealousy among the other ladies and fury among the knights. The Wild Man's amorous adventures proliferate thereafter, provoking lust, competition, and disorder. The king decides to "unwild" the Wild Man, to restore his human appearance, and give him a social status. First he is shaved completely; then he is dressed, taught to speak, taught good manners, and the profession of arms. Finally, he is baptized and given the name Orson, in memory of his former state. He becomes a handsome young man, fights valiantly, and exhibits a good deal of piety, courtesy, and virtue.

The story of Valentin and Orson then turns to romance and the marvelous. It loses its epic and mythical power. The two brothers together accomplish countless exploits. They learn through magic, from the speaking mouth of a bronze head, that they are twins, that their mother is living in exile in Portugal, and that their father is the emperor of Constantinople. Order is gradually restored. On the death of the emperor, a problem of succession arises: Bélissant no longer knows which of the two is the elder twin, the one who should inherit the throne.[56] Several solutions are considered, including having them rule in alternate years. Finally, Valentin dies and Orson becomes emperor of Constantinople. But at the end of seven years, weary of power and of court life, he withdraws deep into the forest and, in solitude, resumes his life as a hermit, if not as a bear. At his death there is talk of canonizing him.[57]

In relation to the subject of this book, this chanson de geste that turns into a novel is interesting in several respects. It points once again to the biological and symbolic kinship between man and bear. But in this case, it is not an animal who mates and procreates with a woman, but a female animal who raises a newborn as her cub and thereby transmits to him a little of her ursine nature. This is exactly what is represented in Greek mythology by the story of Paris—saved, nursed, and protected by a she-bear on Mount Ida. When he reaches adulthood, the bear-man of the forest of Orléans becomes, like Paris, a great seducer. But he is not a ravisher of women like all male bears; he does not abduct the most beautiful woman in the world but makes do with multiplying female conquests at the court of King Pépin. His actions are certainly a cause of disorder but not of ruin, as in the story of Troy.

Another remarkable element is found in the names of the two heroes. The choice of Orson is easily understood, because of the hairy appearance of the young man and his wild childhood.[58] It should be noted, however, that this is the name given to him in the French prose versions. In the original verse chanson de geste, he was called, more symbolically, *Sansnom* (Nameless), preserved in the German adaptation of the first half of the fifteenth century as *Namelos*. This creature situated outside the social order cannot have a name, only a nickname, in this case the strange *Sansnom*, already itself the beginning of a name that gives a glimpse of a future socialization. Valentin, for his part, owes his name to the saint whose feast day is celebrated on February 14, the same day as an important pagan bear festival in the central Alps. Valentin was one of the first bishops of Raetia, particularly honored in Switzerland, Bavaria, and the Tyrol. Nothing in his life and legend brought him into contact with a bear, but his feast day was set for February 14, to "cover" the festival celebrating the end of bear's first hibernation.[59] Farther west, this pagan festival was celebrated on February 2 or 3, but in Bavaria and Austria, it was the 14th, the day that much later became the festival of lovers because, in the rural calendar, it was the day when birds were supposed to begin again to chatter, cuddle, and mate. In the chanson de geste, it was by a kind of osmosis that Valentin was given the strongly ursine name that would have better suited his brother (recall that in the early fifteenth century Valentin was the name of Jean de Berry's favorite bear).

It is worth noting that, in this story of twins and the man of the woods, hair is the sign of animality and the opposite of all civilized life. The first step taken to make the Wild Man a human being is to shave him completely. Then and only then is he dressed, educated, baptized, and finally named. The order in which these operations take place is particularly significant. More than nakedness, which has meaning only in the eyes of others, more than ignorance of language or lack of education, not so infrequent, more than paganism or the lack of a name, which are found outside the Christian world, it is hairiness, excessive hairiness, that turns a man into an animal. Not just any animal, but the one that in the late Middle Ages was taken for the most beastlike of all animals: the bear.

✣ 9 ✣

From Mountain to Museum

AT the dawn of modern times, the bear's status in an emerging new symbolic bestiary was overshadowed by fresh arrivals. Increased knowledge of Greco-Roman mythology and of ancient writers helped to restore to prominence, and then to spread through printed books and carved images, legends and beliefs concerning animals to which the Middle Ages had paid only moderate attention, such as the dolphin, the bull, the monkey, and the elephant. A few decades later, the discovery of far-off worlds in Africa and America brought to zoological knowledge and imagination hitherto little-known, misunderstood, or completely unknown species, such as the rhinoceros and the giraffe. Fauna were reorganized and their value systems revised in all areas. Only the lion—perhaps because it was exotic—resisted the promotion of the newcomers. The bear, in contrast, was often neglected in favor of animals to which was attributed a richer symbolic dimension or one that was more in keeping with new forms of curiosity and sensibility. This was true of emblems, where the bear played a very minor role, and of fables and proverbs, in which it was only a walk-on character.

But the most obvious decline was to be found in the Devil's bestiary. Once its major figure, the very incarnation of the Evil One and the carrier of many vices, the bear faded into the background and, with difficulty, found his place at the intersection of the natural and supernatural worlds, linked in ways that differed from those that prevailed in the heart of the Middle Ages. The witches' sabbath is a perfect example of these changes and the devaluation of the great European beast in the demonic bestiary.

The Witches' Bestiary

Beginning in the fifteenth century, the West experienced recurring episodes of witches and their supposed conspiracies against the Church and Christendom. The oldest manifestations of the phenomenon admittedly occurred earlier: the first trials for witchcraft were held in the thirteenth century or even earlier, but the great witch hunt that was to consume Europe well into the eighteenth century got under way around 1430. The phenomenon seemed at first to be limited to mountain regions and to isolated cases. But it quickly spread in every direction, affecting in the modern period both Catholic and Protestant Europe. Moreover, trials were conducted not only against individuals but against entire communities. A bidding war over orthodoxy impelled various authorities, ecclesiastical and secular, to find witches everywhere and to denounce as a Satanic sect any group that challenged, however slightly, theological, institutional, or legal norms.[1]

In trial records and treatises of demonology, the crimes attributed to witches take on different forms according to period and region. They seem to grow increasingly serious as time passes: first, disguise and metamorphosis, spells and bewitchments, potions and philters, maleficent magical practices causing illness or death; then nocturnal travels and meetings, ritual ceremonies in honor of Satan, sacrilege and blasphemy of every variety; and finally, drinking bouts and group orgies, carnal relations with the Devil, animal and human sacrifices, murders of children, and even cannibalism. Early on, the Sabbath appeared as the major ceremony and the point of convergence for most practices of demon worship. It was particularly dangerous because the Devil was able at will to make it real or illusory and because the actions of judges, exorcists, and inquisitors might be entirely without effect.

By the fifteenth century, the Sabbath was performed as an inverted mass, an antimass, a "black" mass in which the words and gestures of the Christian ritual were parodied and denigrated. The adoration of the lamb, for example, was replaced by the very tangible and pungent adoration of the goat, a greatly devalued animal in medieval symbolism because of its foul odor, aggressive horns, extreme hairiness, and heightened sexuality. There are many accounts of Sabbaths describing the high point of the ceremony as the moment when the participants had to kiss the anus or the genitals of a large black goat with glittering eyes, the incarnation of the Devil. Sometimes the goat was replaced by a cat or a monkey, more seldom by a dog, but the animal was always black.

In one case—only one, as far as I know—a bear played the role of a Satanic animal venerated in obscene fashion. This was a Sabbath supposed to have taken place in 1462 or 1463 in the diocese of Lausanne. The story is known thanks to the trial of Perrissone Gappit in January and February 1464, some of the records of which have been preserved. Suspected first of heresy, then of witchcraft, this "ill-liked" woman of fifty told her judges that during the preceding years she had joined a sect of witches and participated six times, always on Thursday nights, in meetings "of *vauderie.*" The first time, her initiation, she had renounced the Christian faith and paid homage to the Devil, whom she thenceforth acknowledged as her master. The Devil had first appeared to her in the form of a man, but had suddenly changed into a bear, "huge, dirty, and hairy," and she had been required to "kiss its ass." In addition to paying homage, she had also had to promise to give her new lord the little finger of her right hand: the fingernail immediately (which was verified and confirmed at the trial) and the rest after her death. The ceremony of homage "to the ass" was followed by a sacrilegious meal during which they consumed the flesh of children and a general orgy where she copulated with the Devil four times. Questioned about the quality of the sperm of the creature that had taken on the "appearance of a bear," she revealed that it was not "warm and pleasant like that of a man," but "cold and horrible." Perrissone Gappit subsequently confessed to other crimes and misdeeds. She was condemned to death as a heretic and a witch and burned at the stake in February 1464.[2]

This affair, which seems to have originated in a family conflict in which hatred and vengeance took on extreme proportions,[3] differed little from other trials in mountain regions in the second half of the fifteenth century. The Sabbath ritual, in particular, followed the identical pattern, an almost archetypal one. All that was missing was the arrival of witches on their broomsticks, the frenetic dances, the profanation of the host, and the replacement of the wine of the mass with blood.[4] What sets the account by Perrissone Gappit apart is especially the appearance of the Devil in the form of a bear, not a goat, a cat, or a dog. This is obviously an archaic element, inherited from the monastic culture of the feudal period. Why had it persisted in this region, not far from the shores of Lake Geneva in the countryside near Vevey, not in the depths of a mountain valley? The reasons are unknown. But there are few documents of the time that still classify the bear among the demonic animals and even fewer that associate him with the new mythology of witchcraft. Aside from the goat, the major animal of the Sabbath, the witches' bestiary included primarily animals that were nocturnal (cat, wolf, fox, owl), black (crow, dog), slimy (frog, snake), or hybrid (basilisk, dragon, satyr). The bear was usually excluded.

The Bear in Love

The bear did, however, maintain his position with the ladies in the modern period. Many legends and traditions still saw the male bear as a seducer or abductor of girls and young women. In many respects, these legends differed little from those that went back to Greco-Roman mythology and persisted through the Middle Ages. Well into the seventeenth century, the bear was presented as half man, half animal and a lover of female flesh. These traditions were primarily oral, but were sometimes written down and gave rise to original literary creations, echoes of which can be found in the nineteenth century. In some cases, they were based on accounts of "true" stories—or at least accepted as true—that had troubled the life of a village or a valley for some length of time and the memory of which had been transmitted from one generation to the next. An example is the tragic story of the young shepherdess Antoinette Culet, victim of the monstrous passion of a bear. Hers was not, of course, a unique case, but it is one of the best documented of similar stories told in various regions of Europe, always in mountainous regions, under the Ancien Régime.

The tragedy took place in the early seventeenth century in the Duchy of Savoy, deep in a Tarentaise valley. Pierre Culet, a relatively prosperous peasant, lived with his family in the village of Naves, in the diocese of Moûtiers. His eldest daughter, Antoinette, age sixteen, was strikingly beautiful. Awaiting marriage, she helped her family with the farm work and in spring often took the sheep to pasture in the hills, far from the village. One April evening in 1602, Rogation Day, she did not return home. All attempts to find her were futile. She had perhaps fallen prey to a wolf, but no sheep had been devoured. It was not until later, much later, that the terrible adventure that had befallen her came to light.

The animal involved was not a wolf but a bear of great size with light brown fur. At nightfall, he surged into the middle of the flock and seized not one or two sheep but the pretty young shepherdess. He carried her off to his cave, where he blocked the entrance by rolling a huge stone in front of it. He sequestered her in the cave and, overcome with unnatural sexual desire, he ravished the young girl and "had carnal pleasure with her." She fainted. He watched over her, embraced her, licked her, showed true love for her. But this monstrous love was accompanied by even more monstrous sexual commerce that the young girl had to endure almost daily during her long captivity. The bear came to her every night. During the day, he left the cave and stole in the neighboring villages what he thought Antoinette needed: bread, cheese, fruit, and sometimes even clothing.

She remained a prisoner in the cave for almost three years. Early in 1605, three men of the village decided to cut down pine trees higher up and farther away than they usually did. Despite the huge stone closing the entry, Antoinette heard the sound of the axes and, for the first time in a long time, the sound of human voices. She screamed. Her cry was heard, the woodsmen approached, and she was able to tell them who she was and to beg them to help her get out of the cave. One of the men went to get help from the village. He soon returned with a large number of men. The cave entrance was unblocked and the young girl, whose wild appearance was appalling, was taken home to her father. There, once she had been washed, had her hair cut, been comforted, and dressed, she gave a detailed account of her miserable story. She confessed in particular that she had given birth to a monstrous child, half man, half bear, and the father, embracing it too fiercely, had strangled it a few weeks after its birth.

Many people in Naves had trouble believing Antoinette and thought she was mad. Others thought she was lying and that she had simply run off and things had turned out badly. Still others wondered whether she was possessed. The parish priest thought of calling on the exorcist of the diocese. He didn't have the time. The very night that Antoinette was brought home to her father, the bear came down from the mountain and howled outside the Culet farmhouse, demanding that his "little wife" be returned to him. The whole village was terrified. The bear came back the next night, and the next. But on the third night the villagers were waiting for him. The bear was shot dead, but he defended himself ferociously, killing two men. It was the largest bear ever seen in the region. The body was burned and the ashes thrown into a ravine. And young Antoinette, unable to resume a normal life, was taken to a convent far from her village, and even from her diocese, deep in a valley in the Dauphiné.

Today, the bear in love has been completely forgotten. But he was talked about for many years in the Duchy of Savoy and the neighboring regions. Shortly after the event, at the request of his bishop, a priest in the diocese of Moûtiers composed an account of the story of Antoinette Culet. It was printed in Lyon in 1605 and again in Chambéry in 1620 under the title *Discours effroyable d'une fille enlevée, violée et tenue près de trois ans par un ours dans sa caverne* (Appalling Tale of a Girl Abducted, Raped, and Held Captive by a Bear in His Cave for Nearly Three Years).[5] This publication, which gathered dust for many years on library shelves, was not rediscovered by scholars of the Dauphiné and Savoy until three and a half centuries later, but it has since then been a goldmine for ethnologists[6] and excited the fantasies of cryptozoologists,[7] especially because it can be connected to other stories in other times, concerning other regions and other cultures. In the Baltic and Scandinavian countries, to confine the examples to Europe, the traditions that presented the bear as a seducer or a ravisher of women endured until contemporary times and gave rise to copious oral literature, some of which folklorists have collected.

Did Prosper Mérimée find inspiration for his celebrated final story, *Lokis*, published in 1868, in Baltic or Scandinavian traditions?[8] It is probable, although he was more interested in and more familiar with Iberian cultures. Late in life, however, he became interested in Russia, he translated Pushkin and Gogol, and then traveled to Russia and the Baltic countries. *Lokis* takes place in Lithuania, a still-mysterious country whose great forest, untouched until the eighteenth century, was reputedly the most dangerous in Europe. *Lokis* is not just a short story, but above all a black tale, the first version of which was designed to amuse (and frighten) the ladies of the imperial court in Compiègne and Saint-Cloud where Mérimée was frequently in attendance. The second version, although revised for publication, maintains something of the wild strangeness of the original text, written to be read aloud on stormy evenings to a small, captive audience. It is not at all clear whether the ladies of the court grasped all the inner workings of the story, since it is constructed as successive tales within tales, and the monstrous truth is never revealed explicitly but only suggested.[9]

The narrator is a Prussian professor of philology, Kurt Wittenbach, who is staying at a castle belonging to the mysterious and invisible Count Michel Szémioth. The scholar is working in the magnificent library, which contains very old Baltic manuscripts. During his stay, he learns bit by bit the astonishing and appalling story of the owner of the premises, who had disappeared the year before. Forty years earlier, while hunting in the forest two days after her wedding, the count's mother was carried off by a bear and taken to a secret location. Released the next day, she remained troubled by the event throughout her life, and ended by becoming half mad. Meanwhile, nine months after her wedding and her disappearance in the depths of the forest, she gave birth to a son, who seemed normal but whom she soon came to hate. On several occasions she even asked that he be put to death. Her order was never executed and the child, although rejected by his mother, grew up normally, became an attractive, cultivated man, even erudite, but often lost in thought. As the years passed, his strange character gave rise to misunderstanding and later worry. Increasingly misanthropic, he found pleasure only in forests, in the company of woodsmen and wild animals. But he never hunted, and all dogs feared him. Nonetheless, he finally married a ravishing young Polish woman full of life and spirit who, it was thought, would draw him out of his depression. What happened on the wedding night is unknown, but in the early morning the count had disappeared and the woman was found dead in her bed, with a huge bite on her neck that no human being could have caused.

The story of Count Michel is not told in a straightforward way but revealed in scraps that the narrator gradually puts together, causing the reader increasing unease. The story is also interrupted by philological digressions that do not weaken the tale but help give it a strong feeling of strangeness. It is never said that Count Michel is half man, half bear, born from the rape of his mother by the beast that carried her off two days after her wedding. But the reader finally understands that, and if he is cultivated, finds confirmation in the fact that for Russian culture *Mikhail* is the proper name traditionally given to bears, and that in Lithuanian, *lokis* (the licker), the title of the story, is the term usually used to designate the animal. Mérimée seems to have been delighted to tell this tale to frighten the ladies in the entourage of Empress Eugénie, but his story is based on extensive erudition and solid knowledge of bear stories in Slavic and Baltic cultures. In addition, all his talent is expressed in the deliberate contrast between the monstrousness of what is suggested and the almost neutral character of the style.[10] This is certainly one of the finest French short stories of the nineteenth century. But it is also a cruel tale that echoes all the older accounts featuring a male bear seized by a monstrous desire for a young woman.

From Emblem Books to Books of Fables

I have already shown that medieval Europe knew such accounts, mostly drawn from the oral traditions of pagan Germany and Scandinavia, and how they were integrated into various chronicles, some of them turned into genuine literary works.[11] In the early Renaissance, although the bear in love with girls and young women had not completely disappeared, he had lost a good deal of his violence and savagery. He was no longer a beast avid for new flesh or menstrual blood, but a peaceable and courteous animal, almost a delicate lover, careful not to injure the lady he loves. Sometimes the love is shared, as in the story of Orson the Wild Man or in the tales constructed around the theme of Beauty and the Beast.

A French play on words, widespread in the fifteenth and sixteenth centuries, gives an indication of this new relationship between bears and women: it consists of breaking down the syntagm *d'amour* into *dame* + *ours* (lady + bear), turning it into a rebus of the kind that appeared frequently in proverbs and devices as well as in some images.[12] Indeed, starting around 1450, various wooden engravings, tokens, and medals, several miniatures, and even two tapestries showed a woman dancing or conversing with or embracing a bear and seeming to take pleasure in the activity.[13] From a pair of phonemes, at first sight far removed from one another, the play of language had made a pair of lovers and transmitted it to iconography. It may very well be that the mysterious lady des Ursines, supposedly beloved by Duke Jean de Berry,[14] was herself the product of a similar rebus, though not during the duke's lifetime, but rather a few decades after his death in 1416, in the writings of his great-nephew René d'Anjou. The duke's great-nephew was very fond of emblems, allegories, and rebuses. For example, his *Livre du cuer d'amours espris* turned the figures of the lady and the bear (*dame* + *ours* = *d'amours*) into a pair of lovers.[15] A little later, several emblem books and collections of rebuses followed suit, presenting in words and pictures women in love with bears. They sometimes had a harsh moral, condemning through this example all forms of carnal love. An example is found in a manuscript collection of rebuses composed in Picardy toward the end of the sixteenth century, where the image of the couple (woman and bear) is accompanied by the maxim: "Mal est qui se mesle d'amours,"[16] a play on words with multiple meanings *(mal/male)* condemning both human and animal love and urging the reader to prefer divine love, the only one that leads down the path of the good.

But in printed emblem books in the sixteenth century, the figure of the bear was more often associated with anger than with lust or love.[17]

Generally speaking, leaving aside the case of the she-bear licking and shaping her cubs to make them "fully bears" (a symbol of "art stronger than nature," to be compared with the famous saying of Erasmus: "Man is certainly not born, but made man"),[18] the animal remained negative and the carrier of many vices. The vice of *gula* (gluttony) was invariably depicted by the image of a bear trying to steal honey attacked by furious bees. Since bees were particularly prized in Renaissance animal symbolism, their enemy the bear was necessarily a hateful creature, frequently presented as such. To the various vices and five deadly sins the late Middle Ages attributed to the great beast (anger, lust, sloth, envy, and gluttony), sixteenth-century emblems managed to add new ones, particularly those having to do with the idea of trickery *(astutia),* very negative in the medieval value system. Using trickery to gain one's ends was absolutely diabolical conduct, though perhaps regarded in a more ambivalent light in printed emblem books. One of them, published in Heidelberg in 1562 with engravings by Mathias Merian, shows the combat between a bull and a bear. While the bull charges, leading with his horns, the bear rolls on the ground; the caption, *astu haud formidine* (in trickery, not out of fear), emphasizes the bear's intelligence; he has not lain down out of fear of the bull but to avoid his horns and wear him out.[19]

There is nothing like this in proverbs and fables, from which the image of the clever bear is totally absent. Here, the tradition of the *Roman de Renart* had survived, continuing to present the bear as a stupid and clumsy creature, even sometimes accentuating his ridiculousness and misfortune. Illustrations can be found in the three collections of fables by Jean de la Fontaine published between 1668 and 1694. The animals he depicts require no particular zoological knowledge. They are generally "familiar" animals—an essential concept for studying the cultural history of the relations between men and animals—some domestic, some wild, most indigenous, and a few exotic. All of them are part of the most ordinary bestiary of western culture since Antiquity, even the ones, such as the lion and the elephant, that could not be found on European soil.

La Fontaine exercised little originality in presenting this limited bestiary, not only because the fables in which he did not take the matter from one of his predecessors are few in number, but also because he wanted to have each animal maintain its most common traits. Not natural traits, but those attributed by culture. It would indeed be absurd to continue to regard La Fontaine, as he was long viewed, as an attentive observer of the fauna of the French countryside. It would be comparably illusory to believe that the post of *maître des eaux et forêts* of Château-Thierry, which he had had to purchase and which he held for nearly twenty years (did he really spend much time in the forests of Champagne?), enabled him to study that fauna as a naturalist. In the seventeenth century, literary creation was not taken from life, particularly in the highly erudite genre of the fable. Moreover, contrary to received ideas, La Fontaine was never an authentic countryman, and hardly a forester; at most he was a "gardener," that is, someone who frequented gardens.[20] The animals he depicts are therefore not the ones he is said to have frequented in his alleged rural idleness. Most of them were the ones already depicted by ancient and medieval fabulists, tellers of Oriental tales, the *Roman de Renart,* and all the traditions connected to collections of fables and animal poetry. Besides, loving field and forest, seeking out cool streams and shade trees, being neighborly with shepherds and their sheep, observing the sky and the birds, and feeling in harmony with the rhythm of nature, the weather, and the seasons, all come from a poetic tradition. Since Virgil, poets had liked to say it, sing it, proclaim it, but really doing it, in the rain and mud, amid thorns and insects, was out of the question. It was an attitude constructed around book learning whose subject was not nature but one's idea of nature.[21] Its first source is to be found in libraries.[22]

Relying on tradition, books, and images enables the fabulist to save himself from having to provide many unnecessary details, because it is in books and not in elusive nature that the truth of beings and things is to be found. It also enables him, from the first lines of a fable, to change the reader into a tender accomplice. The reader is pleased to find what he already knows: the lion, king of the beasts, is proud and authoritarian; the fox, sly and elusive; the wolf, hungry and cruel; the donkey, stupid and lazy; the crow, talkative and voracious. From one fable to another, the animals maintain their attributes and characters, notably the bear, who is constantly presented in a ridiculous light. He is not, of course, one of the major figures in La Fontaine's bestiary—he has been supplanted in that role by the lion, the wolf, the fox, the donkey, and even the dog—but he nonetheless appears in six fables in which he shows himself to be simultaneously lazy, stupid, greedy, and clumsy, all traits derived from the tradition of animal tales and the *Roman de Renart*.

In the fable *L'Ours et l'Amateur de jardins* (The Bear and the Garden-Lover),[23] perhaps the best known of the fables in which the bear is the hero, he is also ignorant, dangerous, and melancholy. Having established a friendship with an old man who was as bored as he, a bear who has come down from his mountain and out of his forest settles in with his new companion. He contributes to meals by hunting game, and at the time of siesta becomes a "flyswatter": when the old man falls asleep, the bear chases away the flies with his huge paw before they disturb the sleeper. But one day, a fly manages to land on the good man's nose. Thinking he is doing the right thing, the bear crushes the fly by hurling a huge paving stone at his companion's face, killing him immediately. This enables La Fontaine to conclude cruelly: "Rien n'est si dangereux qu'un ignorant ami / Mieux vaudrait un sage ennemi." (Beware the well-inclined but stupid friend / A clever foe is safer in the end). Here as elsewhere, the bear is presented as a stupid, clumsy, and harmful animal.

The Cruelty of Proverbs

La Fontaine did not invent the motif of the *pavé de l'ours*. It can be found in several works of the sixteenth century, and it is attested as a proverb in several European languages in the fifteenth century:[24] "throw the bear's paving stone" or, more often, "do a favor like a bear," meaning behave stupidly, blunder, cause harm when you want to be helpful. The motif can even be found in hagiography. In the *Vita* of Saint Gerold of Feldkirch, compiled sometime between the eleventh and thirteenth centuries, the fairly well-known saint shelters an injured bear in the hermitage he has just established not far from Lake Constance. The animal becomes his companion, helps him in his domestic labors, and protects him from brigands and wild animals. One day as Gerold sleeps, the bear sees a snake creeping toward the saint's bed; he immediately picks up a large stone and throws it at the reptile. But he is clumsy, and not the snake but the saint is mortally wounded, killed like La Fontaine's old man by "the bear's paving stone" *(lapide ursi interfectus).*[25]

In sixteenth- and seventeenth-century collections of sayings and proverbs, the phrase "do a favor like a bear" is both more frequent and more widespread, particularly in German-language compilations: *Jemandem einen Bärendienst erweisen.* The bear is, moreover, one of the principal animals in most of these collections. In the one by Johannes Agricola, a Protestant scholar and theologian close to Luther, sixteen of the 750 proverbs concern bears.[26] Among the most famous, found in all later compilations, can be found (slightly modernized): *Man soll die Bärenhaut nicht verkaufen, ehe der Bär getötet ist* (One shouldn't sell the bearskin before the bear is dead);[27] *sich auf die Bärenhaut legen* (to lie on a bearskin, that is, be idle in the way the ancient Germans or Merovingian kings supposedly were); *Du suchst den Bären und stehst vor ihm* (You're looking for the bear and standing right in front of him); *Allen Tieren Friede gesetzt, ausser Bären und Wölfen* (Peace reigns among all animals except between bears and wolves);[28] *Es ist besser einen Bären loszulassen als einen Bären anzubinden* (It is better to let a bear go than to capture him); *Bär und Büffel können keinen Fuchs fangen* (Bear and buffalo cannot catch a fox). Among the few sixteenth- and seventeenth-century proverbs that seem to be attested only in French are: "Anyone who shares honey with a bear will get the smaller portion"; "A bear not in chains will not dance"; "Anyone who wants to scratch a bear needs iron nails"; "If a branch falls on a bear, he groans; if it's a tree, he is silent."

Of the expressions that refer to the bear, the most common is *un ours mal léché.* It exists in all European languages to describe a coarse, boorish, brutal, bilious person, a rough customer. It obviously alludes to the legend of the bear cubs born unshaped whose mother licks them at length to give them a normal appearance and integrate them into the society of bears. Sometimes the expression is reduced simply to "a bear," proof that the animal was seen primarily as a coarse creature not to be associated with.

Other expressions confirm this unpleasant character: "go to the bear," that is, "go to the devil"; "riding on a bear," fearing nothing; "offer one's bear," try to pass on to someone a task or a burden one wants to get rid of. Comparisons are even more humiliating. Foolish, vile, crude, clumsy, dirty, dark, ugly, wicked, cruel, hairy "like a bear": there is a long list of deprecatory adjectives associated in the sixteenth and seventeenth centuries with the first king of the beasts, in French and in all the neighboring languages. Only the expression "strong as a bear" recalls his former status and presents the animal in a more favorable light.

Despite the unattractive picture of the animal presented by the lexicon and turns of phrase, the bear was still in the modern period a heraldic emblem to which some families and communities remained loyal. He did appear infrequently in armorial bearings, even less often than in the Middle Ages, but some famous shields and banners still proclaimed the strength and prestige of the great beast that was elsewhere so devalued. This was the case, for example, in the coats of arms of three European capitals, in which the bear played the role of a "speaking" figure and a conquering emblem: Bern, Berlin, and Madrid.

The coat of arms of Bern is the oldest and, for heraldry, the most "speaking": the play on words in German between the name of the city *(Bern)* and that of the principal figure *(Bär)* is perfectly clear. The bear of Bern first appeared in an impression of the great seal of the city, appended to a document dated 1224: it is a "free" bear, depicted without a muzzle, *passant* in the seal's field. The same bear is subsequently found on all the seals of Bern, emblazoned or not, on its banners and coats of arms,[29] on coins and medals, insignia and livery, on all public monuments and official objects and documents belonging to the city or under its authority. The heraldic bear can be seen even today everywhere in Bern, in souvenir and confectionery shops where it is the emblematic image of both the city and the canton, the largest in Switzerland. Sometimes, its emblematic function extends to the entire country, and the bear is not only Bernese, but Swiss, since Bern is the capital of the Confederation and has long dominated the other cantons. Propaganda images of the sixteenth and seventeenth centuries were already displaying this "Swiss" bear, alliance with which was sought by the French, the Imperials, the Spanish, and the Italians, because it often provided remarkable soldiers to its allies, although they were often mercenaries. The political bestiary of the time juxtaposed or confronted the imperial eagle; the English leopard; the Spanish, Dutch, Venetian, and Florentine lions; the Milanese snake; the Gallic rooster; and the Swiss bear. Later, in the nineteenth and twentieth centuries, it was the Russian and Soviet bear that occupied center stage and was allied to or an enemy of the eagles and lions of the Western countries.

A Speaking Figure

Bern is not an ancient city. It was founded on the banks of the Aar in 1191 by the powerful Berthold V, Duke of Zähringen, who held large fiefs in southern Germany and northern Switzerland. An old legend, going back to just after the city's founding, says that the duke, who was seeking a name for his new city, decided to give it the name of the first animal his men, who had gone to get wood in the nearby forest, came upon. It was a bear (*Bär* in German), hence Bern. Another version of the legend, more glorious but more recent, says that Duke Berthold, hunting in the Aar forest, had victoriously confronted a bear of exceptional strength in hand-to-hand combat. To commemorate this exploit, he decided to establish on the very spot a city with the name of the bear.[30] These legends, transmitted by several chronicles of the late Middle Ages,[31] are themselves important historical documents. But historians of today cannot fail to remark that the founder of the city of Bern had a given name—traditional in his family—that began with the syllable *Ber-* (*Ber: Bär*). Did he not simply give the new city his own name, abbreviated? It should also be pointed out that Bern is located in a region in which, in the first century before our era, the goddess Artio was particularly venerated. Artio was the Celtic equivalent of the Greek Artemis and, like her, the protector of bears. In 1832, at Muri, in the Bern region, various votive objects were found, among which was a small bronze depicting the seated goddess offering fruit to a bear who approaches her in a familiar manner.[32] The Bern region seems to have celebrated the bear long before the foundation of the city, which suggests that the toponym *Bern,* or its Celtic equivalent, is older than the city.

In any event, it is clear that by the late Middle Ages, the bear was playing the role of a veritable totem. He brought together in a single image the ancestors and the residents of the city, at the same time that he protected, defended, and represented them. Several painted images, accompanying the text of the *Chronicles* of Diebold Schilling in several illuminated manuscripts between 1485 and 1515, show the Bernese making war against Bourguignons, Milanese, or other Swiss cantons. On three occasions, the Bernese are depicted not as men armed from head to toe, but as bears carrying swords, lances, banners, halberds, and feathered helmets. These are images of great symbolic power that echo the famous "bear pit" set in the heart of the city since the fifteenth century. The precise date it was established is unknown, but the pit already existed in 1476, when Duke René II of Lorraine, to thank the Bernese for helping him win victory in his war against Charles the Bold, established a bear pit in Nancy similar to the one that had been visible in Bern for several years, if not several decades. For the occasion, the Bernese gave the duke a splendid red bear *(ursum russum formosum).*[33] The bear pit in Nancy remained until the eighteenth century, when King Stanislas renovated the center of the city.

The more famous pit of Bern still exists and is today the most visited "monument" in Switzerland. Accounting records make it possible to follow its uninterrupted history starting in 1480. From 1513 on, there are records for almost every year of the number of bears in the pit (sometimes with their names and the names of their keepers), the sums spent to feed and care for them, repairs and construction work, and any incidents or accidents that might occur. In addition, at the relevant dates, the death or departure of any particular bear, the arrival of a replacement, the visit of a distinguished guest, or the transfer of the pit (it changed location several times), are all recorded.[34] This is a set of documents of great richness, as well as a unique case. Not only has the city perpetually kept within its perimeter one or more living examples of its totemic animal, but it has preserved their memory in the archival documents that have been kept for more than five centuries. And this animal, obviously, is not just any animal—it is a bear! Could it be anything else?

The bear of Berlin is less totemic and less well documented than the bear of Bern, but it is also "speaking": its presence on the German capital's shield is explained by the play on words between *Bär* and *Berlin*. The oldest example is found on a seal appended to a document dated 1415, but it was only in the modern period, when Berlin definitively became the capital of the Electors of Brandenburg, and then the capital of Prussia, that the Berlin bear became a rallying figure for the residents of the city. Aside from the Nazi period, when the bear was frequently brought to the fore and a contest was even held to give it a more "National Socialist," that is, more expressionist, design, the city's heraldic animal never played a major emblematic and symbolic role comparable to that of the bear of Bern.[35] Besides, Berlin was too cosmopolitan, open, and changeable a city, or too hungry for modernity to be embodied in a single figure, inherited from ancient heraldry and built around a kind of pun.

With regard to the coat of arms of Madrid, of whose bear nonnatives are generally not aware, it is not certain that it is truly "speaking" in the sense in which that word is used in heraldry, at least as far as the animal is concerned. The current shield, which is very charged, shows a tree bearing fruit, a bear standing next to the tree, and a surrounding border strewn with seven stars.[36] The various figures differ in age. The bear appeared first on the oldest seal of Madrid that has been preserved, dated 1381; then came the tree, toward the end of the fifteenth century; and finally the border with stars, almost a century later, in 1572. At that time, the tree was already seen as a speaking figure and identified as an arbutus, whose name in Castilian is *madrono*, and from that to *Madrid* is only a small step. There was nothing of the kind with regard to the bear. Several writers in the sixteenth and seventeenth centuries saw it as a memory of an older bear, the one displayed on the banner of King Alfonso VIII of Castile at his great defeat of the Muslims in the battle of Las Navas de Tolosa in 1212. This thirteenth-century bear was said to be the descendant of another royal bear, belonging to the Visigoth kings who had ruled over the northern Iberian Peninsula from the fifth to the seventh century. The Visigoth bear is purely legendary, but it was believed genuine in the early modern period, even by the most serious French writers.[37] Subsequently, Ancien Régime scholars offered another explanation for the presence of a bear on the arms of Madrid: the old Latin name for the city was said to have been *Ursuria*, a recollection of a Roman legion, the *legio ursa* that allegedly founded the city. There is no documentary evidence of the name or the legion, but for many decades scholarship strove to hide the fact that Madrid was originally not a Roman city but a fortress built by Muslims in the ninth century, called *Majrit*.

The reasons for the choice of the bear remain mysterious. Seeing it as taken from local fauna—the city is ringed by mountains which were long forested—is a rather flimsy explanation. It is better to see the bear as a speaking figure, like the arbutus, and to associate the proper name *Madrid* with the common noun *maderno*, well attested in thirteenth- and fourteenth-century Castilian to designate a virile man, and perhaps by extension, the quintessentially masculine creature, the *masle beste,* the bear.[38]

Naturalists' Confusions

If in the late Middle Ages and throughout modern times, fables, proverbs, and coats of arms present the image of the bear in a relatively coherent form, the same thing is not true of zoology. The discipline did make considerable progress between the fifteenth and the eighteenth century. Printed books and engraved pictures permitted a more rapid spread of knowledge. Iconography was reshaped, libraries specialized, cabinets of curiosities proliferated. Further, the development of postal services and the increase in correspondence fostered exchanges between scholars, and many universities established chairs of zoology, where instruction was no longer only theoretical and speculative but concrete as well, and dissections were conducted for pedagogical purposes. But all animals did not benefit from this progress in equal measure. The sixteenth century was particularly interested in birds and fish; knowledge about the latter, rudimentary in the Middle Ages, made immense progress. Similarly, the seventeenth century, when the microscope was invented, was curious about insects, "worms," and tiny animals. In the eighteenth, when Europeans ventured into new oceans and new worlds, the primary focus was on hitherto unknown species, the discovery of which required a revision and expansion of zoological classifications.

Knowledge of the bear derived little benefit from these advances. One sometimes has the opposite impression that many works of the early modern period display less knowledge than some medieval encyclopedias and especially than the *Livre de la chasse* of Gaston Phébus, Comte de Foix, compiled in 1387 and 1388. The Swiss doctor and naturalist Conrad Gesner (1516–1565), for example, whose knowledge was vast and whose library was even larger, contributed nothing new compared to what had come before. In the first volume of his huge *Historia animalium,* on quadrupeds, published in Zurich in 1551, the chapter on bears is prolix, but deals more with symbolic history than with zoology.[39] That makes it a work of great interest for historians—notably because it is a repository for all the medieval traditions, expressions, beliefs, and legends connected to the bear.[40] It was by no means, however, a turning point in natural history, either for the bear or for most other animals. As a matter of taste, Gesner was more drawn to botany than zoology, and he was most original in his discussion of plants.[41]

A similar negligible advance in knowledge is found in the work of Ulisse Aldrovandi (1522–1605), a well-known doctor and professor at the University of Bologna, who published little about animals in his lifetime. But his students collected his lecture notes in various books printed after his death.[42] The pages on the bear present nothing new.[43] They strive to classify the various species of bear (essentially according to the color of their fur) but create more confusion than order and present an uncertain image of the animal that endured. This image was employed by most writers of the seventeenth century, who, when it came to quadrupeds, tended to plunder the huge collections by Gesner and Aldrovandi. An example is Jan Jonston (1603–1675), a Scottish doctor who settled in Leiden, author of a large zoological encyclopedia that was still almost medieval in conception and organization; only the copper engravings introduce a little novelty in the precision of the pictures.[44]

Generally speaking, knowledge of the brown bear hardly changed between the invention of printing and the major works of natural history of the eighteenth century. Even scientists who performed dissections—usually using the body of a bear from a royal or princely menagerie—had little effect on the level of knowledge. An example was Claude Perrault, better known as an architect and as the brother of Charles, the author of the celebrated tales. Claude had diverse interests, including anatomy and medicine. He had the opportunity, along with some fellow artists and doctors, to dissect several animals that had died in the royal menagerie (now the Jardin des Plantes), among them, in 1667, "a very old bear." But the publication that came out of this dissection contributed no new information about the animal's internal organs,[45] which had long been known to be similar to those of humans.

While knowledge of the brown bear made no progress in the sixteenth and seventeenth centuries, knowledge of the polar bear did develop and achieve greater precision. The animal was unknown to ancient writers and misunderstood by medieval clerics. But there had been polar bears in some royal menageries in the central Middle Ages (they had been sent as gifts with other animals from "the North" by the kings of Norway and Denmark to some monarchs in Western Europe).[46] It was believed at the time that polar bears were only a variety of brown bear with very light-colored fur. Indeed, when removed from the arctic ice fields and the polar cold, the polar bear's fur is never truly white. Subsequently, the animal seems to have been better understood, particularly in Scandinavia and northern Germany, even though authors of bestiaries and encyclopedias did not mention it. However, in the middle of the sixteenth century, in his huge and fascinating "history" of the peoples of the North—a veritable ethnological inquiry concerning the populations of Scandinavia and Lapland—the erudite archbishop of Uppsala, Olaus Magnus (1490–1558), mentions polar bears on several occasions and even devotes a whole chapter to them.[47] He describes them as "very large and very strong" (*ursi albi maximi et fortissimi*), describes the clever way they fish under the ice, and emphasizes the intense trade in their skins. Olaus Magnus did not get his knowledge from books alone. He had been driven from his native Sweden by the Lutheran Reformation and taken refuge in Rome, where incomparable libraries were available to him. But as a young man, in 1518 and 1519, he had made a complete tour of northern Scandinavia, had ventured as far as Lapland and the Lofoten Islands, perhaps even farther north, and had collected in the field a great deal of information concerning daily life, material culture, legends, and beliefs.

In fact, well before Olaus Magnus and succeeding writers who plundered his work, sailors were probably the first to understand that the polar bear was not the same animal as the bear of temperate zones. First came the whale hunters, who had begun to venture far into Arctic waters, sometimes as far as Spitzbergen, by the late fifteenth century, followed a few decades later by adventurers searching in the North Atlantic for a sea passage to East Asia, China, and the Spice Islands. Venturing beyond the Arctic Circle, they saw many polar bears in Greenland, northern Hudson Bay, and on the large islands later named Baffin and Ellesmere. Through their accounts and sketches, as well as through the animals captured and brought back alive to temperate climates, a clearer picture of the polar bear gradually emerged. In works of zoology of the eighteenth century, it is no longer confused with the brown bear.

In Buffon's *Histoire naturelle*, for example, the chapter on the bear was first published in 1756. It clearly distinguishes between the two animals, recognizing two different species in the "land bear" and the "sea bear," the latter inhabiting the "icy seas" and feeding exclusively on fish and sea animals. But Buffon was not well informed about the bear family, at least compared to other writers of the time, such as the eminent Swedish scientist Carl Linnaeus, whom Buffon despised and whose classification system he abhorred. Ill informed and not very curious about the animal, Buffon identified three subspecies of "land bear": brown, black, and white. The first is found in cold and temperate climates, primarily in mountain regions, like those seen in the Alps; it is fierce, carnivorous, a scavenger, stronger than the wolf, and attacks all animals, including the largest, and even humans. The second is more peaceable and is found in the forests of northern Europe and America; timid if not fearful, it does not attack humans and eats primarily vegetables and honey. The third is more omnivorous and dangerous, inhabits the deep forests of Muscovy, Lithuania, and Great Tartary (western Siberia), but has been little studied and remains badly understood. In Buffon's view, then, there were two kinds of white bear, polar and forest bears. But he explains that classifying the various species of bear is not an easy endeavor and that "writers have not varied so much on any other animal."[48]

Despite his uncertainties and hesitations, Buffon delighted in correcting his predecessors' errors, even going as far back as Aristotle and Pliny, who were mistaken on certain points (which had been known for decades, if not centuries): no, bears do not mate *more hominum,* face to face, belly against belly, but like all quadrupeds; no, the female's gestation period is not thirty days but several months; no, cubs are not born shapeless and lifeless, they are perfectly formed and quite alive, but very small. Besides, in Buffon's view, it was not only the cubs that were misshapen, but all bears, young or adult, male or female.

Indeed, the great man did not like bears; in fact he hated them, perhaps because he knew little about them and did not know where to put them in his own classification system. In the *Histoire naturelle,* the chapter on the bear is far removed from those on the lion and other wild animals. Bears fall between marmots and beavers, with the hibernating animals and not the fearsome beasts. In the 1767–1768 edition, Buffon gives it only twenty pages, compared to the forty he devotes to the lion, the bear's old rival for the title of king of the beasts, and even thirty-five for the lowly beaver.[49] In this respect, the *Histoire naturelle* does not differ from other books on zoology in the eighteenth century, which had little to say about bears.

But Buffon's hatred for the animal probably had a different source, in its anthropomorphic appearance and in all the legends still circulating during the Enlightenment about the kinship between bears and men. For Buffon, the animal "closest to man" was not the bear but the horse, to which he was personally devoted and on which he wrote magnificent and justly famous pages. The horse is the first animal given a separate chapter in the *Histoire naturelle,* just after those discussing man. But later, much later in the book, the naturalist is obliged to acknowledge that of all animals the bear is the one that externally most resembles a human being. He has similar hands and feet, he is a "plantigrade," he can sit and stand, he can hold and use tools, he walks, runs, jumps, swims, climbs, and even dances like a man. Buffon cannot conceal these obvious similarities. But once he has enumerated them, he erases them with a venomous final sentence, ending the chapter on the bear on a spiteful note, which I deliberately chose as an epigraph for this book: "But all these rough resemblances with man make the bear all the more deformed and give him no superiority over other animals."[50] This sentence certainly would have delighted the clergy of the Carolingian period struggling against the pagan cults of the bear in the European forests.

A Survivor in the Museum

After Buffon, naturalists' discourse became less vindictive but remained elementary and gave rise to little curiosity or passion. The bear was left out of the great debates of the first half of the nineteenth century over the fixity or the evolution of species. Neither Lamarck (1744–1829), nor Cuvier (1769–1832), nor Geoffroy Saint-Hilaire (1772–1844), much less Darwin (1809–1882), relied on the bear to support their ideas. For them, and for all the zoologists of their time, the animal that was thought of and perceived as the closest to man was the monkey, an idea already more or less put forth by Aristotle but that medieval Christianity had violently rejected and that had not really returned to the forefront of naturalism and philosophy until the Enlightenment. The controversies around transformism and Darwin's groundbreaking work *On the Origin of Species,* published in 1859,[51] gave the idea great currency in the second half of the nineteenth century.

Nothing like this occurred with the bear. When zoologists dwelled on the subject it was to try to distinguish new species and varieties in the bear family. With the brown bear, that had been observed on three continents, differences from one individual to another were so numerous and so frequent (size and general morphology, appearance of the head, fur color, feeding habits, hibernation behavior) that they suggested the existence of several subspecies. In addition, between the late eighteenth and the mid nineteenth century, western zoology seemed to have been afflicted with a taxonomic frenzy in which classifications proliferated, were revised, corrected, completed, and abolished, and new ones proposed, which were in turn constantly reshaped. Families, genera, species, and varieties came and went on winds of speculation. But starting in the period from 1860 to 1880, more numerous discoveries of fossil bears by prehistorians, along with considerable progress in paleontology, made it possible to reconsider these classifications and establish more well-founded genealogies. The tendency was toward grouping together, so that today, for most naturalists, the family Ursidae is divided into only seven species (there were as many as twenty-four around 1850): the giant panda (China, Tibet), the spectacled bear (the Andes cordillera), the sun bear (tropical forests of Southeast Asia), the sloth bear (mountain regions of northern India and Sri Lanka), the black bear (North America), the brown bear (Europe, Asia, North America), and the polar bear (Arctic and sub-Arctic regions). Their kinship has been proved by genetics, but except for the giant panda, clearly individualized, the boundaries separating them are not always very precise. Many cases of hybridization have been observed, for example, between black and brown bears, and even between brown and polar bears, which relativizes the notion of autonomous species in bears, especially because the hybrid offspring have had fertile descendants.

Modern, like medieval, knowledge of the bear long remained uncertain. For reasons difficult to understand, zoologists of the nineteenth and twentieth centuries were uninterested in the animal (while they were passionate about the wolf) until they belatedly realized that it was among the species threatened with extinction.

Obvious evidence of this lack of interest can be found in the status granted to the book by an amateur or an "almost amateur," which was for several decades a required reference work: *L'Ours brun* by Marcel Couturier (1897–1973), published at the author's expense in Grenoble in 1954.[52] Until the 1980s and 1990s, in magazines and learned journals, including those of the most famous English, German, and American universities, this book was cited as the principal authority in the realm of studies of bears. It is indeed a comprehensive survey, the most voluminous ever written, but it is very vague in strictly scientific terms. The exposition adopts scientific airs and is amply developed, particularly with regard to anything that concerns anatomy. But many of the author's assertions are weak, and the critical apparatus is nonexistent. The best part of the book deals with observation of the bear in the field, his behavior, and his eating habits. There is a good reason for this. Marcel Couturier, a medical doctor, a naturalist in his spare time, was a man of the outdoors, and above all a great hunter, one of the most famous in the years between 1930 and 1960, a well-known killer of chamois, ibex, grouse, and bears. Despite his call for the creation of reserves and national parks, his passion for the hunt no doubt contributed to the scarcity of the species he studied. He killed bears on three continents, boasted of the fact in his book, sometimes recounts the hunt in detail, and writes passages that a half-century later seem unbearable in their lack of awareness and their cruelty.[53] He goes even further in printing as plates three large photographs that show him posing proudly in front of the body of the last brown bear he killed (massacred might be more accurate), on August 24, 1953, near Urdos in the Aspe valley of the Pyrenees.[54]

In fact, the bear, once king of the beasts, ancestor or relative of man for many cultures, is an animal that has only a few decades left to live, at least in its wild state. Despite all the protective measures that have been taken in the last quarter-century in Europe, America, and Asia, its disappearance seems inevitable, whether it is black, brown, or white. On this tragic problem, the figures are both eloquent and pathetic. They are also controversial, which adds a pitiful dimension to a terrifying observation.

I will concentrate on the brown bear, the subject of this book. In 2007, the world population of brown bears was between 220,000 and 230,000, very unevenly distributed throughout the temperate zone of the northern hemisphere, between the 30th and 75th parallels. They are most numerous in Alaska (30,000 to 40,000) and in western and northwestern Canada

(25,000), in eastern Siberia (unknown number, perhaps around 60,000 or 80,000), in Japan (about 2,500), in Tibet and China (several thousand), and in the Caucasus (3,000). In Europe, the population is a remnant confined to forest and mountain regions where human activities have been limited. The regions with the largest populations are in northern Russia, Estonia, Karelia, Belarus, the Ural mountains, the Carpathians (particularly Romania), and the Balkans. But the wars in the former Yugoslavia and Albania reduced the bear population in the Balkans, which had been relatively abundant until recently. Several hundred animals perished under the bombs and in fires, others fled to Bulgaria, Greece, Hungary, Slovenia, and even Italy, while still others simply died of hunger. Farther west, the few locations still containing a few dozen brown bears are in Sweden and Norway, Trentino and the Abruzzi, and the Cantabrian mountains.[55]

In France, bears disappeared early on from the Massif Central and the Cévennes, perhaps by the middle of the seventeenth century; from the Vosges in the late eighteenth (the last one was seen near Guebwiller in 1786); from the Jura around 1860. A few dozen remained in the French Alps in the late nineteenth century (whereas the animal had already deserted Piedmont and western Switzerland), but they were reduced to a few isolated individuals after the First World War.[56] The last bear killed in the French Alps was shot in 1921, on August 13, around noon, in Basse-Maurienne, on the heights of La Chambre, at an altitude of about 2,000 meters. It was a very old female, "with worn-down teeth," who had nonetheless stolen a few sheep over the preceding weeks. There were three hunters, and the fatal shot was fired by a man named Théodule André, who immediately became famous as "Théodule the bear-killer." The animal was carried down into the valley and given to a butcher in La Chambre, who butchered it and sold the meat by the kilo.[57] This she-bear was not the last one seen in the French Alps. Several of her fellow creatures seem to have appeared here and there, chiefly in Maurienne and the Chartreuse Massif. It was further south, however, in Vercors, that in September 1937 the last living bear was seen at an altitude of about 1,000 meters above Saint-Martin-en-Vercors. The shepherd who saw it was named Julien Arnaud, and he was accompanied by his two children, his dog, and his flock. They were all terrified. The beast was small, but it was more or less red and therefore terrifying.[58]

Bears have not completely disappeared from the Pyrenees on either the French or the Spanish side. But it is impossible to give an exact number of surviving individuals: perhaps between five and twenty on both sides, including the ones recently imported from Slovenia. In Spain, bears are more numerous in the Cantabrian mountains than in the Pyrenees and are not a source of dispute. In France, as in Trentino in Italy, "reintroductions" have provoked vigorous debates and controversies sometimes verging on mass hysteria. Some enemies of bears have lost all sense of proportion and attributed to them many more harms than they were able to commit (cattle killed, trees torn up, hives and crops ravaged, food stolen, children attacked, and so on). Moreover, they have defended their positions with rather weak arguments in light of what is really at stake.[59] On the other side, the advocates of reintroduction do not explain their reasons clearly and do not explain why they prefer Slovenian to Iberian bears. That the state, local communities, animal defense associations, and shepherds cannot manage to agree on the subject is disheartening, but not very surprising for a historian of the bear. The problem at issue is not so much economic or ecological, nor tied to any particular valley and its ecosystem, as essentially symbolic. For that very reason, it is insoluble. Reintroducing bears will probably accomplish nothing; in any case it will not dissipate a general bad conscience which seems to have reached a deeper level than for any other species. The bear, it cannot be repeated often enough, is not an animal like the others, and relations that human beings have had with it have always been passionate. They still are, as recent disputes have demonstrated (which hardly exist for the wolf or the lynx), and they will remain so whatever measures are taken to try to save the animal. In killing the bear, his kinsman, his fellow creature, his first god, man long ago killed his own memory and more or less symbolically killed himself. It is too late to hope to turn back the clock.

This is why conservation measures adopted around Europe for the last generation or two seem totally futile. Nature parks, reserves, zones for the preservation of habitat, "bear plans," study groups, defense associations, prohibitions,[60] and protections of all kinds will accomplish nothing: the bear is doomed to disappear. He has already symbolically disappeared from the living world of wild animals, since almost everywhere, not only in the Alps and the Pyrenees, but also in Scandinavia, in the Abruzzi, and the Cantabrian mountains, there are now "bear museums." Barely dead, or not even completely dead, and the European brown bear is already an object in a museum.[61] The same fate soon awaits the brown bear of North America, for now enclosed in parks but already subject to the sordid and deadly voyeurism of tourists. Their polar cousin is dying of hunger because of climate change and the melting of the ice fields, which has driven the polar bear for the first time in its history into disturbing cannibal behavior.

The Ethnologists' Favorite

This inexorable march toward extinction and confinement to the museum has been accompanied for thirty years by a proliferation of scholarly studies of the animal, particularly collective and comparative works filling in the gaps in the book by Marcel Couturier and correcting his mistakes and simplifications. Forgotten or neglected by zoologists for several centuries, the bear reawakened their curiosity when he was threatened with extinction. His is not an isolated case, but resembles that of other threatened species (gorillas, tigers, seals, and whales, considering only mammals). Science seems to become interested in certain animals only because it knows that humanity is about to lose them.

Ethnologists were more prescient, not waiting until the number of surviving bears was miniscule to make the bear the unchallenged centerpiece of their bestiary. The bear has been at the center of their thinking and their inquiries for at least a century. Their studies were at first focused on distant (at least for Europeans) societies, where bear cults were carried on with ceremonies and beliefs that were still very much alive in the twentieth century. The Ainu of northern Japan and Sakhalin Island, for example, see the bear as one of the ancestors of their people and practice strongly totemic ursine rituals: hunts, sacrifices, banquets, initiations, taboos. It is not uncommon for a bear cub captured very young to be nursed by a woman who has just given birth to a child: one breast for each. The animal is raised and pampered for three or four years, then sacrificed and eaten at a ritual banquet.[62] This functions to place the tribe under the protection of the animal and to appropriate some of its strength, of its sense of smell and hearing, and even of its soul. Some portions are considered especially beneficial: the liver, the heart, the tongue, the muzzle, the ears, and above all the left forepaw.[63]

Similar practices, more closely tied to the hunt, are found among various peoples of Siberia (Nivkhs, Evenks, Chukchis, Koryaks, Khantys), for whom the bear might represent—by turns or all at once—a divinity, a relative or clan ancestor, an animal in which a human being has been reincarnated, or else a kind of shaman-creature, assisting in the passage between this world and the beyond.[64] The prevalent idea is that the bear killed by the hunters was a voluntary victim. The way in which he is butchered is particularly meticulous, not only because a large number of pharmaceutical products are removed from the body, but also because, if the animal is butchered following the rules, the spirit can separate from the body and the bear be resurrected.[65] Similar rites, practiced by the Yakuts or the Samoyeds, were sometimes described by travelers in the eighteenth and nineteenth centuries, who at best called them "ridiculous," at worst "loathsome" or "demonic."[66] These rites were the subject of scholarly studies in the early 1900s that later fostered fruitful comparisons with those practiced in Inuit societies in Greenland and Canada. They, too, made the bear—the polar bear—a relative, a god, or a totem.[67]

At the same time, studies by ethnologists became more frequent and turned toward European cultures. The Lapps were the first subject for extended analysis, because it was easier in their case than in eastern Siberia to compare accounts from the sixteenth and seventeenth centuries with those from more recent or even contemporary periods.[68] These comparisons showed that ursine rituals were not fixed but evolving: on the basis of the same myths and beliefs, the details of practices and narratives differed in time and space.

Among the Lapps, as among the Ainu and the Siberian peoples, the sacrifice of the bear occupies the central position. It takes the form of a hunt that lasts for several days, from which women are excluded. This hunt is preceded by chants, dances, simulations, and prayers: the great respect borne the bear requires the Lapps to ask the animal to allow himself to be killed. In addition, since the bear is supposed to understand human language and to foresee their intentions, beforehand hunters must refrain from pronouncing his name, do nothing that might offend him, appear uninterested in the hunt, prepare in secret, and especially say nothing to the women, who do not know how to keep quiet and who, if they were to speak, would be the first victims of the animal. The hunt itself is long and complex; it involves a meticulous distribution of roles and concludes with a slow return procession accompanied by chants and miming.[69] The women, dressed in their finest clothes, welcome the hunters by spitting on them to neutralize the dangerous powers acquired from contact with the wild beast. To prepare for this, they have chewed for a long time alder or birch bark, purifying essences. Ritual butchering and the subsequent elaborate cooking are performed by the men. But women are present at the banquet, which produces a meticulous division of the meat and the organs by sex, age, and rank. This division is carried out not by the chief but by the man who first spotted the bear: he, along with the animal, is the hero of the feast. He keeps the heart, the most noble organ, for himself. The gallbladder is carefully set aside, because it is used to make potions that confer strength and health. If there is not enough of it for the whole group of hunters, it is mixed with that of a boar, the animal considered closest to the bear by his virtues, courage, and internal anatomy. There follow the bear's funeral, the burial of his bones (they try to reconstruct his skeleton), various purification rites, and a three-day mourning period before life resumes its ordinary course.[70]

Work by ethnologists in the Balkans and Carpathians has focused primarily on ursine rituals in the depths of winter and during carnival. The principal function of these rituals is to hasten the return of spring and of fertility by making the bear end his hibernation. The animal is supposed to embody the spirit of vegetation and to preside over the growth of grain. In the ritual, a bear is led in a procession, festooned with straw, branches, or leaves. He is given seeds and fruits, he is caressed, made to spin and dance, people climb on his back. Usually, it is not a real bear but a man disguised as a bear, who delights in frightening women and children. Sometimes, notably when it is a straw man, he is made into a scapegoat, symbolically put to death, and then burned. Similar agricultural rites, all connected to fertility, have been attested in all parts of the Slavic and Germanic worlds. They do not always take place at carnival time, but also on Palm Sunday, or even in summer, at the end of the harvest.[71]

But it is farther west, in the Pyrenees and adjacent regions, that European ethnologists have carried out their most recent and most numerous studies. There, in Béarn, Navarre, Catalonia, Roussillon, and a large part of the southern Languedoc, the bear is often the only star attraction of the carnival. A specific celebration is dedicated to him that differs from one village to the next by only a few variations. It usually takes place on Candlemas (February 2) or the following Sunday, sometimes the Thursday before Lent. It almost always follows the same pattern: a man disguised as a bear comes down from the mountain or out of the forest; he seizes a girl who was dancing with the boys, generally the prettiest one, and carries her off to his den; they pursue him, search for him, call him, and find him; he is captured, tied up, and led to the center of the village following a very precise route; but the animal escapes on the way, terrorizes the crowd, and simulates a second abduction; captured again, this time he is chained, humiliated, shaved, and put to death. The very noisy ritual is accompanied by chants and dances, shouts and insults, collective merrymaking and transgressions of all kinds symbolizing the end of winter (which is early in these regions). The sexual dimension of the celebration is obvious from beginning to end: the abduction of the girl by the wild animal recalls the ancestral rivalry between man and bear for the carnal possession of women. On that day, the animal shows particularly ardent desire for the girl he has abducted, and nothing is known—at least in theory—of what happens when he hides her for a few moments in his den until she is freed. Sometimes there is not one but several bears; sometimes all the men of the village "play the bear," for the greater fear—or joy—of the young women.[72]

Misery and Distress of a Wild Animal

These practices, whose roots are sometimes ancient,[73] should obviously be compared to the many stories of bears abducting and raping women recounted throughout this book, stories already present in Greek mythology. They survive in the present not only in more or less quaint and hackneyed festivals, but also in various oral traditions, in iconography and toponymy,[74] as well as in stories.[75] The most famous, the one whose versions and variants are countless and which has been exported to three continents, is not *Goldilocks* but *Jean de l'Ours*. The tale always follows the same pattern: a woman is carried off and raped by a bear; she gives birth to a boy who kills his father but later has trouble finding his place in the world of men; extremely strong, he tries to be helpful but encounters only hostility, suspicion, or ingratitude; after many adventures, all ill-fated, he ends up fleeing human society and goes back to die, alone, in the cave where he was born.[76]

Stories featuring the "son of a bear" are plentiful in all societies in which the animal is or once was present. Sometimes, the child is not half bear but entirely human: he has been abandoned in the forest and nursed with the milk of a she-bear. In most cases, his strength is prodigious and he feels insatiable sexual desire for young women.[77] Other, very different, tales relate incidents or marvels connected to the hunt, or the metamorphosis of a human into a bear, or the way the Devil likes to appear as a bear. Still others show the animal contending with rival animals who attack, deceive, or ridicule him.[78] All emphasize his solitude and melancholy. The bear of oral tradition is almost always an unhappy creature.

The bears who belong to the world of the circus, the fairground, or the zoo are also unhappy, although they are hardly allowed to show it. It has already been shown that as early as the feudal period, bear showmen had appeared at fairs and markets, and the Church, usually hostile to animal spectacles, tolerated these exhibitions because it saw them as a way of desacralizing a wild animal that was overly admired. The bear of the late Middle Ages was thus devalued and transformed into a simple circus animal, in no way recalling the former king of the beasts, or even the lord of the mountain or the forest.

Bear showmen have continued through the centuries and even became more numerous after the animal disappeared from most habitats. Starting in the late eighteenth century, they traveled throughout Europe and introduced the animal to populations that had never seen one.[79] But was this still a wild animal? Engravings, followed by photography and later postcards, have left many images of muzzled bears, sometimes standing on their hind legs, accompanying a vagabond in rags or else trying to dance in a village square in front of a few onlookers. They are often small, thin, with scanty fur. They have a timid, resigned air, in contrast with the ruddy faces and dark looks of their masters.[80] These men are usually called "Turks," "Bohemians," or "Gypsies," at the time generic and imprecise terms designating fairground merchants, musicians, and performers from eastern Europe and the edges of the Ottoman Empire. Bear showmen generally came from the Romanian Carpathians or the Balkan mountains, where bear cubs were captured and trained: they were taught to dance, salute, tumble, roll themselves into a ball, simulate combat, and play dead. Their teeth and claws were filed down, and a ring through their muzzle made it possible to chain them.[81] In France in the nineteenth century, bears from the mountains of Ariège were similarly exhibited in towns and villages in southern regions. Less mistreated than their fellow creatures from the east, they were thought to bring happiness and protect against certain diseases. Children were especially invited to pet them and climb on their backs, which was intended to cure them of all their fears. These bears from the Pyrenees led through the departments of the south disappeared after the First World War.[82]

Bear cubs captured in the mountains of eastern Europe were not intended for fairground show alone. Some of them were part of a lucrative trade and were raised in menageries or intended for circus games. Circus games, which had disappeared with the victory of Christianity in the fourth century, gradually made their reappearance starting in the Renaissance in a less violent and bloody form. The animal stars remained for a long time horses and lions, later replaced by dogs and monkeys. It was not until the late nineteenth century that bears again made their entry into the circus. Before that, they were occasionally displayed in a square or on the outskirts of a town; their presence in exhibitions or animal combats was such a rare curiosity that it was announced with some fanfare. For example, in Paris in 1734, a large, beautiful poster engraved by J. M. Papillon announced for "Tuesday, February 2, in the faubourg Saint-Germain, at the barrière de Sèvres, the combat of a bear against a bull," and even specified that "the bear is large and strong and has good teeth" and that the bull will be assisted by "mastiffs."[83]

Bears did not really appear under the tents of large traveling circuses until a century and a half later, between 1860 and 1880: brown bears, but also polar bears and Asian black bears from the Himalayas. In the middle of the twentieth century, veritable "bear circuses" traveled throughout Europe—the most famous was that of the bear tamer Valentin Filatov. The animals danced and juggled, balanced on a board or a ball, rode a bicycle or a seesaw, imitated a boxing match, or pretended to play the accordion.[84] The contrast was great between their clumsy appearance and what they were able to do, always with that sad, resigned air that they also displayed in zoos. They have been present in zoos since at least the late eighteenth century, since the opening of the old princely menageries and the new municipal gardens to all segments of the public. Admiring them from the other side of the bars of the bears' enclosure—usually much too small for them—became one of the highlights of a visit to the zoo. Like many other wild or exotic animals, they are part of the staging of the living world,[85] a staging that is always cruel and often pathetic.

The Revenge of the Bear

IN the twentieth century, zoo and circus bears were no longer the only types of bear that amused children. The animal gradually entered every house, every bedroom, in the form of a toy, and was becoming the child's closest companion.

Although European children since antiquity had played with models made of straw, leather, felt, or rags in the form of human beings, generically known as "dolls," it was not until much more recently, perhaps in the seventeenth and eighteenth centuries, that the models also adopted animal shapes. Medieval Christianity, which was suspicious of all figurines or any object that might lead to idolatrous or magical practices, particularly wax figures, held back the making of toys in animal forms for several centuries. In the Middle Ages, there were horses carved out of wood, dogs made of hemp stuffed with fiber or bran, or birds made of straw that children could play with, but they were relatively rare and represented a bestiary that was not very diversified.[1] It was only in modern times that animal toys were widely distributed, and only in the early twentieth century that the most famous came into being: the stuffed bear.

Its origin is worth recounting. It was closely linked to the passion for the hunt of President Theodore Roosevelt (1858–1919). A great sportsman, brave soldier, and hero of the Spanish-American War, Roosevelt became governor of New York in 1898 and vice president of the United States in 1900. The assassination of President McKinley by an anarchist placed him at the head of the union in the following year. He strove to fight corruption, to defend the common people, and to offer American arbitration in major world conflicts. Very popular, he was reelected in 1904, and received the Nobel Peace Prize two years later. Four years before that he had already become a legendary figure. In November 1902, he was on a tour through the South, on the border between Mississippi and Louisiana, where he decided to go on a hunt. He hunted for several days in a row without success: every night he came back with no game. The president didn't seem at all affected, but his hosts and his entourage were devastated. Something had to be done to end this humiliation; the head of the nation could not remain empty-handed. One of his subordinates had the distressing idea of capturing a young bear, attaching him discreetly near a tree, and drawing the president's attention to him. But when he saw the cub, Roosevelt, who may have figured out the cruel and ridiculous stratagem, refused to kill the animal. He reportedly pronounced these famous words: "If I shoot that bear, I won't be able to look my boys in the face again." The words were no doubt sincere, but also very clever: repeated by the press, they were broadcast around the United States and the rest of the western world.

Along with the words went a picture. A few days after the event, on November 16, 1902, a cartoonist and political commentator, Clifford Berryman,[2] published a cartoon in the *Washington Star* showing Roosevelt nobly taking pity on and sparing the chained bear cub. The media success was considerable, especially because the cub was black and Roosevelt defended the cause of the Negroes. That might have been the end of the story, a mere contribution to the president's reputation, but there was an aftermath. A man named Morris Michton, a Russian émigré living in New York, had a shop in Brooklyn where he sold sweets, little toys, and rag dolls made by his wife Rose. He had been looking for a way to diversify his production for some time. When he saw the cartoon in the *Star,* he suggested to his wife that she make a stuffed bear cub that would evoke the one whose life the president had just saved. It was an idea of genius. And Michton had another, to ask the White House for authorization to name the new toy Teddy, the president's nickname. After a little hesitation, the request was granted, and the Teddy Bear was born.

Morris Michton sold a large quantity of his bears for Christmas 1902, and the success lasted through 1903. Since Rose could not keep up with the demand, the couple hired workers and tried to increase their business. The two shopkeepers became company directors. But, ill-prepared for this success and their new profession, and inadequately protected by the patents they had filed, they ended up selling their invention to a large toy company, the Ideal Toy Corporation. In 1904, Ideal transformed the craft shop production of Teddy Bears into industrial production, and soon had to deal with competition. When Morris Michton died in 1938, the White House sent its condolences to the family, and the press recalled the events of 1902 and the pretty tale of the origin of the teddy bear.[3] That served some purpose, because a different version had been circulating in Europe for more than three decades, which traced the origin of the toy to a different source: the stuffed bear was not born in America but in Germany, and its real inventor was not Morris Michton but Margarete Steiff.

This woman, paralyzed at a young age by polio, lived in Giengen in Swabia, a town that specialized in the manufacture of felt clothing. Margarete was bored, and in 1901 she came up with the idea of making at home little felt animals that her sisters and nieces sold in the market, with some success. The following year, one of her nephews, who was in art school in Berlin, sent her a drawing of a bear copied from one in the zoo and suggested she make a toy based on it. For this bear, Margarete chose wool rather than felt and came up with the idea of giving the animal articulated arms and legs. This was a great novelty and the wool bear was presented at the Leipzig Toy Fair, the most important one in Europe, in March 1903. European sellers were skeptical about this strange creature, but an American wholesaler, who may already have known about Morris Michton's invention, ordered three thousand of them. The German bear went off to meet the American bear.[4] The competition had been launched and production intensified on both sides of the Atlantic.

It is impossible for historians to determine whether Morris Michton or Margarete Steiff was the first to have the idea for a stuffed bear. It seems there was near-simultaneity of invention and no copying of the creation of one by the other. This suggests that the stuffed bear was in the air in the early twentieth century, and that if the two claimants had not existed, the creature would still have come into existence, a few months or a few years later. Whatever the time or the area concerned, there are never any isolated creators, scientists, artists, or poets.

Indeed, well before the 1900s, perhaps even before the middle of the nineteenth century, bears had frequently appeared in caricatures and satiric drawings, as automata, and in children's books. Moreover, the bear already had a marked anthropomorphic character that was more or less adopted by the first stuffed bears. Until the First World War, they had elongated bodies, with long limbs, narrow shoulders, a stooped or hunch back. Their elongated muzzles made of sewn lightweight felt and their black eyes made out of boot buttons gave them a strange and melancholy appearance that greatly contributed to their success and justified all sorts of transfers and projections: from the beginning, the teddy bear was seen not only as a living creature but as a human being. Starting around 1910, the use of glass for the eyes changed the look somewhat, but it always remained sad and distant. The colors themselves accentuated the general impression of melancholy; made of short-pile wool and stuffed with horse hair, straw, sawdust, or kapok, the first bears were black, gray, or brown. It was not until the 1920s that materials and colors were diversified (there was a fad for red bears). In the 1930s, the shape became less elongated, plumper, the lump on the back disappeared, and the face was not as sad. At the same time, accessories (clothing, hats, objects held in the paws) proliferated,[5] and ingenious systems inside the body enabled the bear to emit sounds when it was squeezed or tilted.

After the Second World War, the teddy bear lost its last wild aspects and, with the use of new synthetic materials, inside and out, became softer and lighter. But despite these improvements and the adoption of increasingly strict safety standards, production began to decline in the 1960s because each year the bear had to confront an ever-larger number of rivals in the toy bestiary.

Until the 1940s, the bear's only rival had been the doll, which had existed much longer and was primarily a girls' toy. Indeed, many doll manufacturers shifted to bears or diversified their products. But after the war—when shortages of appropriate materials led to the inventive creation of substitutes, now much sought after by collectors—other stuffed animals appeared on the market. First there were rabbits, dogs, cats, and elephants; later, pigs, sheep, donkeys, and other farm animals; still later, an entire ex-

otic bestiary, from lions to duck-billed platypuses, and including tigers, giraffes, hippos, and rhinoceroses. They were chiefly mammals—few birds,
few fish, and practically no insects. It would be worth comparing over the
decades the bestiary of stuffed toys with the bestiary of children's books.
In both, the bear held first place, but as time went by the competition
became stiffer. Some of the major bears of children's books, cartoons, or
animated films, like the Teddy Bear, would be worth further study: Baloo,
Winnie the Pooh, Rupert, Prosper, Mishka, Paddington, Gronounours,
and Petit Ours Brun, among others. The list is long and in itself is an important document on the permanence of the relationship between man
and bear. We find its oldest traces in Paleolithic caves and its most recent
manifestations in children's beds. It cannot be said often enough that the
bear is not an animal like the others, and the stuffed bear, like its various
avatars, is different from all other toys.[6]

As psychologists and sociologists have shown, the bear holds the first
odors the infant recognizes and takes pleasure in coming back to. It also
helps awaken children's tactile sensuality—touching, kissing, sucking—
and it enables them to manifest their primitive instincts of possession,
domination, and even sadism—pinching, throwing, twisting, biting. The
teddy bear is the first object over which children have complete mastery.
They can do what they like with it, take it wherever they want: to school,
to hospital, to summer camp. They can even torture or destroy it without
having to explain to anyone. At the same time, the bear is often the confi-
dant, the accomplice, the guardian angel: it substitutes for father, mother,
brother, and sister all together and is a member of the family. It is both a
toy and a person, a bear and a human being.[7]

Sometimes, when childhood ends and the child discards his or her
bear, the parents recover, repair, and store it, prepared to take it out of
the closet or the attic in case the adolescent, psychologically troubled and
feeling an irresistible need for security, asks for old toys. Sometimes even,
when the child has grown up and leaves the family home, the old teddy
bear goes along and, charged with countless memories, ends its life in
another room, another closet, another attic. But in other cases it remains
with the parents and mopes on the departed child's bed. In some cases,

the child's or adolescent's attachment to his bear is excessive or gives rise to an enactment of a split personality or to troubling fetishist rituals, and the bear has to be confiscated by the pediatrician or the parents.[8] In adults, these cases are uncommon but can take the form of obsessive collecting, occasionally producing neurosis.

Teddy bears today are indeed valued collectibles: catalogues and specialized stores, exchange markets, repair shops, and even museums are devoted to them. Some bears are sold for amazing sums at auction. An example is a very old stuffed individual named Mabel that had belonged to Elvis Presley (as a child or an adult?) and had been sold at auction several times after the King's death; it was made in the Steiff workshop in 1909. Its end was exceedingly sinister. Lent by its last owner for an exhibition of stuffed bears in Wells, England, in which it was to be the star attraction, it provoked the hatred or jealousy of a young Doberman accompanying the night watchman after the first day of the exhibition. The dog seized the precious relic and furiously bit and clawed it to pieces.[9]

Dogs do not hold a monopoly on such behavior. Humankind and its societies, as I have pointed out throughout this book, seem haunted by the memory, more or less conscious, of the ancient times when space and prey was shared with bears, when they had the same fears and the same caves, sometimes the same dreams and the same beds. Indeed, humans and bears have always been inseparable, united by a kinship that gradually moved from nature to culture, and they have remained so down to the present.

Notes

Sources and Bibliography

Acknowledgments

Index

Notes

Introduction

1. From a large bibliography of varying quality: J. Grimm, *Deutsche Mythologie*, 4th ed. (Berlin: Dümmlers, 1875–1878); Georges Dumézil, *Les Dieux des Germains* (Paris: PUF, 1959); Jan de Vries, *Altgermanische Religionsgeschichte* (Berlin: de Gruyter, 1970); L. Ejerfeldt, "Germanische Religion," in *Handbuch der Religionsgeschichte*, ed. J. P. Asmussen et al., vol. 1 (Göttingen: Vandenhoeck und Ruprecht, 1971); Régis Boyer, *Le Christ des barbares* (Paris: Cerf, 1987), Régis Boyer, *Yggdrasill: La Religion des anciens scandinaves* (Paris: Payot, 1992); Carole M. Cusack, *Conversion among the Germanic Peoples* (London: Cassell, 1998).

2. Heinrich Büttner, "Mission und Kirchenorganisation des Frankenreiches bis zum Tode Karls des Grosse," in *Karl der Grosse: Lebenswerk und Nachleben*, ed. W. Braunfels (Düsseldorf: Schwann, 1966); Charles de Clercq, *La législation religieuse franque de Clovis à Charlemagne* (Louvain: Bureau du Recueil, Bibliothèque de l'Université, 1939).

3. Michael Tangl, ed., *Die Briefe des heiligen Bonifatius und Lullus* (Berlin: Weidmannsche Verlagsbuchhandlung, 1916), 130 (letter 63); See also F. Flaskamp, "Bonifatius und die Sachsenmission," *Zeitschrift für Missionswissenschaft* 6 (1916), 273–285.

4. *Indiculus superstitionum paganarum* (774), in *Legum nationum germanicarum*, vol. 4, ed. Karl August Eckhardt (Hannover, 1962). See also the capitulary *De partibus Saxoniae* (782 and 785), in *Capitularia regum Francorum*, vol. 3, ed. A. Boretius and V. Krause (Hannover, 1897).

5. Michel Pastoureau, "Le bestiaire héraldique au Moyen Âge," in *L'Hermine et le Sinople: Études d'héraldique médiévale* (Paris: Léopard d'Or, 1982), 105–116.

6. In the front rank of books by pioneering historians must be mentioned that of Robert Delort, *Les animaux ont une histoire* (Paris: Seuil, 1984).

7. Michel Pastoureau, "Le bestiaire héraldique au Moyen Âge."

8. Georges Petit and Jean Théodoridès, *Histoire de la zoologie, des origines à Linné* (Paris: Hermann, 1962), 146–147. The work was published by the old Sixth Section of the École Pratique des Hautes Études in a collection entitled History of Thought. Of its 360 pages, 144 are devoted to Antiquity, 155 to modern times (sixteenth to eighteenth centuries), and 20 to the Middle Ages in the West and its "inanities."

1. The First God?

1. I take the title of this chapter from the book by Christian Bernadac, *Le Premier Dieu* (Neuilly-sur-Seine: M. Lafon, 2000). This is a good work of vulgarization, though unfortunately almost completely lacking in references.

2. On the cave bear: Martina Pacher, "Polémique autour d'un culte de l'ours des cavernes," in *L'Ours et l'Homme,* ed. Thierry Tillet and Lewis Roberts Binford (Liège: Éditions de l'Université de Liège, 2002), 235–246.

3. François Rouzaud, "L'ours dans l'art paléolithique," in *L'Ours et l'Homme,* ed. Tillet and Binford, 201–217.

4. For example, probably the large animal with a black head in the Cosquer cave. See Jean Clottes and Jean Courtin, *The Cave Beneath the Sea,* trans. Marilyn Garner (New York: Abrams, 1996), 119.

5. Jean Clottes, ed., *Chauvet Cave,* trans. Paul G. Bahn (Salt Lake City: University of Utah Press, 2003).

6. For example, in the caves of Combarelles (Dordogne), Montespan (Haute-Garonne), and the Trois-Frères (Ariège).

7. See the pictures in Rouzaud, "L'ours dans l'art paléolithique."

8. For example, the two full-face bears' heads engraved on a wall of the Trois-Frères cave in Ariège.

9. The bear is not the only animal represented in this way; other animals and even men may be shown "wounded": in the "black chamber" of the cave of Niaux (Ariège), for example, many horses and bison seem similarly pierced by arrows.

10. A good summary of the various positions can be found in Jean Clottes and David Lewis-Williams, *The Shamans of Prehistory,* trans. Sophie Hawkes (New York: Abrams, 1998), 61–79.

11. *L'Art des cavernes,* preface by André Leroi-Gourhan (Paris: Imprimerie Nationale, 1984).

12. Clottes and Lewis-Williams, *Shamans of Prehistory,* 81–99.

13. See the tables in Philippe Fosse, Philippe Morel, and Jean-Philippe Brugal, "Taphonomie et éthologie des ursidés pléistocènes," in *L'Ours et l'Homme,* ed. Tillet and Binford, 79–101.

14. Michel Philippe, "L'ours des cavernes de La Balme-à-Collomb," *Mémoires et Documents de la Société savoisienne d'histoire et d'archéologie* 95 (1993): 85–94.

15. At certain sites, the bones found are not those of the cave bear but of its direct ancestor, the *Ursus deningeri,* thereby indicating a very ancient date.

16. See the skeptical summary by André Leroi-Gourhan, *Les Religions de la Préhistoire* (1964; Paris: PUF, 2001), 11–30.

17. Emil Bächler proposed pioneering hypotheses about bear skulls and bones that seemed to have been intentionally deposited in several caves at high altitudes in the Swiss Alps. See Emil Bächler, "Das Drachenloch ob Vättis im Taminatale und seine Bedeutung als paläontologische Fundstätte und prähistorische Niederlassung aus der Altsteinzeit im Schweizerlande," *Jahrbuch der St. Gallischen Naturwissenschaftlichen Gesellschaft* 57 (1920–21): 1–144; reprinted and expanded in *Das alpine paläolithikum der Schweiz im Wildkirchli, Drachenloch und Wildenmannlisloch, die ältesten menschlichen niederlassungen aus der altsteinzeit des Schweizerlandes* (Basel: Birhäuser, 1940).

18. A. Irving Hallowell, "Bear Ceremonialism in the Northern Hemisphere," *American Anthropologist* 28, 1 (1926): 1–175; K. J. Narr, "Bärenzeremoniell und Schamanismus in der älteren Steinzeit," *Saeculum* 10 (1959): 233–272; Hans-Joachim Paproth, *Studien über Das Bärenzeremoniell* (Uppsala: Religionshistorika Institution, 1976); Jean Dominique Lajoux, *L'Homme et l'Ours* (Grenoble: Glénat, 1996). See also the special issue of *Études mongoles et sibériennes* 11 (1980), *L'Ours, l'autre de l'homme*.

19. F. E. Koby, "L'ours des cavernes et les paléolithiques," *L'Anthropologie* 55, 3–4 (1951): 304–308.

20. In particular, eight bear skulls, which were buried under flat stone slabs. See André Leroi-Gourhan, "La grotte des Furtins," *Bulletin de la Société préhistorique française* 44, 1–2 (1947): 43–55; and André Leroi-Gourhan, "La caverne des Furtins," *Préhistoire* 11 (1950): 17–42.

21. André Leroi-Gourhan, *Les Religions de la Préhistoire*, 31–36.

22. See the conclusions and the bibliography by Marina Pacher, "Polémique autour d'un culte de l'ours des cavernes," in *L'Ours et l'Homme*, ed. Tillet and Binford, 235–246.

23. For example, Jean Dominique Lajoux, "Les données ethnologiques du culte de l'ours," in *L'Ours et l'Homme*, ed. Tillet and Binford, 229–234.

24. Among opponents of the cult of the bear, the Swiss historian F. E. Koby occupies the front rank; a large number of his writings consisted of demolishing the hypotheses of his predecessors, notably those of his compatriot Emil Bächler. Among various articles, see F. E. Koby, "Les soi-disant instruments osseux du Paléolithique alpin et le charriage à sec des os d'ours des cavernes," *Verhandlungen der naturforschenden Gesellschaft in Basel* 54 (1943): 59–95, as well as a final clarification: Koby, "L'ours des cavernes et les paléolithiques."

25. F. E. Koby, "Les paléolithiques ont-ils chassé l'ours des cavernes?" *Bulletin de la Société jurassienne d'émulation de Porrentruy* (1953): 30–40.

26. Philippe Morel and Michel-Alain Garcia, "La chasse à l'ours dans l'art paléolithique," in *L'Ours et l'Homme*, ed. Tillet and Binford, 219–228.

27. L. M. Le Tensorer, *La Suisse du Paléolithique à l'aube du Moyen Âge* (Basel: Verlag Schweizerische Gesellschaft für Ur- und Frühgeschichte, 1993), 1:149.

28. Wolfgang Hirschberg, ed., *Neues Wörterbuch der Völkerkunde* (Berlin: Reimer, 1988), 269.

29. It is not impossible that a few of the drawings in the Chauvet cave were made more recently, perhaps between 26,000 and 23,000 BC.

30. The idea was long championed by André Leroi-Gourhan. The geography of artistic centers also must be corrected: Périgord, the Pyrenees, and the Cantabrian Mountains of Spain were not the only major creative centers; Ardèche, the Marseille region (the Cosquer cave was discovered in the *calanques* in 1991), and no doubt other regions were just as significant.

31. Jean Clottes, ed., *Chauvet Cave*, 32–56.

32. Ibid., 98–103 and 192–193.

33. The "skull chamber" itself has pictures of several deer and a horse. More recent artists (Magdalenians?) "scratched out" a deer and added a mammoth.

34. The site of Regourdou and the extraordinary Neanderthal grave still await a monograph; only a few articles have been published, most recently, E. Bonifay, "L'homme de Neandertal et l'ours *(Ursus arctos)* dans la grotte du Regourdou," in *L'Ours et l'Homme*, ed. Tillet and Binford, 247–254.

35. A summary of the soap opera of the conflict between Constant and the authorities can be found in Christian Bernadac, *Le Premier Dieu*, 104–133.

36. H. Begouën, N. Casteret, and L. Capitan, "La caverne de Montespan," *Revue anthropologique* 33 (1923): 333–350.

37. Michel-Alain Garcia and Philippe Morel, "Restes et reliefs: Présence de l'homme et de l'ours dans la grotte de Montespan," *Anthropozoologica* 21 (1995): 73–78.

38. Cited by N. Jadrincev, "O kulte medvedja preimuscestvenno u severnyx inododocev," *Etnografisceskoe Obozrenie* 13 (1980): 101–113. I thank Michel Boccara of the CNRS for this reference and for having drawn my attention to the issue.

39. Aristotle, *History of Animals*, VI, 10, and VIII, 17.

40. The bow of Artemis, goddess of the moon, is often described as having the form of a crescent moon. In several Asiatic cultures, particularly in eastern Siberia, there is a symbolic kinship between the bear and the moon, both of which go to sleep and disappear to be reborn anew.

41. According to some authors, Arcas did not become Ursa Minor, but Arcturus, the guardian of Ursa Major.

42. Apollodorus, *The Library of Greek Mythology*, trans. Robin Hard (1997; Oxford:

Oxford University Press, 2008), 115; Ovid, *Metamorphoses* II, 409–507, and *Fasti* II, 153–192.

43. On the role of bears in different Greek cults of Artemis see Elinor Bevan, "The Goddess Artemis and the Dedication of Bears in Sanctuaries," *Annual of the British School of Athens* 82 (1987): 17–21.

44. Another etymology derives the name Artemis from the Greek *artémès,* "in good health."

45. In modern German the proper name most frequently used to designate Arcadia is *Bärenland.*

46. Pausanias, *Description of Greece,* 8.4 and 10.9. On Arcadian rituals of animal metamorphosis, see Pierre Lévêque, "Sur quelques cultes d'Arcadie: Princesse-ours, hommes-loups, et dieux-chevaux," *L'Information historique* 23 (1961): 93–108.

47. Among other references, see Georges Hacquard, *Guide mythologique de la Grèce et de Rome* (Paris: Hachette, 1990), 75.

48. Bevan, "The Goddess Artemis and the Dedication of Bears in Sanctuaries."

49. Euripides, *Iphigenia in Tauris,* 1448ff. See L. Séchan, "Le Sacrifice d'Iphigénie," *Revue des études grecques* 44 (1931): 368–426.

50. Apollodorus, *The Library of Greek Mythology,* 116–117. See also Ovid, *Metamorphoses* X, 560ff.

51. Apollodorus, *The Library of Greek Mythology,* 124–126.

52. This was recalled by Philippe Walter, *Arthur: L'ours et le roi* (Paris: Imago, 2002), 86, adopting an idea put forward in Otto Rank, *The Myth of the Birth of the Hero,* trans. Gregory C. Richter and E. James Lieberman (Baltimore: Johns Hopkins University Press, 2004), 41. Some philologists associate the name *Paris* itself with one of the words for bear in Sanskrit, constructed around the root **par* ("brown," "brilliant"); the other word, sometimes taboo, was structured around the etymon **ark.*

53. Antoninus Liberalis, *Transformationes* III, 106, in *Scriptores Poeticae Historiae Graeci,* ed. Anton Westermann (Brunswick: G. Westermann, 1843), 200–238.

54. The union of Cephalus and the she-bear is not often recounted in the principal sources for Greek mythology, but it is well known because Aristotle alludes to it twice in his zoological works. See *Brill's New Pauly* (Boston: Brill, 2002), vol. 2, col. 5.

55. M. Sanchez Ruipérez, "La 'Dea Artio' celta y la 'Artemis' griega: Un aspecto religioso de la afinidad celto-iliria," *Zephyrus* 2 (1951): 89–95.

56. Annemarie Kaufmann-Heinimann, *Dea Artio, die Bärengöttin von Muri* (Bern: Bernisches Historisches Museum, 2002). The bronze statuettes and their base are in the Bern Historical Museum.

2. King of the Beasts

1. In general, except for the case of the lion in Europe, the king of the beasts always belongs to the indigenous fauna of each region, country, or continent.
2. Pliny, *Natural History*, VIII, 54.
3. Thomas de Cantimpré, *Liber de natura rerum*, ed. Helmut Boese (Berlin: W. de Gruyter, 1973), 169; Marcel Couturier, *L'Ours brun* (Grenoble: L. Couturier, 1954), 433.
4. Michel Pastoureau, "Tous les gauchers sont roux," *Le Genre humain* 16–17 (1988): 343–354, reprinted in Pastoureau, *Une histoire symbolique du Moyen Âge occidental* (Paris: Seuil, 2004). See also Pierre-Michel Bertrand, *Histoire des gauchers en Occident: Des gens à l'envers* (Paris: Imago, 2002).
5. On forest battles between bears and boars, see Couturier, *L'Ours brun*, 543–550.
6. Otto Keller, *Thiere des klassischen Althertums in kulturgeschichtlicher Beziehung* (Innsbruck: Wagner'schen Universitäts-Buchhandlung, 1887), 106–130; Roland Auguet, *Cruelty and Civilization: The Roman Games* (London: Routledge, 1994); J. M. C. Toynbee, *Animals in Roman Life and Art* (Ithaca: Cornell University Press, 1973).
7. In *Natural History*, VIII, Pliny begins his discussion of quadrupeds with a chapter on the elephant, which he seems to make the king of the beasts, and which he asserts is in any event the strongest.
8. Martial, *Liber de spectaculis*, VIII, 12. Cited and commented on by Toynbee, *Animals in Roman Life and Art*, 17–22, 25–26, 30–31, 71–82, 93–100; and by Otto Keller, *Die antike Tierwelt* (Leipzig: W. Engelmann, 1909), 1:175–181.
9. Georges Ville, "Les jeux de gladiateurs dans l'Empire chrétien," *Mélanges de l'École française de Rome* 72 (1960): 273–335.
10. Toynbee, *Animals in Roman Life and Art*, 93–99.
11. Symmachus, *Epistolae*, II, 76; V, 62; VII, 121; IX, 132, 135, 142.
12. On this subject, see the pioneering and enlightening pages by Jacob Grimm, *Teutonic Mythology*, trans. James Steven Stallybrass (1888; New York: Dover, 1966), 2:667–668; and *Reinhart Fuchs*, ed. Jacob Grimm (Berlin: Reimer, 1834), xlviii–li and ccxcv–ccci.
13. Tacitus, *Agricola; Germany*, trans. A. R. Birley (Oxford: Oxford University Press, 1999).
14. Ammianus Marcellinus, *Rerum gestarum libri qui supersunt*, ed. Wolfgang Seyfarth (Leipzig: Teubner, 1978), liber XXXI, 31, 9, 5.
15. Saxo Grammaticus, *History of the Danes*, trans. Peter Fisher (1979; Cambridge: D. S. Brewer, 1996), 15. On this episode and on Saxo's work in general, see the

remarks by François-Xavier Dillmann, "Chroniques des études nordiques," *Proxima Thulé* 2 (1996), 133–149.

16. On the universal, or nearly universal, character of these rites, see (with caution), Mircea Eliade, *Initiation, Rites, Sociétés secrètes* (Paris: Gallimard, 1959), especially 181–184 and 265–269.

17. Henri Platelle and Denis Clauzel, *Histoire des provinces françaises du Nord* (Dunkirk: Westhoek, 1989), 2:123.

18. Albert of Aachen, *Historia Ierosolimitana, History of the Journey to Jerusalem*, ed. and trans. Susan B. Edgington (Oxford: Oxford University Press, 2007) III, 4, 143–145.

19. Guillaume de Tyr, *Chronicon*, ed. R. B. C. Huygens (Turnholt: Brepols, 1986) 3:18.

20. Horst Schroeder, *Der Topos der Nine Worthies in der Literatur und bildenden Kunst* (Göttingen: Vandenhoeck and Ruprecht, 1971).

21. See Philippe Walter, *Arthur: L'ours et le roi* (Paris: Imago, 2002), 86–87.

22. Régis Boyer, *Le Christ des barbares* (Paris: Cerf, 1987); Régis Boyer, *Yggdrasill: La religion des anciens Scandinaves* (Paris: Payot, 1992); and Carole M. Cusack, *Conversion among the Germanic Peoples* (London: Cassell, 1998).

23. Olaus Magnus, *Description of the Northern Peoples*, trans. Peter Fisher and Humphrey Higgens (London: Hakluyt Society, 1996), 1:257ff.

24. *Le Livre de la colonisation de l'Islande*, ed. and trans. Régis Boyer (Paris: EPHE-VIᵉ Section et Sorbonne, 1973).

25. It is possible that the first bear Odd killed, the one that had massacred his father and brother, was a polar bear. This is at least the hypothesis of several specialists in the sagas who think that the primitive kernel of this story originated in Greenland.

26. Cited by H. R. E. Davidson, "Shape-Changing in the Old Norse Sagas," in *Animals in Folklore*, ed. J. R. Porter and W. M. S. Russell (Ipswich: D. S. Brewer, 1978), 126–142.

27. Bruno Laurioux, "Manger l'impur: Animaux et interdits alimentaires durant le haut Moyen Âge," in *Homme, Animal et Société*, ed. A. Couret and F. Oge (Toulouse: Presses de l'Insitut Politique de Toulouse, 1989), 3:73–87; Marc-André Wagner, *Le Cheval dans les croyances germaniques: Paganisme, christianisme et traditions* (Paris: Champion, 2005), 467–469.

28. "*Et caro ursi ad comedendum homini bona non est, quia si comeditur, hominem ad libidinem incendit et ei mortem apportat.*" Hildegard of Bingen, *Physica*, P.L., 197, col. 1317.

29. Bruno Andreolli, "L'orso nella cultura nobiliare dall' *Historia Augusta* a Chrétien de Troyes," in *Il bosco nel Medioevo*, ed. Bruno Andreolli and Massimo

Montanari (Bologna: CLUEB, 1988), 35–54. An illuminated folio of a manuscript (c. 1450–1460) of the *Chronicle of the Council of Constance* by Ulrich Richental shows a butcher's stall where bears' heads and paws are offered for sale: Rosengarten Museum, Konstanz, Codex 1, fol. 67.

30. Snorri Sturluson, *Heimskringla: History of the Kings of Norway,* trans. Lee M. Hollander (1964; Austin: University of Texas Press, 1995), 10.

31. Neil Stratford, *The Lewis Chessmen and the Enigma of the Hoard* (London: British Museum Press, 1997), 24, fig. 31.

32. Jean Przyluski, "Les confréries de loups-garous dans les sociétés indo-européennes," *Revue de l'histoire des religions* 121 (1940): 128–145.

33. The bibliography devoted to the Berserkers is considerable. If one does not read Scandinavian languages, one should consult primarily: L. Weiser, *Altgermanische Jünglingsweihen und Männerbünde* (Cologne, 1927), 43–82; Otto Höfler, *Kultische Geheimbünde der Germanen* (Frankfurt: Moritz Diesterweg, 1934), and "Berserker," in *Reallexikon der germanischen Altertumskunde* (Berlin: Walter de Gruyter, 1976), 2:298–304; Georges Dumézil, *Les Dieux des Germains* (Paris: PUF, 1959); Hans Kuhn, "Kämpen und Berserker," *Frühmittelalterliche Studien* 2 (1968): 222–234; Régis Boyer, *La Mort chez les anciens Scandinaves* (Paris: Les Belles Lettres, 1994).

34. Claude Lecouteux, *Petit dictionnaire de mythologie allemande* (Paris: Entente, 1991), 30–31. Lecouteux also cites the case of the *Vagynjur* (she-wolves), a female warrior equivalent to the Berserkers and the *Ulfhednir.*

35. Georg Scheibelreiter, *Tiernamen und Wappenwesen* (Cologne: Böhlau, 1976), 101–102.

36. Mircea Eliade, *Shamanism: Archaic Techniques of Ecstasy,* trans. Willard R. Trask (1964; Princeton: Princeton University Press, 2004).

37. Scheibelreiter, *Tiernamen und Wappenwesen,* 58–85.

38. Carola Hicks, *Animals in Early Medieval Art* (Edinburgh: Edinburgh University Press, 1993), 57–78.

39. H. R. Ellis Davidson, *Myths and Symbols in Pagan Europe* (Manchester: Manchester University Press, 1988), 79–80.

40. Gunter Müller, "Germanische Tiersymbolik und Namengebung," in *Probleme der Namenforschung,* ed. Hugo Steger (Darmstadt: Wissenschaftliche Buchgesellschaft, 1977), 425–488.

41. Johannes Wilhelm Wolf, *Beiträge zur deutschen Mythologie* (Göttingen: Dieterich, 1857), 68–69.

42. For example, an archbishop of Mainz as early as the sixth century denounced the custom of German Barbarians who gave their sons names of fearsome

animals to make them strong and invincible: *"Sicut solent et barbarae gentes no-mina filiis imponere ad devastationem respicientia bestiarum ferarum, vel rapacium volucrum, gloriosum putantes filios tales habere, ad bellos idoneos, et insanientes in sanguinem."* Quoted in Müller, "Germanische Tiersymbolik und Namenge-bung," 439.

43. See the fine book by Heinrich Beck, *Das Ebersignum im Germanischen: Ein Be-itrag zur germanischen Tier-Symbolik* (Berlin: Walter de Gruyter, 1965). It would be useful to have a similar work dealing with bear symbolism among the ancient Germans.

44. Henriette Walter and Pierre Avenas, *L'Étonnante histoire des noms de mam-mifères* (Paris: Laffont, 2003), 82–91.

45. Cited by Michel Praneuf, *L'Ours et les hommes dans les traditions européennes* (Paris: Imago, 1989), 30–31.

46. Carl-Martin Edsman, "La fête de l'ours chez les Lapons: Sources anciennes et recherches récentes sur certains rites de chasse aux confins septentrionaux de la Scandinavie," *Proxima Thulé* 2 (1996): 11–49.

47. On these very interesting questions, see the pioneering article by Antoine Meillet, "Quelques hypothèses sur les interdictions de vocabulaire dans les langues indo-européennes," in *Linguistique historique et Linguistique générale* (1921; Paris: Champion, 2003), 1:281–291, in which the principal example is the name of the bear. See also Murray B. Emenau, "Taboos on Animal Names," *Language* 24 (1948): 56–63; and Éveline Lot-Falck, *Les Rites de chasse chez les peuples sibériens* (Paris: Gallimard, 1953).

48. See the references given by Otto Höfler, "Berserker," 298–304. On possible comparisons between Germanic and Celtiberian warriors, see Eduardo Per-alta-Labrador, "Confréries guerrières indo-européennes dans l'Espagne anci-enne," *Études indo-européennes* 10 (1991): 71–123, whose conclusions should be treated with caution.

49. Meillet, "Quelques hypothèses sur les interdictions de vocabulaire dans les langues indo-européennes," 285–286.

50. M. Sanchez Ruipérez, "La 'Dea Artio' celta y la 'Artemis' griega: Un aspecto religioso de la afinidad celto-iliria," *Zephyrus* 2 (1951): 89–95.

51. Salomon Reinach, "Les survivances du totémisme chez les anciens Celtes," in *Cultes, Mythes et Religions* (Paris: E. Leroux, 1908), 1:30–78.

52. William A. Nitze, "Arthurian Names: Arthur," *Publications of the Modern Lan-guage Association* 69 (1949): 585–596; Christian-Joseph Guyonvarc'h, "La pierre, l'ours et le roi: Notes d'étymologie et de lexicographie gauloise et celtique," *Celticum* 16 (1967): 215–238.

53. N. W. Thomas, "La survivance du culte totémique des animaux et les rites agraires dans le pays de Galles," *Revue de l'histoire des religions* 8 (1898): 295–347.

54. *"Artur, latine translatum, sonat ursum terribilem"*; first cited by Edmond Faral, *La Légende arthurienne,* vol. 1, *Les Plus Anciens Textes, des origines à Geoffroi de Monmouth* (Paris: Champion, 1929), 134 n. 3 and 138 n. 3.

55. Unless this particular scholar simply found an echo in the sounds of *Arturus* and *ursus;* but that is hardly likely.

56. There is, however, an early exception in the *Roman de Brut* by Wace (v. 2698–2700): before going to confront a giant on Mont-Saint-Michel, Arthur has a dream vision of "a bear flying through the air; it came from the east and was hideous, colossal, fearsome, and gigantic." *"Que parmi l'air un ours veoit / De vers oriant avolant / Molt let, molt gros, molt fort, molt grand."* *Le Roman de Brut,* ed. Ivor Arnold and Margaret Pelan (Paris: Klincksieck, 1962). A similar dream had already been described by Geoffrey of Monmouth in his *History of the Kings of Britain,* X, ii.

57. R. S. Loomis, *Celtic Myth and Arthurian Romance* (New York: Columbia University Press, 1927), and "Geoffrey of Monmouth and Arthurian Origins," *Speculum* 3 (1928): 16–33. See also Jean-Charles Payen, "L'enracinement folklorique du roman arthurien," in *Mélanges d'Études Romanes du Moyen Âge et de la Renaissance offerts à J. Rychner (Travaux de Linguistique et de Littérature Strasbourg)* 16 (1978), 427–437; Anita Guerreau-Jalabert, "Romans de Chrétien de Troyes et contes folkloriques: Rapprochements thématiques et observations de méthode," *Romania* 104 (1983): 1–48.

58. *La Mort le roi Artu,* ed. Jean Frappier (Geneva: Droz, 1964), § 192.

59. See the illuminating commentary on this passage by Walter, *Arthur: L'ours et le roi,* 208–213.

60. *La Mort le roi Artu,* § 192.

61. Ibid., § 127.

62. It should be noted that the name Martinus, although of Latin origin, seems to contain the Celtic root *art-,* thereby suggesting the name of the bear. Is this the origin of the later tradition in French children's literature that all bears are named Martin?

63. Edmond Faral, "L'île d'Avalon et la fée Morgane," in *Mélanges de linguistique et de littérature offerts à M. Alfred Jeanroy par ses élèves et ses amis* (Paris: Droz, 1928), 243–253; Jean-Christophe Cassard, "Arthur est vivant! Jalons pour une enquête sur le messianisme royal au Moyen Âge," *Cahiers de civilisation médiévale* 32 (1989): 135–146. Like the date of his death, the date of Arthur's birth seems to connect him to the calendar cycle of the bear and to emphasize his animal na-

ture. Several writers tell us that Arthur was born in early August, during the hottest of the dog days, and that he was conceived six months earlier (heroes' mothers have short gestation periods), that is, in early February. February 2 was precisely the date for the great winter festival of the bear: the day when it came out of its den and, depending on the weather, did or did not end its hibernation. It may be noted in passing that, like the bear cubs described by bestiaries, Arthur was born short of a normal gestation period, and for that reason as well has a rather ursine nature.

64. Walter, *Arthur: L'Ours et le roi,* 88–89.

65. Ibid., 89–91.

66. Percy Ernst Schramm and Florentine Mütherich, *Denkmale der deutschen Könige und Kaiser: Ein Beitrag zur Herrschengeschichte von Karl dem Grossen bis Friedrich II, 768–1250* (Munich: Prestel, 1962), 115, no. 5. This bronze she-bear, sometimes with reason identified as a she-wolf, seems to be a Gallo-Roman work of the fourth or fifth century.

67. A throne he refused, as I noted earlier.

68. Otto Keller, *Die antike Tierwelt* I, 277–284.

69. Jacques André, *L'Alimentation et la Cuisine à Rome* (Paris: Klincksieck, 1961), 118–120. It may be noted that the Bible, contrary to Roman traditions, sees the flesh of deer as the purest of all meat (Deuteronomy 15.22), and thereby provided medieval Christianity with solid scriptural arguments to bring out the purity of the animal, very far removed from the savage character of the bear hunt and the bloody rituals of butchering and sharing that followed the death of the animal.

70. Michel Pastoureau, "La chasse au sanglier: Histoire d'une dévalorisation (IVᵉ– XIVᵉ siècle)," in *La Chasse au Moyen Âge: Société, traités, symbols,* ed. Agostino Paravicini Bagliani and Baudouin Van den Abeele (Florence: Sismel, 2000), 7–23.

71. Otto Keller, *Die antike Tierwelt* I, 175–181.

72. Throughout this passage, I use the term "menagerie" in its modern sense, which dates from the seventeenth century. In Old and Middle French, the word designated not a place where wild or unusual beasts were kept and shown, but simply the administration of a farm or a house.

73. On the history of medieval menageries, see Gustave Loisel, *Histoire des ménageries de l'Antiquité à nos jours* (Paris: Doin, 1912), 141–289; K. Hauck, "Tiergarten im Pfalzbereich," in *Deutsche Königspfalzen* (Göttingen: Vandenhoeck und Ruprecht, 1963), 1:30–74; Werner Paravicini, "Tiere aus dem Norden," *Deutsches Archiv für die Erforschung des Mittelalters* 59, 2 (2003): 559–591. The great Percy Schramm also devoted several pages to them in the book

he wrote in collaboration with Florentine Mütherich, *Denkmale der deutschen Könige und Kaiser,* 70–74.

74. Documents have to be collated with other, more numerous documents that can be found, particularly for the late Middle Ages, in iconography and accounting records: payments for food, keepers, veterinary care, the making of cages, chains, collars, clothing, and all kinds of construction.

75. The most common words used to designate a menagerie were *bestiarium, vivarium,* and *claustrum,* but they were used for pits or cages as well as parks or reserves; in addition, they had several meanings: *vivarium,* for example, was used for a menagerie containing wild beasts, a deer park, a rabbit warren, a fishpond, or even an orchard. Terms such as *pardarium, leopardarium,* or *ferarium* were used less frequently but were more precise: they meant a pit containing lions, leopards, or panthers. Similarly, aviaries, unlike fishponds, had an explicit lexicon: *aviarium, columbarium.*

76. Current definitions by zoologists of "domestic" and "domestication" cannot be applied as they stand to medieval culture. In the Middle Ages, all animals that lived in the house *(domus)* or around it were "domestic": *animalia domestica* were therefore considered to include not only dogs, cats, horses, falcons, cattle, and fowl, but also mice, weasels, crows, foxes, and a few others.

77. For the last thirty years I have been developing a census of all the proper names given to animals in France, in literary and narrative texts, in documents in the archives, and in accounting records, for the period from the year 1000 to the end of the fifteenth century; any new information in this area would be welcome.

78. Similarly, there were in the aviaries large numbers of ostriches, parrots, and "India hens" (used for any exotic bird species with even slightly colored plumage); *aviary* did not take on a more precise meaning until the sixteenth century, after the discovery of the New World and the arrival of the turkey *(dindon)* in Western Europe.

79. Unknown to the Ancients, the polar bear seems to have been mentioned for the first time in the Christian West in a saga in the form of a chronicle compiled around 1050–1060: *Morkinskinna: The Earliest Icelandic Chronicle of the Norwegian Kings,* ed. and trans. Theodore M. Andersson and Kari Ellen Gade (Ithaca: Cornell University Press, 2000), 211–212. It was also mentioned a little later by Archbishop Adam of Bremen in his curious treatise on the geography of Denmark and neighboring regions: *Situ Daniae et reliquarum quae sunt trans Daniam sunt regionum natura* (Leiden, 1629), 139: *"Northmannia ursos albos habet"* (Norway has white bears). See Paravicini, "Tiere aus dem Norden," especially 578–579.

80. John Bayley, *The History and Antiquities of the Tower of London* (London: Cadell, 1821), 1:270; Loisel, *Histoire des ménageries de l'Antiquité à nos jours*, 1:155; Paravicini, "Tiere aus dem Norden," 579–580, n. 83. It is possible that King Henry III of England received a second polar bear from the same king of Norway in 1261 or 1262.

81. François Louis Ganshof, ed., *Histoire des relations internationales* (Paris: Hachette, 1953), 1:36–39.

82. *Chanson de Roland*, v. 30–34, 127–135, 183–186.

83. On this elephant, see Einhard, *Life of Charlemagne*, trans. Samuel Epes Turner (Ann Arbor: University of Michigan Press, 1960), 43; Michel Pastoureau, *Les Animaux célèbres* (Paris: Bonneton, 2001), 89–93.

84. According to the *Annales de Vendôme* (*Recueil des Historiens de la France*, vol. XI, 29 D). See R. H. Bautier, "Anne de Kiev, reine de France, et la politique royale au XIᵉ siècle," *Revue des études slaves* 57 (1985): 539–564. See also Frédéric Soehnée, *Catalogue des actes d'Henri Iᵉʳ roi de France* (Paris: Champion, 1907); Jan Dhondt, "Quelques aspects du règne d'Henri Iᵉʳ, roi de France," in *Mélanges d'histoire du Moyen Âge, dédiés à la mémoire de Louis Halphen* (Paris: PUF, 1951), 199–208.

85. *Morkinskinna*, 137–138. The text does not specify the color of the fur of the king of Norway's bears, white or brown. The ones sent with Anna were naturally brown.

3. The Relative of Man

1. Aristotle, *History of Animals*, II, 8; Pliny, *Natural History*, VIII, 54. For Pliny, only the tail distinguishes monkeys from men: "*Simiarum quoque genera plura. Hominis figurae proxima caudis inter se distinguntur.*"

2. Isidore of Seville states that if a pregnant woman looks at a monkey or a picture of a monkey her child will be afflicted with monkey-like ugliness. *Etymologies*, XII.i.60.

3. See, for example, Thomas of Cantimpré, *Liber de natura rerum*, ed. H. Boese (Berlin: W. De Gruyter, 1973), IV.96.1, 162.

4. A sow could even act as surrogate mother for a human embryo for a few hours to permit the performance of an operation. M. F. Rothschild and A. Ruvinsky, eds., *The Genetics of the Pig* (Wallingford: CABI, 1998); P. J. A. Bollen et al., eds., *The Laboratory Swine* (Boca Raton: CRC Press, 2000), extensive bibliography, 117–130. I would like to thank Jean-Louis Lefaix for all the information he has given me on this subject.

5. Among many sources, see Philippe Castan, *Naissance médiévale de la dissection anatomique* (Paris: Sauramps Médical, 1985).

6. See below (note 19) the opinion expressed by the doctor of King Baldwin I of Jerusalem in the early twelfth century, as well as Rudolf Hiestand, "König Balduin und sein Tanzbär," *Archiv für Kulturgeschichte* 70 (1988): 343–360.

7. See, for example, Alexander Neckam, *De naturis rerum,* ed. Thomas Wright (London: Longman, 1863), II, cxxx; Thomas of Cantimpré, *De natura rerum,* IV, 96.

8. It was this diversity of fur color that led some naturalists from the sixteenth to the nineteenth century, including Buffon himself, to distinguish among several brown bear species, whereas present-day zoologists recognize only one: *Ursus arctos.* See, for example, Jean-Michel Parde and Jean-Jacques Camarra, *L'Ours de Pyrénées: Ursus arctos Linnaeus, 1758 (Encyclopédie des carnivores de France,* vol. 5) (Nort sur Erdre: Société française pour l'étude et la protection des mammifères, 1992).

9. See all the excerpts quoted by Vincent of Beauvais, *Speculum naturale* (Douai: Company of Jesus, 1624), XIX, cxviff. See also Corinne Beck, "Approches du traitement de l'animal chez les encyclopédistes du XIIIe siècle: L'exemple de l'ours," in *L'enciclopedismo medievale,* ed. Michelangelo Picone (Ravenna: Longo, 1994), 163–178.

10. Buffon, *Histoire naturelle,* nouvelle édition (Paris: Imprimerie royale, 1769) VIII, 38.

11. But Aristotle drew attention to the bear's truly omnivorous diet. *History of Animals,* VIII, 42.

12. This appears to have been the opinion of William of Auvergne, bishop of Paris, in his *De universo creaturarum,* compiled around 1240. See Franco Morenzoni, "Le monde animal dans le *De universo creaturarum* de Guillaume d'Auvergne," in *Micrologus VIII* (2000): *Il mondo animale,* 1:212–213.

13. Parde and Camarra, *L'Ours de Pyrénées,* 11–13.

14. Knut Schmidt-Nielsen, *Animal Physiology,* 5th ed. (Cambridge: Cambridge University Press, 1997), 12.

15. These virtues of bear grease had already been mentioned and commented on in Pliny's *Natural History,* XXI, 125; XXII, 34; XXVIII, 163, 177, 192, 198, 216, 219, etc.

16. See, for example, Charles Joseph Singer, *A Short History of Anatomy from the Greeks to Harvey* (New York: Dover, 1957), 68–69; Lawrence J. Bliquez and Alexander Kazhdan, "Four Testimonia to Human Dissection in Byzantine Times," *Bulletin of the History of Medicine* 58 (1984): 554–557; Andreas-Holger Maehle and Ulrich Tröhler, "The Debate on Animal Experimentation from

Antiquity to the End of the Eighteenth Century," in *Vivisection in Historical Perspective*, ed. Nicholas A. Rupke (London: Routledge, 1987), 14–47.

17. Hiestand, "König Balduin und sein Tanzbär."

18. See Chapter 2.

19. On Baldwin I of Jerusalem, see Joshua Prawer, *Histoire du royaume latin de Jérusalem* (Paris: CNRS, 1969), 264–299; Hans Eberhard Mayer, "Etudes sur l'histoire de Baudouin Ier, roi de Jérusalem," in *Mélanges sur l'histoire du royaume latin de Jérusalem, Mémoires de l'Académie des inscriptions et belles-lettres*, n.s., 5:10–91.

20. Jean Clédat, "Le raid du roi Baudouin Ier en Égypte," *Bulletin de l'Institut français d'archéologie orientale* 26 (1925): 71–81.

21. Guibert de Nogent, *Gesta Dei per Francos*, Book VII, chapters 11 and 13, in *Recueil des historiens des croisades*, vol. 4, *Historiens occidentaux* (Paris: Imprimerie Royale, 1879), 229–234. English translation by Robert Levine, *The Deeds of God through the Franks* (Rochester: Boydell Press, 1997).

22. *The Autobiography of Guibert*, trans. C. C. Swinton Bland (1925; Westport: Greenwood Press, 1979).

23. On Guibert and his autobiography, see J. Paul, "Le démoniaque et l'imaginaire dans le *De vita sua* de Guibert de Nogent, *Senefiance* 6 (1979): 373–399; Georges Duby, *The Knight, the Lady and the Priest*, tr. Barbara Bray (New York: Pantheon, 1983); John Benton, ed., *Self and Society in Medieval France: The Memoirs of Abbot Guibert of Nogent* (1970; Toronto: University of Toronto Press, 1984).

24. A detailed account of this story was presented by Lambert of Ardres, a priest in service to the lords of Ardres, who compiled a history of the Counts of Guines in the early thirteenth century that is full of information on medieval history and material civilization. See *Historia comitum Ghisnensium*, ed. J. Heller, M. G. H. SS, 24 (1879), 557–642.

25. Pliny, *Natural History*, VIII, 54.

26. Aristotle, *History of Animals*, V, 2; see also VI, 31.

27. It is indeed possible that Pliny misread Aristotle, who says in the quoted passage that the she-bear is "prone," that is, belly to the ground, to receive the male. In that case, Pliny's misreading, not infrequent on his part, would be the only source of the legend that bears couple *more hominum*.

28. Cambridge University Library, MS Kk 4. 25 fol. 32 v°. An analogous idea is found a few decades later in William of Auvergne, *De universo creaturarum*, in *Opera omnia*, ed. Blaise Leferon (Orléans: Praland, 1674), III, 25, col. 1072a.

29. See for example a very fine grisaille miniature found in one of the manuscripts of the *Livre de la chasse* of Gaston Phébus: Paris, BNF, ms. Fr. 14357, fol. 46.

30. See below for its love for debauchery.

31. Oppien, *De la chasse,* ed. Pierre Boudreaux (Paris: Champion, 1908), Book II § 146.

32. Paris, BNF, ms. fr. 14357, fol. 46.

33. See the excerpts and comments of Beck, "Approches du traitement de l'animal chez les encyclopédistes du XIIIᵉ siècle: L'exemple de l'ours," 170–174.

34. Aristotle, *History of Animals,* VI, 30; Pliny, *Natural History,* VII, 54, and X, 174; Ovid, *Metamorphoses,* XV, 379; Aelian, *On the Characteristics of Animals,* II, 19, etc.

35. Hosea 13.8.

36. Rabanus Maurus, *De universo* VIII, 3 (P. L. III, col. 223).

37. Ambrose, *Hexameron* VI, iv, 18 (P. L. 14, col. 263–264).

38. On all of this, see again Beck, "Approches du traitement de l'animal chez les encyclopédistes du XIIIᵉ siècle," 163–178.

39. Isabelle Toinet, "La parole incarnée: Voir la parole dans les images des XIIᵉ et XIIIᵉ siècles," *Médiévales* 22–23 (1992): 13–30; Carla Casagrande and Silvana Vecchio, *Histoire des sept péchés capitaux au Moyen Âge,* trans. Pierre-Emmanuel Dauzat (Paris: Aubier, 2003).

40. Isidore of Seville, *Etymologies,* trans. Stephen A. Barney et al. (Cambridge: Cambridge University Press, 2006), 252.

41. Buffon, *Histoire naturelle,* vol. VIII, 29–30.

42. Aristotle, *History of Animals,* VIII, 17.

43. Marcel Couturier, *L'Ours brun* (Grenoble: L. Couturier, 1954), 456–459. The bear has a litter (one or two cubs, sometimes three) not every year but generally every two years. She is fertile for about fifteen years, between the ages of three and eighteen, and in the course of her life as a mother, therefore gives birth to about twenty cubs.

44. *The Romance of Yder,* ed. and trans. Alison Adams (Cambridge: D. S. Brewer, 1983). This romance, which is interesting for several reasons, has drawn little attention from scholars. Studies of it are few: Gaston Paris, *"Yder,"* *Histoire littéraire de la France* 30 (1888): 199–215; Elaine Southward, "The Knight Yder and the Beowulf Legend in Arthurian Romance," *Medium Aevum* 15 (1946): 1–47; Joël H. Grisward, "Ider et le tricéphale: D'une aventure arthurienne à un mythe indien," *Annales E. S. C.* 33, 2 (March–April 1978): 279–293.

45. *The Romance of Yder,* 132–134 (3301–98).

46. On this echo and the traditions underlying it, see Grisward, "Ider et le tricéphale."

47. "Li ors estut por eventer / Car le veoir out il perdu." *The Romance of Yder,* 3356–57.

48. See Philippe Walter, *Arthur: L'ours et le roi* (Paris: Imago, 2002), 85–86.

49. Arthur's only child is a son, the hidden fruit of incest: the traitor Mordred that he had with his half-sister, the Queen of Orkney, sometimes named Anna, sometimes Morgause.

50. Not until the first versions of the *Prose Tristan* between 1225 and 1230 is Tristan called the "son of Meliodas king of Lyonesse." See Michel Pastoureau, *Les Chevaliers de la Table Ronde* (Lathuile: Éditions du Gui, 2006), 192–193 and 227–230.

51. G. D. West, *An Index of Proper Names in French Arthurian Verse Romances, 1150–1300* (Toronto: University of Toronto Press, 1969), 157.

52. On these questions see Philippe Walter, *Le Gant de verre: Le mythe de Tristan et Yseult* (La Gacilly: Artus, 1990), 187–218.

53. Matthew Paris, *Chronica Majora*, ed. Henry R. Luard (London: Longman, 1874), 2:614–615. On this remarkable figure, see Richard Vaughan, *Matthew Paris* (Cambridge: Cambridge University Press, 1958); Suzanne Lewis, *The Art of Matthew Paris in the Chronica Majora* (Berkeley: University of California Press, 1987).

54. Otto Müller, *Turnier und Kampf in den altfranzösischen Artusromanen* (Erfurt: Ohlenroth, 1907); Michel Pastoureau, *Une histoire symbolique du Moyen Âge occidental* (Paris: Seuil, 2004), 15–16.

55. Matthew Paris writes *"liberaliter,"* that is, "freely, as she pleases," but also "generously." *Chronica Majora* II, 615.

56. Noël Valois, *Guillaume d'Auvergne, évêque de Paris (1228–1249): Sa vie et ses ouvrages* (Paris: Alphonse Picard, 1880).

57. The work of William of Auvergne is unfortunately still partly unpublished and little studied. Some texts are attributed to him that are not his (notably sermons); others that he did write are attributed to others. New editions and new attributions are necessary.

58. On these essential questions, see the excellent article Morenzoni, "Le monde animal dans le *De universo creaturarum.*"

59. On all this, see the enlightening article by Jacques Berlioz, "Pouvoirs et contrôle de la croyance: la question de la procréation démoniaque chez Guillaume d'Auvergne (vers 1180–1249)," *Razo: Cahiers du Centre d'études médiévales de Nice* 9 (1989): 5–27.

60. *De universo creaturarum*, III, 25, col. 1071 b.

61. Morenzoni, "Le monde animal dans le *De universo creaturarum*," 212–214; Berlioz, "Pouvoirs et contrôle de la croyance chez Guillaume d'Auvergne." This passage enables William of Auvergne to emphasize the slight power of demons. For animals as for men, God, in various ways, is the prime mover; it is He who makes possible and "illuminates" life; it is He who causes ac-

tion and procreation. For demons, the Devil plays that role; but his power is limited, and his interventions in human life relatively rare. For this reason, seeing in one place or another the work of the Devil is usually an illusion, a superstition, almost a disease that can be cured by common sense, prayer, and communion.

62. Saxo Grammaticus, *Gesta Danorum* X, xv; see the edition by Jørgen Olrik and Hans Ræder (Copenhagen: Levin and Munksgaard, 1931), 287–288.

63. For example, the anonymous collection of twelfth to sixteenth century narrative texts, *Scriptores rerum germanicarum septentrionalium* (Frankfurt, 1609), 128ff.

64. On these genealogies and the dynastic legends underlying them, see Carl-Martin Edsman, "La fête de l'ours chez les Lapons: Sources anciennes et recherches récentes sur certains rites de chasse aux confins septentrionaux de la Scandinavie," *Proxima Thulé* 2 (1996): 12–49, especially 42–45.

65. Olaus Magnus, *Historia de gentibus septentrionalibus* (Rome, 1555), XVIII, xxx, 627.

66. *Origo et gesta Sivardi ducis*, in *Scriptores rerum Danicarum Medii Aevi*, ed. Jacobus Langebek (Copenhagen: Hafniae, 1774), 3:288–302. Duke Siward was made Earl of Northumbria (1033–1055) and on several occasions had to confront incursions from Macbeth, King of Scotland, into northern England.

67. Axel Olrik, "Siward Digri of Northumberland: A Viking Saga of the Danes in England," *Saga-Book of the Viking Club*, 6:212–237.

68. On the legend of the Orsini, "sons of the bear," see especially Franca Allegrezza, *Organizzazione del potere e dinamiche familiari: Gli Orsini dal Duecento agli inizi del Quattrocento* (Rome: Istituto Storico Italiano per il Medio Evo, 1998), 132–143. See also Sandro Carocci, "I figli dell'orsa," *Medio Evo* (1995): 82–85.

69. On the origin of the Orsini, see Giuseppe Marchetti Longhi, *I Boveschi e gli Orsini* (Rome: Istituto di Studi Romani, 1960).

70. J. Michael Stitt, *Beowulf and the Bear's Son: Epic, Saga, and Fairytale in Northern Germanic Tradition* (New York: Garland, 1992). See also the incisive commentary, quite different from ordinary scholarship, by Jorge Luis Borges, *Cours de littérature anglaise,* trans. Michel Lafon (Paris: Seuil, 2006), 38–59.

71. See the recent bilingual edition with a verse translation by Seamus Heaney (New York: Norton, 1999).

72. Carl-Martin Edsman, "La fête de l'ours chez les Lapons," 43–47.

73. On the problem of animal disguises, see Michel Pastoureau, "Nouveaux regards sur le monde animal à la fin du Moyen Âge," *Micrologus* IV (1996): *Il Teatro della natura,* 41–54.

74. The Aristotelian corpus on animals was translated into Latin from Arabic by Michael Scotus in Toledo around 1230; a few years earlier, the same translator had worked on Avicenna's commentaries on that corpus. About a generation later, it was all combined (almost word for word in some passages) by Albertus Magnus in his *De animalibus*. But several chapters of the corpus were known and had already been translated by the late twelfth century. On the rediscovery of Aristotle's works of natural history, see Fernand van Steenberghen, *Aristotle in the West: The Origins of Latin Aristotelianism*, trans. Leonard Johnston (Louvain: E. Naulewarts, 1955), and *La Philosophie au XIIIe siècle*, 2nd ed. (Louvain: Publications Universitaires, 1991); Charles H. Lohr, *The Medieval Interpretation of Aristotle* (Cambridge: Cambridge University Press, 1982). On the unity of the living world in Aristotle's system, see Pierre Pellegrin, *Aristotle's Classification of Animals: Biology and the Conceptual Unity of the Aristotelian Corpus*, trans. Anthony Preus (Berkeley: University of California Press, 1986).

75. On the legends associating Francis of Assisi with animals, particularly with birds, among many sources see Franco Cardini, "Francesco d'Assisi e gli animali," *Studi Francescani* 78 (1981): 7–46; Jacques Dalarun, *The Misadventure of Francis of Assisi*, trans. Edward Hagman (St. Bonaventure: St. Bonaventure University, Franciscan Institute Publications, 2002).

76. *"Quia et ipsa creatura liberabitur a servitude in libertatem gloriae filiorum dei."*

77. Beginning with Thomas Aquinas himself; see Thomas Domanyi, *Der Römerbriefkommentar des Thomas von Aquin* (Bern and Frankfurt: Peter Lang, 1979), 218–230.

78. The remark is traditionally attributed to William of Auvergne, but it is found in a sermon (c. 1230–1235) that may not be by him; see Albrecht Quentin, *Naturkenntnisse und Naturanschauungen bei Wilhelm von Auvergne* (Hildesheim: Gerstenberg, 1976), 184.

79. Michel Pastoureau, "Une justice exemplaire: les procès intentés aux animaux (XIIIe–XVIe s.)," in *Les Rites de la justice*, ed. Claude Gauvard and Robert Jacob (Paris: Léopard d'Or, 2000), 173–200.

80. *"Nec turpide joca cum urso . . . ante se permittat. . . . Quia hoc diabolicum est et a sacris canonibus prohibitum"*; see the complete text of these prohibitions in P. L. 125, col. 776–777.

81. Philippe Walter, "Der Bär und der Erzbischof: Masken und Mummentanz bei Hinkmar von Reims und Adalbero von Laon," in *Feste und Feiern im Mittelalter*, ed. Detlef Altenburg et al. (Sigmaringen: J. Thorbecke Verlag, 1991), 377–388.

82. To frighten their flocks, some medieval bishops threatened that anyone who disguised himself as an animal would really be transformed into that animal, or else keep a part of the animal's body (particularly ears and feet). William

of Auvergne did not believe that a human being could be transformed into an animal.

83. A festival celebrated at Rome in mid-February in honor of the faun-god Lupercus and supposed to favor the fertility of fields and flocks, as well as preventing female sterility. After sacrificing goats and dogs to him, the god's priests smeared blood over young men who ran through the city half-naked, dressed only in the skins of the sacrificed animals. As they went by they were supposed to strike symbolically all the women, but as time passed, this symbolic blow took on a more licentious, indeed clearly sexual, cast. See the long description in Ovid, *Fasti* II, 267–452; see also Christoph Ulf, *Das Römische Lupercalienfest* (Darmstadt: Wissenschaftliche Buchgesellschaft, 1982).

4. The Saint Stronger than the Beast

1. To repeat, for medieval culture, "domestic" applied to any animal living in or near a human *domus*. Zoologists today consider "truly domesticated" only those animals "that reproduce in captivity and are distinguished from natively wild species by genotypic and phenotypic characteristics resulting from extended and deliberate selection by humans." Jean-Pierre Digard, *L'Homme et les Animaux domestiques: Anthropologie d'une passion* (Paris: Fayard, 1990), 85.

2. Corinne Beck, "Approche des territoires historiques de l'ours en Europe au Moyen Âge," in *Actes du XVIIᵉ colloque de la Société française pour l'étude et la protection des mammifères* (Grenoble, 1993), 94–100.

3. Jean-Jacques Camarra and Jean-Paul Ribal, *L'Ours brun* (Paris: Hatier, 1989), 14. See also, among many others, C. Berducou et al., "Le régime alimentaire de l'ours brun des Pyrénées," *Bulletin mensuel de l'Office national de la chasse* 54 (1982): 34–45; M. Fabbri, *Le abitudini alimentari dell'orso bruno nel Parque Nationale d'Abbruzzo* (Parma, 1988); L. Faliu et al., "Le régime carnivore de l'ours des Pyrénées: Étude préliminaire," *Ciconia* 4, 1 (1980): 21–32.

4. Marcel Couturier, *L'Ours brun* (Grenoble: L. Couturier, 1954), 157–182.

5. Many "festivals of the bear" and associated rituals that are still current today in the valleys of the Pyrenees and some valleys of the Alps go back no further than the late eighteenth century, sometimes not even the mid-nineteenth. It is prudent to be skeptical in this area, as in may others, about the claimed antiquity of folk practices in rural areas.

6. Vincent of Beauvais, *Speculum naturale* (Douai: Company of Jesus, 1624), XIX, cxvi–cxx.

7. Polar bear skins, given as gifts by the kings of Denmark and Norway, were the

most sought after and admired: Percy Ernst Schramm and Florentine Mütherich, *Denkmale der deutschen Könige und Kaiser: Ein Beitrag zur Herrschengeschichte von Karl dem Grossen bis Friedrich II, 768–1250* (Munich: Prestel, 1962),
71–72 and 99–100; Werner Paravicini, "Tiere aus dem Norden," *Deutsches Archiv für die Erforschung des Mittelalters* 59, 2 (2003): 559–591.

8. Alexandre Dumas, *Mon dictionnaire de cuisine*, new ed. (Paris: U. G. E., 1998),
467–469. Elsewhere, Dumas tells how he was served a bear steak in a restau-
rant in Martigny in Switzerland, and on that occasion expresses his opinion
of the bears of Bern and the story of their pits: *Travels in Switzerland*, trans.
R. W. Plummer and A. Craig Bell (London: A. Owen, 1958), 39ff.

9. Gaston Phébus, *Livre de Chasse* (Stockholm: Almqvist och Wiksell, 1971), I, 8.

10. Bruno Andreolli, "L'orso nella cultura nobiliare dall'*Historia Augusta* a Chrétien de Troyes," in *Il bosco nel Medioevo*, ed. Bruno Andreolli and Massimo
Montanari (Bologna: CLUEB, 1989), 35–54. More generally on the bear's paw
as the most symbolic part of the animal's body, see Rémi Mathieu, "La patte
de l'ours," *L'Homme: Revue française d'anthropologie* 24, 1 (January–March
1984): 5–42.

11. Some writers thought they had detected similar feudal dues outside the Alpine crescent, notably in western France, but that is probably due to a paleo-
graphic confusion between the words *ours* (bear) and *oie* (goose).

12. Altan Golkap, "L'ours anatolien, un oncle bien entreprenant," *Études mongoles
et sibériennes* 11 (1980): 215–242; André Miquel, *Les Arabes et l'Ours* (Heidelberg:
C. Winter, 1994), 124–126.

13. An animal could become the iconographic emblem of a saint because of
an episode in the saint's life, often of his passion, but also because of the
saint's name (the lamb [*agneau*] for Saint Agnes, the dove [*colombe*] for Saint
Columba, the wolf for Saint Wolfgang), his work (the fish for Saint Andrew
the fisherman), or because of a patron.

14. An expression used several times by Claude Lévi-Strauss with reference to
totemism and the "savage mind," and adopted and commented on by Dan
Sperber, "Pourquoi les animaux parfaits, les hybrides et les monstres sont-ils
bons à penser symboliquement," *L'Homme* 15, 2 (1975): 5–34.

15. Claude Gaignebet and Jean-Dominique Lajoux, *Art profane et Religion populaire au Moyen Âge* (Paris: PUF, 1985), 240–265 and passim; Armand Tchouh-
adjian, ed., *Saint Blaise, évêque de Sébaste*, 2nd ed. (Paris: L'Harmattan, 2004),
413–420.

16. Louis Réau, *Iconographie de l'art chrétien* (Paris: PUF, 1956) III / 1, 227–233;
Lexikon der christlichen Ikonographie (Freiburg im Breisgau: Herder, 1973), vol.
5, col. 416–419.

17. Johann Joseph Laux, *Der heilige Kolumban: Sein Leben und seine Schriften* (Freiburg im Breisgau: Herder, 1919); Marguerite-Marie Dubois, *Un pionnier de la civilisation occidentale: Saint Colomban* (Paris: Alsatia, 1950).

18. Annibale Maestri, *Il culto di San Colombano in Italia* (Piacenza: Biblioteca storica piacentina, 1955), 330ff.

19. *Vita Columbani abbatis*, P. L. 87, col. 1011–47, and *M. G. H., Scriptores rerum merovingicarum* IV, 1–62 and 65–156 (ed. B. Krusch).

20. The other iconographic emblems of Saint Columban are the spring (which he caused to flow in the cave), the abbey cross, the book, and in modern times the whip (symbol of his severity). See R. Olmi, "L'iconografia di San Colombano," in *Convegno storico Colombiano, 1–2 sett. 1951* (Bobbio, 1953), 33–40.

21. On this episode, see Pierre Boglioni, "Les animaux dans l'hagiographie monastique," in *L'Animal exemplaire au Moyen Âge (V^e–XVe siècle)*, ed. Jacques Berlioz, Marie Anne Polo de Beaulieu, and Pascal Collomb (Rennes: Presses Universitaires de Rennes, 1999), 51–80.

22. F. Blanke, *Der heilige Gallus* (Zurich, 1940).

23. This episode is absent from lives of Saint Gall before the twelfth century. But the same story is found in the *vita* of Saint Aventinus of Troyes. See L. Valle, *Vita di sant'Avventino* (Turin, 1794).

24. See Chapter 7, section "The Fall of a King."

25. L. Knappert, "La Vie de saint Gall et le paganisme germanique," *Revue de l'histoire des religions* 29 (1894): 286–302.

26. Both edited by B. Krusch in *M. G. H. Scriptores rerum merovingicarum* IV, 229–337. The episode of the bear is found in chapter 11 of the *vita* by Walafrid Strabo.

27. Saint Gall Stiftbibliothek, Cod. Sang. 53. On this plate binding, among many sources, see Marguerite Menz-Vondermühll, "Die St. Galler Elfenbeine um 900," *Frühmittelalterliche Studien* 15 (1981): 387–434.

28. F. Gull, "Das Wappenbild der Abtei und der Stadt St. Gallen in älteren Bannern und Siegeln," *Archives héraldiques suisses* (1907): 68–76.

29. The episode is recounted for the first time in the *Vita Corbiniani* compiled by a monk in the monastery of Tegernsee at the turn of the ninth and tenth centuries, but it did not really take its place in the iconography of Saint Corbinian until the late Middle Ages.

30. Lajoux, *L'Homme et l'Ours* (Grenoble: Glénat, 1996), 66–67.

31. See J. Hau, *Sankt Maximin* (Sarrebruck, 1935).

32. In Old French, it is often difficult to determine whether the phrase *l'ours Martin* means "the bear named Martin" or "Saint Martin's bear."

33. See the discussion in Chapter 2, section "Taboos about the Name."

34. It was also not unusual for donkeys to be named Martin, perhaps recalling

Saint Maximinus's donkey devoured by a bear mentioned earlier in this chapter. In some regions of Germany and the Netherlands in the late Middle Ages and the early modern period, November 11 was a day on which gifts were given to children; and Saint Martin riding on a donkey often played the role given elsewhere to Saint Nicholas. See Philippe Walter, *Mythologie chrétienne: Rites et mythes au Moyen Âge* (Paris: Entente, 1992), 77–78.

35. This episode is absent from the earliest life of Eligius, written by his friend Saint Ouen; it is found in later lives and is linked to the legendary origins of Ourscamp abbey. In some versions, it is not Eligius doing the plowing but a priest in his diocese.

36. Paul Benoît, *Vie populaire de saint Claude* (Besançon: Imprimerie Catholique de l'Est, 1924).

37. Lajoux, *L'Homme et l'Ours,* 67.

38. Jean Maury, *Limousin roman* (Saint-Léger-Vauban: Zodiaque, 1990); E. Rupin, *Coffret en cuivre doré et émaillé du XIIIᵉ siècle: Église de Saint-Viance (Corrèze)* (n.p., n.d.).

39. A. de La Vacquerie, *Histoire de la vie et des vertus de saint Florent* (Paris, 1637); Alix de La Frégeolière, *Saint Florent: Sa vie, ses miracles, ses reliques* (Angers: Hervé et Briand, 1878).

40. Stories of young men condemned to be devoured by bears and then spared are, on the other hand, infrequent. Examples that may be cited include Cerbonius (celebrated October 10), the well-known bishop of Populonia in Tuscany and patron saint of the town of Massa Marittima (where a bas relief on the façade of the cathedral of San Cerbone shows him surrounded by lions and bears). The theme of the girl or young woman spared by a male bear should be compared with that of the bear in love, seduced by a woman whom he kidnaps, sequesters, and rapes, or whom he makes his companion and the mother of his children, as discussed in the preceding chapter.

41. The same story is found in the *vita* of Saint Gerold of Feldkirch, a hermit who lived on the border between Switzerland and Austria in the second half of the tenth century. A wealthy lord who had sold all his worldly goods to retire into the wilderness, Gerold tamed a bear who was fleeing hunters; the animal helped him to build a cell and then a real hermitage, which later became the Saint Gerold Priory of Feldkirch in the Vorarlberg. See Josef Anton Amann, *Der heilige Gerold* (Höchst: Schneider, 1950).

42. M. Barth, *Die heilige Kaiserin Richardis und ihr Kult* (Schlettstadt, 1949); Marguerite Corbet, *Sainte Richarde* (Sélestat: Alsatia, 1948); Gaignebet and Lajoux, *Art profane et Religion populaire au Moyen Âge,* 250–251.

43. Albert Martiny, ed., *Textes sur Richarde* (Matzenheim: Collège Saint Joseph,

1989); E. Sommer, *Les Sculptures romanes de l'église abbatiale d'Andlau* (Andlau, 1990).

44. In the Celtic world, the first days of November were devoted to the dead, notably the night from the first to the second, the "night of Samhain," when the souls of the dead were thought to begin their long voyage to the beyond. It was not by chance that in 998, Odilon, the fifth abbot of Cluny, set November 2 as All Souls' Day, a Cluny ritual that gradually became the day of commemoration of the dead for all Christendom. See Françoise Le Roux, "Études sur le festiaire celtique: Samain," *Ogam* 13 (1961): 481–506.

45. In *Pantagruel,* Rabelais uses it as a synonym of *chopiner* and *trinquer* (1532 edition, chapter 18).

46. On popular festivals and celebrations in France connected with Saint Martin, see the various studies by Henri Fromage published in the *Bulletin de la Société de mythologie française* 74 (1969): 75–84 and 93–102; 78 (1970): 83–106; 83 (1971): 164–175; 108 (1978): 1–28.

47. Claude Gaignebet and Odile Ricoux, "Les Pères de l'Église contre les fête païennes," in *Carnavals et Mascarades,* ed. Pier Giovanni d'Ayala and Martine Boiteux (Paris: Bordas, 1988), 43–49.

48. The reader may consult the classic works by Henri Dontenville, *Mythologie française,* 2nd ed. (Paris: Payot, 1973); Claude Gaignebet and Marie-Claude Florentin, *Le Carnaval: Essais de mythologie populaire* (Paris: Payot, 1974); Georges Dumézil, *Fêtes romaines d'été et d'automne* (Paris: Gallimard, 1975); Gaignebet and Lajoux, *Art profane et Religion populaire au Moyen Âge;* Walter, *Mythologie chrétienne.*

49. On this role of the bear in the calendar, see Gaignebet and Florentin, *Le Carnaval,* passim.

50. Philippe Walter, "Der Bär und der Erzbischof: Masken und Mummentanz bei Hinkmar von Reims und Adalbero von Laon," in *Feste und Feiern im Mittelalter,* ed. Detlef Altenburg et al. (Sigmaringen: J. Thorbecke Verlag, 1991), 377–388. These games and simulations *(turpia joca cum ursis)* are alluded to by Archbishop Hincmar in his celebrated sermon denouncing festivals and ceremonies with pagan characteristics. See *P. L.* 125, col. 776.

51. Massimo Montanari, "Uomini e orsi nelle fonti agiografiche dell'alto medioevo," in *Symbole des Alltags, Alltag der Symbole: Festschrift für Harry Kühnel,* ed. Gertrud Blaschitz (Graz: Akademische Druck-und Verlagsanstalt, 1992), 571–587.

52. Among many references, see especially J. Begouen, "L'ours Martin en Ariège," *Bulletin de la Société ariégeoise des sciences, lettres et arts* (1966): 111–175; Daniel Fabre and Charles Camberoque, *La Fête en Languedoc: Regards sur le*

Carnaval aujourd'hui (Toulouse: Privat, 1977); Daniel Fabre, "Réflexions sur l'anthropologie de l'ours dans les Pyrénées," *Cahiers de l'université de Pau et des pays de l'Adour* (June 1977): 57–67; Sophie Bobbé, "Analyse de la fête de l'ours contemporaine en Catalogne française," in *Histoire et Animal,* ed. Alain Couret and Frédéric Ogé (Toulouse: Presses de l'Institut d'Études Politiques de Toulouse, 1989), 3:401–417; Gérard Caussimont, "Le mythe de l'ours dans les Pyrénées occidentales," in *Histoire et Animal,* ed. Couret and Ogé, 367–380; Lajoux, *L'Homme et l'Ours,* 73–86.

53. On this problem, see the pertinent remarks by Jean-Claude Schmitt, "Religion populaire et culture folklorique," *Annales E.S.C.* 31, 5 (1976): 941–953, and "Les traditions folkloriques dans la culture médiévale: Quelques réflexions de méthode," *Archives des sciences sociales des religions* 52, 1 (1981): 5–20.

54. For the Romans, Proserpina was not only the goddess of the underworld, counterpart to the Greek Persephone. She was also an agrarian goddess, whose cult included many fertility rites in the period of germination.

55. Françoise Le Roux, "Études sur le festiaire celtique: Imbolc et Beltaine," *Ogam* 14 (1962): 174–184.

56. Before the fifth century, the Presentation of Jesus at the Temple was celebrated on February 14, and the wedding at Cana was commemorated on the second Sunday after Epiphany. In some dioceses, these customs continued until the ninth century, sometimes even the twelfth.

57. Rafaelle Corso, *L'orso della Candelora* (Helsinki: Suomalainen Tiedeakatemia, 1955); Gaignebet and Florentin, *Le Carnaval;* Julio Caro Baroja, *Le Carnaval,* 2nd ed. (Paris: Gallimard, 1979).

5. The Bear in the House of the Devil

1. While biblical Greek had only the word *leon,* Hebrew used several words to designate the lion. The most frequent was *'arî;* but one also finds with some frequency *labi, layis, sahal,* and, for the lion cub, *kpîr.*

2. More reflection and research on these problems by medieval historians would be welcome. They would deal not only with animals, but also with plants, minerals, numbers, and colors. With regard to colors and the problem of translation into Latin of Hebrew, Aramaic, and Greek terms, see some remarks in Michel Pastoureau, *Blue: The History of a Color,* trans. Markus I. Cruse (Princeton: Princeton University Press, 2001), 7–11.

3. This scene was rather frequently depicted in the late medieval and early modern periods, notably, beginning in the fourteenth century in images related

to the Carmelite order, which considered the prophet Elisha their second founder, after Elijah. See *Lexikon der christlichen Iconographie* (Freiburg im Breisgau: Herder, 1978), vol. 1, col. 613–618.

4. Tertullian, *Adversus Judaeos*, in *P. L.* 2, col. 676; Anonymous, *Vitae prophetarum*, ed. Theodore Schermann (Leipzig: Teubner, 1907), 112–113.

5. *History of Animals* V, 2; VI, 30; VII, 17; IX, passim.

6. See Chapter 3, note 74.

7. *Natural History*, VII–XII.

8. Ibid., XXVIII–XXXII.

9. The work also appeared under the title *Collectanea rerum memorabilium*. See the anonymous edition (of high quality) published in Deux-Ponts in 1794 and the edition of Theodore Mommsen, 2nd ed. (Berlin: Weidmann, 1895).

10. Pliny had, however, already discussed wolves at length in the chapter on basilisks, with a long excursus on the deadly gaze of these two animals.

11. *"Nec alteri animalium in maleficio stultitia sollertior."* *Natural History*, VIII, 54. The meaning of the sentence is clear, though it is difficult to translate.

12. On medieval readers of Pliny, see the scholarly study by Arno Borst, *Das Buch der Naturgeschichte: Plinius und seine Leser im Zeitalter des Pergaments*, 2nd ed. (Heidelberg: Carl Winter, 1995).

13. *Commentarii in Isaiam*, ed. Marc Adriaen (Turnhout: Walter de Gruyter, 1963), 611 (= CCL 73A).

14. On Jerome as a reader of Pliny, see Borst, *Das Buch der Naturgeschichte*, 64–76.

15. Even though several times Augustine claimed the contrary, for example in the second book of *De doctrina christiana*.

16. On Augustine as a reader of Pliny, see Borst, *Das Buch der Naturgeschichte*, 64–76.

17. Many passages in the *Natural History* bring out Pliny's atheism and the vanity of any metaphysical quest; for example, this very powerful affirmation *"effigiem Dei quaerere, imbecillitatis humanae est"* ("I consider it . . . an indication of human weakness to inquire into the form and figure of God"). See the excellent thesis by Valérie Naas, *Le Projet encyclopédique de Pline l'Ancien* (Rome and Paris: École Française de Rome, 2002).

18. See, for example, the commentary on the Epistle to the Romans that Augustine wrote at the request of the monks of Hippo: *Augustine on Romans*, ed. and trans. Paula Fredriksen Landes (Chico, Calif.: Scholars Press, 1982); *P. L.* 39, col. 245–253.

19. See, for example, Augustine's commentaries on the Creation in *On Genesis: Two Books on Genesis against the Manichees; and, On the Literal Interpretation of*

Genesis, an Unfinished Book, trans. Roland J. Teske (Washington: Catholic University of America Press, 1991); *P. L.* 34, col. 173–180 and col. 245–253.

20. *"In istis duabus bestiis idem diabolus figuratus est." Sermones* XVII, 37 (*P. L.* 39, col. 1819).

21. *Polyhistor* (Deux-Ponts, 1794), 103–105 *(Caput XXVI: Numidia. In ea de ursis).* Solinius claims that these Numidian bears are deformed because of rabies.

22. See note 11, above.

23. *Natural History* VIII, 54. This extraordinary notation marks the conclusion of the chapter on bears.

24. See Chapter 3, section "The Sexuality of the Bear."

25. *"Ursus typum diaboli praefigurat; ursus est diabolus." Sermones, appendix sermo 37* (*P. L.* 39, col. 1819).

26. I should note that unlike Pliny and Augustine, Isidore makes no judgment about the bear. He merely expounds on the origin of the word *ursus,* which he connects to the passive past participle *orsus* and to the fact that when the she-bear has stillborn cubs, she restores them to life by licking them *cum ore suo.* See Isidore of Seville, *Etymologies,* trans. Stephen A. Barney et al. (Cambridge: Cambridge University Press, 2006), 252.

27. See Elisabeth Heyse, *Hrabanus Maurus' Enzyklopädie "De rerum naturis": Untersuchungen zu den Quellen und zur Methode der Kompilation* (Munich: Arbeo-Gesellschaft, 1969).

28. *"Ursus ergo aliquando juxta allegoriam significat diabolum insidiatorum gregis Dei, aliquando autem duces saevos et crudeles." De universo* VIII, 1 (*P. L.* 111, col. 223).

29. Ibid.

30. On the notion of image itself and the connections that unite all forms of *imagines* in the feudal period, see Jean-Claude Schmitt, *Le Corps des images: Essais sur la culture visuelle au Moyen Âge* (Paris: Gallimard, 2002), especially 21–62.

31. On dreams in the feudal period, see Jacques Le Goff, "Le christianisme et les rêves," in *Un autre Moyen Âge* (Paris: Gallimard, 1999), 689–738; Jean-Claude Schmitt, "L'iconographie des rêves," in *Le Corps des images,* 297–321.

32. Peter the Venerable, *De miraculis,* ed. Denis Bouthillier (Turnhout: Brepols, 1988), Book I, chapter XVIII: *"De Armanno novicio quem diabolus in specie ursi perterruit."*

33. Unfortunately, there is no recent edition of this work. While awaiting the one that is in preparation, see the old edition edited by Joseph Strange, Caesarius of Heisterbach, *Dialogus miraculorum* (Cologne: J. M. Heberle, 1851).

34. Ibid., 257–258 *("De Henrico cognomento Fikere").*

35. See the examples cited by Pierre Boglioni, "Les animaux dans l'hagiographie

monastique," in *L'Animal exemplaire au Moyen Âge (V^e–XVe siècle)*, ed. Jacques Berlioz, Marie Anne Polo de Beaulieu, and Pascal Collomb (Rennes: Presses Universitaires de Rennes, 1999), 50–80, especially 68–72.

36. A list can be found in Richard Mentz, *Die Träume in den altfranzösischen Karls- und Artus-Epen* (Marburg: N. G. Elwert, 1888). See also Hermann Braet, "Fonction et importance du songe dans la chanson de geste," *Le Moyen Âge* 77 (1971): 405–416.

37. *La Chanson de Roland*, v. 725–737, 2551–54, 2555–67.

38. On the meaning of these animals, see Mentz, *Die Träume in den altfranzösischen Karls- und Artus-Epen*; Karl Josef Steinmeyer, *Untersuchungen zur allegorischen Bedeutung der Träume im altfranzösischen Rolandslied* (Munich: M. Hueber, 1963); Hermann Braet, "Le second rêve de Charlemagne dans la *Chanson de Roland*," *Romanica Gandensia* 12 (1969): 5–19; Wolfgang G. van Emden, "Another Look at Charlemagne's Dreams in the *Chanson de Roland*," *French Studies* 28, 3 (July 1974): 257–271. The interpretations of Jean Bichon in *L'Animal dans la littérature française aux XIIe et XIIIe siècles* (Lille: Service de Reproduction des Thèses, Université de Lille III, 1976), 1:182–188, should be avoided.

39. *La Chanson de Roland*, v. 2555–67.

40. Note that the lineage holds lands in the Ardennes, the old location of worship of the Celtic goddess Arduina, goddess of bears.

41. Marcel Couturier, *L'Ours brun* (Grenoble: L. Couturier, 1954); Jean-Jacques Camarra and Jean-Paul Ribal, *L'Ours brun* (Paris: Hatier, 1989).

42. Today's brown bear has a coat whose color varies greatly depending on the season and on the individual bear, from light beige to dark brown. The bear's diet and area inhabited can also change the tint of its coat, which is neither uniform nor really monochromatic.

43. For medieval culture, up until about the year 1000, there were only three basic colors: white, red, and black; later, from the eleventh and twelfth centuries on, the number increased to six: white, red, black, green, yellow, and blue. See Michel Pastoureau, *Jésus chez le teinturier: Couleurs et teintures dans l'Occident médiéval* (Paris: Léopard d'Or, 1998), passim, and *Blue: The History of a Color*.

44. M.-C. Blanchet, "Des bruns et des couleurs," in *Mélanges Jeanne Lods* (Paris, 1978), 1:78–87; Michel Pastoureau, *Une histoire symbolique du Moyen Âge occidental* (Paris: Seuil, 2004), 197–212.

45. Klaus-Dieter Barnickel, *Farbe, Helligkeit und Glanz im Mittelenglischen* (Düsseldorf: Stern-Verlag Janssen, 1975), 87–102; Barbara Schäfer, *Die Semantik der Farbadjektive in Altfranzösischen* (Tübingen: Narr, 1986), 106–109.

46. *Fuscus, furvus, burrus, badius, brunus*, etc. See Jacques André, *Étude sur les termes*

de couleur dans la langue latine (Paris: Klincksieck, 1949), 123–127. See also M.-C. Blanchet, "Des bruns et des couleurs."

47. Michel Pastoureau, *Une histoire symbolique du Moyen Âge occidental,* 152–156.

48. The phenomenon was identical to what happened during the same period for *Renart* and *goupil* ("fox"). But, in the case of the bear, there was never in any Western language a complete substitution of the proper for the common noun.

49. G. D. West, *An Index of Proper Names in Arthurian Verse Romances (1150–1300)* (Toronto: University of Toronto Press, 1969), and *An Index of Proper Names in French Arthurian Prose Romances* (Toronto: University of Toronto Press, 1978).

50. Vincent of Beauvais, *Speculum naturale* (Douai: Company of Jesus, 1624), XIX, cxvi–cxxi.

51. Ibid., XIX, cxviii.

52. Commenting on this exchange of a birthright for a dish of lentils, Saint Paul speaks of him as "profane" (Hebrews 12.16) and sees in Isaac's paternal blessing of Jacob and not Esau an image of the freedom of divine election (Romans 9.10–13), interpretations that were adopted by most medieval theologians.

53. This appalling nature and tragic fate are embodied in the very name of Isaac's eldest son: in Hebrew, Esau means "hairy" *('e_aw),* and the other name given him, Edom, means "red" *(édom).*

54. This is why, when they give examples of animal disguises that are especially to be prohibited, normative texts coming from ecclesiastical authorities always mention animals with prominent "horns" (stag, bull) or with abundant hair (bear, boar); sometimes they are accompanied by animals with large ears, such as donkeys or hares. For the Church, animality seems to have consisted of protuberances, elements that seemed to come out of the body, that transgressed it the better to attack, wound, or kill (teeth, horns, tail, hair, claws). Some animals were even doubly targeted by bishops and councils: the bull for his horns and his tail, the boar for his bristles and his tusks, the donkey for his ears and his outsized sexual organ.

55. Philippe Walter, "Der Bär und der Erzbischof: Masken und Mummentanz bei Hinkmar von Reims und Adalbero von Laon," in *Feste und Feiern im Mittelalter,* ed. Detlef Altenburg et al. (Sigmaringen: Thorbecke, 1991), 377–388.

56. Johannes Scheffer, *Histoire de la Laponie, sa description, ses mœurs, la manière de vivre de ses habitants,* trans. Augustin Lubin (Paris: Veuve Olivier de Varennes, 1678), 386–388.

57. *Reinhart Fuchs,* ed. Jacob Grimm (Berlin: Reimer, 1834), v. 1577–1612; *Le Roman de Renart,* ed. Armand Strubel et al. (Paris: Gallimard, Bibliothèque de la Pléiade, 1998), Branch Ia, v. 520–727, 16–20.

58. 2 Kings 2.23–24. See note 3 above.

59. The Carmelites, who considered Elisha as one of their legendary founders (along with Elijah), frequently had the prophet depicted, notably the scene in which the bears devour the children. See, for example, Cécile Emond, "L'iconographie carmélitaine dans les anciens Pays-Bas méridionaux," in *Mémoires de l'Académie royale de Belgique* (Brussels, 1961), 79–87.

60. Robert Delort, *Le Commerce des fourrures en Occident à la fin du Moyen Âge* (Rome: École Française de Rome, 1985), passim.

61. In the medieval West, on the other hand, bearskins were used neither as trophies set in front of the hearth nor as bedside rugs on the stone floor. It was American images of the nineteenth century that invented this kind of representation and transmitted it, through movies, cartoons, and comic strips, to European iconography, which, retroactively, sometimes projected it into the Middle Ages.

62. Bruno Andreolli, "L'orso nella cultura nobiliare dall'*Historia Augusta* a Chrétien de Troyes," in *Il bosco nel Medioevo,* ed. Bruno Andreolli and Massimo Montanari (Bologna: CLUEB, 1989), 35–54. It seems that it was in the Val d'Aoste that the feudal custom that required the residents of a parish to provide a dead bear for their lord every year lasted the longest, perhaps until the seventeenth century.

63. James W. Hassell, *Middle French Proverbs, Sentences, and Proverbial Phrases* (Toronto: Pontifical Institute of Medieval Studies, 1982).

6. The Coronation of the Lion

1. Modern zoology sometimes designates it as *Leo persicus.*

2. Pliny, *Natural History* VIII, 1–11.

3. "*Eo quod princeps sit omnium bestiarum*"; Isidore of Seville, *Etymologies,* trans. Stephen A. Barney et al. (Cambridge: Cambridge University Press, 2006), XII. ii.3, 251.

4. In most Indian cultures, the king of the beasts is not the lion but the elephant, sometimes the tiger.

5. Salomon Reinach, *Cultes, Mythes, et Religions,* 5 vols. (Paris: Ernest Leroux, 1905–23); Jan de Vries, *La Religion des Celtes* (Paris: Payot, 1963); Paul-Marie Duval, *Les Dieux de la Gaule,* new ed. (Paris: Payot, 1976); Miranda J. Green, *Animals in Celtic Life and Myth* (London: Routledge, 1992).

6. Ambrose, *Hymni latini antiquissimi,* ed. A. Bulst (Heidelberg: Kerle, 1956), 42; Rabanus Maurus, *De rerum naturis* VIII, 1 (P. L. 112, col. 217–218).

7. Jacques Voisenet, *Bestiaire chrétien: L'imagerie animale des auteurs du haut Moyen Âge (Vᵉ–XIᵉ siècle)* (Toulouse: Presses Universitaires du Mirail, 1994), 115–127.

8. Among many studies, see especially Nikolaus Henkel, *Studien zum Physiologus im Mittelalter* (Tübingen: Niemeyer, 1976).

9. *De bestis et aliis rebus* II, 1 (P. L. 177, col. 57); *Bestiarum: Die Texte der Handschrift MS. Ashmole 1511 der Bodleian Library Oxford*, ed. Franz Unterkircher (Graz: Akademische Druck- und Verlagsanstalt, 1986).

10. Thomas de Cantimpré, *Liber de natura rerum*, ed. Helmut Boese (Berlin: W. de Gruyter, 1973), 139–141; Bartholomaeus Anglicus, *De proprietatibus rerum* (Cologne: Johann Koelhoff, 1489), fol. 208 vb f; Vincent of Beauvais, *Speculum naturale* (Douai: Company of Jesus, 1624), XIX, cxvi–cxxiv.

11. On these various properties—unknown to Aristotle and Pliny—see Henkel, *Studien zum Physiologus im Mittelalter*, 164–167.

12. Robert Viel, *Les Origines symboliques du blason* (Paris: Berg International, 1972), 31–91.

13. Michel Pastoureau, "Figures et couleurs péjoratives en héraldique médiévale," in *Communicaciones al XV Congreso internacional de las ciencias genealógica y heráldica*, Madrid, 1982 (Madrid: Ediciones Hidalguia, 1985), 3:293–309.

14. On the origin and appearance of coats of arms, see Erich Kittel, "Wappentheorien," *Archivum heraldicum* 85 (1971), 18–26 and 53–59; Académie internationale d'héraldique, *L'Origine des armoiries: Actes du IIᵉ colloque international d'héraldique (Brixen/Bressanone, 1981)* (Paris: Le Léopard d'Or, 1983); Lutz Fenske, "Adel und Rittertum im Spiegel früher heraldischer Formen," in *Das ritterliche Turnier im Mittelalter*, ed. Josef Fleckenstein (Göttingen: Vandenhoeck und Ruprecht, 1985), 75–160; Michel Pastoureau, "La naissance des armoiries," *Cahiers du Léopard d'Or*, vol. 3, *Le XIIᵉ siècle* (1994): 103–122.

15. On the extension of the use of coats of arms to society as a whole and, more generally, on the relationship between heraldry and society, see Gustav A. Seyler, *Geschichte der Heraldik*, 2nd ed. (Nuremberg: Bauer und Raspe, 1890), 66–322; Rémi Mathieu, *Le système héraldique français* (Paris: J. B. Janin, 1946), 25–38; Donald L. Galbreath and Léon Jéquier, *Manuel du blason* (Lausanne: Spes, 1977), 41–78; Michel Pastoureau, *Traité d'héraldique*, 2nd ed. (Paris: Picard, 1993), 37–65.

16. Michel Pastoureau, *Armorial des chevaliers de la Table Ronde: Étude sur l'imagination héraldique à la fin du Moyen Âge* (Paris: Léopard d'Or, 2006).

17. Viel, *Les Origines symboliques du blason*; Antonio Quacquarelli, *Il leone e il drago nella simbolica dell'eta patristica* (Bari: Istituto di Letteratura Cristiana Antica, 1975).

18. Manfred Zips, "Tristan und die Ebersymbolik," *Beiträge zur Geschichte der*

deutschen Sprache und Literatur 94 (1972): 134–152; Michel Pastoureau, "Les armoiries de Tristan dans la littérature et l'iconographie médiévales," *Gwéchall*
1 (1978): 9–32.

19. See the statistical results presented in Michel Pastoureau, "Le bestiaire
héraldique au Moyen Âge," *Revue française d'héraldique et de sigillographie* 25
(1972): 3–17, and in *Traité d'héraldique*, 136–143.

20. Pastoureau, "Le bestiaire héraldique," 3–17, and *Traité d'héraldique*, 136–143.

21. Often challenged, this widespread fashion of the lion in medieval coats of
arms has never been clearly explained. There were, of course, many lions in
various emblems and insignia in antiquity and the High Middle Ages, but the
eagle and the boar were at least as frequent. Moreover, between the sixth and
eleventh centuries, compared to its status in the Greco-Roman world, the lion
seemed to be in clear retreat in political symbolism and warrior emblematics throughout the West. But the second half of the eleventh century and all
of the twelfth witnessed a massive invasion of lions and knights of the lion,
first as image motifs and then as literary themes. More than an actual influence of the Crusades (whose cultural importance historiography seems to
me to have always exaggerated), I believe in the role played by fabrics and art
objects regularly imported from Spain and the East on which lions were frequently represented (often in preheraldic attitudes). Sculpture, painting, and
early heraldry found in the lion a figure adaptable to a plethora of formal and
symbolic functions. But that is far from a complete explanation.

22. The strictly heraldic origin of the leopard in heraldry was connected to the
evolution of the coats of arms of the Plantagenets in the second half of the
twelfth century. There is not enough space to dwell on it here; it should just
be said that Richard Lionheart was the first to use a coat of arms with three
leopards, which was adopted by all his successors (Henry II may have had
an escutcheon with two leopards). See Hugh Stanford London, *Royal Beasts*
(East Knoyle, Wiltshire: Heraldry Society, 1956), 9–15; Viel, *Les Origines symboliques du blason*, 46–106 (to be read with caution); Adrian Ailes, *The Origins
of the Royal Arms of England: Their Development to 1199* (Reading: Graduate
Centre for Medieval Studies, University of Reading, 1982). See also Edward
Earle Dorling, *Leopards of England and Other Papers on Heraldry* (London: Constable, 1913); Hugh Stanford London, "Lion or Leopard?" *The Coat of Arms* 2
(1953): 291–296; C. R. Humphrey-Smith and M. Heenan, *The Royal Heraldry
of England* (London: Heraldry Today, 1966); John and Rosemary Pinches, *The
Royal Heraldry of England* (London: Heraldry Today, 1974), 50–63; Michel Pastoureau, "Genèse du léopard Plantagenêt," *Bulletin of the Société des Amis de
l'Institut historique allemand* 7 (2002): 14–29.

23. Pastoureau, *Traité d'héraldique,* 143–146.
24. Michel Pastoureau, "Bestiaire du Christ, bestiaire du Diable," in *Couleurs, Images, Symboles* (Paris: Léopard d'Or, 1989), 85–110.
25. Florence McCulloch, *Medieval Latin and French Bestiaries* (Chapel Hill: University of North Carolina Press, 1960), 150–151; Henkel, *Studien zum Physiologus im Mittelalter,* 41–42. Aristotle does not mention the mating of lioness and leopard; it was Pliny who transmitted this legend to Solinius and thence to medieval culture through the inevitable intermediary of Isidore of Seville: *"leopardus ex adulterio leae et pardi nascitur"* ("The leopard is born from the cross-breeding of a lioness and a pard"), *Etymologies* XII.ii.11, 252.
26. In this connection, it is necessary to point to the contrast between the abundance of anthroponyms and toponyms constructed from a root evoking the bear and the rarity of the animal in coats of arms. This represents powerful reluctance on the part of heraldry, similar to that with respect to the fox and the crow, plentiful in onomastics but rare in coats of arms; the same thing was not true for the rooster. See Pastoureau, *Traité de héraldique,* 146–154.
27. London, British Library, MS Harley 5012, fol. 32.
28. Michel Pastoureau, "L'ours en dehors de l'écu," *Actes du XIIIᵉ colloque international d'héraldique (Troyes 2003),* forthcoming.
29. Pastoureau, *Traité d'héraldique,* 253.
30. It seems that the chronicler Helmold von Bosau was the first to give the margrave of Brandenburg the nickname "Bear" in his *Chronica Slavorum,* compiled between 1163 and 1172. Albert died in 1170, so it is possible the name was given to him while he was alive. But the bear was not part of his repertory of emblems. His coat of arms is unknown—he may not even have had one—and his seal depicts, in the field, an eagle, as did that of his father Count Otton of Ballenstaedt, who died in 1123. See Otto von Heinemann, *Albrecht der Bär* (Darmstadt: G. G. Lange, 1864); Hermann Krabbo, *Albrecht der Bär* (Leipzig: Duncker und Humblot, 1906); Lutz Partenheimer, *Albrecht der Bär: Gründer der Mark Brandenburg und des Fürstentums Anhalt* (Cologne: Böhlau, 2001). Curiously, none of these voluminous and detailed monographs dwells on the nickname "Bear."
31. Beginning in the twelfth century, everywhere in Europe, numerous proper names in one way or another evoked the lion: baptismal names constructed from the root *leo-* (Leo, Leonardus, Leonellus, Leopoldus), family names incorporating the word *lion* (Lionnard, Löwenstein, Leonelli), as well as nicknames given to great personages (Henry the Lion, Richard Lionheart), and to literary heroes (Yvain the Knight of the Lion, Robert the Lion, Lion of

Bourges, Lancelot's cousin Lionel). But the most plentiful documentary material in this area comes not from anthroponomy, but from heraldry.

32. Saint Bernard, for example, who, in a celebrated diatribe delivered between 1125 and 1127, raged against "ferocious lions, disgusting monkeys, spotted tigers, hybrid monsters, strange centaurs, fish with the bodies of quadrupeds, animals riding men or other animals." Saint Bernard, *Apologie à Guillaume de Saint-Thierry*, in *S. Bernardi opera*, ed. Jean Leclercq, C. H. Talbot, and Henri Rochais (Rome: Editiones Cisterciences, 1977), 3:127–128.

33. Another distinctive sign may be the position of the head: raised for the lion, lowered for the bear.

34. See the excellent thesis Raphaël Guesuraga, "Le Thème de la dévoration dans la sculpture romane de France et d'Espagne: Étude iconographique, enjeux politiques, aspects eschatologiques" (Paris: EPHE, IVe section, 2001).

35. Marianne Besseyre, "L'Iconographie de l'arche de Noé du IIIe au XVe: Du texte aux images" (Paris: École Nationale des Chartes, 1997).

36. The text of the thirteenth century Vulgate is just as imprecise as that of modern translations: *"Et ex cunctis animantibus universae carnis bina induces in arcam, ut vivant tecum, masculini sexus et femini. De volucribus juxta genus suum de bestiis in genere suum et de bestiis in genere suo et ex omni reptili terrae secundum genuus suum: bina de omnibus ingredientur tecum, ut possint vivere."*

37. More than a quarter-century ago, with the help of some of my students, I began a study of the bestiary of the ark depicted in medieval images: a corpus of about three hundred miniatures found in manuscripts (Bibles, Psalters, missals, breviaries, universal chronicles, and historical compilations), copied and painted in the West between the late seventh century and the early fourteenth. The study was to have been extended to other media for more data, leading to better geographic and historical distribution and better quantitative evaluation. But as it is, the corpus already provides useful information: it shows in particular that the bestiary of the Carolingian ark is not that of the thirteenth century (and even less that of the late Middle Ages) and that a single animal is always present through the centuries and in all images: the lion.

38. In medieval images, it is often difficult to distinguish between sheep, calves, and dogs with no collar. Some animals are endowed with remarkable iconographic attributes and others not. Among birds, for example, while it is easy to recognize the eagle, the swan, the owl, and the magpie, many other species are undifferentiated and unidentifiable. It would be helpful to have studies on these questions concerning the representation of animal species and the attributes (formal, chromatic, syntactic, and so on) given to them.

39. The study of the arrangement of the animals in the ark is also instructive. There are places that are more honorific than others, and the interplay between center and periphery, high and low, left and right (in relation to Noah in particular) plays a role in this distribution. It evolves from one image to the next over the decades and is worth detailed study.

40. See Chapter 2, section "A Royal Animal."

41. Werner Paravicini, "Tiere aus dem Norden," *Deutsche Archiv für die Erforschung des Mittelalters* 59, 2 (2003):559–591.

42. Ibid., 562.

43. A fine example can be found in Ann Payne, *Medieval Beasts* (New York: New Amsterdam Books, 1990), 20.

44. Laurent Hablot, "La Devise, mise en signe du prince, mise en scène du pouvoir: Les devises et l'emblématique des princes en France et en Europe à la fin du Moyen Âge" (University of Poitiers, 2001), 3:593–601.

45. Gustave Loisel, *Histoire des ménageries de l'Antiquité à nos jours* (Paris: Octave Doin et fils, 1912), 1:145–146; Ernst Kantorowicz, *Frederick the Second, 1194–1250*, trans. E. O. Lorimer (New York: F. Ungar, 1957), 185–187.

46. See Chapter 3, section "Bears and Women."

47. As I write these lines, the inventory of occurrences lies in the future. One can use profitably (and carefully) a well-made biblical concordance (English-Hebrew-Greek-Latin), available on the Internet, Blue Letter Bible. http://www.blueletterbible.org.

48. An excellent edition is Yves Lefèvre, *L'"Elucidarium" et les Lucidaires: Contribution par l'histoire d'un texte à l'histoire des croyances religieuses en France au Moyen Âge* (Paris: E. de Boccard, 1954).

49. *Clavis Physicae*, ed. Paolo Lucentini (Rome: Edizioni di Storia e Letteratura, 1974). Unlike the *Elucidarium*, a work of his youth heavily influenced by the teaching of Anselm of Canterbury, *Clavis Physicae* borrows a good deal on the problem of the resurrection of the flesh from the ideas developed in the ninth century by Johannes Scotus Erigena in several of his treatises, notably in the very arduous *De divisione naturae*. See, in *Clavis Physicae*, chapters 271–273, 301–308, 480–481.

50. On Honorius, see Joseph Anton Endres, *Honorius Augustodunensis: Beitrag zur Geschichte des geistigen Lebens im 12. Jahrhundert* (Munich: J. Kösel, 1906); Eva Matthews Sanford, "Honorius, *Presbyter* and *Scholasticus*," *Speculum* 23 (1948): 397–425.

51. On this central problem of medieval Christian theology, see the beautiful book by Caroline W. Bynum, *The Resurrection of the Body in Western Christianity, 200–1336* (New York: Columbia University Press, 1995).

52. Ibid., 59–114.

53. Johannes Scotus Erigena, *De divisione naturae*, ed. I. P. Sheldon-Williams et al. (Dublin: Dublin Institute for Advanced Studies, 1978–83). A convenient summary of the ideas of this difficult writer can be found in Maïeul Cappuyns, *Jean Scot Érigène: Sa vie, son œuvre, sa pensée* (Brussels: Culture et Civilisation, 1969).

54. Bynum, *The Resurrection of the Body in Western Christianity*, 137–155.

55. See Guesuraga, *Le Thème de la dévoration dans la sculpture romane de France et d'Espagne*.

56. *Elucidarium*, liber I, quaestiones 180–183; *L'"Elucidarium" et les Lucidaires*, 394–396. See also liber II, quaestiones 96; ibid., 440 and 103; ibid., 441–442; and liber III, quaestio 45; ibid., 456.

57. Ibid., liber II, quaestio 96.

58. In addition to Bynum, *The Resurrection of the Body in Western Christianity*, see the excellent and very complete article by A. Challet, "Corps glorieux," *Dictionnaire de théologie catholique* (Paris: Letouzey et Ané, 1938), III, cols. 1879–1906.

59. See the discussion of the legend of Saint Colomban in Chapter 4, section "The Bear as Companion to the Saint."

60. See Bynum, *The Resurrection of the Body in Western Christianity*, 143.

7. A Humiliated Animal

1. Gaston Phébus, *Livre de la chasse*, trans. into modern French Robert and André Bossuat (Paris: P. Lebaud, 1986).

2. Jakob Grimm, *Reinhart Fuchs* (Berlin: Reimer, 1834), an edition of the late twelfth-century Alsatian text and its adaptations in various German dialects, with a long, suggestive introduction.

3. The proper name *Reginhard*, common in Germany from the ninth through the twelfth century, but never that of a ruler, means "of strong counsel," "skilled in giving advice." Originally, it did not in any way suggest the fox, unlike proper names like *Fuchs* or *Füchsel*, well attested during the same period.

4. Between the thirteenth and fifteenth centuries *renard* replaced *goupil* in common speech. The latter word did not completely disappear but became a rare and precious term, and then itself became a proper name, as in the title of the book by Louis Pergaud, *De Goupil à Margot* (1913) and in children's books like *Les Aventures de Maître Goupil*.

5. Gaston Paris, *"Le Roman de Renart,"* in *Mélanges de littérature française du Moyen Âge,* vol. 2 (Paris: Champion, 1912), 2:337–423.

6. Léopold Sudre, *Les Sources du Roman de Renart* (Paris: Émile Bouillon, 1892).

7. Lucien Foulet, *Le Roman de Renard* (Paris: H. Champion, 1914).

8. *Ysengrimus,* ed. Ernst Voigt (Halle: Verlag der Buchhandlung des Waisenhauses, 1884); Nivardus, *Ysengrimus,* trans. Jill Mann (Leiden: Brill, 1987).

9. On this language, see the studies by Gunnar Tilander, chiefly *Lexique du Roman de Renart* (Paris: H. Champion, 1971), and *Remarques sur le Roman de Renart* (Göteborg: Wettergren und Kerber, 1925).

10. On this question, see Michel Pastoureau, "L'animal et l'historien du Moyen Âge," in *L'Animal exemplaire au Moyen Âge (V^e–XVe siècles),* ed. Jacques Berlioz and Marie-Anne Polo de Beaulieu (Rennes: Presses Universitaires de Rennes, 1999), 13–26.

11. On the history of the cat, see Laurence Bobis, *Le Chat: Histoire et légendes* (Paris: Fayard, 2000).

12. On Tibert, see Jean Batany, *Scènes et Coulisses du Roman de Renart* (Paris: Société d'édition d'enseignement supérieur, 1989), 133–138.

13. Hans Robert Jauss, *Untersuchungen zur mittelalterlichen Tierdichtung* (Tübingen: M. Niemeyer, 1959), 24–35; Batany, *Scènes et Coulisses du Roman de Renart,* 167–199; Armand Strubel, *La Rose, le Renard et le Graal: La littérature allégorique en France au XIIe siècle* (Geneva: Slatkine, 1989), 229–233.

14. On this point, see Gabriel Bianciotto, "Renart et son cheval," in *Mélanges Félix Lecoy* (Paris: Champion, 1973), 27–42.

15. On fear of the wolf, see Daniel Bernard, *L'Homme et le Loup* (Paris: Berger-Levrault, 1981); Geneviève Carbone, *La Peur du loup* (Paris: Gallimard, 1991), and *Les Loups* (Paris: Larousse, 2003). On the wolf in the medieval West, see Gherardo Ortalli, *Lupi, genti, culture: Uomo e ambiente nel medioevo* (Turin: Einaudi, 1997).

16. Ortalli, *Lupi, genti, culture;* Jean Delumeau, *Sin and Fear: The Emergence of a Western Guilt Culture,* trans. Eric Nicholson (New York: St. Martin's Press, 1989).

17. Note the absence of the elephant from this short list, although it was often represented in church décor and relatively well known to medieval populations.

18. *Reinaert de Vos,* ed. Jan Frans Willems (Ghent: F. en E. Gyselynck, 1836), 84–85. I would like to thank Richard Trachsler for pointing out to me the role of vice-king played by the bear in some Dutch and Scandinavian traditions.

19. Some readings prefer "Rufanus."

20. Philippe Walter, *Canicule* (Paris: SEDES, 1988), passim; Batany, *Scènes et Coulisses du Roman de Renart*, 199, n. 42.

21. On this tempting hypothesis, see Batany, *Scènes et Coulisses du Roman de Renart*, 93–94, who relies on Karl Ferdinand Werner, "Liens de parenté et noms de personne: Un problème historique et méthodologique," in *Famille et Parenté dans l'Occident médiéval*, ed. Georges Duby and Jacques Le Goff (Rome: École française de Rome, 1977), 13–34 (on the name *Bruno* and the issues it raises, 27–31).

22. See Batany, *Scènes et Coulisses du Roman de Renart*, 72–107.

23. The one exception is in the branch *Renart empereur*, where Brun, who is in command of the fourth battle group of the royal army, is called "most valiant of all" ("Brun li ors / qui molt par estoit coraigous"). See *Le Roman de Renart*, ed. Armand Strubel et al. (Paris: Gallimard, Bibliothèque de la Pléiade, 1998), branch XVI, 612, vv. 2043–44.

24. Ibid., branch XXIV, 818, vv. 1790–92.

25. Ibid., branch X, 319; branch XII, 364; branch XIII, 388; branch XV, 543–545.

26. Ibid., branch Ia, 16–20, vv. 520–727.

27. Ibid., 86, vv.3220–25.

28. *La monstrance du cul, Le Roman de Renard*, ed. Strubel et al., branch XXII, 745–749. On tales with the theme of the castration of the bear, see Antti Aarne and Stith Thompson, "The Gelding of the Bear," in *The Types of the Folktale*, 45–46 (Helsinki: Suomalainen Tiedeakatemia, 1973); Paul Delarue and Marie-Louise Ténèze, *Le Conte populaire français* (Paris: Maisonneuve and Larose, 1976), 3:420–421.

29. *Le Roman de Renard*, ed. Strubel et al., branch XII.

30. Ibid., 333–365, vv. 1–1381.

31. On jongleurs who were not authors of literary works, see Edmond Faral, *Les Jongleurs en France au Moyen Âge* (Paris: H. Champion, 1910); Margit Bachfischer, *Musikanten, Gaukler und Vaganten: Spielmannskunst im Mittelalter* (Augsburg: Battenberg, 1998); Wolfgang Hartung, *Die Spielleute im Mittelalter* (Düsseldorf: Artemis und Winkler Verlag, 2003).

32. Konrad von Megenberg, *Das Buch der Natur*, ed. Franz Pfeiffer (Stuttgart: Verlag von Karl Aue, 1861), 161.

33. It was not until the seventeenth century that the squirrel began to have a better image in encyclopedias and zoological literature. But this revaluation was so swift and so strong that in the following century, Buffon, in a passage full of wonder, made it one of the most admirable and engaging animals in all creation. See Michel Pastoureau, *Jésus chez le teinturier: Couleurs et teintures dans l'Occident médiéval* (Paris: Léopard d'Or, 1998), 29–32.

34. The oldest example of the image of a dancing bear seems to be in an English manuscript of around 1070 or 1080: a jongleur in striped costume, armed with a stick, makes a standing bear turn in circles. London, British Library MS Arundel 91, fol. 47 verso.

35. See Chapter 3 at n. 24.

36. Quoted by Léon Gautier, *La Chevalerie* (Paris: H. Welter, 1897), 152–153.

37. Batany, *Scènes et Coulisses du Roman de Renart*, 190–191.

38. An example is the marginal decoration of a large English Bible of the mid-fourteenth century: London, British Library, MS Harley 4189, fol. 114.

39. Tertullian, *Apology*, chapter IX, in *Ante-Nicene Fathers* (Buffalo: Christian Literature Publishing Company, 1885–96), 3:25.

40. Georges Ville, "Les jeux de gladiateurs dans l'Empire chrétien," *Mélanges d'archéologie et d'histoire* 72, 1 (1960): 273–335.

41. It is hard to know what practices were designated by the expression *joca cum ursis*, used by several writers, councils, and priests of the High Middle Ages (Councils of the Churches of Ireland and England in the seventh and eighth centuries, Hincmar in the ninth century, Regino of Prüm around 900, Burchard of Worms around 1020, and so on) to denounce particularly pagan rituals and spectacles.

42. Gautier, *La Chevalerie*, 83; Jean Bichon, *L'Animal dans la littérature française aux XIIᵉ et XIIIᵉ siècles* (Lille: Service de Reproduction des Thèses, Université de Lille III, 1976), 1:402: *Aye d'Avignon:* "et esgardent le gieu des ours et des lions."

43. Maria Giuseppina Muzarelli, "Norme di comportamento alimentare nei libri penitenziali," *Quaderni medievali* 13 (1982): 45–80. On medieval obesity and the sin of *gula*, see Carla Casagrande and Silvana Vecchio, *I sette vizi capitali: Storia dei peccati nel Medioevo* (Turin: Einaudi, 2000), 124–148.

44. Guillaume de Tocco, *L'Histoire de Saint Thomas d'Aquin*, trans. Claire Le Brun-Gouanvic (Paris: Cerf, 2005). See also François-Xavier Putallaz, *Le Dernier Voyage de Thomas d'Aquin* (Paris: Salvator, 1998), passim.

45. For a French-speaking reader, the name "Baloo" given to the bear by Rudyard Kipling in *The Jungle Book* (1894) seems to echo the clumsiness *(balourdise)* traditionally attributed to the animal. Obviously, the actual etymology of the proper name is different: it is derived from the Hindi *bhalu*, sloth bear.

46. Augustine, *De civitate Dei*, ed. Bernhard Dombart and Alfonse Kalb (Leipzig: Teubner, 1928), 1:129.

47. Michel Pastoureau, "Une justice exemplaire: les procès intentés aux animaux (XIIIᵉ–XVIᵉ siècle)," *Cahiers du Léopard d'Or* 9 *(Les Rites de la Justice)* (2000): 173–200.

48. Peter Damian, *De bono religiosi status*, P. L. 145, col. 763–92, esp. chapter XXIV.

49. *Physica seu liber subtilitatum diversarum naturarum creaturarum*, P. L. 197, col. 1117–1352; in English, *Hildegard von Bingen's Physica*, trans. Priscilla Throop (Rochester: Healing Arts Press, 1998).

50. Élisabeth Klein, "Un ours bien léché: Le theme de l'ours chez Hildegarde de Bingen," *Anthropozoologica* 19 (1994): 45–54. See also Laurence Moulinier-Brogi, "L'ordre du monde animal selon Hildegarde de Bingen," in *L'Homme, l'Animal domestiques, et l'Environnement du Moyen Âge au XVIIIᵉ siècle*, ed. Robert Durand (Nantes: Ouest Éditions, 1993), 51–62.

51. Huon de Méry, *Le Tournoi de l'Antéchrist*, trans. Stéphanie Orgeur, 2nd ed. (Orléans: Paradigme, 1995).

52. Max Prinet, "Le langage héraldique dans le *Tournoiement Antéchrist*," *Bibliothèque de l'École des Chartes* 83 (1922): 43–53.

53. de Méry, *Le Tournoi de l'Antéchrist*, 60.

54. *La Vengeance Radiguel*, trans. Sandrine Hériché-Pradeau (Paris: Honoré Champion, 2010).

55. Pierre Michaud-Quantin, *Sommes de casuistique et Manuels de confession au Moyen Âge* (Louvain: Nauwelaerts, 1962); Cyrille Vogel, *Le Pécheur et la Pénitence au Moyen Âge* (Paris: Éditions du Cerf, 1969), 82–107.

56. Morton W. Bloomfield, *The Seven Deadly Sins*, 2nd ed. (Lansing: Michigan State University Press, 1967); Carla Casagrande and Silvana Vecchio, *Histoire des sept péchés capitaux au Moyen Âge*, trans. Pierre-Emmanuel Dauzat (Paris: Aubier, 2003).

57. Mireille Vincent-Cassy, "L'envie au Moyen Âge," *Annales E. S. C.* 35, 2 (1980): 253–271; Aimé Solignac, "Péchés capitaux," in *Dictionnaire de spiritualité ascétique et mystique* 12, 1 (Paris: Beauchesne, 1984), col. 853–862.

58. Even though the book does not go past the thirteenth century, it is still worth reading Adolf Katzenellenbogen, *Allegories of the Vices and Virtues*, trans. Alan J. P. Crick (New York: Norton, 1964). See also Jérôme Baschet, "Les sept péchés capitaux et leurs châtiments dans l'iconographie médiévale," in Casagrande and Vecchio, *Histoire des sept péchés capitaux au Moyen Âge*, 387–400.

59. Richard Newhauser, *The Treatises on Vices and Virtues in Latin and the Vernacular* (Turnhout: Brepols, 1993); Franz-Josef Schweitzer, *Tugend und Laster in illustrierten didaktischen Dichtungen des späten Mittelalters* (Hildesheim: Olms, 1993); Nigel Harris, *Etymachie-Traktat* (Munich: Lengenfelder, 1995). Most treatises on etymachia derive from *Lumen animae*, an allegorical work compiled by Mathias Farinator, an Austrian Franciscan, in the 1330s. The author describes a series of jousts between the vices and virtues that appeared to him in a dream.

60. Jürgen Leibbrand, *Speculum bestialitatis: die Tiergestalten der Fastnacht und des Karnevals im Kontext christlicher Allegorese* (Munich: Tuduv, 1989).

61. Two examples involving the bear are lust and gluttony. Lust usually rides a goat, shows a bear on his shield, and a pig on his banner, and features a rooster or a fox on his crest, while gluttony rides a bear, features a bear on his shield, and a pike on his banner, and wears a vulture as his crest.

62. Bloomfield counts 115 different animals associated with the seven major sins: *The Seven Deadly Sins*, 244–245.

63. Michel Pastoureau, *Une histoire symbolique du Moyen Âge occidental* (Paris: Seuil, 2004), 33–36 and 42–46.

8. Princes' Whims, Ladies' Fantasies

1. On Gaston Phébus, see Pierre Tucoo-Chala, *Gaston Fébus et la Vicomté de Béarn* (Bordeaux: Bière, 1959), and *Gaston Fébus, prince des Pyrénées (1331–1391)*, 2nd ed. (Pau: J. et D. Éditions, 1994); on Jean Froissart's stay at the court of Orthez, see Pierre Tucoo-Chala, "Froissart dans le Midi pyrenéen," in *Froissart Historian*, ed. John J. N. Palmer (Totowa, N.J.: Rowman, 1981), 118–131.

2. Gaston Phébus, *Livre de chasse*, ed. Gunnar Tilander (Karlshamm: Johansson, 1971), book I, ch. 8, and book III, ch. 52.

3. Jean Froissart, *Chronicles*, trans. Geoffrey Brereton (New York: Penguin, 1968), 275–279.

4. Ibid., 278 ("Tu me chaces et si ne te veuil nul dommaige, mais tu mourras de male mort").

5. Michel Zink, "Froissart et la nuit du chasseur," *Poétique* 41 (February 1980): 60–77. On the story of Pierre de Béarn told by Froissart, see also Laurent Harf-Lancner, "La merveille donnée à voir: la chasse fantastique et son illustration dans le livre III des *Chroniques* de Froissart," *Revue des Langues Romanes* 100, 2 (1996): 91–110; Joël H. Grisward, "Froissart et la nuit du loup-garou. La 'fantaisie' de Pierre de Béarn: modèle folklorique ou modèle mythique," in *La Modèle à la Renaissance*, ed. Laurie Balavoine, Jean Lafond, and Pierre Laurens (Paris: Vrin, 1986), 21–34.

6. Froissart, *Chronicles*, 278–279. On the myth of Actaeon in Froissart, see Laurent Harf-Lancner, "La chasse au blanc cerf dans le *Méliador* de Froissart: Froissart et le mythe d'Actéon," in *Mélanges Charles Foulon* (Liège, 1980), 2:143–152.

7. See the fine study by Joël Grisward, "Ider et le tricéphale: D'une aventure arthurienne à un mythe indien," *Annales E. S. C.* 33, 2 (March–April 1978): 279–293.

8. Gaston Phébus is said to have killed his own son (also named Gaston) by stabbing him. Did he do it purposely or accidentally? The opinions of medieval chroniclers and modern historians are divided. But all agree that the Count of Foix suspected his son of trying to poison him. The account of this tragic death can be found in *Chronicles*, 268–274.
9. Froissart explains that Pierre de Béarn can consider one-quarter of his wife's possessions as his. *Chronicles*, 276.
10. *La Chace dou cerf* (*Cynegetica*, vol. 7), ed. and trans. Gunnar Tilander (Stockholm, 1960). I should also mention William Twich, great huntsman of King Edward II of England and author, around 1315 or 1320, of an *Art de vénerie*, published under the title *La Vénerie de Twiti: Le plus ancien traité de chasse écrit en Angleterre* (*Cynegetica*, vol. 2), ed. Tilander (Uppsala, 1956).
11. *Livre de chasse*, 52.
12. In this reversal of the prestige of different hunts between the High and late Middle Ages, it is also necessary to consider the locations of the hunt. The stag was hunted with horse and hounds, like the deer, the fox, and the hare, and thus required more space than the boar hunt. As time passed, the legal system governing the *foresta*, that is, hunting rights controlled by the power of dynasts or reserved for the suzerain alone were extended in the kingdoms and great fiefs of the West. As a result, starting in the twelfth century, in many countries and regions only kings and princes possessed enough territory to hunt stags. Not owning huge forests where they could hunt stags lawfully or by feudal right, petty lords had to be satisfied with the boar hunt. They thereby helped to diminish the prestige of that hunt, while the stag hunt, once less valued, became fully royal. The prestige of the stag hunt was especially enhanced because it was conducted on horseback, while the boar hunt began the same way but ended on foot. Starting in the twelfth and thirteenth centuries, few kings and princes would agree to hunt on foot, like valets and villeins.
13. Among many sources, see Thomas Szabo, "Die Kritik der Jagd, von der Antike zum Mittelalter," in *Jagd und höfische Kultur im Mittelalter*, ed. Werner Rösener (Göttingen: Vandenhoeck und Ruprecht, 1997), 167–230.
14. *Acta sanctorum*, sept. VI, 106–142.
15. On the legend of Saint Hubert, see *Historia sancti Huberti principis Aquitani*, ed. Jean Robert (Luxembourg: Hubertus Reulandt, 1621); *Le Culte de saint Hubert au pays de Liège*, ed. Alain Dierkens and Jean-Marie Duvosquel (Liège: Crédit Communal, 1991); *Die Verehrung des heiligen Hubertus im Rheinland: Ein Handbuch*, ed. Klaus Freckmann and Norbert Kühn (Cologne: RVDL Verlag, 1994).

16. As in Greco-Roman Antiquity, the stag in the Middle Ages remained a powerful symbol of lustfulness and sexuality. It was not uncommon for priests to prohibit their flock from "playing the stag" *(cervum facere)*, that is, during carnival or ritual festivals, disguising oneself as a stag and displaying a huge male sexual organ with which one simulated intercourse. In the late Middle Ages, "playing the stag" was a virile, transgressive disguise almost as frequent as "playing the bear."

17. *"Et iis [cervis] est cum serpente pugna. Vestigant cavernas, nariumque spiritu extrahunt renitentes. Ideo singulare abigendis serpentibus odor adusto cervino cornu."* (The stag, too, fights with the serpent: it traces out the serpent's hole, and draws it forth by the breath of its nostrils, and hence it is that the smell of burnt stags' horn has the remarkable power of driving away serpents.) Pliny, *Natural History*, VIII, 50.

18. *"Quaemodum desirat cervus ad fonts aquarum ita desirat anima mea ad te, Deus."* (As a hind longs for the running streams, so do I long for thee, O God.) Psalms 42, 1. See the long commentary on this psalm and the symbolism of the stag by Saint Augustine, *Ennaratio in Psalmos, P. L.* 36, col. 466. This verse explains why the stag is so often pictured on baptismal fonts and in depictions of baptism: it evokes the Christian soul drinking from the source of life.

19. Marcelle Thiébaux, *The Stag of Love: The Chase in Medieval Literature* (Ithaca: Cornell University Press, 1974).

20. Colette Beaune, "Costume et pouvoir en France à la fin du Moyen Âge: les devises royales vers 1400," *Revue des Sciences Humaines* 183 (1981): 125–146.

21. Hervé Pinoteau and Jean de Vaulchier, *La Symbolique royale française, V^e–XVIIIe siècle* (LaRoche-Rigault: PSR, 2003), 467–470.

22. On the "chamber of the stag" in the papal palace in Avignon and its political and ideological meaning, see Fausto Piola Caselli, *La costruzione del palazzo dei papi di Avignone (1316–1367)* (Milan: A. Giuffre, 1981); Étienne Anheim, "La Forge de Babylone: Culture et Pouvoir pontifical: L'exemple de Clément VI (1342–1352)" (Ph.D. diss., École Pratique des Hautes Études, IVe section, Paris, 2004).

23. Étienne Baluze, *Vitae paparum avenionensium*, ed. G. Mollat (Paris: Letouzey and Ane, 1920), 2:300–310; Eugène Déprez, "Les funérailles de Clément VI et d'Innocent VI d'après les comptes de la cour pontificale," *Mélanges d'histoire et d'archéologie publiés par l'École Française de Rome* 20 (1900): 235–250; Frédérique-Anne Costantini, *l'Abbatiale Saint-Robert de La Chaise-Dieu: Un chantier de la papauté d'Avignon* (Paris: Honoré Champion, 2003), 21–24.

24. Perhaps also because of a word play between *cervus* and *servus servorum*, an expression frequently designating Christ and sometimes the pope.

25. Françoise Autrand, *Jean de Berry: L'art et le pouvoir* (Paris: Fayard, 2000), 182–192.

26. On Jean de Berry, in addition to Autrand, see Françoise Lehoux, *Jean de France, duc de Berri: Sa vie, son action politique,* 4 vols. (Paris: Picard, 1966–68).

27. Around the same time, three bear heads appeared for the first time on the armorial bearings of the powerful lords of Berwick, who held large fiefs in northeast England on the Scottish border but also frequented the court of Edward III. See D. H. B. Chesshyre and Thomas Woodcock, eds., *Dictionary of British Arms: Medieval Ordinary* (London: Society of Antiquaries of London, 1992), 1:289–290 and 295.

28. On "speaking" armorial bearings, see Jorge Preto, *Des armoiries qui parlent: Propos sur la science du blason et la linguistique* (Lisbon: Instituto Português de Heraldica, 1986); Michel Pastoureau, "Du nom à l'armoirie: Héraldique et anthroponymie médiévale," in *Genèse médievale de l'anthroponymie moderne,* vol. 4, *Discours sur le nom: Normes, usages, imaginaire (VIᵉ–XVIᵉ siècle),* ed. Patrice Beck (Tours: Université de Tours, 1997), 83–105, and "Les armoiries parlantes," *Revue de la Bibliothèque nationale de France* 18 (2004): 36–45. A study of speaking armorial bearings in German-speaking countries would be welcome. For France, forthcoming is the excellent thesis B. Jalouneix, "Les Armoiries parlantes" (Ph.D. diss., École Pratique des Hautes Études, IVᵉ section, Paris, 2002).

29. Louis Douët d'Arcq, *Archives de l'Empire: Collection de Sceaux* (Paris: Plon, 1863), vol. 1, no. 423.

30. Ibid., no. 421.

31. *Le livre du cuer d'amours espris,* ed. Susan Wharton (Paris: Union Générale d'éditions, 1980). The author has Jean de Berry say: "Je fus ardemment d'estre amoureulx espris / d'une dame anglaise suivante du dieu d'amours" (I was smitten with burning love / for an English lady devoted to the god of love).

32. On this marriage, which provoked a great deal of talk among contemporaries (the duke was 49, Jeanne 12), see Autrand, *Jean de Berry,* 261–274.

33. The mysterious "Swan Knight" was said to be the grandfather of Godfrey of Bouillon. Many princes and lords claimed to be his descendants and, with their emblems and conduct, participated in the mythology surrounding the figure. See Anthony R. Wagner, "The Swan Badge and the Swan Knight," *Archaeologia* 97 (1959): 127–138; Claude Lecouteux, *Mélusine et le Chevalier au Cygne* (Paris: Imago, 1982); Laurent Hablot, "Emblématique et mythologie médiévale: Le cygne, une devise princière," *Histoire de l'art* 49 (December 2001): 51–64.

34. It is noteworthy that in the notebook of drawings of the architect from

Picardy, Villard de Honnecourt, from 1230–1235, a bear and a swan of large size are drawn on the same page. Paris: BNF, ms. fr. 19093, fol. 4.

35. Jules Guiffrey, *Inventaires de Jean de Berry (1401–1416)*, 2 vols. (Paris: E. Leroux, 1894–96), with a particularly thorough index.

36. Ibid., 2:251.

37. *Petites Heures*, Paris: BNF, ms. latin 18014, fol. 288 v°.

38. *Très Riches Heures du duc de Berry*, Chantilly: musée Condé, ms. 84, fol. 22 v°, 51 v°, 52.

39. Guiffrey, *Inventaires*.

40. Ibid., vol. 1, cxxiii. On polar bears in princely menageries and collections in the Middle Ages, see Werner Paravicini, "Tiere aus dem Norden," *Deutsches Archiv für Erforschung des Mittelalters* 59, 2 (2003): 559–591, especially 578–579.

41. Jules Guiffrey, "La menagerie du duc Jean de Berry (1370–1403)," *Mémoires de la Société des Antiquaires du Centre* 23 (1899): 63–73.

42. See the accounts preserved in the National Archives in Paris, KK 254, fol. 115 v°, 138 v°, and so on.

43. Émile Le Goazre, comte de Toulgoët-Tréanna, "Les comptes de l'hôtel du duc de Berry (1370–1413)," *Mémoires de la Société des Antiquaires du Centre* 18 (1889–1890): 65–175, passim.

44. Louis Douët d'Arcq, *Comptes de l'hôtel des rois de France aux XIVᵉ et XVᵉ siècles* (Paris: Renouard, 1865), 312.

45. On Jean de Cambrai, see Alain Erlande-Brandenburg, "Jean de Cambrai, sculpteur de Jean de France, duc de Berry," *Fondation Eugène Piot: Monuments et mémoires* 63 (1980): 143–186.

46. Françoise Lehoux, "Mort et funérailles de Jean de Berri," *Bibliothèque de l'École des Chartes* 114 (1956): 76–96.

47. On the Sainte-Chapelle of Bourges, see Béatrice de Chancel-Bardelot and Clémence Raynaud, eds., *Une fondation disparue de Jean de France, duc de Berry: La Sainte-Chapelle de Bourges* (Bourges: Somogy, 2004).

48. Accounting records show that Amédée VIII had a she-bear that, like those of his father-in-law Jean de Berry, accompanied him in his travels. An entry on April 17, 1399, mentions: "delivered to Mermet Marchand, to cover expenses for going from Morge to Chambéry to take my lord's she-bear, 8 sous in coin." Turin: Archives de la Chambre des comptes de Savoie, Comptes du Trésorier general, vol. 44, fol. 264. I thank my friend Anne Ritz for bringing this document to my attention.

49. On the king's madness, see Françoise Autrand, *Charles VI: La folie du roi* (Paris: Fayard, 1986); Bernard Guenée, *La Folie de Charles VI, roi Bien-Aimé* (Paris: Perrin, 2004).

50. Froissart provides a detailed and moving account in the *Chronicles*. See also Pierre Gascar, *Charles VI: Le Bal des Ardents* (Paris: Gallimard, 1977).

51. Aimé Champollion-Figeac, *Louis et Charles ducs d'Orléans: Leur influence sur les arts, la littérature et l'esprit de leur siècle*, 3 vols. (Paris: Comptoir des Imprimeurs Réunis, 1844); Émile Collas, *Valentine de Milan, duchesse d'Orléans* (Paris: Plon, 1911).

52. On Louis d'Orléans, see Bernard Guenée, *Un meurtre, une société: L'assassinat du duc d'Orléans 23 novembre 1407* (Paris: Gallimard, 1992).

53. On the theme of the wild man and the vogue for him in the late Middle Ages, see Richard Bernheimer, *Wild Men in the Middle Ages: A Study in Art, Sentiment, and Demonology* (Cambridge: Harvard University Press, 1952); Timothy Husband, *The Wild Man: Medieval Myth and Symbolism* (New York: Metropolitan Museum of Art, 1980); Claude Gaignebet and Jean-Dominique Lajoux, *Art Profane et Religion populaire au Moyen Âge* (Paris: PUF, 1985), 79–136.

54. Froissart, *Chroniques*, ed. Kervyn de Lettenhove, vol. 13, 112–113; quoted by Autrand, *Jean de Berry*, 262.

55. There is no complete edition of the French text. An edition is forthcoming from Danielle Régnier-Bohler. For now, see Arthur Dickson, *Valentine and Orson: A Study in Late Medieval Romance* (New York: Columbia University Press, 1929); Danielle Bohler, "Jumeaux par contrat," *Le Genre humain* 16–17 (Winter 1987–88), 173–187.

56. The theme of twins is not infrequent in late chansons de geste *(Maugis d'Aigremont, Lion de Bourges)* and is generally connected to dynastic questions: which of the two should inherit, become king, duke, or count? On this problem, the jurist Philippe de Beaumanoir, in his *Coutumes du Beauvaisis* (completed in 1283), answers "the one who is the elder." It is up to the mother to say which child came out of the womb first—Beaumanoir even explains that if the mother no longer remembers, the midwives must be questioned. See Bohler, "Jumeaux par contrat."

57. Gaignebet and Lajoux, *Art profane et religion populaire au Moyen Âge*, 115–119.

58. For a long time in Middle French, the term for designating the offspring of the bear, *ourson*, was in competition with *oursin;* and it was the resemblance between the stiff hair of the young bear and the sea animal's spikes that led to it being given the name oursin in the sixteenth century. See Albert Dauzat, "l'étymologie d'Oursin," *Revue de linguistique romane* 18 (1954): 192–200.

59. And perhaps to hide the last remnants of the Roman Lupercalia, which took place around February 15. On Valentin and his feast day, see P. Müller-Dieffenbach, *Der heilige Valentin, erster Bischof von Passau und Rhätien* (Mainz, 1889).

9. From Mountain to Museum

1. On witchcraft in the late Middle Ages and the early modern period, among many sources (of varying quality), see particularly Norman Cohn, *Europe's Inner Demons: The Demonization of Christians in Medieval Christendom,* rev. ed. (Chicago: University of Chicago Press, 2000); Richard Kieckhefer, *European Witch Trials: Their Foundations in Popular and Learned Culture, 1300–1500* (Berkeley: University of California Press, 1976); Andreas Blauert, ed., *Ketzer, Zauberer, Hexen: Die Anfänge der europäischen Hexenverfolgungen* (Frankfurt: Suhrkamp, 1990); Nathalie Nabert, ed., *Le Mal et le Diable: Leurs figure à la fin du Moyen Âge* (Paris: Beauchesne, 1996).

2. See the excellent study by Georg Modestin, *Le Diable chez l'évêque: Chasse aux sorciers dans le diocèse de Lausanne (vers 1460)* (Lausanne: Université de Lausanne, 1999), especially 99–111 and 276–317.

3. Ibid., 99–107.

4. On the Sabbath in the fifteenth century, see Martine Osterero et al., eds., *L'Imaginaire du Sabbat: Édition critique des textes les plus anciens (c. 1430–c. 1440)* (Lausanne: Université de Lausanne, 1999).

5. In the BNF in Paris, under call number 8-LN27-5223.

6. See Charles Joisten, *Récits et Contes populaires de Savoie* (Paris: Gallimard, 1980).

7. For example, Jean Roche, *Sauvages et velus: Enquêtes sur des êtres que nous ne voulons pas voir* (Chambéry: Exergue, 2000).

8. The most recent edition is in Mérimée, *Théâtre de Clara Gazul; Romans et Nouvelles,* ed. Jean Mallion and Pierre Salomon (Paris: Gallimard, Bibliothèque de la Pléiade, 1978), 1049–90; in English: Mérimée, *Carmen and Other Stories,* trans. Nicholas Jotcham (New York: Oxford University Press, 2008), 291–332.

9. On *Lokis,* see Raymond Schnittlein, *Lokis: La dernière nouvelle de Prosper Mérimée* (Baden-Baden: Art et Science, 1949); Daniel Leuwers, "Une lecture de *Lokis,*" *Europe* 557 (Sept. 1975): 70–76.

10. On Mérimée's style, see Jean Decottignies, "*Lokis:* Fantastique et dissimulation," *Revue d'histoire littéraire de la France* 71 (1971): 18–29.

11. See Chapter 3, section "Sons of Bears."

12. Jean-Claude Margolin, "Sur quelques figures de l'ours à la Renaissance," in *Le Monde animal au temps de la Renaissance,* ed. Marie-Thérèse Jones-Davies (Paris: Touzot, 1990), 219–242.

13. Ibid., 231–235.

14. See Chapter 8 regarding Jean de Berry, in the section "A New System of Emblems."

15. *Œuvres complètes du roi René*, ed. T. de Quatrebarbes (Angers: Cosnier et Lachèse, 1846), 3:117–118.

16. Paris: BNF, ms. fr. 5658, fol. 83. See Jean Céard and Jean-Claude Margolin, *Rébus de la Renaissance: Des images qui parlent* (Paris: Maisonneuve et Larose, 1986), 2:235.

17. On the image of the bear in sixteenth century emblem books, see Margolin, "Sur quelques figures de l'ours à la Renaissance."

18. Erasmus, *On Education for Children / De pueris instituendis*, in *The Erasmus Reader*, ed. Erika Rummel (Toronto: University of Toronto Press, 1990), 72. The image of the she-bear licking her cub to give it a harmonious body appears several times in Erasmus and was adopted by various emblem books.

19. Julius Wilhelm Zincgref, *Emblematum ethico-politica*, ed. Dieter Mertens and Theodor Verweyen (Tübingen: Niemeyer, 1993).

20. Not hothouses and vegetable gardens, but the "labyrinths of greenery," like the one in the park of Versailles, whose decisive role in the development of the fables is now known. The image of the poet as natural scientist, however, seems indelible; it is part of the legend of "old man La Fontaine" and concerns primarily his alleged observations of dogs, cats, donkeys, rats, mice, and . . . ants—according to legend, his careful study of ants made him late for a meal. See Alain-Marie Bassy, "Les fables de La Fontaine et le labyrinthe de Versailles," *Revue française d'histoire du livre* 12 (1976): 1–63.

21. Which is very far from the ambiguous notion of "natural" as articulated in the fine book by Patrick Dandrey, *La Fabrique des Fables: Essai sur la Poétique de La Fontaine* (Paris: Klincksieck, 1992), 155–166.

22. Some older works are disconcerting, such as Damas-Hinard's *La Fontaine et Buffon* (Paris: Perrotin, 1861); they present La Fontaine as the first real French natural scientist. More recently, an approach like that of H. G. Hall, "On Some of the Birds in La Fontaine's Fables," *Papers on French Seventeenth Century Literature* 22 (1985): 15–27, which compares the descriptions of some birds by La Fontaine and current zoological knowledge of avifauna, seem to me anachronistic and questionable.

23. This fable, published in 1678 in the second collection, is the tenth fable of Book VIII. See the edition by Alain-Marie Bassy (Paris: Garnier-Flammarion, 1995), 240–242. For a translation, see *The Complete Fables of Jean de La Fontaine*, trans. Norman R. Shapiro (Urbana: University of Illinois Press, 2007), 200–201.

24. See, for example, Lutz Röhrich, *Lexikon des sprichwörtlichen Redensarten*, 5th ed. (Freiburg: Herder, 1994), 1:146.

25. Laurenz Burgener, *Helvetia sancta* (Einsiedeln: Benziger, 1860), 1:272–274; Josef Anton Amman, *Der heilige Gerold* (Höchst: Schneider, 1950), 26–27.

26. Johannes Agricola, *Sybenhundert und fünfftzig teütscher Sprichwörter,* 2nd ed. (Haguenau: Braubach, 1534).

27. The proverb seems to be very old, but I have not been able to find its Latin form. More common in English in the seventeenth century was "Don't count your chickens before they hatch."

28. On the traditional hostility between bears and wolves, see Sophie Bobbé, *L'Ours et le Loup: Essai d'anthropologie symbolique* (Paris: Éditions de la Maison des sciences de l'homme, 2002), 61–76.

29. Since the early fourteenth century, the coat of arms of Bern has been emblazoned *de gueules à la bande d'or chargée d'un ours de sable* (red with a golden band charged with a black bear). The bear is sometimes *armé et langué de gueules* (armed, with a red tongue).

30. On the foundation of the city of Bern and the legends surrounding it, see, among many sources, Friedrich Volmar, *Das Bärenbuch* (Bern: Haupt, 1940), 208–231; Hans Schadek and Karl Schmid, eds., *Die Zähringer: Anstoss und Wirkung* (Sigmaringen: Thorbecke, 1991), 245–250.

31. Notably the famous chronicles of Diebold Schilling, preserved in several illuminated manuscripts showing images of the city's foundation. The best preserved manuscript, known as the *Spiezer Bilderchronik* (1485), is in the Burgerbibliothek of Bern, Ms. Hist. Helv. I, 16. Among several facsimiles and collections of images taken from these chronicles, see Hans Haeberli et al., eds., *Die Schweiz im Mittelalter in Diebold Schillings Spiezer Bilderchronik* (Lucerne: Faksimilie Verlag, 1991).

32. This famous object is now in the Bern Historical Museum. It is the subject of many studies, the most recent of which is Annemarie Kaufmann-Heinimann, *Dea Artio, die Bärengöttin von Muri* (Bern: Bernisches Historisches Museum, 2002). See Chapter 1 at n. 56.

33. Gustave Loisel, *Histoire des ménageries de l'Antiquité à nos jours* (Paris: O. Doin et fils, 1912), 1:242–243.

34. On the history of the Bern bear pit, see Volmar, *Die Bärenbuch,* 247–329.

35. On the Berlin coat of arms, see Ottfried Neubecker, "Der Bär von Berlin," *Jahrbuch des Vereins für die Geschichte Berlins* 1–3 (1951–53): 4–16, and 4 (1954): 37–50.

36. The traditional French emblazonment of the arms of Madrid is *d'argent à l'arbousier de sinople, terrassé du meme, fruité de gueules et accosté d'un ours rampant de sable; à la bordure d'azur à sept étoiles d'or* (silver with a green arbutus,

on a green hill, with red fruit and accosted with a sable bear rampant; with an azure border strewn with seven gold stars).

37. For example, the great André Du Chesne and Jules Chifflet in the seventeenth century, who viewed the Visigoth kings as the ancestors of the counts of Toulouse and attributed to them a banner featuring a bear.

38. But this sound hypothesis is contradicted by several fifteenth and sixteenth century documents that view the heraldic animal standing next to the fruit tree not as a bear but as a she-bear. On Madrid's coat of arms, see the recent excellent presentation Pierre Canavaggio, *Madrid-Accueil* 50 (1999): 17–22.

39. Conrad Gesner, *Historia animalium. Liber I: De quadrupedibus viviparis* (Zurich: Froschauer, 1551), fol. CLXXII.

40. Gesner's *Historia animalium* is in fact a huge dictionary of natural and cultural history. The animals are classified in alphabetical order according to their Latin names, and the very copious chapter devoted to each one is divided into eight sections: lexicon, habitat, appearance and anatomy, behavior, usefulness for humans, food and cooking, medicine, and *varia* (proverbs, expressions, etymologies, fables, coats of arms, legends, beliefs, and the like).

41. Gesner's huge botanical treatise, *Opera botanica,* where the space given to mountain flora is considerable, is unfortunately still only in manuscript.

42. Giuseppe Olmi, *Ulisse Aldrovandi: Scienza e natura nel secondo Cinquecento* (Trento: Università di Trento, 1976).

43. Ulisse Aldrovandi, *De quadrupedibus digitatis viviparis et de quadrupedibus digitatis oviparis libri duo. Bartholomaeus Ambrosinus collegit* (Bologna: Bernia, 1637).

44. Jan Jonston, *Historia naturalis,* 4 vols. (Frankfurt: Merian, 1650).

45. *Description anatomique d'un caméléon, d'un castor, d'un dromadaire, d'un ours et d'une gazelle* (Paris: F. Léonard, 1669), with beautiful copper engravings.

46. Werner Paravicini, "Tiere aus dem Norden," *Deutsches Archiv für de Erforschung des Mittelalters* 59, 2 (2003): 559–591, especially 578–579. See also Else Ebel, "Der Fernhandel der Wikingerzeit bis in das 12. Jahrhundert in Nordeuropa nach altnordischen Quellen," in *Untersuchungen zu Handel und Verkehr der vor- und frühgeschichtlichen Zeit in Mittel- und Nordeuropa,* ed. Klaus Düwel et al. (Göttingen: Vandenhoeck und Ruprecht, 1987), 4:266–312.

47. Olaus Magnus, *Historia de gentibus septentrionalibus* (Rome, 1555), XVIII, xxIIII, 621.

48. Buffon, *Histoire naturelle* (Paris: Imprimerie royale, 1769), vol. 8, 18.

49. Ibid., 39–74.

50. Ibid., 38.

51. Extended and completed in 1871 by *The Descent of Man,* where Darwin clearly describes how humans descended from monkeys.

52. Marcel Couturier, *L'Ours brun* (Grenoble: L. Couturier, 1954).
53. I am thinking in particular of the long passages on the hunt, the wounded bear, the stuffing of the animal and trophies. Ibid., 585–705.
54. Ibid., plates 63, 71, 77.
55. See the various figures offered by Claude Dendaletche, ed., *L'Ours brun: Pyrénées, Abruzzes, monts Cantabriques, Alpes du Trentin* (Pau: Claude Dendaletche, 1986); James M. Peek et al., "Grizzly Bear Conservation and Management: A Review," *Wildlife Society Bulletin* 15, 2 (Summer 1987): 160–169; O. J. Sorenson, "The Brown Bear in Europe in the Mid 1980s," *Aquilo Series Zoologica* 27 (1990): 3–16; Jean-Michel Parde and Jean-Jacques Camarra, *L'Ours (Ursus arctos, Linnaeus, 1758)* (Nantes: Société française pour l'étude et la protection des mammifères, 1992), 3–6; Paul Ward and Suzanne Kynaston, *Bears of the World* (Boston: Blandford, 1995).
56. Bernard Prêtre, *Les Derniers Ours de Savoie et du Dauphiné, de Genève à Barcelonette: Essai sur la triste fin des ours alpins* (Grenoble: Belledonne, 1996).
57. Couturier, *L'Ours brun*, 163–164; Prêtre, *Les Derniers Ours de Savoie*, 79–83 and 177–178.
58. Couturier, *L'Ours brun*, 164–166; Prêtre, *Les Derniers Ours de Savoie*, 182–183.
59. A good presentation of these problems can be found in Farid Benhammou et al., *Vivre avec l'ours* (Saint-Claude-de-Diray: Éditions Hesse, 2005).
60. Notably the prohibition on selling its skin (Europe, Canada); its gallbladder (Asia), supposedly having many therapeutic qualities; and its paws, still used as amulets on three continents. See Claude Dendaletche, *La Cause de l'ours* (Paris: Sang de la Terre, 1993).
61. In France, I might mention the Musée de l'Ours in Etsaut, in the Aspe valley (Pyrénées-Atlantiques), and the one in Entremont-le-Vieux (Savoie).
62. B. Scheube, *Das Bärencultus und die Bärenfeste de Aïnos* (Yokohama, 1880); John Batchelor, *The Ainu and Their Folklore* (London: Religious Tract Society, 1901), 474–500.
63. On everything concerning the symbolism of the various parts of the bear, particularly the prestige attached to the paws, see Rémi Mathieu, "La Patte de l'ours," *L'Homme* 24, 1 (1984): 5–42.
64. See especially two collections of articles: a special issue of *Études mongoles et sibériennes* 11 (1980), *L'Ours, l'autre de l'homme*; E. V. Ivanter and D. I. Bibikov, eds., *Medvedi-Bears* (Moscow, 1993), with a very large bibliography. Both supplement the pioneering study by A. Irving Hallowell, "Bear Ceremonialism in the Northern Hemisphere," *American Anthropologist* 28 (1926): 1–175.
65. Among many sources, see especially Uno Harva, *Die religiösen Vorstellungen der altaischen Völker*, trans. Erich Kunze (Helsinki: Suomalainen Tiedeakate-

mia, 1938); and Éveline Lot-Falck, *Les Rites de chasse chez les peuples sibériens* (Paris: Gallimard, 1953).

66. See, for example, the contemptuous and troubled remarks by Jean-Baptiste Barhthelemy de Lesseps, *Travels in Kamchatka during the Years 1787 and 1788,* 2 vols. (London: J. Johnston, 1790). See especially, for Siberia as a whole, the travel accounts published in the huge *Recueil de voiages au Nord, contenant divers mémoires très utiles au commerce et à la navigation,* 8 vols. (Amsterdam: Jean Frédéric Bernard, 1727).

67. I should mention here the pioneering work by Knud Rasmussen, *Across Arctic America: Narrative of the Fifth Thule Expedition* (1921–24; Fairbanks: University of Alaska Press, 1999). See also the recent book by Vladimir Randa, *L'Ours polaire et les Inuits* (Paris: SELAF, 1986).

68. See the remarks by G. Hasselbrink, "La chanson d'ours des Lapons: Essai d'interprétation d'un manuscrit du xviiie siècle concernant la chasse et le culte de l'ours," *Orbis: Bulletin international de documentation linguistique* 13 (1964): 420–480.

69. Among the Lapps, as among most Finno-Ugric peoples, ursine rituals are accompanied by a large number of chants and poems. An exemplary repertory has been compiled by Lauri Honko, Senni Timonen, and Michael Branch, *The Great Bear: A Thematic Anthology of Oral Poetry in the Finno-Ugrian Language* (1993; New York: Oxford University Press, 1994).

70. On all of this, see the fundamental study by Carl-Martin Edsman, *Jägaren och makterna: Samiska och finska björnceremonier* [Hunter and Powers: Sami and Finnish Bear Ceremonies] (Uppsala: Dialekt-och Folkminnesarkivet, 1994). A helpful and lengthy summary in French is: "La fête de l'ours chez les Lapons: Sources anciennes et recherches récentes sur certains rites de chasse aux confins septentrionaux de la Scandinavie," *Proxima Thulé: Revue d'études nordiques* 2 (1996): 11–49 (adapted and translated from the Swedish by François-Xavier Dillmann). On very similar hunting rituals, see also Hans-Joachim Paproth, *Studien über das Bärenzeremoniell: Bärenjagdriten und Bärenfeste bei den tungusischen Völkern* (Munich: Renner, 1976).

71. Michel Praneuf, *L'Ours et les Hommes dans les traditions européennes* (Paris: Imago, 1989), 63–70 and 128–133.

72. On these bear festivals in the Pyrenees and neighboring provinces, there is a large and often disappointing bibliography. Among the most helpful studies, for a historian, are Daniel Fabre and Charles Camberoque, *La Fête en Languedoc: Regards sur le Carnaval aujourd'hui* (Toulouse: Privat, 1977); Fabre, "Réflexions sur l'anthropologie de l'ours dans les Pyrénées," *Cahiers de l'université de Pau*

et des pays de l'Adour (June 1977): 57–67; Sophie Bobbé, "Analyse de la fête de l'ours contemporain en Catalogne française," in *Homme, Animal, Société: Actes du colloque de Toulouse, 1987*, ed. Alain Couret and Frédéric Ogé (Toulouse: Presses de l'Institut d'Études Politiques, 1989), 401–417; Gérard Caussimont, "Le mythe de l'ours dans les Pyrénées occidentales," in *Homme, Animal, Société*, ed. Couret and Ogé, 367–380. See also studies of Candlemas and Carnival, notably Raffaele Corso, *L'orso della Candelora* (Helsinki: Suomalainen Tiedeakatemia, 1955); Claude Gaignebet, *Le Carnaval* (Paris: Payot, 1974); Julio Caro Baroja, *Le Carnaval*, trans. Sylvie Sésé-Léger (1965; Paris: Gallimard, 1979).

73. The oldest documented bear festival in Catalonia goes back to 1444. See Bobbé, "Analyse de la fête de l'ours contemporain en Catalogne française," 402.

74. Arnold Lebeuf, "Des évêques et des ourses: Étude de quelques chapiteaux du cloître de Saint-Lizier-en-Couserans," *Ethnologia polona* 3 (1987): 257–280.

75. Marianne Mesnil, "Quatre contes sur l'ours," *Semiotica* 20, 1–2 (1977): 49–79; Michel Bornaud, *Contes et Légendes de l'ours* (Saint-Claude-de-Diray: Éditions Hesse, 1996). Compare to Pertev N. Boratav, "Les histoires d'ours en Anatolie," *Folklore Fellows' Communications* 152 (1955).

76. Daniel Fabre, *Jean de l'Ours: Analyse formelle et thématiques d'un conte populaire* (Carcassonne: Éditions de la Revue *Folklore*, 1973).

77. See Carl-Martin Edsman, "The Story of the Bear Wife in Nordic Tradition," *Ethnos* 21 (1956): 36–56.

78. Concerning the typology and thematics of bear tales, in addition to the works cited in note 75, see especially Hans-Joachim Paproth, "Bär, Bären," in *Enzyklopädie des Märchens*, ed. Kurt Ranke (Berlin: Walter de Gruyter, 1977), vol. 1, col. 1194–1203.

79. G. Berg, "Zahme Bären, Tanzbären, Bärenführer," *Der zoologische Garten (Berlin)*, n.F., 35, 1–2 (1968): 37–53.

80. See, for example, the collection of Raymond Vinot, *Mémoire en images: Des ours et des hommes* (Saint-Cyr-sur-Loire: A. Sutton, 2005), 9–70.

81. T. P. Vukanovitch, "Gypsy Bear-leaders in the Balkan Peninsula," *Journal of the Gypsy Lore Society*, 3rd ser., 38 (1959): 43–54; Françoise Cozannet, *Mythes et Coutumes religieuses des Tsiganes* (Paris: Payot, 1973); Praneuf, *L'Ours et les hommes dans les traditions européennes*, 70–78.

82. François-Régis Gastou, *Sur les traces des montreurs d'ours des Pyrénées et d'ailleurs* (Toulouse: Loubatières, 1987); Praneuf, *L'Ours et les hommes dans les traditions européennes*, 66–70.

83. Lyon, Musée de l'Imprimerie.
84. Pierre Robert Lévy, *Les Animaux du cirque* (Paris: Syros/Alternatives, 1992), 57–65.
85. Eric Baratay and Elisabeth Hardouin-Fugier, *Zoo: A History of Zoological Gardens in the West,* trans. Oliver Welsh (London: Reaktion, 2002).

Epilogue

1. On medieval toys, see Pierre Riché and Danièle Alexandre-Bidon, *L'Enfance au Moyen Âge* (Paris: Seuil, 1994); Annemarieke Willemsen, *Kinder delijt: Middeleeuws speelgoed in de Nederlanden* (Nijmegen: Nijmegen University Press, 1998).
2. Claudia Rabel has pointed out that the cartoonist had a name that predestined him to draw a bear.
3. On Morris Michton and the invention of the teddy bear, see Constance Ellen King, *The Century of the Teddy Bear* (Woodbridge: Antique Collectors' Club, 1997); Pat Rush, *The Teddy Bear Story* (London: Museum Quilts, 1998); Brian Gibbs, *Teddy Bear Century* (Newton Abbott: David and Charles, 2002).
4. Günther Pfeiffer, *100 Jahre Steiff Teddybären* (Königswinter: Heel, 2001), and *125 Jahre Steiff Firmengeschichte* (Königswinter: Heel, 2005).
5. When Margarete Steiff died in the sinking of the *Titanic* in 1912, her company marketed a bear wearing a black armband. It had great success in Germany and Great Britain.
6. On the history of the stuffed bear, see Peter Bull, *The Teddy Bear Book* (Winscombe: Nisbet, 1983); Gérard Picot, *L'Ours dans tous ses états* (Paris: Chêne, 1988); Pauline Cockrill, *The Teddy Bear Encyclopedia* (London: DK, 1993); Peter Ford, *Teddybären für Liebhaber und Sammler* (Cologne: Delphin-Verlag, 1993).
7. Matty Chiva, ed., *L'Enfant et la Peluche: Le dialogue par la douceur* (Nanterre, 1984), passim. See also Donald O. Hebb, *Psychophysiologie du comportement* (Paris: PUF, 1958), 123ff.; P.-H. Plantain, "Les relations de l'enfant et de l'ours en peluche," in *L'Homme et l'Animal: Premier colloque d'ethnozoologie,* ed. Raymond Pujol (Paris: Institut International d'Ethnoscience, 1975), 352–355; Hubert Montagner, *L'Attachement: Les débuts de la tendresse* (Paris: Odile Jacob, 1988).
8. Chiva, ed., *L'Enfant et la Peluche,* 12–64.
9. *Daily Telegraph,* August 1, 2006, 8.

Sources and Bibliography

Principal Written Sources

Listed here are only the principal written sources on which this study is based. Other textual sources, greater in number but referred to only occasionally, are cited in the notes. The same is true of archeological, iconographic, archive, and ethnological sources that have been used in the preparation of various passages and chapters.

Ancient Texts

Aelian. *On the Characteristics of Animals.* 3 vols. Ed. and trans. A. F. Scholfield. Cambridge, Mass.: Harvard University Press, 1958–59.

Ambrose. *Hexameron. Patrologia Latina (P. L.),* vol. XIV.

Ammianus Marcellinus. *Histoires.* Ed. Guy Sabbagh et al. Paris: Belles Lettres, 1968–99.

Apollodorus. *The Library of Greek Mythology.* Trans. Robin Hard. Oxford: Oxford University Press, 2008.

Aristotle. *History of Animals.* In *Complete Works,* ed. Jonathan Barnes. Princeton: Princeton University Press, 1984.

Augustine. *Sermones.* Turnhout, 1954.

Oppien. *De la chasse.* Ed. Pierre Boudreaux. Paris: Champion, 1908.

Ovid. *Fasti.* Trans. Betty Rose Nagle. Bloomington: Indiana University Press, 1995.

———. *Metamorphoses.* Trans. David R. Slavitt. Baltimore: Johns Hopkins University Press, 1994.

Pausanius. *Graecae descriptio.* 3 vols. Ed. F. Spiro. Leipzig, 1903.

Pliny the Elder. *The Natural History of Pliny.* 6 vols. Trans. John Bostock and H. T. Riley. London: Bohn, 1855–57.

Solinius. *Collectanea rerum memorabilium.* Ed. Theodor Mommsen. Berlin, 1895.

Tertullian, *Apology. Ante-Nicene Fathers,* vol. 3. Buffalo: Christian Literature Publishing Company, 1885–96.

Xenophon. *L'Art de la chasse.* Ed. Édouard Delebecque. Paris: Les Belles Lettres, 1970.

Medieval Texts

Adelard of Bath. *De cura accipitrum*. Ed. A. E. H. Swaen. Amsterdam, 1937.

Albertus Magnus. *De animalibus libri XXVI*. 2 vols. Ed. Hermann Stadler. Münster: Aschendorff, 1916–20.

Alexander Neckam. *De naturis rerum*. Ed. Thomas Wright. London: Longman, 1863.

Bartholomaeus Anglicus. *De proprietatibus rerum*. Frankfurt, 1601.

Bede, The Venerable. *De natura rerum*. Ed. Charles W. Jones. *Corpus christianorum, Series latina*, vol. 123A, 173–234. Turnhout, 1975.

Bestiari medievali. Ed. Luigina Morini. Turin: Einaudi, 1996.

Bestiarum (Bodleian Library, MS Ashmole 1511). Ed. Franz Unterkircher. In *Die Texte der Handschrift MS Ashmole 1511 der Bodleian Library Oxford. Lateinisch-Deutsch*. Graz: Adeva, 1986.

Brunetto Latini. *Li livres dou Tresor*. Ed. Francis J. Carmody. Berkeley: University of California Press, 1948.

Capitularia regum Francorum. 7 vols. Ed. Alfred Boretius and Victor Krause. Hanover: Hahn, 1883–1897.

Chace dou cerf, La. Ed. Gunnar Tilander. Stockholm: Almkvist and Wiksell, 1960.

Chanson de Roland, La. 2nd ed. Ed. G. Moignet. Paris: Bordas, 1969.

Ferrières, Henri de. *Les Livres du roy Modus et de la royne Ratio*. 2 vols. Ed. Gunnar Tilander. Paris: Société des Anciens Textes Français, 1932.

Frederick II. *De arte venandi cum avibus*. Ed. Carl Arnold Willemsen. Leipzig: In aedibus Insulae, 1942.

Froissart, Jean. *Chronicles*. Trans. Geoffrey Brereton. New York: Penguin, 1968.

Gace de la Buigne. *Le Roman des deduis*. Ed. Åke Blomqvist. Karlshamm: E. G. Johansson, 1971.

Gaston Phébus, *Livre de la chasse*. Trans. Robert and André Bossuat. Paris: P. Lebaud, 1986.

Gervaise. *Bestiaire*. Ed. Paul Meyer. In *Histoire littéraire de la France*, vol. 34, 379–381. Paris: Imprimerie nationale, 1915.

Guillaume le Clerc. *Le Bestiaire divin*. Ed. C. Hippeau. Caen: A. Hardel, 1852.

Hardouin de Fontaine-Guérin. *Le Trésor de vénerie*. Ed. Henri Victor Michelant. Metz: Rousseau-Pallez, 1856.

Honorius. *De imagine mundi*. P. L. 172, col. 115–188.

Huon de Méry. *Le Tournoi de l'Antéchrist*. 2nd ed. Trans. Stéphanie Orgeur. Orléans: Paradigme, 1995.

Isidore of Seville. *Etymologies*. Trans. Stephen A. Barney et al. Cambridge: Cambridge University Press, 2006.

Konrad von Megenberg. *Das Buch der Natur.* Ed. Franz Pfeiffer. Stuttgart: Verlag von Karl Aue, 1861.

Legum nationum germanicarum. 5 vols. Ed. Karl August Eckhardt. Hannover, 1962.

Liber monstrorum. Ed. Moriz Haupt. In *Opuscula*, vol. 2, 218–252. Leipzig, 1876.

Matthew Paris. *Chronica Majora.* Ed. Henry R. Luard. London: Longman, 1874.

Peter Damian. *De bono religiosi status, P. L.* 145, col. 763–792.

Peter the Venerable. *De miraculis.* Ed. Denis Bouthillier. Turnhout: Brepols, 1988.

Philippe de Thaon. *Bestiaire.* Ed. Emmanuel Walberg. Paris: Welter, 1900.

Pierre de Beauvais. *Bestiaire.* Ed. C. Cahier and A. Martin. In *Mélanges d'archéologie, d'histoire et de literature*, vol. 2 (1851), 85–100, 106–232; vol. 3 (1853), 203–288; vol. 4 (1856), 55–87.

Pseudo-Hugh of Saint-Victor. *De bestiis et aliis rebus, P. L.* 177, col. 15–164.

Rabanus Maurus. *De universo, P. L.* III, col. 9–614.

Raoul de Houdenc (?). *La Vengeance Radiguel.* Trans. Sandrine Hériché-Pradeau. Paris: Honoré Champion, 2010.

Reinhart Fuchs. Ed. Jacob Grimm. Berlin: Reimer, 1834.

Richard de Fournival. *Bestiaire d'Amours.* Ed. Cesare Segre. Milan and Naples: Ricciardi, 1957.

Roman de Renart, Le. Ed. Armand Strubel et al. Paris: Gallimard, Bibliothèque de la Pléiade, 1998.

Saxo Grammaticus. *History of the Danes.* Trans. Peter Fisher. Cambridge: D. S. Brewer, 1996.

Thomas of Cantimpré. *Liber de natura rerum.* Ed. H. Boese. Berlin: W. De Gruyter, 1973.

Twiti, *La Vénerie de Twiti.* Ed. Gunnar Tilander. Uppsala, 1956.

Vincent of Beauvais. *Speculum naturale.* Douai: Company of Jesus, 1624.

William of Auvergne. *De universo creaturarum.* In *Opera omnia*, ed. Blaise Leferon. Orléans: Praland, 1674.

Yder, The Romance of. Ed. and trans. Alison Adams. Cambridge: D. S. Brewer, 1983.

Modern Texts

Aldrovandi, Ulisse. *De quadrupedibus solipedibus: Volumen integrum Ioannes Cornelius Uterverius collegit et recensuit.* Bologna, 1606.

———. *De quadrupedibus digitatis viviparis et de quadrupedibus digitatis oviparis libri duo. Bartholomaeus Ambrosinus collegit.* Bologna: Bernia, 1637.

Buffon, G. L. Leclerc, comte de. *Histoire naturelle, générale et particulière.* 12 vols. Paris: Imprimerie royale, 1749–64.

Discours effroyable d'une fille enlevée, violée et tenue près de trois ans par un ours dans sa caverne. Chambéry, 1620.

Gesner, Conrad. *Historia animalium. Liber I: De quadrupedibus viviparis.* Zurich: Froschauer, 1551.

———. *Icones animalium quadrupedum viviparorum et oviparorum, quae in Historiae animalium Conradi Gesneri libro I et II describuntur.* Zurich, 1553.

Jonston, Jan. *Historia naturalis.* 4 vols. Frankfurt: Merian, 1650.

La Fontaine, Jean de. *The Complete Fables of Jean de La Fontaine.* Trans. Norman R. Shapiro. Urbana: University of Illinois Press, 2007.

Mérimée, Prosper. *Lokis.* In *Théâtre de Clara Gazul; Romans et Nouvelles,* ed. Jean Mallion and Pierre Salomon, 1049–90. Paris: Gallimard, Bibliothèque de la Pléiade, 1978.

Olaus Magnus. *Historia de gentibus septentrionalibus.* Rome, 1555.

Scheffer, Johannes. *Histoire de la Laponie, sa description, ses mœurs, la manière de vivre de ses habitants.* Trans. Augustin Lubin. Paris: Veuve Olivier de Varennes, 1678.

Topsell, Edward. *The History of Four-Footed Beasts and Serpents.* 2 vols. London: E. Cotes, 1658.

Bibliography

This bibliography is divided into two parts. The first, addressing the brown bear and its cultural history in Europe, is not exhaustive but aims to be relatively complete. The second, containing works by historians on the animal world, is obviously merely a selection relevant to this book. Its purpose is only to enlighten readers who might wish to supplement their knowledge or broaden their thinking about any particular point. I have deliberately emphasized studies of the Middle Ages, because it is the subject of the largest part of this book.

The Bear and Its History

1. Generalities

Bobbé, Sophie, and Jean-Pierre Raffin. *Abécédaire de l'ours.* Paris: Flammarion, 1997.

Camarra, Jean-Jacques, and Jean-Paul Ribal. *L'Ours brun.* Paris: Hatier, 1989.

Catani, V., and F. Osti, eds. *L'orso nelle Alpi.* Tranto, 1986.

Caussimont, Gérard. *L'Ours brun à la frontière franco-espagnole: Pyrénées occidentales.* Pau, 1991.

Couturier, Marcel. *L'Ours brun.* Grenoble: L. Couturier, 1954.

Dendaletche, Claude, ed. *L'Ours brun: Pyrénées, Abruzzes, monts Cantabriques, Alpes du Trentin.* Pau: Claude Dendaletche, 1986.

Kazeeff, W. N. *L'Ours brun, roi de la forêt.* Paris: Dellamain et Boutelleau, 1934.

Krementz, Anton. *Der Bär.* Berlin: Wilhelm Baensch Verlagshandlung, 1888.

Lajoux, Jean Dominique. *L'Homme et l'Ours.* Grenoble: Glénat, 1996.

LeFranc, Maurice N., ed. *Grizzly Bear Compendium.* Missoula, Mont.: Interagency Grizzly Bear Committee, 1987.

Miquel, André. *Les Arabes et l'Ours.* Heidelberg: Winter, 1994.

Ours, L', l'autre de l'homme. Special issue of *Études mongoles et sibériennes* 11 (1980).

Paproth, Hans-Joachim. "Bär, Bären." In *Enzyklopädie des Märchens,* ed. Kurt Ranke, vol. 1, col. 1194–1207. Berlin: Walter de Gruyter, 1977.

Parde, Jean-Michel, and Jean-Jacques Camarra. *L'Ours (Ursus arctos, Linnaeus, 1758).* Nantes: Société française pour l'étude et la protection des mammifères, 1992.

Petter, Francis. *D'ours en ours.* Exhibition catalogue. Paris: Muséum national d'histoire naturelle, 1988.

Peuckert, Hermann. "Bär." In *Handwörterbuch des deutschen Aberglaubens,* ed. Eduard Hoffman-Krayer and Hans Bächtold-Stäubli, vol. 1, col. 881–905. Leipzig: Walter de Gruyter, 1927.

Praneuf, Michel. *L'Ours et les Hommes dans les traditions européennes.* Paris: Imago, 1989.

Stauch, L. "Bär." In *Reallexikon zur deutschen Kunstgeschichte,* vol. 1, col. 1442–49. Stuttgart: J. B. Metzler, 1937.

Volmar, Friedrich. *Das Bärenbuch.* Bern: Haupt, 1940.

Ward, Paul, and Suzanne Kynaston. *Bears of the World.* Boston: Blandford, 1995.

2. Prehistory

Bächler, Emil. "Das Drachenloch ob Vättis im Taminatale und seine Bedeutung als paläontologische Fundstätte und prähistorische Niederlassung aus der Altsteinzeit im Schweizerlande." *Jahrbuch der St. Gallischen Naturwissenschaftlichen Gesellschaft* 57 (1920–21): 1–144.

Begouën, H., N. Casteret, and L. Capitan. "La caverne de Montespan." *Revue anthropologique* 33 (1923): 333–350.

Bernadac, Christian. *Le Premier Dieu.* Neuilly-sur-Seine: M. Lafon, 2000.

Bonifay, E. "L'homme de Neandertal et l'ours *(Ursus arctos)* dans la grotte du Regourdou." In *L'Ours et l'Homme,* ed. Tillet and Binford, 247–254.

Bosch, Robert. *L'Ours-Totem d'Arles-sur-Tech.* Arles-sur-Tech: R. Bosch, 1987.

Clottes, Jean, ed. *Chauvet Cave.* Trans. Paul G. Bahn. Salt Lake City: University of Utah Press, 2003.

Clottes, Jean, and Jean Courtin. *The Cave beneath the Sea*. Trans. Marilyn Garner. New York: Abrams, 1996.

Fosse, Philippe, Philippe Morel, and Jean-Philippe Brugal. "Taphonomie et éthologie des ursidés pléistocènes." In *L'Ours et l'Homme*, ed. Tillet and Binford, 79–101.

Garcia, Michel Alain, and Philippe Morel. "Restes et reliefs: Présence de l'homme et de l'ours dans la grotte de Montespan. *Anthropozoologica* 21 (1995): 73–78.

Koby, F. E. "Les paléolithiques ont-ils chassé l'ours des cavernes?" *Bulletin de la Société jurassienne d'émulation de Porrentruy* (1953): 30–40.

Morel, Philippe, and Michel-Alain Garcia. "La chasse à l'ours dans l'art paléolithique." In *L'Ours et l'Homme*, ed. Tillet and Binford, 219–228.

Narr, K. J. "Bärenzeremoniell und Schamanismus in der älteren Steinzeit." *Saeculum* 10 (1959): 233–272.

Pacher, Martina. "Polémique autour d'un culte de l'ours des caverns." In *L'Ours et l'Homme*, ed. Tillet and Binford, 235–246.

Philippe, Michel. "L'ours des cavernes de La Balme-à-Collomb." *Mémoires et Documents de la Société savoisienne d'histoire et d'archéologie* 95 (1993): 85–94.

Tillet, Thierry, and Lewis Roberts Binford, eds. *L'Ours et L'Homme*. Liège: Éditions de l'Université de Liège, 2002.

3. Antiquity

Bachofen, Johann Jakob. *Der Bär in den Religionen des Altertums*. Basel: Meyri, 1863.

Bertandy, F. "Remarques sur le commerce des bêtes sauvages entre l'Afrique du Nord et l'Italie." *Mélanges de l'École française de Rome: Antiquité* 99, 1 (1987): 211–241.

Bevan, Elinor. "The Goddess Artemis and the Dedication of Bears in Sanctuaries." *Annual of the British School of Athens* 82 (1987): 17–21.

Bomgardner, David. "The Trade in Wild Beasts for Roman Spectacles: A Green Perspective." *Anthropozoologica* 16 (1992): 161–166.

Goguey, Dominique. "Les Romains et les animaux: regards sur les grands fauves." In *Homme et Animal dans l'Antiquité romaine*, 51–66. Tours, 1995.

Kaufmann-Heinimann, Annemarie. *Dea Artio, die Bärengöttin von Muri*. Bern: Bernisches Historisches Museum, 2002.

Lévêque, Pierre. "Sur quelques cultes d'Arcadie: Princesse-ours, hommes-loups, et dieux-chevaux." *L'Information historique* 23 (1961): 93–108.

Sanchez-Ruipérez, M. "La 'Dea Artio' celta y la 'Artemis' griega: Un aspecto religioso de la afinidad celto-iliria." *Zephyrus* 2 (1951): 89–95.

Ville, Georges. "Les jeux de gladiateurs dans l'Empire chrétien." *Mélanges de l'École française de Rome* 72 (1960): 273–335.

Zenker, S. "Bär." In *Reallexikon für Antike und Christentum*, vol. 1, col. 1143–47. Stuttgart: Hiersemann, 1950.

4. Middle Ages

Andreolli, Bruno. "L'orso nella cultura nobiliare dall' *Historia Augusta* a Chrétien de Troyes." In *Il bosco nel Medioevo*, ed. Bruno Andreolli and Massimo Montanari, 35–54. Bologna: CLUEB, 1988.

Beck, Corinne. "Approche des territoires historiques de l'ours en Europe au Moyen Âge." In *Actes du XVIIᵉ colloque de la Société française pour l'étude et la protection des mammifères*, 94–100. Grenoble, 1993.

———. "Approches du traitement de l'animal chez les encyclopédistes du XIIIᵉ siècle: L'exemple de l'ours." In *L'enciclopedismo medievale*, ed. Michelangelo Picone, 163–178. Ravenna: Longo, 1994.

Bernheimer, Richard. *Wild Men in the Middle Ages: A Study in Art, Sentiment, and Demonology.* Cambridge, Mass.: Harvard University Press, 1952.

Boglioni, Pierre. "Les animaux dans l'hagiographie monastique." In *L'Animal exemplaire au Moyen Âge (Vᵉ–XVᵉ siècles)*, ed. Jacques Berlioz, Marie Anne Polo de Beaulieu, and Pascal Collomb, 51–80. Rennes: Presses Universitaires de Rennes, 1999.

Gaignebet, Claude, and Jean-Dominique Lajoux. *Art Profane et Religion populaire au Moyen Âge.* Paris: PUF, 1985.

Grisward, Joël H. "Ider et le tricéphale: D'une aventure arthurienne à un mythe indien." *Annales E. S. C.* 33, 2 (March–April 1978): 279–293.

Hauck, K. "Tiergarten im Pfalzbereich." In *Deutsche Königspfalzen*, vol. 1, 30–74. Göttingen: Vandenhoeck und Ruprecht, 1963.

Hiestand, Rudolf. "König Balduin und sein Tanzbär." *Archiv für Kulturgeschichte* 70 (1988): 343–360.

Höfler, Otto. "Berserker." In *Reallexikon der germanischen Altertumskunde*, vol. 2, 298–304. Berlin: Walter de Gruyter, 1976.

Husband, Timothy. *The Wild Man: Medieval Myth and Symbolism.* New York: Metropolitan Museum of Art, 1980.

Klein, Élisabeth. "Un ours bien léché: Le theme de l'ours chez Hildegarde de Bingen." *Anthropozoologica* 19 (1994): 45–54.

Kuhn, Hans. "Kämpen und Berserker." *Frühmittelalterliche Studien* 2 (1968): 222–234.

Montanari, Massimo. "Uomini e orsi nelle fonti agiografiche dell'alto medio-evo." In *Symbole des Alltags, Alltag der Symbole: Festschrift für Harry Kühnel,* ed. Gertrud Blaschitz, 571–587. Graz: Akademicsche Druck- und Verlagsanstalt, 1992.

Pastoureau, Michel. "Nouveaux regards sur le monde animal à la fin du Moyen Âge." *Micrologus* 4 (1996): 41–54.

———. "Pourquoi tant de lions dans l'Occident medieval." *Micrologus* 8 (2000): 11–30.

———. "Quel est le roi des animaux?" In *Le Monde animal et ses representations au Moyen Âge,* 133–142. Toulouse: Université de Toulouse-Le Mirail, 1985.

Walter, Philippe. "Der Bär und der Erzbischof: Masken und Mummentanz bei Hinkmar von Reims und Adalbero von Laon." In *Feste und Feiern im Mittelalter,* ed. Detlef Altenburg et al., 377–388. Sigmaringen: J. Thorbecke Verlag, 1991.

Wehrhahn, L., and L. Stauche. "Bär." In *Lexikon der christlichen Ikonographie,* vol. 1, col. 242–244. Freiburg im Breisgau: Herder, 1974.

Zink, Michel. "Froissart et la nuit du chasseur." *Poétique* 41 (February 1980): 60–77.

5. Modern Times and Ethnology

Begouen, J. "L'ours Martin en Ariège." *Bulletin de la Société ariégeoise des sciences, lettres et arts* (1966): 111–175.

Benhammou, Farid, et al. *Vivre avec l'ours.* Saint-Claude-de-Diray: Éditions Hesse, 2005.

Bobbé, Sophie. "Analyse de la fête de l'ours contemporain en Catalogne française." In *Homme, Animal, Société: Actes du colloque de Toulouse, 1987,* ed. Alain Couret and Frédéric Ogé, 401–417. Toulouse: Presses de l'Institut d'Études Politiques, 1989.

———. *L'Ours et le Loup: Essai d'anthropologie symbolique.* Paris: Éditions de la Maison des sciences de l'homme, 2002.

Boratav, Pertev N. "Les histoires d'ours en Anatolie." *Folklore Fellows' Communications* 152 (1955).

Bouchet, Jean-Claude. *Histoire de la chasse dans les Pyrénées (XVIᵉ–XXᵉ siècles).* Pau: Éditions Marrimpouye, 1990.

Bull, Peter. *The Teddy Bear Book.* Winscombe: Nisbet, 1983.

Chichlo, Boris. "L'ours-chaman." *Études mongoles et sibériennes* 11 (1980): 35–112.

Chiva, Matty, ed. *L'Enfant et la Peluche: Le dialogue par la douceur.* Nanterre, 1984.

Cockrill, Pauline. *The Teddy Bear Encyclopedia.* London: DK, 1993.

Corso, Rafaelle. *L'orso della Candelora.* Helsinki: Suomalainen Tiedeakatemia, 1955.

Dendaletche, Claude. *La Cause de l'ours.* Paris: Sang de la Terre, 1993.

Edsman, Carl-Martin. "La fête de l'ours chez les Lapons: Sources anciennes et recherches récentes sur certains rites de chasse aux confins septentrionaux de la Scandinavie." *Proxima Thulé* 2 (1996): 11–49.

———. "The Story of the Bear Wife in Nordic Tradition." *Ethnos* 21 (1956): 36–56.

Fabre, Daniel. *Jean de l'Ours: Analyse formelle et thématiques d'un conte populaire.* Carcassonne: Éditions de la Revue *Folklore,* 1973.

———. "Réflexions sur l'anthropologie de l'ours dans les Pyrénées." *Cahiers de l'université de Pau et des pays de l'Adour* (June 1977): 57–67.

Gastou, François-Régis. *Sur les traces des montreurs d'ours des Pyrénées et d'ailleurs.* Toulouse: Loubatières, 1987.

Hallowell, A. Irving. "Bear Ceremonialism in the Northern Hemisphere." *American Anthropologist* 28, 1 (1926): 1–175.

Hasselbrink, G. "La chanson d'ours des Lapons: Essai d'interprétation d'un manuscript du XVIIIe siècle concernant la chasse et le culte de l'ours." *Orbis: Bulletin international de documentation linguistique* 13 (1964): 420–480.

Honko, Lauri, Senni Timonen, and Michael Branch. *The Great Bear: A Thematic Anthology of Oral Poetry in the Finno-Ugrian Language.* New York: Oxford University Press, 1994.

Ivanter, E. V., and D. I. Bibikov, eds. *Medvedi-Bears.* Moscow, 1993.

Krohn, Kaarle. "Bär, Wolf und Fuchs." *Journal de la société finno-ougrienne* 6 (1988): 1–132.

Maleyran, Dominique. "Les Ours: Situation actuelle en France à l'état sauvage et en captivité." Ph.D. diss., Maisons-Alfort, 1995.

Margolin, Jean-Claude. "Sur quelques figures de l'ours à la Renaissance." In *Le Monde animal au temps de la Renaissance,* ed. Marie-Thérèse Jones-Davies, 219–242. Paris: Touzot, 1990.

Marliave, Olivier de. *Histoire de l'ours dans les Pyrénées.* Toulouse: Éditions Sud-Ouest, 2000.

Mathieu, Rémi. "La Patte de l'ours." *L'Homme* 24, 1 (1984): 5–42.

Merlet, François. *L'Ours, seigneur des Pyrénées.* Pau: Marrimpouey Jeune, 1971.

Paproth, Hans-Joachim. *Studien über das Bärenzeremoniell: Bärenjagdriten und Bärenfeste bei den tungusischen Völkern.* Munich: Renner, 1976.

Prêtre, Bernard. *Les Derniers Ours de Savoie et du Dauphiné, de Genève à Barcelonette: Essai sur la triste fin des ours alpins.* Grenoble: Belledonne, 1996.

Randa, Vladimir. *L'Ours polaire et les Inuits.* Paris: SELAF, 1986.

Scheube, B. *Das Bärencultus und die Bärenfeste de Aïnos.* Yokohama, 1880.

Zetterberg, Hilmer. *Björnen i Sägen och verkligheten.* Uppsala: Lindblad 1951.

Animals in History

1. Generalities

Abel, Othenio. *Animali del passato.* Rome: Mondadori, 1940.

Animal, L': Son histoire et ses droits. Special issue of *Le Débat* 27 (November 1983).

Animaux, Les: Domestication et representation. Special issue of *L'Homme* 38, 4 (October–December 1988).

Bodson, Liliane, ed. *L'Animal dans l'alimentation humaine: Les critères de choix.* Paris: Laboratoire d'Anatomie comparée, Muséum d'Histoire naturelle, 1988.

———. *L'Animal de compagnie: Ses roles et leurs motivations au regard de l'histoire.* Liège: Université de Liège, 1997.

———. *Les Animaux exotiques dans les relations internationales: espèces, fonctions, significations.* Liège: Université de Liège, 1998.

———. *L'Histoire de la connaissance du comportement animal.* Liège: Université de Liège, 1993.

———. *Le Statut éthique de l'animal.* Liège: Université de Liège, 1996.

———, and Roland Libois, eds. *Contributions à l'histoire de la domestication.* Liège: Université de Liège, 1992.

Bousquet, Georges-Henri. "Des animaux et de leur traitement selon le judaïsme, le christianisme et l'islam." *Studia islamica* 9 (1958): 31–48.

Chaix, Louis, and Patrice Méniel. *Archézoologie: Les animaux et l'archéologie.* Paris: Éditions Errance, 2001.

Cohen, Esther. "Law, Folklore and Animal Lore." *Past and Present* 110 (1986): 6–37.

Couret, Alain, and Frédéric Ogé, eds. *Homme, Animal, Société: Actes du colloque de Toulouse, 1987.* 3 vols. Toulouse: Presses de l'Institut d'Études Politiques, 1989.

Crosby, Alfred W. *Ecological Imperialism: The Biological Expansion of Europe, 900–1900.* Cambridge: Cambridge University Press, 1996.

De Gubernatis, Angelo. *Zoological Mythology, or The Legends of Animals.* 2 vols. London: Trübner, 1872.

Dekkers, Midas. *Dearest Pet: On Bestiality.* Trans. Paul Vincent. London: Verso, 1994.

Delort, Robert. *Les animaux ont une histoire.* Paris: Seuil, 1984.

Desse, Jean, and Frédérique Audoin-Rouzeau, eds. *Exploitation des animaux sauvages à travers le temps.* Juan-les-Pins: Éditions APDCA, 1993.

Digard, Jean-Pierre. *L'Homme et les Animaux domestiques: Anthropologie d'une passion.* Paris: Fayard, 1990.

Durand, Robert, ed. *L'Homme, l'Animal domestiques, et l'Environnement du Moyen Âge au XVIIIᵉ siècle.* Nantes: Ouest Éditions, 1993.

Evans, E. P. *The Criminal Persecution and Capital Punishment of Animals.* London: Heinemann, 1906.

Fontenay, Élisabeth de. *Le Silence des bêtes: La philosophie à l'épreuve de l'animalité.* Paris: Fayard, 1998.

Franklin, Alfred. *La Vie privé d'autrefois: Les Animaux.* 2 vols. Paris: Plon, 1897–99.

Grieser, Dietmar. *Im Tiergarten der Weltliteratur.* Munich: Langen Müller, 1991.

Hennebert, Eugène. *Histoire militaire des animaux.* Paris: Hatier, 1893.

Klingender, Francis D. *Animals in Art and Thought to the End of the Middle Ages.* Cambridge: M.I.T. Press, 1971.

Laffont, Robert, and Jacques Boudet. *L'Homme et l'Animal: Cent mille ans de vie commune.* Paris: Éditions du Pont Royal, 1962.

Lenoble, Robert. *Esquisse d'une histoire de l'idée de nature.* Paris: Albin Michel, 1969.

Lévi-Strauss, Claude. *The Savage Mind.* Trans. John and Doreen Weightman. Chicago: University of Chicago Press, 1966.

Lewinsohn, Richard. *Animals, Men and Myths.* New York: Harper, 1954.

Loevenbruck, Pierre. *Les Animaux sauvages dans l'histoire.* Paris: Payot, 1955.

Loisel, Gustave. *Histoire des ménageries de l'Antiquité à nos jours.* Paris: Doin, 1912.

Marino Ferro, Xosé-Ramon. *Symboles animales.* Paris: DDB, 1996.

Pastoureau, Michel. *Les Animaux célèbres.* Paris: Bonneton, 2001.

Petit, Georges, and Jean Théodoridès. *Histoire de la zoologie des origines à Linné.* Paris: Hermann, 1962.

Planhol, Xavier de. *Le Paysage animal: L'homme et la grande faune: Une zoographie historique.* Paris: Fayard, 2004.

Porter, Joshua R., and William M. S. Russell, eds. *Animals in Folklore.* Ipswich: D. S. Brewer, 1978.

Rozan, Charles. *Les Animaux dans les proverbs.* 2 vols. Paris: Ducrocq, 1902.

Sälzle, Karl. *Tier und Mensch: Das Tier in der Geistesgeschichte der Menschheit.* Munich: Bayerischer Landwirtschaftsverlag, 1965.

Vartier, Jean. *Les Procès d'animaux du Moyen Âge à nos jours.* Paris: Hachette, 1970.

Zeuner, Frederick E. *A History of Domesticated Animals.* New York: Harper and Row, 1963.

2. Prehistory

Bandi, H. G., et al., eds. *La Contribution de la zoologie et de l'éthologie à l'interprétation de l'art des peuples chasseurs préhistoriques.* Fribourg: Éditions Universitaires, 1984.

Cauvin, Jacques. *The Birth of the Gods and the Origins of Agriculture.* Trans. Trevor Watkins. Cambridge: Cambridge University Press, 2000.

Clottes, Jean, and David Lewis-Williams. *The Shamans of Prehistory.* Trans. Sophie Hawkes. New York: Abrams, 1998.

Gautier, Achilles. *La Domestication.* Paris: Éditions Errance, 1990.

Leroi-Gourhan, André. *Les Chasseurs de la Préhistoire.* 2nd ed. Paris: PUF, 1992.

———. "Chronologie zoologique." In *La Préhistoire,* ed. Leroi-Gourhan, 298–306. Paris: PUF, 1966.

———. *Les Religions de la Préhistoire,* 5th ed. Paris: PUF, 2001.

Vialou, Denis. *L'Art des grottes.* Paris: Scala, 1998.

3. Antiquity

Amat, Jacqueline. *Les Animaux familiers dans la Rome antique.* Paris: Belles Lettres, 2002.

Anderson, John K. *Hunting in the Ancient World.* Berkeley: University of California Press, 1985.

Arbogast, Rose-Marie, Patrice Méniel, and Jean-Hervé Yvinec, eds. *Une histoire de l'élevage: Les animaux et l'archéologie.* Paris: Éditions Errance, 1987.

Aymard, Jacques. *Essai sur les chasses romaines des origines à la fin du siècle des Antonins.* Paris: E. de Boccard, 1951.

Beiderbeck, Rolf, and Bernd Koop. *Buchers Bestiarium: Berichte aus der Tierwelt der Alten.* Lucerne: C. J. Bucher, 1978.

Bible de A à Z, La: Animaux, plantes, minéraux et phénomènes naturels. Turnhout: Brepols, 1989.

Borgeaud, Philippe, Yves Christe, and Ivanka Urio, eds. *L'Animal, l'Homme, le Dieu dans le Proche-Orient ancien.* Louvain: Peeters, 1985.

Bouché-Leclercq, Auguste. *Histoire de la divination dans l'Antiquité.* 4 vols. Paris: Ernest Leroux, 1879–82.

Calvet, Jean, and Marcel Cruppi. *Le Bestiaire de l'Antiquité classique.* Paris: F. Lanore, 1955.

Cassin, Barbara, and Jean-Louis Labarrière, eds. *L'Animal dans l'Antiquité.* Paris: Vrin, 1998.

Cassin, Elena. "Le roi et le lion." *Revue de l'histoire des religions* 198, 4 (1981): 355–401.

Détienne, Marcel, and Jean-Pierre Vernant. *The Cuisine of Sacrifice among the Greeks.* Trans. Paula Wissing. Chicago: University of Chicago Press, 1989.

Dierauer, Urs. *Tier und Mensch im Denken der Antike.* Amsterdam: Gruner, 1977.

Dumont, Jacques. *Les Animaux dans l'Antiquité grecques.* Paris: L'Harmattan, 2001.

Gonthier, Thierry. *L'Homme et l'Animal: La philosophie antique.* Paris: PUF, 2001.

Homme et Animal dans l'Antiquité romaine: Actes du Colloque de Nantes, 1991. Tours: Centre de recherches André Piganiol, 1995.

Jennison, George. *Animals for Show and Pleasure in Ancient Rome.* Manchester: Manchester University Press, 1937.

Keller, Otto. *Die antike Tierwelt.* 2 vols. Leipzig: W. Engelmann, 1909–13.

Lévêque, Pierre. *Bêtes, Dieux et Hommes: L'imaginaire de premières religions.* Paris: Messidor, 1985.

Manquat, Maurice. *Aristote naturaliste.* Paris: Vrin, 1932.

Pangritz, Walter. *Das Tier in der Bibel.* Munich: E. Reinhardt, 1963.

Pellegrin, Pierre. *Aristotle's Classification of Animals.* Trans. Anthony Preus. Berkeley: University of California Press, 1986.

Prieur, Jean. *Les Animaux sacrés dans l'Antiquité.* Rennes: Ouest-France, 1988.

Rudhardt, Jean, and Olivier Reverdin, eds. *Le Sacrifice dans l'Antiquité.* Geneva: Fondation Hardt, 1981.

Sauvage, André. *Étude de themes animaliers dans la poésie latine.* Brussels: Latomus, 1975.

Schouten van der Velden, Adria. *Tierwelt der Bibel.* Stuttgart: Deutsche Bibelgesellschaft, 1992.

Toynbee, J. M. C. *Animals in Roman Life and Art.* Ithaca: Cornell University Press, 1973.

Trinquier, Jean. "Localisation et fonction des animaux sauvages dans l'Alexandrie lagide: La question du zoo d'Alexandrie." *Mélanges de l'École française de Rome: Antiquité* 114, 2 (2002): 861–919.

Vernus, Pascal, and Jean Yoyotte. *Bestiaire des pharaons.* Paris: Perrin, 2005.

4. Middle Ages

A. GENERALITIES

Audoin-Rozeau, Frédérique. *Hommes et Animaux en Europe de l'époque antique aux temps modernes: Corpus de données archéozoologiques et historiques.* Paris: CNRS éditions, 1993.

Berlioz, Jacques, Marie Anne Polo de Beaulieu, and Pascal Collomb, eds. *L'Animal exemplaire au Moyen Âge (V^e–XVe siècles).* Rennes: Presses Universitaires de Rennes, 1999.

Colardelle, Michel, ed. *L'Homme et la Nature au Moyen Âge.* Paris: Éditions Errance, 1996.

Flores, Nora C., ed. *Animals in the Middle Ages: A Book of Essays.* New York: Routledge, 1996.

Monde animal et ses representations au Moyen Âge (XIe–XVe siècles), Le: Actes du XVe

congers de la Société des historiens médiévistes de l'enseignement supérieur publique (1984). Toulouse: Université de Toulouse-Mirail, 1985.

Paravicini, Walter. "Tiere aus dem Norden." *Deutsches Archiv für die Erforschung des Mittelalters* 59, 2 (2003): 559–591.

Paravicini Bagliani, Agostino, ed. *Il mondo animale. The World of Animals*. Special issue of *Micrologus* 8 (2000).

Pastoureau, Michel. "L'animal et l'historien du Moyen Âge." In Berlioz et al., eds. *L'Animal exemplaire au Moyen Âge*.

Salisbury, Joyce E., ed. *The Beast Within: Animals in the Middle Ages*. New York: Routledge, 1994.

Uomo di fronte al mondo animale, L': Settimane di studio del Centro italiano di studi sull'alto Medioevo (1982). Spoleto: Centro italiano di studi sull'alto Medioevo, 1984.

B. PATRISTICS, THEOLOGY, HAGIOGRAPHY

Anti, Elisa. *Santi e animali nell'Italia padana (secoli IV–XII)*. Bologna: CLUEB, 1998.

Bernhart, Joseph. *Heilige und Tiere*. Munich: Josef Müller, 1937.

Boglioni, Pierre. "Les animaux dans l'hagiographie monastique." In *L'Animal exemplaire au Moyen Âge (V^e–XVe siècles)*, ed. Jacques Berlioz, Marie Anne Polo de Beaulieu, and Pascal Collomb, 51–80. Rennes: Presses Universitaires de Rennes, 1999.

Bousquet, Georges-Henri. "Des animaux et de leur traitement selon le judaïsme, le christianisme et l'islam." *Studia islamica* 9 (1958): 31–48.

Cardini, Francesco. "Francesco d'Assisi e gli animali." *Studi Francescani* 78 (1981): 7–46.

Guilbert, Lucille. "L'animal dans la *Légende Dorée*." In *Legenda aurea: sept siècles de diffusion*, ed. Brenda Dunn-Lardeau, 77–94. Montreal: Bellarmin, 1986.

Hesbert, René-Jean. "Le bestiaire de Grégoire." In *Grégoire le Grand*, ed. Jacques Fontaine, Robert Gillet, and Stan Pellistrandi, 455–466. Paris: Éditions du CNRS, 1986.

Miquel, Dom Pierre. *Dictionnaire symbolique des animaux: Zoologie mystique*. Paris: Léopard d'Or, 1991.

Nitschke, August. "Tiere und Heilige." In *Festgabe für Kurt von Raumer*, 62–100. Münster: Aschendorff, 1966.

Penco, Gregorio. "Il simbolismo animalesco nella letteratura monastica." *Studia monastica* 6, 1 (1964): 7–38.

Voisenet, Jacques. *Bestiaire chrétien: L'imagerie animale des auteurs du haut Moyen Âge (V^e–XIe siècles)*. Toulouse: Presses Universitaires du Mirail, 1994.

————. *Bêtes et hommes dans le monde médiéval: Le bestiaire des clercs du Ve au XIIe siècle.* Turnhout: Brepols, 2000.

Waddell, Helen. *Beasts and Saints.* London: Constable, 1934.

C. BESTIARIES AND ENCYCLOPEDIAS

Abeele, Baudoin van den, ed. *Bestiaires médiévaux: Nouvelles perspectives sur les manuscrits et les traditions textuelles.* Louvain-La-Neuve: Collège Érasme, 2005.

Allen, Lillian G. *An Analysis of the Medieval French Bestiaries.* Chapel Hill: University of North Carolina Press, 1935.

Baxter, Ron. *Bestiaries and Their Users in the Middle Ages.* Stroud: Sutton, 1998.

Borst, Arno. *Das Buch der Naturgeschichte: Plinius und seine Leser im Zeit des Pergaments.* 2nd ed. Heidelberg: Winter, 1995.

Boüard, Michel de. *Une nouvelle encyclopédie médiévale: Le Compendium philosophiae.* Paris: E. de Boccard, 1936.

Clark, Wilene B., and Meredith T. McNunn, eds. *Beasts and Birds of the Middle Ages: The Bestiary and Its Legacy.* Philadelphia: University of Pennsylvania Press, 1989.

Febel, Gisela, and Georg Maag, eds. *Bestiarien im Spannungsfeld: Zwischen Mittelalter und Moderne.* Tübingen: Gunter Narr Verlag, 1997.

George, Wilma B., and William B. Yapp. *The Naming of the Beasts: Natural History in the Medieval Bestiary.* London: Duckworth, 1991.

Hassig, Debra. *Medieval Bestiaries: Text, Image, Ideology.* Cambridge: Cambridge University Press, 1995.

Henkel, Nikolaus. *Studien zum Physiologus im Mittelalter.* Tübingen: Niemeyer, 1976.

Heyse, Elisabeth. *Hrabanus Maurus' Enzyklopädie De rerum naturis: Untersuchungen zu den Quellen und zur Methode der Kompilation.* Munich: Arbeo-Gesellschaft, 1969.

James, Montague Rhodes. *The Bestiary.* Oxford: Oxford University Press, 1928.

Kitchell, Kenneth F., and Irven M. Resnick. *Albertus Magnus on Animals: A Medieval Summa Zoologica.* 2 vols. Baltimore: Johns Hopkins University Press, 1999.

Langlois, Charles V. *La Connaissance de la nature et du monde au Moyen Âge.* Paris: Hachette, 1911.

Lauchert, Friedrich. *Geschichte des Physiologus.* Strasbourg: Trübner, 1889.

McCullough, Florence. *Medieval Latin and French Bestiaries.* Chapel Hill: University of North Carolina Press, 1960.

Meyer, Paul. "Les bestiaires." *Histoire littéraire de la France* 34 (1915): 362–390.

Muratova, Xenia. *The Medieval Bestiary.* Moscow, 1984.

Picone, Michelangelo, ed. *L'enciclopedismo medievale.* Ravenna: Longo, 1994.

Ribémont, Bernard. *De natura rerum: Études sur les encyclopédies médiévales.* Orléans: Paradigme, 1995.

Steel, Carlos, Guy Guldentops, and Pieter Beullens, eds. *Aristotle's Animals in the Middle Ages and Renaissance.* Louvain: Leuven University Press, 1999.

D. HUNTING

Abeele, Baudoin van den. *La Fauconnerie dans les lettres françaises du XIIe au XIVe siècle.* Louvain: Leuven University Press, 1990.

———. *La littérature cynégétique.* Turnhout: Brepols, 1996.

———. *Les Traités de fauconnerie latins du Moyen Âge.* Louvain-la-Neuve: Collège Érasme, 1991.

Chasse au Moyen Âge, La: Actes du Colloque de Nice (juin 1979). Paris: Belles Lettres, 1980.

Cummins, John. *The Hound and the Hawk: The Art of Medieval Hunting.* New York: St. Martin's Press, 1988.

Galoni, Paolo. *Il cervo e il lupo: Caccia e cultura nel Medioevo.* Rome-Bari: Laterza, 1993.

Lecouteux, Claude. *Chasses fantastiques et Cohortes de la nuit au Moyen Âge.* Paris: Imago, 1999.

Lindner, Kurt. *Die Jagd im frühen Mittelalter.* Berlin: W. de Gruyter, 1940.

Picard, Étienne. "La vénerie et la fauconnerie des ducs de Bourgogne." *Mémoires de la Société éduenne* 9 (1980): 297–418.

Rösner, Werner. "Jagd, Rittertum und Fürstenhof im Hochmittelater." In *Jagd und höfische Kultur im Mittelalter,* ed. Rösner, 123–147. Göttingen: Vandenhoeck und Ruprecht, 1997.

Strubel, Armand, and Chantal de Saulnier. *La Poétique de la chasse au Moyen Âge: Les livres de chasse du XIVe siècle.* Paris: PUF, 1994.

Verdon, Jean. "Recherches sur la chasse en Occident durant le haut Moyen Âge." *Revue belge de philologie et d'histoire* 56 (1978): 805–829.

E. LITERATURE

Bichon, Jean. "L'Animal dans la littérature française aux XIIe et XIIIe siècles." 2 vols. Ph.D. diss., Université de Lille III, 1977.

Buschinger, Danielle, ed. *Hommes et Animaux au Moyen Âge.* Greifswald: Reineke, 1997.

Dicke, Gerd, and Klaus Grubmüller. *Die Fabeln des Mittelalters und der frühen Neuzeit: Ein Katalog der deutschen Versionen und ihrer lateinischen Entsprechungen.* Munich: Wilhelm Fink, 1987.

Flinn, John. *Le Roman de Renart dans la littérature française et dans les littératures étrangères au Moyen Âge*. Paris: PUF, 1963.

Harf-Lancner, Laurence, ed. *Métamorphoses et Bestiaire fantastique au Moyen Âge*. Paris: École normale supérieure de jeunes filles, 1985.

Hensel, Werner. "Die Vögel in der provenzalischen und nordfranzösischen Lyrik des Mittelalters." *Romanische Forschungen* 26 (1891): 584–670.

Hervieux, Léopold. *Les fabulistes latins depuis le siècle d'Auguste jusqu'à la fin du Moyen Âge*. 5 vols. Paris: Firmin Didot, 1884–99.

Jauss, Hans Robert. *Untersuchungen zur mittelalterlichen Tierdichtung*. Tübingen: M. Niemeyer, 1959.

Knapp, Fritz Peter. *Das lateinische Tierepos*. Darmstadt: Wissenschaftliche Buchgesellschaft, 1979.

Lecouteux, C. "Les Monstres dans la littérature allemande du Moyen Âge (1150–1350)." 3 vols. Ph.D. diss., Paris IV, 1980.

Rombauts, Edward, and Andries Welkenhuysen, eds. *Aspects of the Medieval Animal Epic*. Louvain: Leuven University Press, 1975.

Wüster, Gustaf. "Die Tiere in der altfranzösischen Literatur." Ph.D. diss., Göttingen, 1916.

F. ART AND ICONOGRAPHY

Benton, Janetta R. *The Medieval Menagerie: Animals in the Art of the Middle Ages*. New York: Abbeville Press, 1992.

Bestiaire roman: Textes médiévaux. Trans. Élisabeth de Solms. La Pierre-qui-Vire: Zodiaque, 1977.

Camus, Marie-Thérèse. *Les Oiseaux dans la sculpture du Poitou roman*. Poitiers: Société des antiquaires de l'Ouest, 1973.

Debidour, Victor Henry. *Le Bestiaire sculpté du Moyen Âge en France*. Paris: Arthaud, 1961.

Doridot, Caroline, Danièle Thibault, and Anne Zali, eds. *Bestiaire médiéval: Enluminure*. Paris: Bibliothèque nationale de France, 2005.

Druce, George C. "The Medieval Bestiaries and Their Influence on Ecclesiastical Decorative Art." *Journal of the British Archaeological Association* 25 (1919): 41–82 and 26 (1920): 35–79.

Evans, Edward P. *Animal Symbolism in Ecclesiastical Architecture*. London: Heinemann, 1896.

Gathercole, Patricia M. *Animals in Medieval Manuscript Illumination*. Lewiston, N.Y.: E. Mellen Press, 1995.

Hicks, Carola. *Animals in Early Medieval Art*. Edinburgh: Edinburgh University Press, 1993.

Houwen, L. A. J. R., ed. *Animals and the Symbolic in Medieval Art and Literature.* Groningen: Egbert Forsten, 1997.

Malaxecheverria, Ignacio. *El bestiario esculpido en Navarra.* Pamplona: Gobierno de Navarra, 1982.

Michel, Paul. *Tiere als Symbol und Ornament.* Wiesbaden: L. Reichert, 1979.

Muratova, Xenia. "Adam donne leurs noms aux animaux: L'iconographie de la scène dans l'art du Moyen Âge." *Studi Medievali* 3rd ser., 18, 2 (1977): 367–394.

Pastoureau, Michel. "Le monde animal." In *Le Moyen Âge en lumière: Manuscrits enluminés des bibliothèques de France,* ed. Jacques Dalarun. Paris: Fayard, 2002.

Payne, Ann. *Medieval Beasts.* New York: New Amsterdam Books, 1990.

Randall, Lilian M. C. *Images in the Margins of Gothic Manuscripts.* Berkeley: University of California Press, 1966.

G. EMBLEMATICS AND SYMBOLISM

Blankenburg, Wera von. *Heilige und dämonische Tiere: Die Symbolsprache der deutschen Ornamentik im frühen Mittelalter.* Leipzig: Koehler und Amelang, 1943.

Charbonneau-Lassay, Louis. *The Bestiary of Christ.* Trans. (abridged) D. M. Dooling. New York: Parabola Books, 1991.

Laurioux, Bruno. "Manger l'impur: Animaux et interdits alimentaires durant le haut Moyen Âge." In *Homme, Animal et Société,* ed. Couret and Ogé, 3:73–87. Toulouse: Presses de l'Insitut Politique de Toulouse, 1989.

Lecouteux, Claude. *Les Monstres dans la pensée médiévale européenne: Essai de presentation.* Paris: Presses de l'Université de Paris-Sorbonne, 1993.

Pastoureau, Michel. "Bestiaire du Christ, bestiaire du Diable: Attribut animal et mise en scène du divin dans l'image médiévale." In *Couleurs, Images, Symboles: Études d'histoire et d'anthropologie.* Paris: Léopard d'Or, 1986.

———. "Le bestiaire des cinq sens." *Micrologus* 9 (2000): 5–19.

———. *Une histoire symbolique du Moyen Âge occidental.* Paris: Seuil, 2004.

———. "Nouveaux regards sur le monde animal à la fin du Moyen Âge." *Micrologus* 4 (1996): 41–54.

Rowland, Beryl. *Animals with Human Faces: A Guide to Animal Symbolism.* Knoxville: University of Tennessee Press, 1973.

———. *Birds with Human Souls: A Guide to Bird Symbolism.* Knoxville: University of Tennessee Press, 1978.

Schmidtke, Dietrich. "Geistliche Tierinterpretation in der deutschsprachigen Literatur des Mittelalters (1100–1500)." Ph.D. diss., Freie Universität, Berlin, 1966.

Steinen, Wolfram von den. "Altchristlich-mittelalterliche Tiersymbolik." *Symbolum* 4 (1964): 218–243.

Vincent-Cassy, Mireille. "Les animaux et les péchés capitaux: De la symbolique à l'emblématique." In *Le Monde animal et ses representations au Moyen Âge (XIᵉ–XVᵉ siècle): Actes du XVᵉ congers de la Société des historiens médiévistes de l'enseignement supérieur public (1984)*, 121–132. Toulouse: Presses Universitaires du Mirail, 1985.

H. LAW

Amira, Karl von. "Thierstrafen und Thierprocesse." *Mitteilungen des Instituts für Oesterreiche Geschichtsforschung* 12 (1891): 546–606.

Berkenhoff, Hans Albert. *Tierstrafe, Tierbannung und rechtsrituelle Tiertötung im Mittelalter.* Leipzig: Heitz, 1937.

Chêne, Catherine. *Juger les vers: Exorcismes et procès d'animaux dans le diocèse de Lausanne (XVᵉ–XVIᵉ siècles).* Lausanne: Cahiers lausannois d'histoire médiévale, 1995.

Ménabréa, Léon. *De l'origine, de la forme et de l'esprit des jugements rendus au Moyen Âge contre les animaux.* Chambéry: Puthod, 1846.

Pastoureau, Michel. "Une justice exemplaire: Les procès intentés aux animaux (XIIIᵉ–XVIᵉ siècles)." *Cahiers du Léopard d'or* 9 (2000): 173–200.

5. Modern Times

Baratay, Eric. *L'Église et l'Animal (France, XVIIᵉ–XXᵉ siècle).* Paris: Éditions du Cerf, 1996.

Baratay, Eric, and Elisabeth Hardouin-Fugier. *Zoo: A History of Zoological Gardens in the West.* Trans. Oliver Welsh. London: Reaktion, 2002.

Baümer, Änne. *Zoologie der Renaissance, Renaissance der Zoologie.* Frankfurt: Peter Lang, 1991.

Campardon, Émile. *Les Spectacles de la foire.* 2 vols. Geneva: Slatkine Reprints, 1970.

Daudin, Henri. *Les Classes zoologiques et l'Idée de série animale en France à l'époque de Lamarck et de Cuvier (1790–1830).* 2 vols. Paris: Alcan, 1926–27.

Delaunay, Paul. *La Zoologie au XVIᵉ siècle.* Paris: Hermann, 1963.

Dittrich, Sigrid, and Dittrich, Lothar. *Lexikon der Tiersymbole: Tiere als Sinnbilder in der Malerei des 14.–17. Jahrhunderts.* 2nd ed. Petersberg: Imhof, 2005.

Haupt, Herbert, Eva Irblich, Théa Vignau-Wilberg, and Manfred Staudinger. *Le Bestiaire de Rodolphe II.* Paris: Citadelles, 1990.

Lacroix, Jean-Bernard. "L'approvisionnement des ménageries et les transports d'animaux sauvages par la Compagnie des Indes au XVIIIᵉ siècle." *Revue française d'histoire d'outre-mer* (1978): 153–179.

Leibbrand, Jürgen. *Speculum bestialitatis: die Tiergestalten der Fastnacht und des Karnevals im Kontext christlicher Allegorese.* Munich: Tuduv, 1989.

Lloyd, Joan Barclay. *African Animals in Renaissance Literature and Art*. Oxford: Clarendon Press, 1971.

Moriceau, Jean-Marc. *L'Élevage sous l'Ancien Régime (XVIe–XVIIIe siècle)*. Paris: SEDES, 1999.

Nissen, Claus. *Die zoologische Buchillustration, ihre Bibliographie und Geschichte*. 2 vols. Stuttgart: Hiersemann, 1969–78.

Paust, Bettina. *Studien zur barocken Menagerie in deutschsprachigen Raum*. Worms: Wernersche Verlagsgesellschaft, 1996.

Risse, Jacques. *Histoire de l'élevage français*. Paris: L'Harmattan, 1994.

Salvadori, Philippe. *La Chasse sous l'Ancien Régime*. Paris: Fayard, 1996.

Thomas, Keith. *Man and the Natural World: A History of the Modern Sensibility*. New York: Pantheon, 1983.

6. Contemporary Period

Albert-Llorca, Marlène. *L'Ordre des choses: Les récits d'origine des animaux et des plantes en Europe*. Paris: Éditions du C. T. H. S., 1991.

Blunt, Wilfrid. *The Ark in the Park: The Zoo in the Nineteenth Century*. London: Hamish Hamilton, 1976.

Burgat, Florence. *Animal, mon prochain*. Paris: Odile Jacob, 1997.

Couret, Alain, and Caroline Daigueperse. *Le Tribunal des animaux: Les animaux et le droit*. Paris: Thissot, 1987.

Diolé, Philippe. *Les Animaux malades de l'homme*. Paris: Flammarion, 1974.

Domalain, Jean-Yves. *L'Adieu aux bêtes*. Paris: Arthaud, 1974.

Hediger, Heini. *The Psychology and Behavior of Animals in Zoos and Circuses*. Trans. Geoffrey Sircom. 2nd ed. New York: Dover, 1968.

Laissus, Yves, and Jean-Jacques Petter. *Les Animaux du Muséum, 1793–1993*. Paris: Imprimerie nationale, 1993.

Lévy, Pierre Robert. *Les Animaux du cirque*. Paris: Syros / Alternatives, 1992.

Paietta, Ann C., and Jean L. Kauppila. *Animals on Screen and Radio*. Metuchen, N.J.: Scarecrow Press, 1994.

Rothel, David. *The Great Show Business Animals*. San Diego: A. S. Barnes, 1980.

Rovin, Jeff. *The Illustrated Encyclopedia of Cartoon Animals*. New York: Prentice-Hall, 1991.

Thétard, Henry. *Les Dompteurs*. Paris: Gallimard, 1928.

———. *La Merveilleuse Histoire du cirque*. 2nd ed. Paris: Julliard, 1978.

Acknowledgments

Before it became a book, this cultural history of the bear was for several years the subject of my seminars at the École Pratique des Hautes Études and the École des Hautes Études en Sciences Sociales. I thank all my students and auditors for the fruitful discussions we had. I would also like to thank all the friends, relatives, colleagues, and students who accompanied me through these "ursine" years, provided me with information and documents, and gave me the benefit of their comments, advice, and suggestions. I would like to thank in particular Emmanuelle Adam, Jacques Berlioz, Michel Boccara, Thierry Buquet, Pierre Bureau, Perrine Canavaggio, Massimo Carassi, Yvonne Cazal, Teresa Dunin-Wasowicz, Anita Guerreau, Éliane Hartmann, François Jacquesson, Laurence Klejman, Jean-Dominique Lajoux, Odile Lépinay, Caroline Masson-Voss, Jean-Michel Mehl, Massimo Montanari, Maurice Olender, Laure Pastoureau, François Poplin Anne Ritz, Pierre Sineux, Baudouin Van den Abeele, Olga Vassilieva-Codognet, Inès Villela-Petit, and Marguerite Wilska.

Finally, I would like to acknowledge my enormous debt to Claudia Rabel, who constantly provided me with her sage advice, constructive criticism, and scrupulously accurate proofreading. This book belongs in part to her.

Index